# net.seXXX

Steve Jones
*General Editor*

Vol. 23

**PETER LANG**
New York • Washington, D.C./Baltimore • Bern
Frankfurt am Main • Berlin • Brussels • Vienna • Oxford

# net.seXXX

## Readings on Sex, Pornography, and the Internet

Dennis D. Waskul,

EDITOR

PETER LANG
New York • Washington, D.C./Baltimore • Bern
Frankfurt am Main • Berlin • Brussels • Vienna • Oxford

**Library of Congress Cataloging-in-Publication Data**

Net.seXXX: readings on sex, pornography, and the Internet /
edited by Dennis D. Waskul.
p. cm. — (Digital formations; v. 23)
Includes bibliographical references and index.
1. Computer sex. 2. Internet pornography. I. Title: Net sex.
II. Waskul, Dennis D. III. Series.
HQ23.N47    306.7′02854678—dc22    2004006747
ISBN 0-8204-7072-4
ISSN 1526-3169

Bibliographic information published by **Die Deutsche Bibliothek**.
**Die Deutsche Bibliothek** lists this publication in the "Deutsche
Nationalbibliografie"; detailed bibliographic data is available
on the Internet at http://dnb.ddb.de/.

Cover design by Sophie Boorsch Appel

© 2004 Peter Lang Publishing, Inc., New York
275 Seventh Avenue, 28th Floor, New York, NY 10001
www.peterlangusa.com

# ❖ Table of Contents

# ❖ Acknowledgments

*Net.SeXXX* began as an idea generated in e-mail with Steve Jones; were it not for his efforts and encouragement this book would not have been possible. I am sincerely grateful to Steve Jones for his long-term unwavering support. In addition, I am appreciative for the outstanding assistance I received from Peter Lang—especially Damon Zucca, whose efforts epitomized the phrase "beyond the call of duty." I am also in debt to Angela Norton and Crystal Kennard, my two exceptional student assistants, who spent many hours nitpicking, editing, tweaking, and generally providing marvelous feedback. A special thanks to the authors who contributed original materials for this book—Trudy Barber, Phillip Vannini, Joel Powell Dahlquist, Lee Garth Vigilant, Keith Durkin, Jim Thomas, Lauren Langman, Erica Owens, and Stephen Roberds—I've never worked with a more amiable and competent batch of scholars; I hope each of you enjoyed working on this project as much as I have enjoyed working with you. Thanks also to Taylor Marsh, Lewis Perdue, and Howard Rheingold for their gracious permissions. I must also express my profound appreciation for the support and tolerance I have received from the two most important people in my life: my wife Michele and my daughter Mikayla, without whom neither this nor anything else matters much to me.

## ❖ Introduction

# Sex and the Internet: Old Thrills in a New World; New Thrills in an Old World

Dennis D. Waskul

In the early 1980s sociologists Charles Edgley and Kenneth Kiser (1981:59) published a witty and insightful analysis of the Polaroid camera—as a *sexual* technology.

> [I]nstant photography and instant pornography were invented...at the same time...Polaroid sex, then, may be defined as the use of instant photography devices to create homemade pornography. Prior to the development and mass distribution of the Polaroid camera, homemade pornography was almost impossible to achieve, unless one of the participants had access to a developing laboratory and the skill with which to process his own prints.

Edgley and Kiser explore how resourceful uses of instant photography rapidly altered the nature of swinging subcultures (in all likelihood, it was not accidental that the first mass-produced low-cost Polaroid camera was named "The Swinger"), became a popularized means for couples to creatively liven up a monogamous sexual relationship, and bore a veritable bonanza of amateur pornography ("Hustler Beaver Hunt" and "The Girl Next Door: Gallery's Amateur Photo Contest," for example). Without a doubt, this most improbable of wholesomely marketed technologies has a history of uses that are far more salacious than most people care to publicly recognize—Polaroid notwithstanding.

Of course, that was the late 1970s and early 1980s. With times changing so fast in what has undoubtedly been an era of rapid technological development, "Polaroid sex" might now seem quaint—perhaps charmingly cute—if not downright silly. It wouldn't be long before innovative sexual uses of the Polaroid camera would be taken to entirely new levels on the heels of a rapid succession of other technological innovations such as the VCR, camcorder, scanners, online chat, the World Wide Web, video chat, and virtual reality. Yet Edgley and Kiser's analysis is not nearly as antiquated as it might seem; even the most casual readers cannot miss the point: "Polaroid sex" is a lens into something else—something that predates *and* proceeds the Polaroid camera.

"Every technological innovation creates deviant as well as respectable possibilities," wrote Edgley and Kiser (1981:59), adding that "the machine itself does not dictate the moral choice; human beings do that." Yet Edgley and Kiser (1981:59) were equally aware of the obvious: "it would be foolish to believe that the availability of certain technologies did not make possible certain moral choices that were previously difficult or impossible to arrange." As skilled observers of human social life, these sociologists (1981:62) understood that Polaroid sex was a small part of "the technological explosion that has influenced our society in virtually every area of life offer[ing] a variety of truly mind-boggling possibilities." Thus, Edgley and Kiser (1981:63) make their point unambiguous: "Polaroid Sex" is really all about "sexual relationships in a changing society," "popular culture as an agent of change," and cultural dynamics found at the intersection of "technology, deviance, and respectability." To be sure, these same themes appear repeatedly in the contents of this book.

This book is all about sex and pornography on the Internet. Yet, ironically, each reading consistently turns into something else. Discussions of Internet sex rapidly become occasions for pondering beliefs, values, worldviews, morality, ethics, deviance, social relationships, gender, economics, technology, social change, culture, the shifting power of social institutions, and people caught in the ebb and flow of these highly contested social currents. Truly, things have not changed so much. Like "Polaroid sex," Internet sex is more than the latest use of high technology for low ends; Internet sex is a lens into precarious dynamics of what continues to be a changing society. This book seeks to refine that lens, harness insights, offer critical assessments, and raise new questions.

There is little doubt that sex has provided the major motivation and the financial resources for the development of cutting-edge computer-networking technologies. In the process, the Internet has also brought about a plethora of new sexual possibilities, opened new markets for entrepreneurs of pornography, challenged the boundaries of social institutions, obscured the borders of social relationships, and created a novel arena for asking important questions about the people who may or may not be grounded in this emerging matrix of computer-mediated meaning. Now is a perfect time to take stock of these changes.

## High Technology and Low Ends

The use of high technology for low ends is nothing new, although there is no consensus about either. Definitions of "high" technology consistently prove obsolete and definitions of "low" ends are persistently contested. Even so, the rich history of pornography repeatedly illustrates how prurient interests characteristically appropriate sophisticated technology.

In 1839 Louis Daguerre revealed his innovative method for capturing images to the French Academy of Science (Pollack 1977). Published in eight languages, Daguerre became the most famous of several people to invent photography. The first nude "daguerreotype" image was taken less than two years later. Evidence suggests that these early forays into nude photography were as much a commercial enterprise as a personal hobby: "The practice of producing and selling 'artistic studies'...was so successful that less than three years after the invention of the daguerrerotype, the United States Congress passed the Customs Act of 1842, which specifically forbade the importation of 'obscene or immoral...pictures'" (Lane 2000:43). Almost 150 years later, at the 1998 Consumer Electronics Show in Las Vegas, Sony executives admitted that the key reason their technologically superior Betamax lost the VCR war to VHS is attributable to Sony's refusal to cooperate with the pornography industry—a mistake neither Sony nor Pioneer intend to make with DVD technology (Perdue 2002). When phone sex lines were first introduced in the 1980s, the volume of calls caused telephone networks in several countries to collapse on the first night (O'Toole 1998). With each technology the situation seems oddly familiar.

Polaroid sex, commercial nude photos, phone sex, adult videos—the pattern appears prone to historical repetition. Thus, we ought not be surprised by how computer-networking technologies have been appropriated by prurient interests, nor should we be surprised by how similar technologies will be employed in comparable ways for a long time to come. For example, we can rest assured that many people have already contemplated wild and creative sexual uses of cutting-edge video cell phones—for personal as well as commercial erotic activities. Quite possibly, the success of video cell phones might hinge on their affordability *and* these kinds of sexual applications. We can expect, if video cell phones become less cost-prohibitive, this technology—like those that preceded it—will open new doors of opportunity for sex, pornography, and erotic entrepreneurial endeavors while, in the process, acquiring the potential to revolutionize telecommunications. After all, with the possible exception of cordless and cell technologies, the consumer experience of telephones has remained essentially unchanged; we are still fundamentally experiencing the same communication technology pioneered by Alexander Graham Bell. Telephones are due for a revolution and perhaps sex will once again help turn the wheels of technology. If this prediction sounds a little far-fetched, one would be wise to more carefully examine the history of the VCR, photography, the Internet, and perhaps the contents of this book.

## The New and the Old

The fact that high technology has always been in service to low ends (and vice-versa) does not mean that history is a monotonous repetition of something that has already happened. Certainly, on one hand, anyone who surveys pornography on the Internet or explores the steamy world of cybersex will not be surprised by what is found: Internet sex is largely composed of images, systems of meaning, and forms of interaction that are conspicuously familiar. In many respects this "new world" of seemingly infinite varieties of innovative sexual possibilities remains organized around old themes of cultural gender roles, androcentric sexuality, the usual characteristics of a male-dominated pornography industry, and predictable moral concerns.

Still, there *is* something new going on here. At its core, what is most new about Internet sex is its unprecedented access. Never before have so many people had such easy access to so much sexually explicit material. Previous technologies made sexually explicit materials available, but adult movie theaters, pornographic bookstores, the dank and dimly lit back room of neighborhood video rental shops, the embarrassment of purchasing a nudie magazine at a local gas station, and similar controls have always kept the availability of these materials somewhat limited and rather tightly confined. The Internet has significantly changed that. From the comfort of one's own home and under a dense veil of anonymity, an enormous range of sex is readily available at one's fingertips—and no one is embarrassingly exposed for their curious cyberpeepings.

The loosening of these formal and informal controls has encouraged greater numbers of people to view Internet pornography or participate in cybersex, including those who would not otherwise. Yet, the significance is not in the number of people who can now easily consume sexually explicit materials, but the variety. The pornography industry has long dominated the production and distribution of sexually explicit materials, and it is no secret that the industry has been decidedly androcentric and heterosexist—often appealing to the most juvenile level of male adolescent fantasy. As greater varieties of people gain access to sexually explicit materials, one can easily predict changes to the nature of those materials. Always willing to respond to the profit incentive of new markets, sex on the Internet most certainly displays a diversity that has historically eluded the pornography industry.

On the Internet, taboos of the mainstream pornography industry are routinely dismissed. Gays, lesbians, bisexuals, and transsexuals can gain access to materials and support networks specifically designed for them—regardless of whether they live in the most conservative rural regions, or the most liberal urban environments. On the Internet the voices, interests, and desires of women—long disregarded by the pornography industry—prove to play a significant role in Internet sex. Indeed, with women currently comprising more than 50 percent of all Internet users, most entrepreneurs of Internet pornography are eager to appeal to this substantial new market. In either cybersex environments or Internet pornography sites people of all genders, sexual orientations, fetish interests, or finicky desires can find ready opportunities to explore the surfaces and depths of their erotic interests, as well as find others who share similar tastes.

Ease of access makes all of this possible, and much more. Of course there are potential problems. Public libraries, schools, workplace computers, and the ever-curious eyes of children may well represent domains where easy access to Internet sex has forced difficult decisions. But even so, these potential problems are not always so clearly affixed to computer networking technologies—often they are just as easily explained by our collective cultural uneasiness with sex, a preponderance of mixed messages about sex, and the micro politics surrounding changing, and often ambiguous, sexual norms. Thus, even in these problematic scenarios, easy access to Internet sex pushes the boundaries of the old and the new as it opens a dialogue on subjects that are all too often addressed only with silence.

We would be mistaken to believe that Internet sex represents an entirely new realm of sexual experience. We are also mistaken to believe that Internet sex is simply the newest regurgitation of the same old themes that have always been a part of the pornography industry. The situation is both but neither. The old and the new are reconfigured, sometimes in ways that are predictable and sometimes in ways that surprise. Either way, the significance of this reconfiguration—beyond personal amusement and titillation—depends largely on how the story of Internet sex is told.

## A Tale of Multiple Endings

Laurence O'Toole (1998:246) once wrote, "There are two leading stories told about pornography and the new media technologies...One account finds a dispute between cyber-skeptics dreading a further alienation of people from 'real' life and those cyber-boosters who proclaim a new dawn of sexual rapture via telecommunications." This dispute results in two narratives about future sex. On one hand, as O'Toole (1998:273–274) explains,

> there are those perplexing images of newfangled sexy gimmicks like virtual reality grop-
> ings—also known as "teledildonics"—promising us sex such as we've never had sex be-
> fore, and where we often find our carnal futures looking rather like an American science-
> fiction B-movie from the fifties, featuring body suits with Velcro sensors and computer
> cables hooked up to the groin and chest. These are visions that people find simultane-
> ously alarming and comically hard to believe in.

On the other hand,

> The counter-narrative to such way-out visions of future sex features a big dose of
> technofear, and associated misgivings…concerning excess, the decline of real flesh ex-
> periences, and a dread of what happens when men and machines fall in love.

One story with two competing narratives: one about blissful promise another about impending doom. While all narratives are drama, clearly both of these stories are *melo*drama. They are sensational tales built of crude appeals to emotion. Whether it is hopes or fears, fantasies or nightmares, both stories exaggerate: neither are especially convincing. Either version primarily concerns the values and apprehensions of the story*teller*.

"Meanwhile, the other new tech and porn story concerns risk and danger, illegality and censorship" (O'Toole 1998:273). This is a narrative of fear and distrust—not of technology, but of the people who use it and even one self. These are tales of addiction, compulsivity, abuse, exploitation, victimization, and similar hazardous risks. Concerned moralists have been telling this story from the earliest days of the Internet. The story is brought to life by a variety of frightening characters: pedophiles that use the Internet to steal children from the safety of their home; hapless lonely hearts that unwittingly become addicted to Internet sex; or stable marital relationships that are torn apart by a spouse's "virtual infidelities" on the Internet—regardless, each tale is linked by familiar themes of fear and control.

Of course, these are stories about human activity—not descriptions of a coin. There are more than two sides. In fact, O'Toole (1998:274) suggests a third way of thinking about sex, pornography, and new media technologies:

> Between rosy visions of a new age of sexual rapture in "cyberville" and alternative,
> darker tales of machine alienation, there does exist another less heralded, less quantifiable
> tale of connectivity, a story of how in an era of convergence, where computers, televi-
> sions, phones, cables, video and compact disk technology are starting to merge in multi-

media harmony, more people than ever before are gaining access through new technology
to sexual materials and communities of like-minded types.

This is a story that is rarely heard in first-person, though pieces of the tale can be
found here and there. The stigma of pornography—the fear of being exposed as
someone who at least occasionally enjoys explicit sexual experiences—prevents
open admissions. Even so, we can rest assured: for many people the Internet has
proved an important and valuable sexual resource. For example, in spite of fears
concerning the dangers of Internet sex for youth, have we thought to ask what
those resources might mean to a rural adolescent who struggles to come to grips
with his or her homosexuality in an environment far removed from the support
structures of the city? In spite of our continuing paternalistic attitudes toward
women—as frail creatures who require protection from sexual exploitation—
have we thought about how Internet anonymity might provide the only context
where women can freely explore sexual interests without paying the price of
stigma and shame remunerated courtesy of a deeply entrenched and insidious
double standard? While concerns about "virtual infidelity" are often stated, has
anyone thought to ask how couples have used easy access Internet sex to spice
up an otherwise monogamous relationship? How about the disabled, the socially
inept, the unattractive, and other people who might have found Internet sex a
meaningful context to cultivate a positive sense of sexual self-worth? These tales
of connectivity and self-exploration, though seldom heard, are at least as important as narratives of blissful promise or danger.

This book is filled with narratives that come from all three points of view. In
themselves, none contain the truth; collectively we get a little closer. However,
"the" truth is quite relative. After all, we're talking about sex and pornography—
something defined, experienced, interpreted, and made meaningful in the context
of a plurality of differences. The very same experience of Internet pornography
or cybersex will elicit diverse responses from different people, and even the
same person at different times. For this reason alone, this book does not seek to
expose "the" truth about Internet sex. Instead, this book explores various truths
and places them in a context where readers can assess them for themselves. Perhaps some will be drawn to articulations of risk and danger. Others might be
fond of the ways the Internet has provided resources for connectivity and personal kinds of sexual self-exploration. Some might even be inspired by the eroticism of it all, or intrigued by way-out visions of funky future techno-sex. That,
of course, is the beauty of it. Like the very subject of this book, responses will
vary. Some ideas are bound to "turn you on" and others will surely leave you
dissatisfied. The point, however, is to peer into what is frequently defined as a

forbidden world of often secretive computer-mediated erotic activity; the value of what you see might well be assessed by how it uniquely moves you.

## References

Edgley, C., and K. Kiser. 1981. "Polaroid Sex: Deviant Possibilities in a Technological Age." *Journal of American Culture*. 59–64.

Lane, F. 2000. *Obscene Profits: The Entrepreneurs of Pornography in the Cyber Age.* New York, NY: Routledge.

O'Toole, L. 1998. *Pornocopia: Porn, Sex, Technology, and Desire.* London: Serpents' Tail.

Perdue, L. 2002. *EroticaBiz: How Sex Shaped The Internet.* New York, NY: Writers Club Press.

Pollack, P. 1977. *The Picture History of Photography.* New York, NY: Harry N. Abrams, Inc.

# Part One

# Personhood and Internet Sex

On the Internet, everyone can be anyone: personhood is transformed into an ostensibly unlimited discursive performance. Even seemingly stable elements of self—race, ethnicity, age, gender, sexual orientation, and physical appearance—are made into infinitely mutable self-selected variables to be toyed with as part of an elaborate kind of "self-game" (Waskul and Douglass 1997; Waskul 2003). Apparently, forms of personhood are put on and taken off as eagerly as virtual clothing in a steamy episode of cybersex; perhaps nowhere are people more free to be without being. Indeed, only on the Internet is Cleo Odzer's (1997:43) frank admission even remotely understandable:

> With the freedom to be and do anything, I had sex with three men at once. I had sex with a woman. I had sex with three men and a woman once. Posing as a man, I had sex with a woman. Posing as a gay man, I had sex with a man. Posing as a man, I had sex with a man who was posing as a woman. I learned all about S&M, as the sadist and the masochist. I had all sorts of sex in every new way I could think of.

The apparent self-fluidity of Internet environments is largely attributable to one central characteristic: the Internet is an utterly disembodied medium of communication. For all the pornography and cybersex that can be found on the Internet, one can never encounter a corporeal body—one only comes across words and images that *represent* bodies. On the Internet, the whole of one's communicative presence is represented in one place, while the entirety of one's physical body is located elsewhere. Thus, to whatever extent the Internet dislocates communicative presence from the corporeal body, everybody can claim to be anybody—and no one is wiser to differences between truth and fiction.

These conditions have provided social scientists a lens into examining complex questions concerning the nature of personhood—not only on the Internet but, more generally, in a society and culture that is permeated by similar technologies of communication and conditions of self-fluidity (see Gergen 1991; Lifton 1993; Meyrowitz 1985). In this respect, Internet sex is an *ideal* context for exploring provocative questions concerning at least one dimension of this new landscape of technology and personhood: because sex is among the most embodied of all imaginable human activities *and* computer-mediated communications are so clearly disembodied, Internet sex potentially exposes new dynamics about the experience of self in an age of rapidly accelerating technologies of communication. The readings in Part One explore these complex dynamics.

In their study of text cybersex, Dennis Waskul, Mark Douglass, and Charles Edgley (2000) raise questions about personhood in an environment where everybody is no-*body*. In text cybersex participants cannot see their cyberlover(s); instead, they interactively type words that represent actions, touches, and utterances. Consequently, as Waskul, Douglass, and Edgley point out, text cybersex "is a kind of experience that explicitly contradicts its form"—something they call "outercourse"—a communicative encounter where "semiotic icons (in this case typed words, emotions, and utterances) represent and replace corporeal sexual intercourse. Whereas the pleasures of corporeal sexual intercourse are encapsulated in physical contact, the pleasures of cybersex are encapsulated in erotic text communication." However, as Waskul, Douglass, and Edgley find out, text cybersex does not escape claims of the flesh; instead, it depends on them. Text cybersex is crafted from compressed social and cultural symbols of beauty and sexiness and, because no one needs to be seen ugly, every man has an enormous penis, every woman is big-busted, everybody is beautiful, and everyone is expertly skilled in ever-pleasing sexual techniques. In the end, the freedom to "be without being" merely allows text cybersex participants to redefine themselves—sometimes to a ridiculous extreme—according to standards programmed by society and culture.

What happens when people have cybersex but can see live images of the other participant(s) involved? Contemporary cost effective and user-friendly technology make this a ready possibility: easy to use digital cameras and client software have made programs like CUSeeMe and ICU a boon for exhibitionist and voyeur cybersex enthusiasts everywhere. Obviously, watching and being watched in televideo cybersex magnifies the role of the body in an environment that is still, ironically, disembodied. However, these extremely provocative Internet sex encounters transform the dynamics of personhood much more than one would expect: participants are made into spectators unto themselves in a manner that intensifies the looking-glass of personhood. Dennis Waskul's study of televideo cybersex explores these complex dynamics.

As these readings suggest, Internet sex can be used as a lens for asking questions about the nature of personhood in contemporary society. Experiences of self-fluidity, experimentation, and exploration (of the surfaces—and depths—of selfhood) are all latently a part of the kinky fun-and-games of Internet sex. These readings further suggest that Internet sex has much to teach us about the nature of personhood—regardless of whether we partake of this kind of erotic activity.

## References

Gergen, K. 1991. *The saturated self: Dilemmas of identity in contemporary life*. New York, NY: Basic Books.

Lifton, R. 1993. *The protean self: Human resilience in an age of fragmentation*. New York, NY: Basic Books.

Meyrowitz, J. 1985. *No sense of place: The impact of electronic media on social behavior*. New York, NY: Oxford University Press.

Odzer, C. 1997. *Virtual spaces: Sex and the cyber citizen*. New York, NY: Berkley Books.

Waskul, D. 2003. *Self-games and body-play: Personhood in online chat and cybersex*. New York, NY: Peter Lang.

Waskul, D., and M. Douglass. 1997. Cyberself: The dynamics of self in online chat. *Information Society: An International Journal* 13(4):375–97.

Waskul, D., M. Douglass, and C. Edgley. 2000. Cybersex: Outercourse and the enselfment of the body. *Symbolic Interaction*. 23(4):375–97.

❖ Chapter One

# Outercourse: Body and Self in Text Cybersex

Dennis D. Waskul, Mark Douglass, and Charles Edgley[*]

*Dennis Waskul, Mark Douglass, and Charles Edgley interview participants of text cyber-sex encounters and seek to understand what these experiences can teach us about the na-ture of selfhood in an age increasingly characterized by rapidly expanding technologies of communication and ever-increasing opportunities for self-fluidity. Never before have people been so able to change who they are, and never before has there been an envi-ronment like the Internet where it is so easy to experiment with being someone else. Thus, Waskul, Douglass, and Edgley explore what the Internet—seen through the lens of text cybersex—can teach us about contemporary selfhood.*

For most people most of the time, sexual intercourse represents the ultimate in embodiment—a corporeal experience in which physical bodies interact. The consequences of these corporeal sexual encounters evidence themselves in bod-ily matters (e.g., sexual intercourse is wet, odoriferous, and teeming with bio-logical organisms). Cybersex, in contrast, is a kind of experience that explicitly contradicts its form.[1] Like traditional print, photo, and video pornography, chat-based cybersex is an experience that simulates tactile sex through a nontactile medium. In chat-based cybersex, semiotic icons emerge in a process of commu-nication and replace all interactions between people.

Similar to phone sex, chat-based cybersex is purely communicative. There are no copresent bodies, actions, touches, and (unlike phone sex) spoken words or utterances—the whole of the experience emerges in typed words that repre-sent actions, touches, and utterances. For this reason, on-line chat environments represent an ultimate experience of disembodiment (Waskul and Douglas 1997). This is part of the erotic appeal of cybersex: typed words necessarily communi-cate taken-for-granted actions, movements, romantic settings, and utterances. In

[*] Waskul, Dennis, Mark Douglass, and Charles Edgley. 2000. "Cybersex: Outercourse and the Enselfment of the Body." *Symbolic Interaction* 23 (4): 375–97.

cybersex the eroticism of detailed intimate description and communication re-places the physical pleasures of sexual intercourse.

Because cybersex explicitly contradicts its form, part of its erotic appeal emerges from this contradiction. Furthermore, by pressing the corporeal experi-ence of sexual intercourse through the disembodied medium of computer net-work technologies, a McLuhanesque transformation alters cybersex into something different—an experience that we may call sexual "outercourse." In sexual outercourse, semiotic icons (in this case typed words, emotions, and ut-terances) represent and replace corporeal sexual intercourse. Whereas the pleas-ures of corporeal sexual intercourse are encapsulated in physical contact, the pleasures of cybersex are encapsulated in erotic text communication. This study examines the nature of these cybersexual semiotic icons. And, in the context of on-line communication environments, we raise questions regarding traditionally conceived relationships among bodies, selves, and society.

### Self, Body, Society, Sex, and the Problem of Virtual Experience

Most people interpret sexual intercourse as a bodily activity, yet we recognize that the sexual interplay between bodies has neither a fixed nor a necessarily normative state. Sexuality can assume a stunning range of expression between individuals. In fact, sexuality is such a complex and multifaceted dimension of human experience because sexual expression is rooted in the interplay between the selves that we are, selves in relation to our physical bodies, and ourselves situated in a sociocultural context. These three aspects of self together form the core of any sexual encounter and converge to form explicit body-to-self-to-society relationships when considering human sexual activity. Yet each of the components of this body-self-society relationship is fundamentally distinct; we interpret and respond differently to each.

The self is a symbolic referent of a human being—a fluid system of mean-ings that refers to the person. These meanings emerge only through interrelation-ships with others in the context of particular social situations, roles, and encounters. In other words, a self emerges only as one interacts with another and transfers the meanings of those actions to this person. Selfhood is multiple and dynamic. A self can change (or be changed) as one moves from situation to situation, role to role, place to place, developmental stage to developmental stage. All persons enact a wide range of selves, as we are one thing to one person and something else to another.

The body, however, is not simply a fluid set of meanings. It is an empiri-cally verifiable and objectively real *thing*. Unlike selfhood, the body manifests itself in objective qualities that occupy space and time. As such, the physically verifiable corporeal body has at least two important functions in traditional conceptions of selfhood. First, because selfhood is multiple, dynamic, and fluid, "the nebulousness of personal identity has caused it to be commonly conceived in concrete form as coextensive with the physical body" (Davis 1983:112). We commonly associate (or affix) systems of meaning to the corporeal body that collectively comprise the self. Or, as Goffman (1959:253) describes, the "body merely provide[s] the peg on which something of collaborative manufacture will be hung for a time." According to traditional Western views, a body provides the "peg" on which to associate or affix a stable set of meanings that we comprehend as a person.

Second, the corporeal body, more than the stable "thing" to which we associate fluid systems of meaning that collectively comprise the self, is also commonly conceived as that which *contains* the self. In spite of the fluidity of selfhood, the fixed and veritable existence of a physical body always limits the range of selves that an individual may enact. Although the human body is decorated and otherwise altered along a seemingly infinite range, the body still limits self-to-social-world relationships. We know, for example, that to have a male or female body will exert a strong influence on the range of potential self-enactments available to the person. Although bodies are modified and self-enactments vary greatly, the physical existence of one's body restricts the range of one's selfhood.

The body *exists* as an important and fundamental element of selfhood—instrumental to our sense of being, who we think we are, and what others attribute to us. "Being a *body* constitutes the principle behind our separateness from one another and behind our personal presence. Our bodily existence stands at the forefront of personal identity and individuality" (Heim 1991:74).

While there is a clear relationship between selfhood and one's body, there is also an important relationship between one's body and society. As Stone (1995) suggests, the body is the unambiguous core of taken-for-granted conceptions of a comprehensible person and politically recognized citizen. For this reason, we can best understand and interpret self-to-body relationships in the context of broader body-to-social-world relationships that exert an independent influence.

...This perspective suggests that we negotiate selfhood according to prevailing interpretive discourses; it resides in the Goffmanian (1968) "cracks" between the relationships of one's body to one's social world. Experiences of selfhood emerge, are negotiated, and are then validated as one's body enters the scene of interaction in the context of preestablished sociocultural systems of meaning. This process occurs in the framework of a *triadic* body-to-self-to-society relationship. Selfhood is contained and affixed to the corporeal body, which society acts on, and is interpreted according to prevailing societal discourse. Indeed, bodies represent a fundamental element of personhood, the experience of which is caught in the precarious margins between body-to-social-world relationships.

...The body represents the grounded referent of selfhood. The body is a necessary condition for all of action and interaction (Strauss 1993). "It is the medium through which each person takes in and gives out knowledge about the world, object, self, others, and even about his or her own body" (Merleau-Ponty 1962; quoted in Strauss 1993:108–9). The body is a medium for the self—an agent to the self, the object of action, and the fulcrum of societal reaction.[2]

However, in the social worlds of on-line computer-mediated environments, there are no corporeal bodies. There are only symbolic representations of bodies (at best), in spite of millions of Internet participants and widely available pornography. In on-line communication a corporeal body is usually necessary to access and interact with others. However, in this communication the body is left at the keyboard *behind the scene* of the interactions that transpire; participants are literally disembodied. Because no physically verifiable or empirically measurable bodies exist anywhere in cyberspace, actions and interactions are entirely disassociated from the corporeal body. Instead, bodies are transformed into symbol alone—representations, images, descriptive codes, words of expectations, appearance, and action. In these on-line social worlds, traditional assumptions about self and body do not apply: the activities of participants and experiences of self are neither contained by nor affixed to corporeal bodies. In on-line communication environments both bodies and selves exist only as socially constructed representations—sets of meanings that emerge in a process of interaction.

In light of the important role of the body in traditional conceptions of selfhood, the disembodied nature of on-line interaction presents ideal conditions for examination of body-to-self-to-social-world relationships. Furthermore, because sex is among the most embodied of all imaginable activities, an activity that focuses on an interplay between bodies, sex is the peg on which we hang our brief examination of body-to-self-to-social-world relationships revealed in computer-mediated forms of leisure social interaction. This study examines the very means by which experiences of "self" and "body" are produced and how these constructs function in on-line social environments of a sexual nature. The study is cast in the context of cybersex, focusing on the negotiation of processes among individuals, selfhood, on-line leisure situations, and physical bodies that may or may not be grounded in an emerging matrix of virtual experience.

## A Dramaturgical Approach to the Problem of Virtual Reality

Many scholars have discussed the difficulties of assessing what is "real" with regard to the unique situations posed by electronic media environments (see Altheide and Snow 1991; Chayko 1993; Eco 1986; Zerubavel 1991). Scholars of computer-mediated communication have noted how these problems are most extreme in the environments of on-line social worlds (see Jones 1995; Rheingold 1991; Stone 1995; Turkle 1995). Out of these ontological challenges, the term "virtual reality" has emerged in the lexicon of both popular and academic discourse. Although it has become common practice to refer to all computer-mediated environments as "virtual," this term reflects an oversimplified understanding and overlooks the complex nuances of virtual reality.

Laurel offers an illuminating perspective on virtual experiences:

> The adjective virtual describes things—worlds, phenomena, etc.—that look and feel like reality but lack the traditional physical substance. A virtual object, for instance, may be one that has no real-world equivalent, but the persuasiveness of its representation allows us to respond to it as if it were real. (1993:8)

To Laurel, virtual "things" are persuasive representations that allow persons to respond to them as if they were physically real. "Virtual" merely refers to things, situations, and experiences that are dislocated from the frame of the empirically real; they do not necessarily draw reference from, nor are they necessarily a part of, that which can be empirically verified or that which can be made subject to direct measurement. From this perspective, the reality of virtual things emerges from interactions with the representations, not a quality of the things themselves. This approach to virtuality is quite similar to dramaturgical social reality. In this sense, we may borrow from Goffman (1959) to suggest that the reality of on-line environments is a product of a scene that comes off, not the cause of this reality or a quality of the scene itself. Or, we may borrow from W. I. Thomas (1966) to suggest that the things of virtual environments are persuasive representations that become real in their consequences. Like elements of social reality, the "things" of virtual reality may not have an objective or empirical manifestation, yet as representations they exert real influence that allows people to respond to them as if they were real. By eliciting these responses, virtual "things" assume a pragmatic and experiential reality that transcends the frame of the empirically real. Indeed, whether virtual or otherwise, all realities are far more than a mere collection of things: reality is produced, and it is the process of production that is important.

Approaching cybersex in this framework, this study does not concern itself directly with the empirically "real" persons or "real" experiences of sexual arousal, or the orgasms behind these virtual sexual trysts.[3] Rather, it seeks to understand how persons create sexual encounters that have the privilege of being responded to "as if they were real" and the forms of body and selfhood that emerge in these circumstances. What is important to this study is that on-line environments dislocate the physical body from the context of social interaction. In this respect, they are "virtual" encounters. By removing the frame of the empirically real, on-line communication environments potentially allow for the enactment of new forms of selfhood and provide insights into new relationships among bodies, selves, and social situations. What is the relationship among bodies, selves, and social interaction when selfhood is situationally freed from the empirical shell of the body?

## Research Methods

We used firsthand qualitative methods to conduct this research. Interviews and participant observations were conducted in a wide variety of sexually oriented on-line chat forums on commercial servers, Internet Relay Chat, bulletin board systems, and the World Wide Web. Interviews were the primary source of data collection, and a majority of interviews occurred in the chat forums of a large commercial server. ...We accessed on-line chat areas explicitly devoted to the experience of cybersex. (All chat channels are given a name that is generally indicative of the topic for discussion or purpose for communication.) At any given time (but particularly at night), hundreds of channels intended for the purpose of cybersexual encounters can be accessed.

...All of these chat areas were "publicly" available to anyone with access to the system. We did not access sexually explicit chat areas where participants intended to carve out "private" electronic spaces (e.g., membership-based on-line sex locations, private chat rooms, or chat channels that require secret passwords). In each of these chat channels participants made no effort to hide the explicit sexual purposes of their communication forums.

...Over the course of a total of three months, sixty-two nonstandardized e-interviews were conducted. Initially, we conducted and analyzed thirty-two interviews. Later, we conducted an additional thirty interviews to check the validity and elaborate on ideas that emerged from our analysis. ...

## Cybersex: The Simmelian Adventure of Outercourse

The first fully functional teledildonic system will be a communication device, not a sex machine. You will probably *not* use erotic telepresence technology in order to have sexual experiences with machines. ...[P]eople will use them to have sexual experiences with other *people,* at a distance, in combinations and configurations undreamed of by pre-cyberneric voluptuaries.

—Howard Rheingold, *Virtual Reality*

Cybersex is a form of coauthored interactive erotica (Reid 1994). It is a written conversation by which participants transform a computer-mediated communication environment into a personalized interactive arena for sexual experience. In the anonymity of electronic space, individuals engage at least one other participant and type erotic actions, utterances, feelings, and happenings to one another. Like phone sex, cybersex entails a process of provoking, constructing, and playing out sexual encounters through a single interactive mode of communication. In this process participants draw from a vast repertoire of sociocultural symbols to construct a drama that compresses large amounts of information into the very small experiential space of a text medium (Stone 1995). A single channel of dense interactive text compresses and conveys the enormous range of bodily sensations that typically accompany sex (gestures, appearances, expressions, odors, utterances, and physical sensations). Consequently, as many participants indicated, to be "good," cybersex requires a great deal of sexual literacy and communication skills:

An active imagination and expansive vocabulary help. Using predictable expressions is a little ho-hum. Just saying "I want to suck your dick" is unlikely to arouse many people.

There are only so many ooohs and mmm hmmms you can type.

Good typing skills and creativity are fundamental for the scene to come off well in cybersex, which is not surprising considering the challenge of compressing such an intense experience into text.

Cybersex occurs in on-line chat environments that many acknowledged as relatively anonymous forms of interaction (see Jones 1995; Myers 1987; Reid 1991; Turkle 1995; Waskul and Douglas 1997). Participants choose levels of anonymity and exercise selectivity in the personal information that they report to other participants. Emergent from this generally anonymous form of on-line interaction, cybersex participants feel little need to anchor themselves to a physically fixed manifestation of self. Not surprisingly, numerous respondents indicate that the anonymity of the on-line context allows for a fluidity of self-presentations that represent an important element of cybersexual encounters:

Cybersex allows the freedom of sexual expression. Cybersex allows a person to be whoever or whatever they want to be!!

> It's erotic, it turns—me on—the mystery of it. Not knowing who is really on the other end is really erotic—you can be anything. I may stretch truth, and live out fantasies. ...It allows you to be with who ever you want—no inhibitions.

Similar to other forms of role-playing and vicarious experience, the anonymity of on-line chat allows participants to play various selves in the drama of a socially constructed virtual situation. In this case, participants may assume a wide variety of roles in the enactment of an interactive sexual drama. This range of roles is an important element of the eroticism of cybersex, because it allows participants to playfully toy with alternative vicarious experience:

> Sometimes I pretend I'm a woman, I've also invented experiences (like 3 somes). ...Cybersex enables me to play out fantasies. ...It allows you to take your dreams one step closer to reality.

> You can do anything you want and you can picture anybody you wish. It's not real. People can take any identity they want, and they do. People lie about who they are to create sexual illusions.

The anonymity of the medium allows the participants to experiment with sexual adventures. As an added bonus, if the adventure is deemed unpleasant or uncomfortable, the participant can delete his or her screen name or nick and create a new one. The capacity to delete one's nick allows participants to choose another virtual identity under another alias, starting completely anew:

> I deleted my previous screen name because I tried something that went beyond my normal comfort range.

> It's more anonymous. And you can disappear much easier if it doesn't work well.

Anonymity in conjunction with the power to delete and re-create nicks contributes to the emergence of a social environment in which participants feel free to experiment with new social roles and presentations of self. Participants tend to perceive these interactions as a kind of "self-game" (Waskul and Douglas 1997) in which anonymous leisure interactions become a form of recreation and communication play. By "self-game," we generally refer to forms of amusement, simulation, or recreation that involve the alteration of identity, character, or qualities of the person. As one participant stated, "We enjoy it more than some folks enjoy bridge! So, what's the big deal, it's merely another form of entertainment."

Although these alterations during self-games may be intentional, they need not be. Likewise, although these alterations may be playful, they need not be (for more discussion on the nature of self-games, see Waskul and Douglas 1997:390–91). To an extent, we all engage in self-games any time we knowingly attempt to portray ourselves as this-or-that kind of person (e.g., at a job interview). Sometimes, however, we take this experience to an overtly playful level for the purposes of the sheer amusement or pleasure that these self-alterations can provide (e.g., many online cybersex participants).

On-line chat environments allow participants to interact with others from a wide array of socially constructed personae, with no necessary commitment to that which is veritable. This observation, however, is nothing new. Not only have numerous scholars examined the fluidity of selfhood in the context of cyberspace (see Jones 1995; Myers 1987; Reid 1991, 1994; Stone 1995; Turkle 1995; Waskul and Douglas 1997), but in many regards this kind of fluidity and self-multiplicity is not unique to the on-line environment. A "cyberself," like any self, is situationally defined. Persons "have" as many selves as they have meaningful situations to interact in. What makes on-line environments unique is how the remoteness of a physical body expands the fluidity of self-enactments.

When on-line one can not only enact a multiplicity of selves but also enact selves beyond an individual's range of possibility due to constraints the physical body normally imposes. As a result, on-line leisure communication environments present an opportunity for a hyperfluidity of self-enactments due to the ability to transcend gender, skin pigment, age, weight, and all other socially meaningful characteristics of the physical body. In this context all fixed bodily features become variables—self-selected interaction utensils in the enactment of a self-not taken-for-granted constants or givens.

To say that cyberself enactments reveal the potential for hyperfluidity does not lessen their experiential importance to participants. A self, by its very nature, is symbolic—a necessarily fluid and situationally defined system of meaning.[4] Therefore, there is no reason to conclude that cyberselfhood is any less meaningful than other forms of self-enactment—perhaps more transitory or more liminal but not necessarily any less meaningful. In fact, through coauthored erotic fantasy with anonymous others, many cybersex participants claim to learn new sexual techniques, discover new sexual turn-ons, and vicariously experience sexual arousal in ways that they would not (or could not) experience in "real" face-to-face sexual encounters. Consequently, the experience is not only meaningful but also sometimes highly valued:

> With cybersex I learned about stuff I didn't know, like maybe how to do some things better. Everyone should try it!

Since I've started chatting with people on-line, I've been walking around in this perpetual
state of arousal! It's wonderful! I mean, perpetual, never ending, I'm always thinking
about sex, coming up with new ideas, listening to other peoples' fantasies and expressions and learning things I never knew existed!

Although some describe cybersex in terms such as "virtual" or "fantasy,"
and might consider it experientially liminal (i.e., outside the assumed realities of
everyday life), participants often insist that the experience is meaningful and
highly valued. On the surface this appears paradoxical. However, this apparent
inconsistency makes perfect sense when considering the degree to which cybersex represents a Simmelian "adventure," and how both sex and fantasy are important enclaves in which persons create "free areas" for self-expression and
identity work.

Simmel (1911) describes "the erotic" as a supreme example of "the adventure" as a form of experience. To Simmel, the adventure is a form of experiencing that involves "dropping out of the continuity of life...in contrast to that
interlocking of life-links." Although an adventure falls outside the context of
life, it remains connected to it. "It is like an island of life which determines its
beginning and end according to its own formative powers and not—like the part
of a continent—also according to those adjacent territories" (Simmel 1911;
quoted in Levine 1971:189). "The adventure" is an experience that occurs outside the context of taken-for-granted everyday life. Yet, by being outside daily
conventions, the experience uniquely allows persons to synthesize, comprehend,
and provide new meaning to everyday experiences that "the adventure" stands
over and against.

Cohen and Taylor (1992) extend Simmel's "adventure" by illustrating the
ways that sex and fantasy culminate in "activity enclaves" by which persons cultivate a safe place for identity work apart from routinized realities of everyday
life. Both fantasy and sex can be "cultivated as a free area when it is regarded as
a portion of life in which we feel ourselves free of the routine nature of the rest
of existence[,] ...regarded as an activity in which we may 'be ourselves' or 'get
away from everyday life'" (Cohen and Taylor 1992:125–26). Cybersex certainly
constitutes one such "activity enclave." The anonymous nature of on-line leisure
interaction, in conjunction with both the fantasy and the sexual dimensions of
cybersex encounters, creates situational conditions similar to Simmel's form of
adventure and thus potentially creates free spaces for identity work. Although
distinct from the structures of everyday life, there is an intimate relationship between those structures and these experiences. Hence, cybersexual experiences
may become quite meaningful and highly valued by participants, not in spite of
their "virtual" and "fantasy" elements, but *because* of them. One participant

states very clearly how cybersex provides an experience of Simmelian adventure—an activity enclave—in which virtual experiences provide a context for renegotiating self:

> Whether a guy or a girl sends me a private message and wants to talk, it's usually very exciting. I am 32 years old and think I am only now reaching my sexual prime, and I don't know that I'd have discovered certain things about myself without it. I never thought I could be so free with my emotions and fantasies, and it's even spilled over into my real life, I mean, now I feel free about talking about my sexuality (bisexuality) with other people openly, now that I've discussed it with myself first (which basically is what I'm doing here, talking to a nameless, faceless person, i.e., ME!).

Most often, cybersex resembles a Simmelian "island of experience" that is related to everyday life through participants' appeals to physical bodies—as a novel masturbatory innovation, a way to learn about sexual techniques, a means for examining one's sexuality and the sexuality of others. Cybersex participants commonly interpreted the experience by appealing to the physical body. However, the absence of physical bodies promotes the perception of cybersex as a safe form of communication play—an experience in which the emotional baggage of face-to-face sex does not complicate enjoyment. Therefore, participants perceive cybersex as rich in therapeutic effects. For this reason, participants can easily maintain the distinction between cybersex and "real sex" that underlies the experience of a Simmelian "adventure":

> I guess the reason I do [it] is because it is a safe medium by which to explore sexually. To experiment with those aspects of sex that you have not yet explored. To enhance your sex life through the use of new ideas that are learned with a new sexual partner, without risk. It is also a way to be excited sexually without the performance anxiety that is present in face-to-face encounters. It is a way to express yourself sexually in a way you may not feel comfortable doing in a relationship.

> For me, cybersex is an opportunity to give someone else stimulation and fulfillment in about the safest way there is right now—no commitments, no diseases, just good clean nasty fun.

> Acting out of fantasies can be very healthy and therapeutic. It can actually help your real sex life. It helps you do things that you might find difficult to do in real sex. Try things out. Actually find out what the opposite sex likes.

The virtual context and hyperfluidity of self-enactments allow users to engage others in a sexual self-game that intentionally relates to the physical body and interprets cues on that pretext (i.e., sexual arousal). Thus, the con-

text of cybersex upholds the basic triadic body-to-self-to-social-world relationship. Despite the lack of physical bodies, cybersex is still a body-game
enacted by participants according to prevailing sociocultural interpretive discourses. As one respondent states, "It's a paradox. People say that what they
like about [cybersex] is that people are not judging them by their appearance,
but after age/sex checks, it is the first thing everyone wants to know."

## Cybersex and the Social Production of the Virtual Body

The hyperfluidity of selfhood, afforded by the absence of a corporeal body,
does not eliminate the important role of the body in on-line sexual interaction. In fact, the role of the body remains quite important—yet its importance is
almost entirely symbolic. By far the most common phrase in on-line chat environments is some version of the question Are you a male or female? The second
most commonly occurring phrase is usually one of the following: "What do you
look like?" "How old R U?" or "Where do you live?" Ironically, by means of
this complex and technologically sophisticated network of communication, people ask some of the most fundamental body questions imaginable—questions
that are unnecessary or seem inappropriate in face-to-face interaction.

Physical presence does not determine how a person "looks" to another online participant. Rather, appearances depend entirely on information participants
choose to disclose. Or, as one participant states, "What you read is what you
get." Because this convention frees the body from any necessary or verifiable
physical manifestation, it is transformed into complete symbol—a "virtual body"
made manifest in words that emerges from communication and yet remains detached from the frame of the empirically verifiable. In on-line leisure interaction,
both bodies and selves become systems of meaning emergent in a process of
communication, and they associate with whatever semiotic performance participants currently enact. The corporeal body remains at the keyboard—behind the
dramaturgical curtain—engrossed in actions that are only remotely a part of the
scene that comes off. When the corporeal body disappears behind the dramaturgical scene, it no longer contains and holds selfhood. In short, the body is no
longer directly connected to the enacted self.

These conditions often lead people to believe that they are "more free."
Once released from the sociocultural shackles of the physical body, people often
assume that cultural and social meanings associated with bodies somehow magically vanish (i.e., presumptions about gender, race, obesity, ugliness, etc.). Or, in
other words, many seem to believe that the basic triadic body-to-self-to-social-
world relationship becomes a dyadic body-to-self relationship—with the self in

complete control of (and not limited by) the appearance and actions of the body. This kind of "release from the tyranny of selfhood" is a common theme in the rhetoric surrounding the medium. A 1996 MCI television advertisement, entitled "Anthem," promotes this seductive vision: "There is no race. There is no gender. There is no age. There are no infirmities. There are only minds. Is this utopia? No, the Internet."

This happy vision of egalitarianism probably sells a lot of Internet service and remains common currency in the rhetorical harangue that often surrounds major technological innovations. "Some people mistake any discussion of the 'breaking down of boundaries among people' for a prophecy of a utopian society of harmony and bliss" (Meyrowitz 1985:317). However, this egalitarian vision does not stand up to empirical muster, nor does it make reasonable sense. It is more reasonable to suggest that because on-line chat participants can present any body they choose, they will be more likely to do so in a manner supportive of the situational self they are currently enacting. These on-line self-enactments are dramaturgical performances that do not materialize out of thin air. Rather, they occur on a metaphorical stage that contains scripted sociocultural performances to which participants tend to adhere.

Therefore, we should expect the performance of virtual bodies to emerge as a part of a participant's presentation of self, and in highly predictable forms. As communicated elements of a self-enactment, bodies are more likely to adhere to cultural and social prescriptions appropriate to the situation—not as a variable but as a prerequisite to the situation. In this sense, the disembodied on-line context confines, rather than frees, the body.

In cybersex, as long as relationships remain on-line, participants never so much as see each other, regardless of how many words they exchange.[5] The self, the body, and the whole scene of interaction amount to a shared consensual hallucination (Gibson 1984) substantiated and validated in textual dramaturgies that involve other disembodied participants. Each participant contributes to the performance of the other in a negotiated agreement that determines the desires, expectations, and requirements of the situation. Or, as one respondent succinctly stated, "Looks and communication all tie together." Thus, the disembodied context enables participants to sidestep cultural specifications of beauty, glamour, and sexiness, but it does not subvert these concepts (Reid 1994). The fluidity of both body and self-presentation does not free participants from the shackles of the beauty myth but only allows them to redefine themselves in accordance with that myth.

When everyone can be beautiful, there can be no hierarchy of beauty. This freedom, however, is not necessarily one that undermines the power of such conventions. Indeed, such freedom to be beautiful tends to support these conventions by making beauty not unimportant but a pre-requisite[,] ...free from the stigma of ugliness not because appearance ceases to matter but because no one need be seen to be ugly. (Reid 1994:64)

Because participants can present a virtual body that supports a cyberself enactment and because these enactments contain culturally prescribed standards of beauty and sexiness, it should not be surprising to observe a conspicuous absence of fat, ugly persons with pimples, small breasts, or tiny penises. Consider, for example, these typical descriptions of self and body that participants on a commercial on-line system anonymously report:

I have brown hair, blue eyes, average height, average build, bigger-than-average cock!

I'm 22, 6'0" tall, about 176 pounds, long brown hair (mid back). ...Good shape, and love to have a good time. I'm not stuck up, but I am very attractive.

My hobbies include workin' out; I have a 46" chest, 32" waist, and 22" biceps/ great ass nice and firm and a thick 9" cock.

The above are typical descriptions. However, participants do not have to claim either actual or typical appearances. When on-line, persons can present a virtual body that is strikingly attractive, has hyperbolic sexual organs, and absolute specialties in sexual techniques. Take, for example, the following:

My hobbies include using my 13" LONG 4" THICK [sic] Penis on Women. Selectively meeting attractive Women and sexing them with my 13" penis.

I'm a 21 year old single female 5'7" with bluegray eyes.124lbs, 44DD-28-30.

I'm 5'7, Long Black Hair, Brown Eyes, 46DD-30-36,125lbs.

I am 5'2,110, blnde/brn waist length hair, green eyes, 48DD.

Granted, it might be possible, as one of the above participants suggests, to have a 13-inch penis that is 4 inches thick. However, such a penis is improbable. Likewise, it might be possible for a woman to have 48DD breasts—even if she's only 5'2" and weighs a mere 110 pounds. Yet such a woman would have breasts that constitute an improbable amount of her entire body weight. Participants more likely exaggerate the proportions of these virtual bodies in the direction of sociocultural prescriptions for beauty and sexiness. And many on-line participants are acutely aware of this possibility. As one participant stated: "If they really were 6'2,185, with 3 % body fat, and a 8" unit—would they be on-line trying to pick up a gorilla like me?"

Some participants (perhaps a majority) likely embody the sexual performance of a virtual body with exaggerated physical appearances, abilities, and dimensions of sexual organs. Furthermore, these embodiments probably will adhere to (if not extend) social and cultural standards of beauty and sexiness. This is certainly the case when one considers commonly reported breast sizes. One large on-line commercial service allows users to create a "profile"—a brief summary of simple demographic and biographical information. The users of the system create all profiles, and persons can include anything they wish to tell other electronic participants about themselves. Although there is no category for reporting the dimensions of one's virtual body, nonetheless some people do. A keyword search of member profiles revealed that more than 4,250 persons reported a personal bra size. One out of every three persons listing a bra size (32.7%) identified themselves as either D or DD cup.[6] This would indicate that either an inordinate number of large-breasted women spend time on-line or people who claim to be women tend to exaggerate the breast size of their socially constructed virtual body. The latter interpretation seems far more plausible.

Instead of subverting the beauty myth (Wolf 1990), participants *perform a body* that they most often define in accordance with it. When they transform the body into a discursive performance without necessary commitment to the physically real, performances become ideal—a reflection of cultural and social definitions of appropriateness or desirability. These performances of the "virtual body" draw meaning from well-established sociocultural scripts for behavior. Such performances serve to *strengthen* the "beauty myth" and bestow it with more legitimacy. In this respect, the power and freedom to define oneself in accordance with cultural standards of beauty is neither a power nor a freedom; it is what Wolf (1990) calls "the Iron Maiden" of the beauty myth that contains participants within the tight confines of what is culturally acceptable. Indeed, the absence of the corporeal body in cybersex only serves to heighten its symbolic importance. As one respondent explained, "People are playing out a fantasy and the fantasy needs a face and body. Actually, people seem only interested in the body part." More to the point, another respondent simply stated, "Don't you know that everyone on-line is gorgeous?"

These findings blatantly contradict the claim of an on-line egalitarian utopia. While the rhetoric of the medium suggests equality, it only accomplishes this lofty claim by eliminating diversity through the hegemonic power of culture made "high tech." As Nakamura (2000:20) succinctly states, "If technology will indeed make everyone, everything, and every place the same, as 'Anthem' claims in its ambivalent way, then where is there left to go?"

Even when entirely disembodied, self-enactments are still subject to the sociocultural constraints we impose on bodies. As Heim (1991:74) states, "The stand-in self can never fully represent us. The more we mistake the cyberbodies for ourselves, the more the machine twists our selves into the prostheses we are wearing." However, in cybersex, the prostheses that Heim refers to are not technological, they are cultural. The body is not only an empirical object, it is also a symbolic subject that is presented to others and interpreted according to prevailing systems of sociocultural meaning—even when the body is not present in the scene of interaction.

Sex is an act that requires, or is at least dependent on, physical bodies. One's body in relation to the bodies of others forms the essence of a sexual encounter. Yet in cyberspace there can be no body, or fixed physical entity of the person. Nonetheless, cybersex does not escape claims of the flesh. Indeed, it fundamentally depends on them, extends them, and latently supports cultural and social standards for interpreting them. In text-based on-line leisure environments, participants transform their bodies into symbol alone—representations, descriptive codes, and words that embody expectations, appearances, and actions. Thus, they transform their bodies into a dramaturgical performance. What participants send to and from computer terminals are not merely words and self-enactments but body performances. Thus, cybersex is based on claims of the flesh in a discursive embodiment of sociocultural meanings that connect with a performance and emerge from the interactions between participants.

## Conclusions

Because computer-networking technologies allow persons to dislocate selfhood from the corporeal body, one can transform himself or herself into someone else. This represents a classic case of vicarious experience—involvement in a role without commitment to that role. In a society where people are expected to be what their role implies, computer-networking technologies can have a kind of liberating potential that we can easily see in on-line chat environments. As numerous respondents in this study indicate, one can be who one might like to be, what one might like to experiment with being, or even who one does not think one is. Many examples of screen personae that prove untrue further substantiate this observation. In leisure on-line forums, persons may not even know something as simple as the actual gender of the person with whom they are communicating (see Van Gelder 1985). Indeed, self-games abound in the personae playground of on-line chat environments. However, the findings of this study also conclude with equally important evidence that contradicts this observation. Cybersex participants clearly confine their body presentations within the narrow margins of prevailing cultural norms of beauty and sexual attractiveness. On-line interaction clearly facilitates *both* a greater degree of fluidity and greater limitations on the presentation of self. That is, participants' experiential sense of fluid, open, discursive horizons of multiple potentials for being exists primarily as a freedom to define themselves in accordance with the prevailing standards of what others expect, desire, or mandate by the situation.

**The Enselfment of the Body**

When we tear apart the taken-for-granted seamless surface of reality as exemplified by on-line experiences of virtuality, we find a liminal creature existing within the nuts and bolts of the situation (Stone 1995). In on-line leisure environments, this liminal experience falls within the boundaries of disembodiment and hyperfluidity of selfhood. Although the societal imperative is to have one primary persona, that prescription appears firmly affixed to the physical body. In other words, in spite of widely diverse self-enactments, the self-evident, matter-of-fact, physical existence of the body can comfortably maintain consistency between selves in everyday life. As long as one's physical body is present, one can always be certain of oneself—no matter what one is doing. The experience of fluid disembodiment, characteristic of leisure on-line chat, does not provide this kind of cognitive consistency. Quite simply, in cyberspace no physical form exists on which to affix or contain a self.

In many ways this situation encourages the creation of forms of selfhood and body presentations that characterize the postmodern condition. "It is pastiche, a borrowing from diverse imagery, styles, and traditions, including both 'high' and 'low,' mundane and special, and past, present and future, wherever these seem usable: a form of contextless quotation" (Glassner 1990:217). Or, as Trachtenberg (1985:7) describes, it becomes "performative rather than revelatory, superficial rather than immanent, aleatory rather than systematic, dispersed rather than focused." Yet the fluid and diverse forms by which participants present, negotiate, and validate self and body in on-line communication environments do not merely reflect or simply illustrate the postmodern condition. Rather, we can see these conditions as *accommodations* to the postmodern condition.

Glassner's (1990) analysis of the contemporary fitness movement as "an attempt to reconstruct the self (and in particular the self-body relationship) in a manner that is more felicitous to life in contemporary American culture" (p. 218) bears an uncanny similarity to the findings of this study. To Glassner, the heart of the contemporary fitness movement is a "salvation of the self" "an intimate and holistic marriage between self and body"—through *being* fit, as a means by which "selves are truly embodied." To Glassner, this accommodation allows participants to reconcile the Cartesian twins and resolve principal dualities (i.e., "male-female," "insideoutside," "mortality-immortality"). We may extend this to suggest that both the "fit body" and the "virtual body" of on-line chat environments may be regarded as "a postmodern object par excellence, its image perpetually reconstructed of pieces and colorations added on then discarded" (Glassner 1990:228). Whereas Glassner argues that the fit "embody the self," we may similarly argue that on-line chat participants "enself the body." The on-line "virtual body," like the self, becomes an object of pure meaning—a fluid construct that emerges, like the self, as a product of the scene that comes off. Both the "embodiment of the self" and the "enselfment of the body" locate personhood in a safety zone by neutralizing, reducing, or containing meaning. Both accommodations join together the self and the body in a manner that resolves the Cartesian twins and related dualities. Both are totalizing, one in the direction of the corporeal and the other in the direction of the symbolic. Yet in spite of these differences, these two accommodations are remarkably similar because they are both mere images that are more real than the "real" things they reference (see Glassner 1990). The accommodations are opposite; the effects of grounding selfhood are nearly identical.

In cybersex (and other forms of leisure on-line interaction), participants playfully toy with the virtual actualization of multiple potentials of being. In leisure forms of on-line interaction, bodies, selves, and situations become emergent symbolic elements contingent on interaction. Yet when participants interact, meaning simply does not arise out of thin air. We find the answers to questions such as Who am I? What is going on here? How shall I apprehend this other person? in a broader sociocultural context. Although disembodied, participants are not separate from the sociocultural interpretive apparatus that provides meaning to self, body, situation, and other. On-line participants fashion a self and body through the same symbolic stock of images that provide meaning in everyday life. Thus, in the dislocated and disembodied context of on-line interaction the dramaturgies of producing a meaningful self and body assume new salience, yet still remain rooted in the same symbolic milieu, using the same sets of resources as any other self and body performance.

What does this indicate about the contemporary relationship between selves and bodies? First, the issues noted in this article go beyond the confines of certain recreational dimensions of cyberspace. Rather, they reveal (and are extensions of) much broader shifts in sociocultural beliefs, practices, and technologies. "These include repeated transgressions of the traditional concept of the body's physical envelope and the locus of human agency" (Stone 1995:16). Numerous authors have noted the increasingly pervasive experience of multiplicity (see Gergen 1991; Lifton 1993; Stone 1995). In this regard, *disembodiment is the embodiment of the experience of multiplicity.* That is, if multiple potentials of being have proliferated in technologies of communication and if the citizens of contemporary media culture are indoctrinated with a multitude of selves, then disembodiment provides the ultimate experience of multiplicity. Thus, participants can tacitly resolve contradictions between a singular corporeal body and self amid their experiences of self-multiplicity.

...Within these technosocial arenas of experience, the meaning of the body-self relationship manifests itself in a transformed and/or transforming state. What emerges is not merely a body-as-container-of-self, or body-as-dramaturgical-prop relationship. Rather, evident in this study (and suggestive of broader sociocultural changes) is a body-as-*performance* relationship. The body is more than a prop that is used in a variety of ways to support a multiplicity of self-enactments. Increasingly, the meanings of the actions taken by human agencies define both bodies and selves. As this study suggests, the most stable personal characteristic—our sense of who we are and where we are in space—is now open to redefinition. Given the possibilities of selfhood made manifest in the emerging datasphere as a new arena for human experience, and the relationship of these experiences to the bodies that may or may not be grounded in this matrix of virtual experience, new questions arise about what constitutes a person.

## Notes

1.  This study examines and uses the term "cybersex" to refer to what is sometimes called "netsex," "tinysex," and "net.sleaze." For our purposes, cybersex is a chat-based, interactive, coauthored, text fantasy. Cybersex participants log on to computer networks, meet others in electronic space, and type sexually explicit messages to one another. Although many associate cybersex with adult CD-ROM technologies, interactive games, and pornographic images available in computer formats (see Robinson and Tamosaitis 1993), here we use the term strictly to refer to erotic forms of real-time chat communication predominantly found on Internet Relay Chat, chat areas of commercial on-line services, multi-user games, and bulletin board services.

2.  We must acknowledge that we cannot seamlessly resolve the interplay among self, body, and social world. Distinctions between self and body, body and social world, self and social world, are fundamentally wedded to the basic Cartesian mind-body distinction that perme-

ates the social sciences, and relate to the general bifurcation between that which is "objective" and that which is "subjective."

3. In the context of this study, we are not concerned with whether cybersex is more or less like "real sex." In fact, we contend that distinctions between cybersex and "real sex" are far less concrete than are often assumed. To a certain extent, even corporeal sexual intercourse has always entailed elements of virtual experience. What is the point of sexy lingerie, romantic music, scented candles, and soft-spoken words if not to produce a "virtual" environment for the experience of "real" sexual pleasure?

4. The illusion of stability (i.e., "core self," "personality," etc.) is a social-psychological consequence of stable sets of social relations. If the self is an entity of pure meaning, then, like any system of meanings, it cannot possibly have a singular fixed form.

5. Certainly some cybersex relationships progress to off-line meetings. We acknowledge that these kinds of relationships bring about new dynamics as on-line body and self-games confront the corporeal reality of a living person. For this reason, some people may consider our analysis an "artificial" separation of an act (cybersex) from the relationship in which it is embedded (the ongoing progression of a relationship). However, not all on-line cybersex relationships progress to off-line meetings. In fact, we argue that the majority of on-line cybersexual encounters never result in off-line meetings. Yet *all* cybersex encounters occur on-line, and, at least initially, most cybersex encounters exist entirely in response to what occurs online. For this reason (in addition to the fact that our analysis seeks to focus on the dynamics of what occurs *on-line)*, we do not believe that our overall analysis is in any way "artificial."

6. It should be noted that this keyword search only allowed for a maximum of 250 matching entries. Twelve bra sizes produced more than 250 matching entries. This means that there is no way to determine exactly how many persons actually report a bra size and the exact number of matches for the bra sizes that exceed the maximum 250. However, we feel confident of our interpretation of the data, since nine of the twelve bra sizes that exceeded the limits of 250 maximum matches were large (384) C or D cups.

# References

Altheide, D. and R. Snow. 1991. *Media Worlds in the Postjournalism Era.* New York, NY: Aldine.

Chayko, M. 1993. "What is Real in the Age of Virtual Reality? 'Reframing' Frame Analysis for a Technological World." *Symbolic Interaction 16(2): 171–81*

Cohen, S. and L. Taylor. 1992. *Escape Attempts: The Theory and Practice of Resistance to Everyday Life.* 2d ed. New York, NY: Routledge.

Davis, M. 1983. *Smut: Erotic Reality/Obscene Ideology.* Chicago, IL: University of Chicago Press.

Eco, U. 1986. *Travels in Hyperreality.* Orlando, FL: Harcourt Brace Jovanovich.

Gergen, K. 1991. *The Saturated Self: Dilemmas of Identity in Contemporary Life.* New York, NY: BasicBooks.

Gibson, W. 1984. *Neuromancer.* New York: Ace.

Glassner, B. 1990. "Fit for Postmodern Selfhood." Pp. 215–43 in *Symbolic Interaction and Cultural Studies,* edited by H. Becker and M. McCall. Chicago, IL: University of Chicago Press.

Goffman, E. 1968. *Asylums: Essays on the Social Situation of Mental Patients and Other Inmates.* New York: Anchor.

———. 1959. *The Presentation of Self in Everyday Life.* Garden City, NY: Doubleday Anchor.

Heim, M. 1991. "The Erotic Ontology of Cyberspace." Pp. 59–80 in *Cyberspace: First Steps,* edited by M. Benedikt. Cambridge, MA: MIT Press.

Jones, S. 1995. *Cybersociety: Computer-mediated Communication and Community.* Thousand Oaks, CA: Sage.

Laurel, B. 1993. *Computers as Theater.* Reading, MA: Addison-Wesley.

Lifton, R. 1993. *The Protean Self: Human Resilience in an Age of Fragmentation.* New York, NY: Basic Books.

Merleau-Ponty, M. 1962. *Phenomenology of Perception.* Translated by C. Smith. London: Routledge and Kegan Paul.

Meyrowitz, J. 1985. *No Sense of Place: The Impact of Electronic Media on Social Behavior.* New York, NY: Oxford University Press

Myers, D. 1987. "'Anonymity Is Part of the Magic': Individual Manipulation of Computer-Mediated Communication Contexts." *Qualitative Sociology* 10(3):251–66.

Nakamura, L. 2000. "Where Do You Want to Go Today? Cybernetic Tourism, the Internet, and Transnationality." Pp. 15–26 in *Race in Cyberspace,* edited by B. Kolke, L. Nakamura, and G. Rodman. New York, NY: Routledge.

Reid, E. 1994. *Cultural Formations in Text-based Virtual Realities.* M.A. thesis, University of Melbourne.

———. 1991. "Electropolis: Communication and Community on Internet Relay Chat." Honors thesis, University of Melbourne.

Rheingold, H. 1991. *Virtual Reality.* New York, NY: Touchstone.

Robinson, P. and N. Tamosaitis. 1993. *The Joy of Cybersex: An Underground Guide to Electronic Erotica.* New York, NY: Brady.

Simmel, G. 1971 [1911]. "The Adventurer." Pp. 187–98 in *Georg Simmel: On Individuality and Social Forms,* edited by D. Levine. Chicago, IL: University of Chicago Press.

Stone, A. 1995. *The War of Desire and Technology at the Close of the Mechanical Age.* Cambridge, MA: MIT Press.

Strauss, A.1993. *Continual Permutations of Action.* Hawthorne, NY: Aldine.

Thomas, W. I. 1966. "The Relation of Research to the Social Process." Pp. 289–305 in W. I. *Thomas on Social Organization and Social Personality,* edited by M. Janowitz. Chicago, IL: University of Chicago Press.

Trachtenberg, S. 1985. *The Postmodern Movement: A Handbook of Contemporary Innovation in the Arts.* Westport, CT: Greenwood Press.

Turkel, S. 1995. *Life on the Screen: Identity in the Age of the Internet.* New York, NY: Simon and Schuster.

Van Gelder, L. 1985. "The Strange Case of the Electronic Lover." *Ms.,* October:pp. 94–95.

———. 1996. "Virtual Sisterhood." *CompuServe Magazine,* February (15):30–33.

Waskul, D. and M. Douglass. 1997. "Cyberself: The Dynamics of Self in Online Chat." *Information Society: An International Journal* 13(4):375–97.

Wolf, N. 1990. *The Beauty Myth: How Images of Beauty Are Used against Women.* New York, NY: William Morrow.

Zerubavel, E. 1991. *The Fine Line: Making Distinctions in Everyday Life.* New York, NY: Free Press.

# Chapter Two

# The Naked Self: Body and Self in Televideo Cybersex

## Dennis D. Waskul[*]

*When cybersex participants include digital cameras as part of the communicative sexplay, the experience is fundamentally transformed. When one can see one's cyberlover(s) in live moving video, one can also assess (with relative accuracy) gender, race, ethnicity, age, physical attractiveness, and other "fleshy" variables of personhood—no longer can everybody be anybody. And, as one might well imagine, these erotic episodes can be extremely "fleshy"—filled with nudity, frank genital displays, voyeurism, exhibitionism and, often, mutual masturbation. In these provocative encounters participants not only see others but also, as Waskul explores, see themselves in the looking-glass of technology and the way others respond to seeing their naked body. By virtue of this "naked self" participants claim to get more than just an orgasm out of the experience.*

In any form of interaction, the body becomes an object to one's self and others, presenting itself as an acting subject and a viewed object. This characteristic of the body is explicit in sex, making it a distinctively and pleasingly embodied experience, for in order to have sex a body is necessary. In sex our bodies become objects for the purpose of pleasure in our partner(s) and ourselves. Yet sex is not merely about bodies; it is inextricably infused with subjective meaning. As Simmel (1950:131) suggests, "Sexual intercourse is the most intimate and personal process, but on the other hand, it is absolutely general. ...[T]he psychological secret of this act lies in its double character of being both wholly personal and wholly impersonal." For these reasons, sex is an ideal context for examining the interplay between the objective and subjective qualities of the body and the self and how these are mediated by situated social interaction.

Cybersex is a form of experience that makes these relationships especially salient. After all, the Internet is among the most dislocated and disembodied contexts for real-time human interaction. "The body—or its absence—is central to contemporary notions of 'cyberspace,' 'the Internet,' 'virtuality': computer-mediated communications (CMC) are defined around the absence of physical

[*] Waskul, Dennis. 2002. "The Naked Self: Being a Body in Televideo Cybersex." *Symbolic Interaction* 25(2):199–227.

presence, the fact that we can be interactively present to each other as unanchored textual bodies without being proximate or visible as definite physical objects" (Slater 1998:91). On the Internet, participants interact with others in separate electronic space removed from the immediate presence of the body. Because sex requires a body, cybersex participants must evoke them, and in this process the role and nature of the body is necessarily magnified. In text-based cybersex, participants evoke a subjective semiotic body through typed words. In televideo cybersex, participants interact through digital cameras that display live images of their bodies. Thus televideo cybersex participants evoke the body as an image; they quite intentionally display their bodies as *objects* to be seen. What is the relationship among bodies, selves, and society in these complex erotic forms of social interaction? What can these relationships tell us about the interplay among bodies, selves, and society in everyday life?

### Cybersex and the Body: Textual Enselfment and Video Embodiment

"Cybersex" has rapidly become a catchall term used to refer to an enormous range of computer-mediated sexually explicit material, including adult CD-ROMs, interactive games, and pornographic sound, image, and video files often available over the Internet (Robinson and Tamosaitis 1993). However, in spite of these commercial uses of the term, we find that cybersex is only marginally related to pornography and is more squarely situated in a specific kind of interactive erotic *experience*.[1]

Among experienced cybersex participants, little ambiguity exists as to what constitutes cybersex. It refers strictly to erotic forms of real-time computer-mediated communication. Through typed text or live video (and sometimes spoken voice) cybersex participants meet one another for erotic encounters in the ether of computer-mediated environments. Regardless of the form, however, cybersex always entails meeting someone else in these decidedly liminal "places" where real people interact with other real people for the purposes of sexual arousal and gratification. This study is concerned only with televideo cybersex—casual and usually anonymous televideo sexual encounters between participants who do it for fun.[2]

Although televideo cybersex entails considerable text communication, it differs from text cybersex in that one can *see* the other person(s) involved in live streaming video. By using relatively inexpensive digital cameras and client software, in televideo, live images of one's partner(s) accompany "hot chat." What they look like, what they are (or are not) wearing, where they are, their moment-by-moment expressions, and what they are doing (often to themselves) are all apparent. For this reason, televideo contrasts with text cybersex: it *is an embodied experience.* Televideo cybersex participants embody themselves in the images that represent them. Indeed, the purpose of televideo cybersex is to see images, the bodies of other people, and to be seen.

Thus one cannot, as in the case of text cybersex, simply create a body of unbounded dimensions and attributes. In televideo the body is not a "pure object of meaning" (Waskul, Douglass, and Edgley 2000:394); instead it is presented as an object—a visible *thing,* an image attached to the corporeal person, put on display with the intention of being seen for the purposes of giving and receiving sexual attention or arousal.

## The Object and Subject Body: Sex, Objects, and Sex Objects

I make myself flesh in order to impel the Other to realize *for herself* and *for me* her own flesh, and my caresses cause my flesh to be born for me insofar as it is for the Other *flesh causing her to be born as flesh. I* make her enjoy my flesh through her flesh in order to compel her to feel herself flesh.

—Jean-Paul Sartre, *Being and Nothingness*

Being treated as an object—a physical body—is a necessary part of human sexuality.[3] In sex we have little choice in this matter of being an object, but neither do we have this choice in any other form of interaction. The very nature of personhood is to be both perceiver and perceived, subject and object. Indeed, the "the self has the characteristic that it is an object to itself" (Mead 1934:136). Likewise, the body is always both a noun and a verb; we inhabit an object body (noun) that is subjectively experienced in embodiment (verb).

...While the body may be *present* as an empirical *object,* its meaning and our ability to conceive of it is no more or less innately determined by the qualities of its "thingness" than any other object. In fact, "the body cannot be a direct object to itself. It is an object only to some actor" (Strauss 1993:110). This "actor" can be an individual or a group of individuals who act toward the body in some fashion (Strauss 1993). It is through a process of interpreting, assigning meaning, and internalizing these interactions that we come to indirectly interpret, know, and understand the body.

In this way, as Mead (1934:136) might argue, the body can be an object unto itself but only insofar as a self is involved: "bodily experiences are for us organized about a self." It is "the self [that] makes possible the body as meaning" (Gadow 1982:89), for only by virtue of a self may we see and act toward our bodies as others might. We decorate it through clothing, adorn it through accessories, have sex with it through masturbation, and, in extreme duress, even kill it through suicide. In other words, we may extend Mead's overall point: the body and the self are not merely two separate entities; we can only experience either of them indirectly and symbolically by taking the role of the other.

The body and bodily states are experienced only indirectly in a process by which corporeal objective and subjective conditions are socially shaped. "Physiological sensations are only the raw material out of which bodily experiences are socially constructed" (Cahill 2001:47). As Mason-Schrock (1996) contends, transsexuals explicitly illustrate this relationship among the body, the self, and society. They believe they are born into the wrong body and must look elsewhere for signs of their true gendered selves. But it would be a mistake to understand this problem as limited to transsexuals and others in similarly extreme conditions. For all of us, the conceptual frameworks by which we interpret the body, the language we use to describe it, the narratives we tell about it, the situations in which we find it, and the definitions we impose on it have an influence on the body as an object and mediate how we experience it as a subject. While we may often apprehend the body in various physiological states—in sexual arousal, a drug high (Becker 1963, 1967), pain (Baumeister 1991), critical illness (Frank 1991), or any other corporeal condition—these are experiences, mediated by social structure, culture, interaction, and social situation. ...

...However, the body is a special kind of object, "because it must represent the self in a special sense" (Strauss 1993:111). Because selfhood is symbolic and cannot be directly observed, it is all too easy to directly equate the self with the body and remain oblivious to distinctions between the two and to the broader relationships among bodies, selves, society, and the situations in which we interact. "Embodiment connotes personification, but it also can refer to the body itself as the materialization of otherwise invisible qualities. ...[T]he body continues to be an omnipresent material mediator of who we are or hope to be" (Holstein and Gubrium 2000:197), and therefore this tendency to equate body and self is not entirely without merit.

To be sure, an immediate and undeniable relationship exists between the self and the body. This relationship takes vivid form when the severely stigmatized body negatively affects the self (see Goffman 1963b). More generally, a body is an obvious and necessary prerequisite to having a self; one can hardly speak of a self that has no body (after all, the loss of a body is tantamount to death; a self without a body is not a person; in common parlance we only refer to people as bodies when they are dead). As Simmel (1950:322, 344) suggests, the body is our "first property." We unconditionally possess our body, it obeys our will, and others may categorize it as belonging to us alone. But even so, "body and self, though inseparable, are not identical" (Gadow 1982:86). The body does not represent the whole of the self, and the self is not a physiological component of the body. As William James reminds us:

> Our bodies themselves, are they simply ours, or are they us? Certainly men have been ready to disown their bodies and to regard them as mere vestures, or even as prisons of clay from which they should someday be glad to escape. ([1892] 1961:44)

While Strauss argues that the distinction between the body and the self "is only an analytic artifact" (1993:113; original emphasis), we can remain this conceptually casual only if we ignore the significance of the body in relation to the self (Goffman 1963b; Mason-Schrock 1996) or the degree to which the body can become an independent object or subject completely detached from the self in social situations (Waskul, Douglass, and Edgley 2000). In addition, the increasing prevalence of social interaction technologies makes it possible to transcend the empirical shell of the body, thus severing its traditional connection to the self and the situatedness of both in social contexts. Technologies of communication, especially interaction on the Internet, make it increasingly possible to dislocate selfhood from the body, precariously situating and/or dislocating one or the other from the context of interaction. In some cases, these technologies permit the body to be "enselfed" (Waskul, Douglass, and Edgley 2000); in others (such as televideo cybersex) it permits participants to embody the self. These separations potentially relocate the subject *and* object of interactions and potentially transform or expose relationships between them.

## Nudity and the Net: Voyeurs and Exhibitionists

It is easy to imagine what goes on in televideo cybersex. Participants meet one another in televideo environments (sometimes one on one, sometimes in groups), disrobe (partly or completely, if they are not already naked), display their bodies before others, and comment on what they are seeing. This experience typically leads to sexual arousal, self-touching, and masturbation—all of which participants usually (but not always) put on display for others to see. Often these provocative encounters become an emergent "conversation of gestures": one participant disrobes and flaunts his or her body; if pleased, the other participant may say so, disrobe, and do the same. One participant may begin to masturbate, inviting the other to join in. This conversation of gestures continues until its climactic conclusion. Couples (heterosexual or homosexual) will sometimes connect with individuals or other couples. Most often these erotic encounters occur between people who do not know one another and intend to have casual and immediate sexual gratification. Once satisfied, the interaction typically ends and participants disconnect. However, in spite of various differences, the eroticism of televideo cybersex emerges from a process of intentionally displaying one's body before others in an explicitly sexual manner.

On the surface, televideo cybersex may appear similar to other forms of public or semipublic nudity. It would seem to share much in common with nude beaches (Douglas 1977), nudist resorts (Weinberg 1965, 1966, 1967), the naturist movement (Bell and Holliday 2000), Finnish saunas (Edelsward 1991), streaking (Toolan et al. 1974), and the practice of exposing female breasts at Mardi Gras in New Orleans (Forsyth 1992). Like those who engage in other forms of semipublic nudity, televideo cybersex participants blatantly violate obvious cultural norms. In addition, cybersex occurs in an environment that shares a similar "liminal" (Turner 1969) stigma-suspending quality with other forms of public nudity. "Clothing modesty is a *ceremony* of everyday life that sustains a nonintimate definition of relationships, and with its voluntary suspension relationships are usually [redefined]" (Weinberg 1966:21; original emphasis). The Finnish sauna, like nude beaches, resorts, Mardi Gras, and televideo cybersex, "represents a symbolic separation from the ordinary, a liminal period characterized by separate space, separate time, and separate activities" (Edelsward 1991:193). This separation and liminality is marked by physical, temporal, normative, and symbolic territories. Televideo cybersex occurs in the already liminal world of "cyberspace," a place without space. On the Internet participants, from the comfort of their "space" at home (where nudity is permissible), interact with others in a semipublic "place" (where nudity is generally not permissible). The Internet juxtaposes these "spaces" and "place," and thereby creates a natural environment for liminality: a place separate from one's space where the ordinary norms of everyday life easily may be suspended.

In the final analysis, however, televideo cybersex differs markedly from other forms of public nudity (if we can call it "public" at all). Unlike saunas, nude beaches, and resorts, where nudity is purposely antierotic (Douglas 1977; Edelsward 1991; Weinberg 1981), the nakedness of televideo cybersex is intended to be read sexually. In the former, participants rigidly practice "studied inattention" (Douglas 1977:108), or what Goffman (1963a) calls "civil inattention." In contrast, televideo cybersex participants do not desexualize their nudity, they do not practice "civil inattention" toward the naked bodies of others, and they do not loathe the opportunistic gaze of those who may be watching. Instead they revel in attention. Unlike naturism, there is no "problematic relationship to sex" (Bell and Holliday 2000); nudity and sex are irrevocably intertwined. Nudity in the context of televideo cybersex has nothing to do with "a 'philosophy' which is all about bodies in nature" (Bell and Holliday 2000:127). It does not entail defying social norms and values (Toolan et al. 1974) or the freedom of naturism (Douglas 1977), and it does not involve a lifestyle among others who share strong bonds of solidarity (Edelsward 1991; Weinberg 1965, 1966, 1967). In televideo cybersex, being naked is undeniably and unambiguously about sex. Stripping and being seen nude is meant to be erotic, and there is no pretense of other motivation.

The eroticism of televideo cybersex is related to the pleasures of voyeurism and exhibitionism. However, in the objectified sense of the terms, the participants in this study are *not* true voyeurs or exhibitionists. Voyeurism is the practice of observing others in sexually arousing activities or postures. "Most of us are voyeurs to some extent or at some times: we enjoy looking at people, their visual depiction, or reading about sexual activities" (Kupfer 1983:94). Likewise, exhibitionism is the practice of putting our bodies on display as an object to be seen for the purposes of sexual arousal and attention. We are all exhibitionists to some extent or at some times: we enjoy being looked at, made to feel desirable, sexy, and attractive. Although sexual gazing and being looked upon makes up part of our sex lives, they do not substitute for our actual physical participation. Certainly exhibitionism and voyeurism often aroused participants in this study, but the experience was interactive. Because participants could see and respond to each other, little gap existed between what they watched and how it aroused them (and vice versa). Therefore, the voyeurism and exhibitionism of televideo cybersex closely approximates the voyeurism and exhibitionism of *any* sexual experience.

If the majority of participants in this study are not true voyeurs or exhibitionists, then what accounts for the eroticism of cybersex? How do televideo participants play with the natural tendencies of voyeurism and exhibitionism in their experiences of cybersex? Because both voyeurism and exhibitionism are focally related to the body, what are the implications and consequences of this experience on the self? Because televideo cybersex participants explicitly display their bodies as objects for the subjective sexual interpretation of voyeuristic glare, to what extent may we conclude that televideo cybersex is merely a playful extension of the same social processes by which all bodies are experienced in the interstices of being both object and subject?

## Sexuality, Alter-Sexuality, and Cybersex

In this study I use televideo cybersex as a strategic lens to allow us to see, further understand, and contemplate relationships among the body, the self, and situated social interaction. Sexuality may not be the direct topic of interest in this study: however, it is essential to address it. "Sexuality" is a general term that potentially can refer to almost anything that we may regard as sexual in relation to the person. Yet "sexuality" is commonly used in specific and concrete ways. We commonly speak of *"our* sexuality," or *"their* sexuality," but seldom do we think of it as merely *"a* sexuality." Thus people often assume that sexuality is connected directly to the person, as something that, although influenced or shaped by others, is within individuals and pertains to their bodies with regard to sex. Given that computer-mediated interaction is a distinctively dislocated and disembodied form of interaction, framing sexuality in this way poses serious problems for the study of sex on the Internet.

As Rival, Slater, and Miller indicate (1998:301), the cardinal attraction to sex on the Internet is the "license simply to float pleasurably through a shamelessly eroticized space." The key point, however, is that

> these pleasures and transgressions evidently depend upon *a clear separation of sexuality from "real life":* they are without commitment or consequence; the material resources on which they depend (finance, technology, symbolic capital, labour) are obscured from view and experienced as beyond any scarcity. ...[T]here are no material cares or dangers (including disease); no enduring commitments; performance is unproblematic; desire is inexhaustible, as is desirability (everyone is desired and included). Bodies neither fail, nor make non-sexual demands. (Rival, Slater, and Miller 1998:301; emphasis added)

In short, the dislocated and disembodied nature of computer-mediated communications makes cybersex an experience that potentially expresses a sexuality separate from and transgressive of the person, the body, and everyday life.

For these reasons, it remains unclear whether cybersex participants act out vicarious fantasies directly related to their sexuality or merely engage in cybersex as a form of communicative play only marginally related to sexuality. Whether we can ever tell the difference between the two is even more unclear. On the Internet, an otherwise heterosexual female could "go gay" for a fifteen-minute cybersex encounter. Possibly her lesbian cybersex experience is related to her sexuality, but equally possibly, it may not. In fact, Slater's (1998:99) research on sexpic trading on Internet Relay Chat (IRC) found that "most informants were clear that one of the greatest pleasures and attractions of the IRC sexpics scene was not so much the direct indulgence of their own desires as a fascination with the diversity of human sexuality." Slater (1998:106–7) cites at length participants who find "both sexpics and cybersex very boring" and states, "Both are merely occasions or opportunities for other pleasures of the scene." Clearly these kinds of situations raise complex questions, but at the very least they suggest the need to conceive of the relationship between sexuality and cybersex differently.

In addition to an expression of sexuality, cybersex may constitute a form of *altersexuality,* referring to sexual experiences that differ from those in "real" life. They are a special category of sexual experiences that stand over and against, bounded within a sphere of experiences that can be comfortably maintained as separate and distinct from everyday life and may not be related directly to a person's "real" sexuality. Altersexuality is a kind of liminal experience in which both intimacy and sexuality may be reinvented in the context of loosened temporal, physical, and normative constraints.

How can we frame sexuality so that it may be dynamic enough to include the enormously varied and rich experiences that are made possible in cybersex? We may look to Goffman for a promising approach to framing sexuality and altersexuality in relation to cybersex. For Goffman (1959:252–53), the self "is a *product* of a scene that comes off, and it is not a *cause* of it. The self, then, as a performed character, is not an organic thing that has a specific location. ...[I]t is a dramatic effect arising diffusely from a scene that is presented, and the characteristic issue, the crucial concern, is whether it will be credited or discredited" (original emphasis). Similarly we can argue that sexuality is the product of a scene that comes off, not a cause of it. Sexuality is a dramatic effect arising diffusely from the presented scene, and the crucial issue is whether sexuality is credited or discredited, not whether it is a genuine part of the individual. Framing sexuality in this fashion obliterates the problem of connecting cybersex to the person. As Goffman (1959:252) might argue, "while this [sexuality] is...*concerning* the individual, [it] does not derive from its possessor, but from the whole scene of his action, being generated by that attribute of local events which renders them interpretable by witnesses."

For the purposes of this research, sexuality is something that we *do,* not something that we *are.* Thus this research focuses on how participants "do" sexuality in televideo cybersex, with specific attention to how it is related to the body, the self, and situated social interaction.

## Methods and Data

...Open-ended qualitative interviews with televideo cybersex participants generated the data for this study. I spent several months and uncounted hours exploring and generally "hanging out" in televideo environments where people meet, chat, and watch each other in real time.

I accessed televideo environments that participants explicitly used for sexual purposes and invited them to contact me (via televideo) for a live online interview. Whenever possible, I avoided soliciting specific individuals for interviews so as not to disrupt the social and sexual context of these erotic environments. All respondents agreed to participate, were informed of the nature of the study, were guaranteed anonymity, and were given an opportunity to ask questions. Participants were told that they could withdraw from the interview at any time.

Because televideo cybersex participants are not particularly accessible for research, large samples are difficult to obtain. Even in adult televideo chat environments, not all participants are interested in sex or in answering intimate questions from a researcher. Still, over four months, I conducted thirty-one interviews. Interviews lasted between fifteen minutes and one hour. All participants in this study identified themselves (or could be recognized) as adults. Twenty-four participants were male, and seven were female. Nineteen identified themselves as heterosexual, six as homosexual, and six as bisexual. No additional identifying information was asked of the participants. Of course, given the size of the sample, the findings are merely suggestive. ...

### Televideo Cybersex: Being a Body and Ephemeral Self-Reduction

Televideo cybersex is a hybrid form of erotica—part pornography and part live erotic entertainment. It is pornography to the extent that participants see or hear objective and computer-mediated sexually explicit sounds and images that are dislocated from the people they represent. People look at and listen to sexual sounds and images, giving televideo cybersex much the same voyeuristic appeal as any other kind of pornography, with the added twist of being live, fully interactive, and starring honest-to-goodness "amateurs":

> What I like most is seeing hot studs!

> It's just for fun. I like looking at other people. More like a game to see if you can guess what they're gonna look like with no clothes on.

> Of course, I find the whole thing with televideo exciting and men are the reason. ...It is exciting from one click to the next to see what is going to pop up in front of you.

> I'm just like most males, I get hard just watching a pretty girl putting on a show.

Because televideo cybersex participants are not just watching but also being watched, the experience becomes more than pornography. They are live erotic performers and consumers, casual voyeurs, and exhibitionists all at once. The televideo cybersex norm is "you can watch me in exchange for me watching you"—a norm that can cause uneasiness. One woman explained, "I've only done it [televideo cybersex] for two different guys, but I didn't feel comfortable doing it so now I just flash a booby here or there."

Why would anyone feel compelled to show her body in a circumstance that makes her uncomfortable? All participants seem acutely aware of a very simple reciprocity, or "gift exchange" (Simmel 1950:392–93), that underlies the experience. Like nude beaches, there is in televideo cybersex a "reciprocity of nude exposure" (Douglas 1977:138). As Simmel (1950:392) points out, "Once we have received something good from another person ...we are obliged ethically; we operate under a condition which, though neither social nor legal but moral, is still a coercion. ...I am caused to return a gift, for instance, by the mere fact that I received it." Thus to the extent that participants are curious, interested, or aroused by what they see, they may feel compelled to make an equivalent exchange—to return the "gift"—so that they may continue to watch. As one participant stated, "I'd rather watch than show, but people want to see me in return for me seeing them."

Although being watched makes some televideo cybersex participants uncomfortable, for the vast majority, it makes the experience fun, exciting, and erotic. Many participants are excited by the simple fact that someone wants to see their naked bodies. As one man explains, "Knowing that someone wants to watch you is a turn-on." Or, as simply stated by another, televideo cybersex involves a kind of looking-glass eroticism: "Being watched makes me feel sexy that someone would want to even watch." Similarly, for other participants the interactions that ensue while being watched make the experience exciting. For example: "I prefer to be watched and know I'm watched, with audience participation and involvement."

## The Eros of Stripping, *Being* Naked, and the Naked Self

Stripping and being seen naked is what televideo cybersex is all about. Stripping exposes the "body's erotic generators" (Davis 1983:51)—genitals and other body parts that have been culturally sexualized (buttocks, breasts, legs, and other sexual generators ordinarily kept covered or concealed). The mere sight of them can be very arousing. Consequently, in nonsexual circumstances where nudity is sometimes required, such as medical examinations, others evoke dramaturgical techniques to neutralize the power of erotic generators or create distance between the body and those who are looking at it (Henslin and Biggs 1971; Smith and

Kleinman 1989). Thus simply exposing one's "erotic generators" for the viewing pleasure of someone else can be erotic for several related reasons. First, it excites those who are watching and in doing so interactively stimulates our exhibitional imaginations. Second, it is the quickest way to turn *any* situation into a sexual one. Third, it is part of the condition of sex, and therefore we commonly associate it with sex. Indeed, "there is a strong element of sexuality in nudity and the very fact of the genitals being uncovered suggest[s] symbolically that they are more accessible" (Bryant 1982:26). And fourth, revealing what is normally concealed is in and of itself a rush, a "sneaky thrill" (Katz 1988), or a feeling of liberation that comes from blatantly violating a cultural norm.[4]

If that were not enough, stripping reduces the self to an object. As one man indicated, sexual nudity with others fosters full embodiment; the self and the body are unified in a moment of negotiated sexual pleasure:

> Showing yourself in an excited state separates me from the real world. It becomes a focus, no reality, just a sexual moment and a focus on your sexuality. A focus on the sexual organs and also the body seen through the eyes of others.

"Just the act of removing one's clothes can help strip away symbolic identity and work roles, allowing one to become merely a body, which is the prerequisite for sexual pleasure" (Baumeister 1991:38). Stripping involves a "break through identity boundaries" (Davis 1983:51), in which we dispose of "all the grand, complex, abstract, wide-ranging definitions of self and become just a body again" (Baumeister 1991:12). A male participant refers to this identity breakthrough:

> I enjoy the freedom of being nude. I have a stressful vocation and it seems the pressures come off with the clothes. ...Many of us are defined by what we wear. This causes others to pull on you or give you more to do. Such as a doctor's outfit, a nurse's outfit, etc. When naked there is no distinguishing way of identification or anything to link me or anyone else to work. Nudity is a great equalizer. Freedom to just be comes to the front.

For this reason, sex in general and stripping in particular "must at least have the potential of being one of life's boundary experiences" (Davis 1983: xx). Because stripping and being seen nude breaks through identity boundaries, many televideo cybersex participants claim to get much more than a mere orgasm from the experience. Precipitated in part by a viewing audience, *being* naked becomes an experiential state separate and distinct from the clothed world. Furthermore, nakedness is a condition in which one can *be* that is separate and distinct from the clothed selves of everyday life. Unlike nudity in private, being naked in semipublic places becomes a state in which one is placed as a social object—

literally a thing—a body to be seen. Thus one becomes a "naked self," an objectified nude body presented for the purpose of being seen and interpreted as a sexual body.

## Playing with the Object/Subject Body: Erotic Looking Glasses and the Reenchantment of the Sexual Body

By virtue of the naked self, many televideo cybersex participants are quick to point out "being naked" provides not only sexual benefits but also a variety of other benefits such as increasing appreciation for and assessment of their bodies:

> When someone is turned on by watching me, it makes me feel that I'm sexier than I truly believe I am. ...It's nice to get compliments on...the body. ...I just think it's sexy that people can masturbate and think of me, little ol' me.

> Having a few dozen guys tell you how hot you are, etc., really gives you a great outlook on how you see yourself sexually. Positive reinforcement!

For these participants, the excitement that others receive from seeing them nude is repaid unto the self by the indirect yet comforting knowledge that one's body is appealing and desirable. Although a common theme for most participants, this reenchantment of the sexual body assumes special importance for those who, for various reasons, claim to be disenchanted with their bodies.

For some participants, this disenchantment has to do with perceptions of their appearances, especially with regard to age and weight—cultural standards of beauty and sexiness that refer directly to assessment of the corporeal body. The body may be disappointing to the self, but the sexual attention the individual receives in televideo cybersex serves to undermine that disappointment and reenchant the sexual body. As one man states, "It feels good when others compliment me. I feel like, even though I am overweight, I am accepted by them." A female participant explained that her weight normally disenchants her feelings of physical attractiveness. She also indicated an acute awareness that many men in televideo cybersex will merely tell her what she wants to hear to get what they want (presumably, a sexual performance). But interestingly, she voluntarily suspended her suspicions of deceit and found the trade-off is worthwhile because the attention she received served to reenchant feelings of sexiness and physical attractiveness:

> [To be seen naked] feels wonderful! Of course, it makes me feel like he desires my body. I know in my head that he is going to say what I want to hear so he can get what he wants, but in turn I get what I want. ...As you can see, I'm a pretty good size woman. I'm

not uncomfortable about it on here. I feel as desirable as the ladies who are much smaller
than me. As a matter of fact, I feel very sexy and seductive on here.

Others experience more ambiguous disenchantment and make vague reference to "self-esteem"—a self-imposed assessment of their selves, of which the
body is merely a part. Like the participants cited above, the sexual attention to
their bodies that they receive is repaid unto the self, but in this case the appearance of the body is less significant than the value they attribute to the self. In
these conditions, the self is disappointing unto itself, but because the body and
the self are inescapably connected, the positive sexual attention to the body increases the value they attribute to the self, as one woman indicated: "I enjoy most
the emotional uplift I get from people telling me I am beautiful. I need to feel that I
am still attractive. ...It's just good to have people tell you [that] you are still attractive especially when I have a low self-esteem."

All of these participants suggest that at times the ways they conceive of the
body and self is disenchanting and being naked in televideo cybersex reenchants
these internal conceptions of the self and body. However, for some participants,
the source of disenchantment has less to do with these kinds of intrapsychic assessments of the body and self and more to do with interpersonal social relations.
In fact, overwhelmingly these participants connected the problem to marriage and
long-term partnerships. For some, the problem is related to the routinization of
their normal sexual activities and the desire for a different experience: "My main
reason for being here is to be sociable, hoping to meet that Mr. Right even though
I'm married and have a very active routine sex life at home. The routine part
sucks!" For other participants, the problem is related to the monotonous "mono" of
monogamy and the desire for someone different: "I've been in a long-term relationship for almost five years, and this way I can remain faithful to that while still
getting off with hot guys from around the world." For many televideo cybersex
participants, monotonous routinization of monogamous sexual relations intersects
with their experiences of body and self and disenchants them.

Davis (1983:119) argues that "marriage seems almost intentionally designed
to make sex boring." Long-term sexual relationships also tend to make our bodies
boring. In time, being seen nude by one's lover becomes so commonplace or taken
for granted that sexual generators simply run out of gas or otherwise lose their
erotic power. When our own nudity no longer generates appreciative erotic power,
a classic looking-glass (Cooley [1902] 1964) process may compel us to feel unde-
sirable, unattractive, inadequate, and thoroughly unsexy. Thus some participants
find televideo cybersex helpful in refueling a connection to their corporeal sexual
body and the power of that body to generate eroticism:

I've been with my wife for so long now that our bodies aren't as exciting as they once were. Our sex life is OK, but without that special quality I sometimes feel like a piece of furniture around the house. When someone is excited about seeing me in all my nudity I suddenly feel sexually awake again.

Hubby is older than I am. He knows nothing of this. I'm not a complainer, but he does not have the passion or the desire, or at least he doesn't know how to show me. ...It's hard for him to tap into the part of my brain that triggers the stimulation. I'm a very erotic person. The feeling of being naughty is a turn-on too. See I'm bad, but I love it.

These participants claim "therapeutic" value to the experience of interacting with others as a naked sexual object. This "nude therapy trip" is a relatively common theme among nude beachers also: "[A] lot of people got into traditional nudism for the nude therapy trip, a kind of commonsense, self-help therapy" (Douglas 1977:158). The use of nudity as a therapeutic tool in self-help groups, although not a common practice, is documented (Symonds 1971). To the extent that one attributes "therapeutic value" to the revealing of intimate secrets, being seen nude before others would constitute a dramatic context for such "therapy." More specifically (and less ideologically), being naked before others is a novel condition that shrinks selfhood to the body. A person sheds normal abstract and multifaceted symbolic layers of selfhood with the clothing as he or she becomes a body to be seen. Such a situation begs for interpretation and a redefinition of self that can be harnessed for "therapeutic" purposes, regardless of whether this occurs in the formal context of a self-help group (Symonds 1971) or in more casual experiences such as nude beaches and televideo cybersex.

For other participants, televideo cybersex offers little more than a new and novel mechanism for exploring and cultivating sexuality. For them, nudity is simply a condition of televideo cybersex, and the eroticism engulfs the experience of being naked. The novelty of the medium and the unique circumstances of being seen and interacting with others in the nude combines to form a potentially powerful erotic experience that builds from fantasies of promiscuous casual sex, orgies, and similar circumstances in which one's body is offered up as a piece of semipublic property. Thus first-timers and those who have just recently discovered "the joys of televideo sex" state:

I just tried this on a friend's advice and last night I met a guy named___. ...I mean to be honest, I have never been to that height before, even in actual sex. ...I had several orgasms, no man has done that before.

Can I tell you a secret? I get more turned on here than I do with my husband.

Regardless of the specific motivations and personal benefits that televideo cybersex participants claim, all indicate that being naked in the presence of others reduces the whole of the self to the body. Being naked in the presence of others is a totalizing experience wherein selves are truly embodied. Awareness shrinks to the body and the immediate present (Baumeister 1991). Thus televideo cybersex does not remove the self but rather shrinks it down to a bare minimum. "The minimum self that a person can have is the body" (Baumeister 1991:17).

Further, selfhood not only shrinks to the body but also is made into an object—a naked sexual body to be looked at and commented on. Clearly these participants play with the experience of being object/subject and in the process often gain much more than just sexual gratification. In televideo cybersex "the body becomes a focus of interaction and hence a key constituent of the 'me' of the experience" (Glassner 1990:222). Yet these erotic naked episodes provide looking glasses to experience the body and thus create a space "where the 'I' does stand a chance, where one can both participate in and respond to the informational overbearance of the body" (Glassner 1990:223). As these participants indicate, the tension between the acting body and interpreting self (the "I") and the viewed body (the "me") functions as a kind of personal ritual of self-renewal (Davis 1983): by manipulating the relationships between them, one may temporarily enfeeble the self by being a body in order to return to selfhood reaffirmed.

### Just Another Body: The Face, the Self, and the Body

Although selfhood may shrink to its bare minimum, that "shrinking" is only temporary, ephemeral, and squarely situated in the liminal online environment. In everyday life we can rarely separate the body so clearly from the self, and therefore in everyday life we remain far more accountable for what we do with, to, and by our bodies. It should be no surprise, then, that in "real life" these participants rarely, if ever, indulge in this kind of explicit and promiscuous sex play. As one woman reported, "I would not dare flirt like this in public. The men seem more open and flirtatious as well." A male participant expressed the same sentiment: "There is no way in hell that I'd do anything like this in real life!"

In televideo cybersex being a body is a prerequisite for preserving the integrity and dignity of the self. Although long-term friendships and intimate real-life relationships can and do sometimes emerge from televideo encounters, most of the time the experience is fleeting, anonymous, and casual. Being seen naked (and often masturbating) in anonymous and casual semipublic social situations is, after all, taboo, and therefore, as Douglas (1977:58) reported with regard to nude beaches, many people are "afraid of being seen by friends or associates and branded a weirdo or a sexual pervert." So as not to implicate the self in the promiscuous virtual encounters, great efforts are usually taken to keep identity detached from the body. Because televideo cybersex participants can control the angle and zoom of the digital camera, this delicate dramaturgical task is most commonly achieved by simply not showing one's face. As one man explained, "It's all very anonymous, at least for me. I rarely show my face, therefore I am just another body. Once I show my face, it becomes too personal—I'm not just a body anymore!"

As televideo cybersex participants have discovered, a body without a face is a body without a self: it is "just another body."[5] Televideo cybersex participants are not the only ones to have learned this. Parts Models, a New York agency that specializes in modeling body parts, does not supply models for erotica, but when asked to find a female, fifty to sixty years old, willing to expose her nude chest for a health article in *Self* magazine, the editor claimed: "I screened the magazine very carefully and once they assured me they wouldn't use the model's face it was no problem" (Norwich 1987:51). David Roos of Gilla-Roos, Ltd., an agency that also specializes in parts modeling, described a similar circumstance: "We just shot a commercial for an airline. They wanted a 'chubby man who would stand in the water. Naked.' Of course we found their man, ...but only because everything would be exposed except his face" (Norwich 1987:53).

Clearly the face occupies a supreme position in connecting or disconnecting the self with the body. One's face is the most identifiable feature of one's body and self; it is the single human physiological feature that concretely conjoins the corporeal body with the self. Although the face is just another part of our bodies, we tend to regard it as more uniquely ours than any other part. Significantly, the face is the one part of the body that is almost always seen naked, and therefore televideo cybersex makes it extremely vulnerable. Because the face represents the most critical identifier of who we are, some fear recognition. As one woman stated, "I am afraid to show my face. I live in a small town and someone could notice me." A man said, "I do show my face, but not when I am getting to know someone. ...I am well known in my community and also around the state where I live. You never know who might be online and checking in." Indeed, as this man makes poignantly clear, the vulnerability of "showing face" makes even the safest sex potentially risky:

> I don't show my face at first. I started doing that after an embarrassing situation with a coworker not long after installing the camera and software. ...I had been putting on a show for someone with no cam for several days. A guy at work finally told me it was him [and he] wanted to play in real time. It was very embar-

rassing. ...Since then, I've just felt more secure not showing face. [I] still do show
face, but only after I'm sure I don't know the other person.[6]

Many televideo cybersex participants are concerned that their images
can be saved, reproduced, and distributed. The images can be collected and
used to incriminate the self. Two men manage their anxieties by concealing
their faces:

I don't show my face because [the image] can be saved.

I don't show my face just to protect my privacy. If this could not be saved, I
would show my face more.

Not "showing face" conceals the greater and most significant aspect of
one's identity, thereby making the process of being a body experientially
complete. By detaching the face from the body, televideo cybersex environments often become a virtual meat locker of neck-down naked people.
No two bodies are alike, of course, but without a self or an identity attached to them, they are *just* penises, breasts, buttocks, and torsos, making
the experience exceedingly impersonal.

Some participants dislike the impersonal element of televideo cybersex; others thrive on it. As one participant indicated, those who like the
impersonality refer to the need to be a *thing* from time to time: "Yes, it's
impersonal and therefore not very fulfilling. But sometimes being impersonal is exactly what I crave! To simply be seen, looked at, desired, and for
someone to comment on what they are seeing."

Those who dislike the impersonal virtual meat locker of televideo cybersex state that sex (even on the Internet) is much more fun when shared
with a person rather than a mere object. This point would seem obvious,
but it is often overlooked. For example, the cultural critic Mark Dery
(1992:42–43) claims that "the only thing better than making love *like* a
machine, it seems, is making love *with* a machine." Dery is wrong. No matter how technologically advanced or expensive, or what gee-whizzery it
promises, machines and objects are no match for people in sexual affection.
Almost everyone would rather have sex with a person because machines do
not and cannot have a self, as some televideo cybersex participants remind
us:

Most of the time, I personally do not continue to carry on conversations with men
who will not show me their face, with a few exceptions. However, it does become
very impersonal when all they want from you is to help them masturbate, without ever

seeing their face or expressions. I have connected before and just watched without feeling any sense of connection at all. [In these situations it was] very impersonal, and I wondered if the satisfaction they felt was comforting at all.

It's a bit impersonal. When I get to know the other person more, I show face.

My face is my best feature. How can people tell that you are happy doing what you do online if they can't see your expressions? The eyes, they are not alone as gateways to the soul, all language of the body shows the soul's words and wishes. ...[Showing your face] lets people into your world a little more. ...[T]o let them look into more of my world through my face and my expressions, brings them closer to the reason that I am masturbating online—not because I'm horny, or want attention, but because it makes me feel good to share the experience.

While nudity in and of itself transforms one's self and body into a unified object, nudity in the context of these semipublic televideo environments makes the objectification even more extreme. Objectification results in part from the medium itself. Televideo lacks the qualities of touching and feeling another body, and therefore, as one man described, televideo cybersex is "like looking at a live magazine." Even more, being a body is also a function of the social context. Social taboos against nudity and masturbation in public and semipublic places lead participants to conceal their identities and to present themselves as only a body or body part—a detached penis, vagina, or pair of breasts. At one level, being a body acts back unto the self in an erotic looking-glass process of ritual self-renewal. At another level, when one presents oneself as a body with no self, everything that makes one sexy, desirable, and interesting is stripped away, and having sex with a selfless body is not much different from having sex with any other object.

**The Gendered Body in Televideo Cybersex**

Although "you can watch me if I can watch you" may be the norm of televideo cybersex, in practice the sexual exchange is rarely this egalitarian. By virtue of their bodies some people have more power to "call the sexual shots" and many can command a performance without having to do so themselves. In televideo cybersex this power is undeniably available to *women*.[7] Further, although all women have this power, the more attractive they are, the more sexual power they may wield.

Because there are fewer women than men in casual televideo cybersex environments, men compete with other men to attract the interest of women, and this competition can get fierce. As one man casually remarked, "The fight for attractive people is awful." Key ways that men attempt to attract women are through advertising themselves by their screen names, or nicks, and, when additional fields are available, providing detailed descriptions of their physical features and special talents. Thus screen names and identifying fields become spaces for men to boast about themselves. Consider, for example, the following listings (all of which have been modified to protect participants' anonymity):

| | | |
|---|---|---|
| HardWood | 25 year old STUD | 6', 185, Muscles, HUNG |
| BadMAN | Fit, BIG COCK | Cum watch me j/o |
| BoyinNylon | Very Submissive | Spank me! |
| HungDude | 8" plus a lil' more | Cute and playful! |

Women are far less likely to advertise their physical features but instead tend to advertise their *preferences* so as to attract the right applicant for the job. The following are examples of such listings (again, modified to protect the participants' anonymity):

| | | |
|---|---|---|
| BeHARD | Want HOT men | I like BIG dicks! |
| Bi_ANN | Prefer petite | Tempt Me—NO MEN! |
| Drippingpussy | 4 BIG cock | Must be CUT! |

Beyond attracting the initial attention of a woman, a man must be prepared to please her and in many cases to listen, obey, and follow her instructions. With so many men to choose from, women do not need to tolerate someone they find rude, offensive, unimaginative, ugly, uncooperative, or otherwise inadequate. In addition, the distance afforded by the computer-mediated context adds an element of safety—for all participants, not just women. Not surprisingly, many women feel a sense of liberation that is related to this combination of distance, control, and what seems to be a reversal of sexual power:[8]

It's sometimes empowering cuz I know I have the power to block someone I don't like or whatever.

I think it's liberating. I have more power to choose and flirt with men without worrying about physical repercussions to me. It is functional.

Being watched is erotic, and if they make me feel like a piece of meat, I have control.

You choose who you want to see you, so you have a good idea how it will turn out.

Like other aspects of televideo cybersex, this privilege and power comes at a cost, which, unfortunately, ends up making televideo cybersex more *like* the everyday micropolitics of sex than a departure from them. Because men compete with other men for the attention of women, some men become too brazen, rude, and just plain offensive. Consequently, women sometimes find the heightened attention excessive. As one woman explained, "I think it is harassing sometimes the way they are so bold to just say or show something without knowing who or what is on the other end!" Another participant made the situation clear: "I think it's appalling. How worse could you treat someone than as a slab of fuck-flesh to be beaten off for?" One woman has gone so far as to categorize men on televideo according to how annoying their behavior is. She described the kind of excesses that women commonly encounter in these environments:

> I kinda got an order of which I perceive these men who are clamoring for attention. 1. Normal: fully dressed, at work or home, for chat or looking for love. 2. Semi's: without shirt with a big grin, usually married waiting to play with someone who is willing. 3. Regulars: showing nothing but their penis with an erection waiting for an orgasm (some are there every day). Some say they have two or three orgasms a day. Wow. They must never have real sex. 4. Kinkys: either doms, subs, bis, each are wanting something out of the ordinary in order for them to become excited. 5. Pervs: these are some sick mf's. They do ungodly things with their bodies, want to do really sick things—example, shove a Pepsi can up his ass (I couldn't believe it), have sex with animals, etc. Overall it is very exciting when you are dealing with types 1, 2, and sometimes 3. But when it comes to the last two they harass the shit out of you, bothering you the whole time …until you finally have to just put them on your ignore list.

The naked body is, in glaring clarity, a *gendered* body.[9] Many social roles can be shed along with the clothing worn to play them, but some roles are permanently fashioned into our skin—and the more of that skin we show, the more salient that role becomes. While McCormick and Leonard (1996:110) claim that in cyberspace "we are freed from our physical bodies," that so-called freedom (see Waskul, Douglass, and Edgley 2000) is no more or less possible to obtain in televideo environments than in everyday life. In fact, it should be no surprise that the traditional micropolitics of sex become paramount—even exaggerated—when genders interact in the nude on the Internet, or anywhere else.

## Conclusion

Computer-mediated communication is a dislocated form of interaction that occurs in a social "place" without necessary connection to geographic "space," where the activities of participants and experiences of self are not necessarily contained or affixed to corporeal bodies (Waskul, Douglass, and

Edgley 2000). These characteristics create a context in which online interaction may assume unique forms that have the potential to challenge traditional understandings of self, body, and social situations and the relationships among them.[10] As previous studies have indicated, the dislocated nature of online interaction may be related to experiences of "ultimate disembodiment" (e.g., Waskul, Douglass, and Edgley 2000). As this study suggests, the same quality of the medium may also allow for experiences of "total embodiment"—a condition in which one is embodied within an image of one's own body. In the final analysis, computer-mediated communication is like all other forms of human interaction: it *is emergent* from the purposes of the communication within *situated* contexts that are *negotiated* with others. Although important, the medium is just one of many variables that intersect with the experience of online interaction.

In any scene of interaction, the body is both an experienced subject and a viewed and acted-upon object. How that body appears affects the definition of the situation, the interactions that transpire, and the scene that ensues. Consequently, most of the time we are quite conscious of how others view our bodies, and although we may sometimes intentionally manage that image, we always make certain that we have some clothing on when in public or in the public view.

At a very young age we are socialized to society's proscriptions and prescriptions concerning the situations, circumstances, and purposes of allowable and forbidden genital exposure (Henslin and Biggs 1971). We learn that only three general categories of persons can legitimately approach the naked body of someone else: authorized sex partners, medical practitioners, and the parents of very young children. We also learn that all these persons must be very careful about how they approach the naked body: parents and sex partners must be careful lest they be guilty of rape, abuse, or misconduct; medical practitioners make certain to use elaborate dramaturgical tactics to assure that the context is desexualized and, if possible, the person is detached from the body completely (Henslin and Biggs 1971; Smith and Kleinman 1989). In addition, the treatment of and deference to the naked body is deeply ritualistic, and by adhering to these rituals the naked body achieves a sacred status.[11]

Beneath the facade of clothing is a sacred sexual body—compartmentalized segments of flesh that we may touch only in private and share only with the closest of intimates. This body is protected by stringent rules and filled with profound meaning to the individual, to those who may see it, and to the larger culture. Under normal circumstances, access to the sacred naked body of others means power and privilege and therefore connotes specific rights and responsibilities. The naked body is surrounded by rules that protect it from being profaned, that dictate who may approach it and under what conditions, and what may (and may not) be done in these circumstances (Durkheim [1912] 1965). As Goffman (1971) and Durkheim might suggest, adherence to these rituals maintains the "sacred" sexual body as an object of ultimate value, and while threats of profanation occasionally may occur, we can comfortably maintain the sacredness of the naked body so long as we abide by the rules.

A large part of the eroticism and feelings of liberation that come from televideo cybersex stem precisely from the cultural heresy of breaking these rules. Participants may reap the benefits and remain relatively safe from the potential consequences of revealing what is normally secret and profaning and what is normally sacred. By revealing their naked body, participants create an intensely personal interaction, yet suspend the self as a spectator by concealing their identities. Thus televideo cybersex participants reap the same benefits as fitness enthusiasts—"an intimate and holistic marriage between self and body" (Glassner 1990:221). However, to achieve this benefit, televideo cybersex participants reduce the whole of the self to the body and thus profane the sacred and assure that the complex and multidimensional self is made into an image to be seen and therefore not a person at all.

In both text and televideo cybersex, the body is a virtual object of which one may only be a spectator. Significantly, participants themselves are spectators unto their own bodies, as they must see and respond to the images of their bodies and thus act toward, manage, and interpret that image as others might. In most televideo cybersex environments the image of one's own body appears in a window beside the images of others and is clearly visible to the individual as a mirror-like reflection. Participants must manipulate the images of their bodies in order to prevent "showing face" and to assure the appropriate camera angle, zoom, and focus necessary to perform the "conversation of gestures" inherent in the mutual masturbation of televideo cybersex.

These erotic looking glasses of televideo cybersex influence how one conceives of one's self and body, but this does not differ fundamentally from the ways in which the body manifests itself in everyday life. Instead televideo cybersex simply exaggerates it. In any scene of interaction the body will be placed as a social object and we will most often manipulate its appearance—as is essential to the overall definition of the situation and the self we claim within it. By virtue of literal and metaphorical looking glasses, we manipulate how others perceive the corporeal body in everyday life through clothing and cosmetics, and in doing so, in everyday life the body assumes a virtual ontological status not much different from the images sent and received by televideo cybersex participants.

Like everyday life, in these televideo interactions others symbolically reflect the body back onto the self; these reflections influence how the self conceives, appreciates, and apprehends the body. Hence we can understand the body as an object and subject distinct from the self. However, it would be a mistake analytically to sever the connection between selfhood and body. The boundaries between the self, the body, and situated social interaction will never be clearly demarcated, and any attempt to do so would lack credibility. A better approach is to understand the varied dynamics of the relationships among bodies, selves, and the contexts in which both are located. In a culture seemingly obsessed with bodies, it would be a serious mistake to ignore these and the myriad other relationships among the body, the acting individual, and society.

I do not argue that self and body are separate and distinct entities but rather that one does not automatically imply the other and that neither are simple innate things that the individual has. Surely, the body, unlike the self, is an empirical entity that can be observed, measured, and seen to exist in time and space independent of our own conscious awareness of it. But even so, what that body means is no more or less innately predetermined or any more or less socially shaped than any other object. As the participants in this study have illustrated, the body is not just a thing that exists; it is something that people read, interpret, present, conceal, and make meaningful in an ongoing negotiated process of situated social interaction.

## Notes

1. Researchers overlook this fact. Many define cybersex as broadly as possible to support the notion that it is common, widespread, and usually a problem (or at least a potential problem that may cause disaster in participants' lives). For example, in a recent book on cybersex addiction and recovery, Schneider and Weiss (2001:7) define cybersex sweepingly as "any form of sexual expression that is accessed through the computer or the Internet." Researchers such as Schneider and Weiss (2001) and Cooper, Delmonico, and Burg (2000) fail to distinguish between looking at pornography online and participating in cybersex and thus exploit the ambiguities of the term to support their preconceived conclusions about "cybersex compulsivity."

2. Televideo has been used widely for the pursuit of profit in the Internet pornography industry (Lane 2000). "Live" webcam performances are a relatively common and apparently lucrative service for the entrepreneurs of virtual pornography. However, these webcam services differ from televideo cybersex in that its performers are paid to put on a show, the audience pays to watch, and the performers can rarely if ever see their customers. Those that pay the fee can "peep" in on the show and sometimes communicate with the performer through typed text, but there is little interactivity and the motives of the performers are at

least partly financial. This study focuses on persons who use televideo for sex, for fun, and for free (not considering ISP fees, cost of the digital camera, and cost of the client software) with other participants who are doing the same.

3.  Although "sex object" has become a stigmatizing label, being treated as an object—a physical body—is a necessary part of sexuality. Many feminists argue legitimately that patriarchal social and cultural structures reduce women to mere objects. I do not ignore this criticism by feminists but suggest that there is a fundamental difference ·between being made into an object and choosing to be an object. The former is domination; the latter is a necessary element of sex.

4.  "Social theorists have resisted strongly the recognition that deviance is not merely a reaction against something negative in a person's background but a reaching for exquisite possibilities. ...[D]eviant persons also appreciate the economy of doing evil for characterizing the self generally: it is literally wonderful. Through being deviant for a moment, the person may portray his or her general, if usually hidden, charismatic potential" (Katz 1988:73).

5.  A fascinating exception appears in *Le Viol* (1934), a painting by the Belgian surrealist Rene Magritte. In this surreal anatomical rearrangement, a woman's face and body are one in the same: a portrait of a face that is a woman's torso wrapped in hair; eyes are represented by breasts, the nose by a bellybutton; the mouth is a patch of pubic hair. Not surprisingly, this painting has been subject to substantial feminist criticism for the manner in which it "fragments the female by turning her into a sexual body" (Gubar 1989:49). Some have argued that the female face is erased by the torso, making her sightless, senseless, and dumb, an abject and obscene artistic rendition of female submission and servitude (Gubar 1989). According to Gracyk (1991:125), it is "one of the most graphic subordinations of a woman to an object, for it reduces her to genitalia." What is fascinating about this image (and the controversy surrounding it) is that few seem to ponder whether Magritte intended to (super)impose a body on a face, a face on a body, or both. When critics look at *Le Viol* they see a body in place of a face—one dimension of Magritte's surreal and philosophical riddle. It is interesting that they do not see a face in place of a body, or both at once. Even if Magritte had not intended, *Le Viol* impressively mines the fascinating relationship between bodies and faces—one part of the object and subject of embodiment—revealing (at the very least) the taken-for-granted cultural tendency to see the image as one thing and not another.

6.  Televideo cybersex participants reverse the traditional expressive order of the body normally experienced in the ritual of courtship. Usually, lovers become familiar with one another's faces first and genitals last. As these participants indicate, in televideo cybersex genitals come first and faces are seen last, if at all.

7.  Obviously this section refers strictly to heterosexual one-on-one televideo cybersex. I am confident that the relationship differs among couples that connect with other couples, gay men, and gay women. In each category, the distribution of sexual power is likely to assume different forms in relation to the body and the context of interaction. I focus here on one-on-one heterosexual encounters for several reasons. First, these are the most common sexual relations in televideo cybersex. Second, a full analysis of sexual preference in relation to televideo cybersex is not necessary for my overall argument; this one component is sufficient. Third, and most significantly, I had no difficulty collecting data from gay men, but gay women and couples were not at all interested in talking to me, and therefore I have little data on them. Apparently gay women and couples are all too familiar with the deceptive tactics of heterosexual men who often try to cop a peek or con them into a brief encounter.

Such tactics are not uncommon. One participant in this study gloated when she told me how she used pictures in a magazine (combined with a slight blurring on the focus of the cam) to temporarily con people into thinking she was something she was not. Of course, the picture did not move and therefore the con was short-lived, but deceitful tactics such as these have made gay women and couples *very* suspicious and almost impossible for this man to interview.

8.   This perception of feminine sexual liberation and power in televideo cybersex is actually far more complicated than suggested here and is experienced as real for reasons that are more legitimate than this analysis suggests. Although I am skeptical about much of what passes for "sexual freedom" in cybersex, it is worth reminding ourselves that we are a society in which women continue to be punished or otherwise found guilty for actively seeking sexual pleasure and overtly acting on sexual desire, as opposed to "following their hearts" (Williams 1989:209, 259–60). Further, at least some of the controversy over contemporary high-tech, easy-access, in-the-comfort-of-your-home pornography is attributable to the fact that it is now brought not only into locations where children might wander but also "into the domain of traditional female space" (Williams 1989:283). There is little doubt that sex and pornography on the Internet pose unprecedented opportunities for women to indulge sexual interests. Where else do women find "license simply to float pleasurably through a shamelessly eroticized space" (Rival, Slater, and Miller 1998:301)? Where else do women find equivalent opportunities to explore sexual interests and desires without paying the price of stigma, punishment, and shame charged by the sexual double standard? In short, the analysis presented here is critical of the extent of sexual freedom given the form in which it appears on the Internet, but even so, I have to acknowledge that the freedoms expressed by the women in this study are quite real—even if the forms of those sexual expressions adhere to what appears to be the same old androcentric sexuality.

9.   A similar analysis could be done on the role of race and age in the body politics of the nude in televideo cybersex. Just as one's gender cannot be removed by clothing, neither can race or age (although the latter can be faked to some extent). Many televideo cybersex environments displayed relatively common themes that build off race and age stereotypes. Particularly evident are fantasies of the experienced (and often dominant) elder mistress with her boy-toy and fantasies that build on the mythical girth of the African penis.

10.  What is unique about online interaction and cybersex is that the corporeal body is located in one place and a symbolic representation of it is located elsewhere. This, in itself, is not without precedence (see Flowers 1998), but the quintessence of cybersex—the remarkable interaction among the corporeal body, its virtual representation, and the situated communicative context—surely is. In reference to erotic CD-ROM "games," Williams (1989:312) describes the body in these virtual environments as "felt to be in two places at once. ...[P]leasure consists in a body that is uncannily both *here...and there.* ...[T]here is a sustained simultaneous dividedness of attention and blurring of the distinction between the virtual bodies on screen—one of which is now presumed to be 'my' own—and my own 'carnal density' here where I sit before the screen" (original emphasis). As this study seeks to emphasize, this body—precariously perched in "two places at once"—is not only a unique characteristic of cybersex, it is also what makes the experience ideal for the kind of social psychological analysis that can fundamentally inform or transform the ways in which we think about bodies, selves, situated social interaction, and the nature of personhood because it renders opaque relationships that are normally quite transparent.

11. This is overly simplified. Both the naked body and the clothed body may be considered "sacred" (in the Durkheimian and Goffmanian sense). The naked body achieves sacred status as a result of the rules that govern it and the deference to which it is treated. But the deference and rules regarding the treatment of the naked body exist and persist because clothing is "one of the most basic and pervasive symbols of civilization" (Douglas 1977:390). It is basic and pervasive because it is, in part, through clothing that we physically and symbolically transcend ourselves. Clothing fails to cover the body. It is merely a partial synthetic exterior skin with the delightful capacity to accentuate specific parts of the body while concealing others. Although man comes into the world "covered in a skin[,] ...[he] soon discovered that he could make himself not only one additional skin, but practically as many as he liked, an endless variety of them, to meet his every need and fancy" (Langner 1991:4–5). Of course, these "skins" are produced in societal, cultural, and institutional contexts, in accordance with those formal and informal social mandates. Consequently, "adornment creates a highly specific synthesis of the great convergent and divergent forces of the individual and society" (Simmel 1950:344). Through clothing, in part, we are no longer akin to the animal world but to the world of gods, spirits, and society (Langner 1991). Hence the source of sacredness of the naked body lay in its ever-present potential to subvert society itself—an antisacred—because it is the clothed body that is sacred to social order.

# References

Baumeister, R. 1991. *Escaping the Self: Alcoholism, Spirituality, Masochism, and Other Flights from the Burden of Selfhood.* New York, NY: Basic Books.

Becker, H. 1967. "History, Culture, and Subjective Experience." *Journal of Health and Social Behavior* 8:163–76.

———. 1963. *Outsiders: Studies in the Sociology of Deviance.* New York, NY: Free Press.

Bell, D. and R. Holliday. 2000. "Naked as Nature Intended." *Body and Society* 6(3–4):12–40.

Bryant, C. 1982. *Social Deviancy and Social Proscription: The Social Context of Carnal Behavior.* New York, NY: Human Sciences Press.

Cahill, S. 2001. *Inside Social Life: Readings in Sociological Psychology and Microsociology.* Los Angeles, CA: Roxbury.

Cooley, C. H. [1902] 1964. *Human Nature and the Social Order.* New York, NY: Scribner's.

Cooper, A., D. Delmonico, and R. Burg. 2000. "Cybersex Users, Abusers, and Compulsives: New Findings and Implications." Pp. 5–29 in *Cybersex: The Dark Side of the Force*, edited by A. Cooper. Philadelphia, PA: Brunner-Rutledge.

Davis, M. 1983. *Smut: Erotic Reality/Obscene Ideology.* Chicago, IL: University of Chicago Press.

Dery, M. 1992. "Sex Machine, Machine Sex: Mechano-Eroticism and Robo-Copulation." Pp. 42–43 in *Mondo 2000.* New York, NY: HyperPerennial.

Douglas, J. 1977. *The Nude Beach.* Beverly Hills, CA: Sage.

Durkheim, E. [1912] 1965. *The Elementary Forms of Religious Life.* New York, NY: Free Press.

Edelsward, L. M. 1991. "We Are More Open When We Are Naked." *Ethnos* 56 (3–4):189–99.

Flowers, A. 1998. *The Fantasy Factory: An Insider's View of the Phone Sex Industry.* Philadelphia, PA: University of Pennsylvania Press.

Forsyth, C. 1992. "Parade Strippers: A Note on Being Naked in Public." *Deviant Behavior: An Interdisciplinary Journal* 13:391–403.

Frank, A. 1991. *At the Will of the Body: Reflections on Illness.* Boston. MA: Houghton Mifflin.

Gadow, S. 1982. "Body and Self: A Dialectic." Pp. 86–100 in *The Humanity of the Ill: Phenomenological Perspectives,* edited by V. Kestenbaum. Knoxville, TN: University of Tennessee Press.

Glassner, B. 1990. "Fit for Postmodern Selfhood." Pp. 215–43 in *Symbolic Interaction and Cultural Studies,* edited by H. Becker and M. McCall. Chicago, IL: University of Chicago Press.

Goffman, E. 1971. *Relations in Public: Microstudies in Public Order.* New York: Basic Books.

———. 1963a. *Behavior in Public Places: Notes on the Social Organization of Gatherings.* New York: Free Press.

———. 1963b. *Stigma: Notes on the Management of Spoiled Identity.* Englewood Cliffs, NJ: Prentice Hall.

———. 1959. *The Presentation of Self in Everyday Life.* Garden City, NY Doubleday Anchor.

Gracyk, T. 1991. "Pornography as Representation: Aesthetic Considerations:" Pp. 117–37 in *Pornography: Private Right or Public Menace?,* edited by R. Baird and S. Rosenblum. Buffalo, NY: Prometheus.

Gubar, S. 1989. "Representing Pornography." Pp. 47–67 in *For Adult Users Only: The Dimensions of Violent Pornography,* edited by S. Gubar and J. Hoff. Bloomington: Indiana University Press.

Henslin, J. and M. Biggs. 1971. "Dramaturgical Desexualization: The Sociology of the Vaginal Examination." Pp. 243–72 in *Studies in the Sociology of Sex,* edited by J. Henslin. New York, NY: Appleton-Century-Crofts.

Holstein, J. and J. Gubrium. 2000. *The Self We Live By: Narrative Identity in a Postmodern World.* New York, NY: Oxford University Press.

James, W. [1892] 1961. *Psychology: The Briefer Course.* New York, NY: Harper and Brothers.

Katz, J. 1988. *Seductions of Crime: Moral and Sensual Attractions in Doing Evil.* New York, NY: Basic Books.

Kupfer, J. 1983. *Experience as Art: Aesthetics in Everyday Life.* Albany, NY: State University of New York Press.

Lane, F. 2000. *Obscene Profits: The Entrepreneurs of Pornography in the Cyber Age.* New York, NY: Routledge.

Langner, L. 1991. *The Importance of Wearing Clothes.* Los Angeles, CA: Elysium.

Mason-Schrock, D. 1996. "Transsexuals' Narrative Construction of the 'True Self.'" *Social Psychology Quarterly* 59(3):176–92.

Mead, G. H. 1934. *Mind, Self, and Society.* Edited by C. Morris. Chicago, IL: University of Chicago Press.

McCormick, N. and J. Leonard. 1996. "Gender and Sexuality in the Cyberspace Frontier." *Women and Therapy* 19(4):109–19.

Norwich, C. 1987. "Parts Plus." *Photo/Design* (July–August):51–54.

Rival, L., D. Slater, and D. Miller. 1998. "Sex and Sociality: Comparative Ethnographies of Sexual Objectification." *Theory, Culture, and Society* 15(30):295–321.

Robinson, P. and N. Tamosaitis. 1993. *The Joy of Cybersex: An Underground Guide to Electronic Erotica.* New York, NY: Brady.

Sartre, J. P. 1956. *Being and Nothingness.* New York, NY: Philosophical Library.

Schneider, J. and R. Weiss. 2001. *Cybersex Exposed: Simple Fantasy or Obsession?* Center City, MN: Hazelden.

Simmel, G. 1950. *The Sociology of George Simmel.* Edited by K. Wolf. New York, NY: Free Press.

Slater, D. 1998. "Trading Sexpics on IRC: Embodiment and Authenticity on the Internet." *Body & Society* 4(4):91–117.

Smith, A. and S. Kleinman. 1989. "Managing Emotions in Medical School: Students' Contacts with the Living and the Dead." *Social Psychology Quarterly* 52(1):56–69.

Strauss, A. 1993. *Continual Permutations of Action.* Hawthorne, NY: Aldine. ·

Symonds, C. 1971. "A Nude Touchy-Feely Group." *Journal of Sex Research* 7(2):126–33.

Toolan, J., M. Elkins, D. Miller, and P. D'Encarnacao. 1974. "The Significance of Streaking." *Medical Aspects of Human Sexuality* 8:152–65.

Turner, V. 1969. *The Ritual Process: Structure and Anti-Structure.* Ithaca, NY: Cornell University Press.

Waskul, D., M. Douglass, and C. Edgley. 2000. "Cybersex: Outercourse and the Enselfment of the Body." *Symbolic Interaction* 23(4):375–97.

Weinberg, M. 1967. "The Nudist Camp: Way of Life and Social Structure." *Human Organization* 26(3):91–99.

———. 1966. "Becoming a Nudist." *Psychiatry* 29(1):15–24.

———. 1965. "Sexual Modesty, Social Meanings, and the Nudist Camp." *Social Problems* 12(3):311–18.

———. 1981. "Becoming a Nudist." Pp. 291–304 in *Deviance: An Interactionist Perspective*, edited by E. Rubington and M. Weinberg. New York, NY: Macmillian.

Williams, L. 1989. *Hard Core: Power, Pleasure, and the "Frenzy of the Visible."* Los Angeles, CA: University of California Press.

# Part Two

# Culture and Internet Sex

Part One explored the various ways Internet sex presents a novel context for the experience and expression of personhood. While personal and interpersonal implications were explored, we have not directly examined implied cultural characteristics of these uniquely situated experiences. If Internet sex does, in fact, reconfigure personhood in new and innovative ways, then these reconfigurations presume equally important cultural dynamics that have everything to do with broad questions of how meaning is made. Investigations into the experience of personhood have loosely addressed these subjects, but only in reference to questions about how individuals apprehend themselves in these erotic Internet environments. In Part Two we will broaden our scope.

Most generally, culture refers to patterns of belief and behavior that are symbolic, generally shared, and flexibly adaptive. Culture is something that people not only learn but also actively *use* to understand and act upon the world. Any social environment—on the Internet or elsewhere—will contain implicit cultural forms and, likewise, any cultural environment will contain implicit social structures. Therefore, words like "society" and "culture" are somewhat interchangeable—but not synonymous. When referring to culture we are specifically addressing collectively shared symbolic structures that provide meaning, structure, and coherence to human experience.

Internet sex raises provocative new questions about culture. Sex and pornography on the Internet potentially illuminate close relationships between technology and experiences of life in contemporary society, the ways cultural constructs have been appropriated in an era heavily influenced by communication technologies. They also magnify important shifts in meaning at a time when the electronic circuit has replaced the machine as the dominant metaphor for understanding social and cultural life. Examination of such issues in the context of sex and pornography grounds these somewhat lofty dynamics in an evocative context that is both intimate and broadly shared.

Claudia Springer examines the uniquely contemporary "tendency in popular culture to associate computer technology with sexuality, creating a contradictory discourse that simultaneously predicts the obsolescence of human beings and a future of heightened erotic fulfillment." Springer examines the cyborg—part human and part machine—as a precariously timely object of cultural fascination and erotic desire. As we have already learned, the unique blend of embodiment and disembodiment, human and technological, intimacy and distance, characterize the experience of Internet sex; Springer expands these ideas into a much broader cultural context as she explores the nuances of "electronic eros."

Phillip Vannini presents a sophisticated analysis of pornography on the Internet. However, Vannini's analysis is as clever as it is sophisticated: positing a conceptual framework that inverts Dante's nine layers of hell as a means for exploring various forms of Internet sex, Vannini's framework is as evocative as it is enlightening. Vannini suggests that the Internet represents a potent "synopticon" organized around the power of seduction and populated by people who are gazed upon in a fluid context where the boundary between surveyed and surveyor is porous and interchangeable. Yet, for all its potential pleasures, the pornographic synopticon of the Internet is no place of pure utopia; Vannini discovers the Ultimate Destroyer in the most unlikely of places.

While much has been written about sex and pornography on the Internet, comparatively little investigation has focused on hentai—erotic adaptations of Japanese animated cartoons—the subject of Joel Powell Dahlquist and Lee Vigilant's long overdue investigation. The strange mix of manga (Japanese comics) and erotic images, often involving explicit violence and characters that appear both young and androgynous, begs for analysis. As Powell and Vigilant point out, because cartoons are not "real" they are morally distancing. Yet also because they are cartoons, these images become "way better than real": hentai need not concern itself with limitations of real flesh, cultural taboos, or other limitations of *this* world. In this way, hentai becomes a postmodern sexual phantasmagoria, fully reflective of contemporary cultural ambiguities.

These readings clearly indicate various ways that Internet sex and pornography reflect significant cultural change in contemporary society: an embracement of technology to such an extent that the boundaries between human, machine, and electronic circuitry have blurred in an erotic stew of potent ambiguity; where surveillance, seduction, and appearance occupy a central role; where pornographied images loosely associated with non-Western cultures embody conflicting aesthetics at multiple levels. Here, more so than anywhere else, we clearly see the ways that Internet sex does not so much compel social change, but reflect those changes in creative and sometimes unsettling forms of expression.

## ❖ Chapter Three

# Electronic Eros: Bodies and Desire in the Postindustrial Age

## Claudia Springer[*]

*In her book,* Electronic Eros, *Claudia Springer examines how computers "have intensi-fied, not diminished, our culture's fascination with sexuality." Springer suggests that the computer is a resource for the expression of "a powerful attraction in contemporary cul-ture to the idea of bodiless sexuality." As Springer writes, "Electronic technology is erotic because it makes possible escape from both the confines of the body and the boundaries that have separated organic from inorganic matter." These are themes that have already resonated with both experiences of cybersex and forms of personhood found in these evocative communication environments. However, Springer raises new questions about the general cultural significance of these experiences and posits provocative in-sights. Whereas earlier readings explored the experience of Internet sex, Springer exam-ines what these experiences mean from the lens of a broad cultural analysis.*

At the intersection of technology and eroticism lies techno-eroticism, the pas-sionate celebration of technological objects of desire. Artistic renderings of technology since the early twentieth century have often expressed techno-erotic impulses. ...Social commentators have detected a heavy dose of techno-eroticism running throughout twentieth-century Western culture.

...Industrial-age techno-eroticism focused in particular on the automobile, an object of fascination for generations. Cars represent the culmination of indus-trial technology, combining engines, gears, wheels, and chrome into a beauti-fully streamlined device, extending and transforming the human body so that it can experience exhilarating blasts of speed and power. Industrial technology still surrounds us, but it has been superseded in the late twentieth century by the miniaturized intricacy of electronic circuitry. ...As an object of erotic attraction, electronic technology is of a different order from the industrial technology ex-emplified by the car. Whereas industrial technology has robust physical presence and moves visibly through space, the workings of computers and other electronic equipment are encased within plastic boxes and hidden behind opaque screens.

[*] Springer, Claudia. 1996. *Electronic Eros: Bodies and Desire in the Postindustrial Age.* Austin, TX: University of Texas Press. Pages 3, 4–5, 8–10, 16–18, 28–29, 34–35, 40, 80–82, 91, 126, 161.

Additionally, the glory of industrial technology was its enormousness combined with power; enthusiasts were transfixed by big, bold, and fast machines. Electronic technology, in contrast, is dwindling in size; personal computers, for example, are becoming increasingly portable and inconspicuous. These postindustrial "machines of reproduction rather than of production," in the words of Fredric Jameson [1984:79], do not have the same forceful presence as their industrial forebears. ...In many ways industrial technology and postindustrial electronic technology are complete opposites.

...I argue that the newer electronic technologies have inspired changes in techno-erotic imagery...[and] other [aspects of popular culture] recycle techno-erotic conventions derived from Western society's industrial past, refusing to come to terms with the new postmodern social order and all the transformations it has brought. ...[What interests me is] the tendency in popular culture to associate computer technology with sexuality, creating a contradictory discourse that simultaneously predicts the obsolescence of human beings and a future of heightened erotic fulfillment.

Technology has no sex, but representations of technology often do. Historians of technology have pointed out that new inventions have been accompanied by sexual impulses throughout history. John Tierney [1994:2] writes, "Sometimes the erotic has been a force driving technological innovation; virtually always, from the Stone Age sculpture to computer bulletin boards, it has been one of the first uses for a new medium." ...Tierney goes on to state that "the oldest known literature, recorded by the Sumerians in cuneiform on clay tablets, includes poetry celebrating the sweetness of a woman's lips and vulva." He documents the use of communications media for sexual expression from the invention of the printing press to the introduction of the novel, photography, films, videocassette recorders, computers, and pay-per-call telephone services. Tierney's analysis illustrates that the histories of technology and the erotic are closely linked.

...The industrial-age tendency to apply gendered metaphors to machines continues in the electronic age but is complicated by the computer's ambiguous relationship to gender. The design of a computer does not immediately evoke either male or female attributes; if anything, it presents a bland and asexual surface. But the urge to assign gender to machines persists. Consequently, in an attempt to masculinize their products, manufacturers refer to their computers' power and strength. ...At the same time, however, other computer enthusiasts invest computers with attributes they consider feminine: small size, fluid and quiet functioning, and the ability to absorb the user's ego in an empathic bond. Still others celebrate the computer's supposed gender-bending capabilities that allow users to create their on-line personae: men can become women and vice versa.

There is no consensus, then, on the computer's metaphoric gender, but there is cultural acceptance of the idea that computers can be gendered. ...I argue that popular culture plays out contemporary cultural conflicts over sexuality and gender roles in its representations[.] ...What results is a popular culture arena where cultural debates over sexuality and gender are played out in both literal and metaphoric guise. Debates about what it means to be male or female and how sexuality should be expressed often find their way into popular culture's techno-erotic imagery. The imagery sometimes explores alternative types of sexuality and gender roles and at other times retreats to conventional stereotypes from the past.

### Deleting the Body

...The seventeenth and eighteenth centuries bequeathed to subsequent generations a belief in the uniqueness of human beings. Humans, according to Enlightenment philosophy, are blessed with reason and thus enjoy superiority over animals and human-made artifacts. ...During the height of industrialization, however, in the late nineteenth century, perceptions of the relationship between humans and machines changed. Machines were increasingly described as superior to the human body. ...A shift had occurred in how humans were differentiated from machines...: machines were described as if they were human, and humans were characterized as fundamentally mechanical.

In the late twentieth century the distinction between human beings and machines has become even more blurred. Human dependence on technology has started to efface the line between the two. ...The figure of the cyborg—part human and part machine—is now common in fiction, films, television, comic books, magazines, computer games, and video games and can also be found in the works of scientists and contemporary cultural theorists.

...Ancient Greek myths and the sixteenth-century story of Joseph Golem, who was created from clay by an enterprising rabbi in Prague, are among the better-known tales about simulated life to have survived to the present day, but there have been many other such mythic tales, as well as actual attempts to simulate life over the course of the centuries. J. David Bolter [1984:201] writes that "there was perhaps never a moment in the ancient or modern history of Europe when no one was pursuing the idea of making a human being by other than the ordinary reproductive means." The desire to simulate human life is thus deeply rooted in Western culture.

The craft of building humanoid automata flourished during the late seventeenth and eighteenth centuries, when the mechanistic worldview reigned. It reached its peak during the eighteenth century. ...[Even] Rene Descartes himself had a female automaton named Francine. ...Some things have clearly remained the same since the time when Descartes traveled with his artificial female companion; the male desire to construct an ideal woman by artificial means dates back at least to the ancient Greek myth of Pygmalion and Galatea and continues to this day in films...and on television.

...The relationship between human beings and technology has changed dramatically since the seventeenth century, however, achieving an intimacy that was inconceivable until only recently. Human fusion with artificial devices has become a fact of life; prosthetic limbs and artificial organs are just two examples of how the human body incorporates technology's products. ...By watching television and using computers we have all become dependent on the interface with electronic technology.

...When the boundary between human and artificial collapses, all of the other dualities also dissolve, and their two parts become indistinguishable, displacing humans from the unique and privileged position they maintained in Enlightenment philosophy. Transgressed boundaries, in fact, are a central feature of postmodernism, and the cyborg is the ultimate transgressed boundary.

...Technology allows cyber...characters to alter themselves in any way they choose, abandoning any semblance of their original identities. ...Their identities, moreover, are often technological constructs without origin in human consciousness. ...What results is the world of simulations theorized by Jean Baudrillard [1983:4], a hyperreality where "it is no longer a question of imitation, nor of reduplication, nor even of parody. It is rather a question of substituting signs of the real for the real itself." ...Minds and bodies change like chameleons..., going beyond the merely fragmented subjectivity found in other postmodern texts to display complete instability.

Postmodern consumer society is an all-encompassing marketplace of products; everything in it has been commodified, and it surrounds us with advertising, packaged images, and ever-changing fashions in clothes, music, and "lifestyles." Images and sounds bombard postmodern humans and create a phantasmagoria of idealized human bodies. The endless depictions of human bodies have in effect replaced actual human bodies in the public imagination, and it can thus be argued, as do postmodern cultural critics Arthur and Marilouise Kroker [1987:22, emphasis in original], that the human body is already obsolete. They ask, "why the concern over the body today if not to emphasize the fact that the (natural) body in the postmodern condition has *already* disappeared, and what

we experience as the body is only a fantastic simulacra of body rhetorics?"
...Even our experience of space and time...has been transformed under postmodernism. Time has collapsed into a perpetual present, in which everything
from the past has been severed from its historical context in order to circulate
anew in the present, devoid of its original meanings but contributing to the clut-
tered texture of our commodified surroundings.

...In the inhospitable clutter of commodified postmodern space, human perception is invited to skim the surface rather than explore meaningful depths. This
postmodern depthlessness is exemplified by the flatness of the television and
computer screens that pervade our lives and encourage a flattening of all percep-
tual experiences. Jean Baudrillard [1983:7] explains how postmodern computerized existence differs in fundamental ways from earlier experience[:]

> We used to live in the imaginary world of the mirror, of the divided self and of the stage,
> of otherness and alienation. Today we live in the imaginary world of the screen, of inter-
> face and the reduplication of contiguity and networks. All our machines are screens. We
> too have become screens, and the interactivity of men has become the interactivity of
> screens. Nothing that appears on the screen is meant to be deciphered in depth, but actu-
> ally to be explored instantaneously, in an abreaction immediate to meaning—or an im-
> mediate convolution of the poles of representation.

...Postmodern humans experience themselves as surface phenomena without
depth and experience their interactions with each other as occurring without distance, as if all life were reduced to immediacy and the flat surface of the computer or television screen.

### Virtual Sex

...VR [virtual reality] is by no means the first technological innovation to be
aligned with sexual impulses; early filmmaking was motivated in part by a desire
to gaze surreptitiously at women's bodies, a phenomenon that Linda Williams
[1986; 1989] has described in her essay "Film Body" and her book *Hard Core*.
Now, a century after the introduction of moving pictures, we are witnessing a
new technology, virtual reality, take shape. Development is still in an early
stage, so that what people envision for VR far surpasses anything that is currently possible. The visionary discourses surrounding VR are consequently more
interesting than the technology itself.

...Virtual reality is a concept dating back to the late 1960s that has become
fashionable in the 1990s, receiving widespread media coverage while several
companies develop its capabilities and design marketing strategies. ...It would
be inappropriate to call virtual reality an escape from reality, since what it does

is provide an alternative reality where "being" somewhere does not require physical presence and "doing" something does not result in any change outside the virtual system. Virtual reality undermines certainty over the term *reality,* ultimately abandoning it altogether, along with all the other certainties that have been discarded in postmodern times.

...It is widely recognized that VR is often associated with sex. An article in the *Boston Globe,* for example, bemoans the growing interest in cybersex and predicts that it will replace old-fashioned physical sex in the near future [Raymo 1992]. In an article in the book *Cyberspace* Allucquere Rosanne Stone [1994:105] acknowledges that "erotic possibilities for the virtual body are a significant part of the discussions of some of the groups designing cyberspace systems." John Perry Barlow [1990:42] writes, "there is the ...sexual thing. I have been through eight or ten Q & A sessions on virtual reality and I don't remember one where sex didn't come up." Mike Saenz comments, "when I explain virtual reality to the uninitiated, they just don't get it. But they warm immediately to the idea of virtual sex." Just how warm people have gotten to the idea is revealed by Howard Rheingold [1991], author of the book *Virtual Reality,* whose fanciful article on what he called teledildonics became an international sensation nearly overnight.

...[Vivian] Sobchack [1991:25] is not surprised that the desire to escape into virtual worlds has taken hold as strongly as it has: "In an age in which temporal coordinates are oriented toward computation rather than toward human beings, and spatial coordinates have shrunk to the brief occupation of 'here,' in an age in which there is too much perceived risk to living and too much information for both body and mind to contain and survive, need we wonder at the desire to transcend and escape where and who we are."

...Computers, it seems, have intensified, not diminished, our culture's fascination with sexuality. ...[H]owever, computers have inspired flights of fantasy that remain firmly grounded in our current cultural preoccupation with sex and gender.

...Conventional ways of defining what makes each one unique have started to give way, and the human body has become a terrain of dispute. Ambivalence about the human body has manifested itself in various ways in the past, but at no other time has serious speculation about bodily obsolescence been joined by a glut of mass-media imagery depicting a posthuman future. Nevertheless, despite the prevalence of posthuman imagery, a desire to preserve bodily pleasures clearly remains.

# References

Barlow, J. P. 1990. "Being in Nothingness." *Mondo 2000.* 2:34–43.

Baudrillard, J. 1983. *Simulations.* Translated by Foss, Paul, Patton, Paul, and Beitchman. New York, NY: Semiotext(e).

Bolter, J. D. 1984. *Turing's Man: Western Culture in the Computer Age.* Chapel Hill, NC: University of North Carolina Press.

Jameson, F. 1984. "Postmodernism or the Cultural Logic of Late Capitalism." *New Left Review.* 146 (July–August).

Kroker, A., and M. Kroker. 1987. *Body Invaders: Panic Sex in America.* New York, NY: St. Martin's.

Raymo, C. 1992. "Flights of Cyber-fancy." *Boston Globe.* March 23.

Rheingold, H. 1991. *Virtual Reality.* New York, NY: Touchstone.

Sobchack, V. 1991. "New Age Mutant Ninja Hackers." *Artforum International.* 29 (8):24–25.

Stone, A. 1994. "Will the Real Body Please Stand Up? Boundary Stories about Virtual Cultures." Pp 81–118 in *Cyberspace: First Steps,* edited by M. Benedikt. Cambridge, MA: MIT Press.

Tierney, J. 1994. "Porn, the Low-Slung Engine of Progress." *New York Times.* January 9:Section 2.

Williams, L. 1989. *Hard Core: Power, Pleasure, and the "Frenzy of the Visible."* Los Angeles, CA: University of California Press.

———. 1986. "Film Body: An Implantation of Perversions." *Cine-Tracts.* 12 (winter); reprinted in *Narrative, Apparatus, Ideology: A Film Theory Reader* (edited by P. Rosen), pp. 507–534.

# Chapter Four

# Così Fan Tutti:[1] Foucault, Goffman, and the Pornographic Synopticon

## Phillip Vannini

*Sex and pornography on the Internet are all about looking at other people, being looked upon by other people, or both. That is the point: to gaze upon the bodies of others and, perhaps, to have one's own body gazed upon. Similar dynamics have captured the interest of many social theorists, not the least of whom include Michel Foucault and Friedrich Nietzsche. Phillip Vannini's refined analysis reexamines these dynamics and posits new insights on the "pornographic synopticon" of Internet sex.*

### Prologue

I discovered pornography in my pre-teens. I was raised Catholic in a Catholic country where parents send children to after-school Bible classes. My friends and I would often show up early for class and play outside the church; on good days one of us would somehow "score" a porn mag and bring it along to share with friends. We had to be careful. In class we were taught to fight desire, lust, and impurity, in both morality and aesthetics. While priests would push the New Testament in Bible classes, teachers would praise Dante's Divine Comedy in school. But, as our souls were restrained, our bodies strove to grow. It was then that school bathrooms and parking lots became temporary autonomous zones of resistance. In these spaces we could marvel at the embodiment of pleasure represented in our secret glimpses of pornographic imagery. We could fantasize about a utopian space where sins became joys and spiritual shackles crumbled beneath the power of full-grown bodies. We were contesting, without full awareness of doing so; we were challenging the notion of a body that is separate from mind and, along with it, the ideology of a heaven and hell that is separate from *this* embodied existence.

Years have gone by, and the carnal treasures of voyeurism that we could only obtain through the complicity of an older sibling or the absent-mindedness of a news-kiosk clerk are now a simple mouse click away. No stratagems are now needed; all I have is to do is choose. Brunettes, construction workers, redheads, well-hung firefighters, midget couples, bukkake aficionados, watersports buffs, German exhibitionists, all await my choice on the virtual shelves of the mall of flesh known as Internet porn. Now, no longer am I a slave of ascetic morality or apparatchik literature. No longer are the prying eyes of the master scavenging through my soul to cleanse me of my desires. All I have is choice. I am catching glimpses of a utopian, yet all-too-real and all-too-human space: the pornographic *Synopticon*.

### Abandon All Spirituality Ye Who Enter: My Journey through the Pornographic Synopticon

The doors to heaven are now open: my god must have finally died! And along with him have died all his truths (see Nietzsche 1967). At last, free is my body: freed of my imposing soul and freed of my rational mind. With the death of God, and the consequent demise of morality, there are no spirits in the Synopticon. That is why bodies but not souls dwell in the Synopticon, thus turning Dante's ideology upside down. Residents of this heavenly space seem to have shed their clothes and all the shrouds used to cover shame. I learn that all of the dwellers of this pagan heaven are here for having embraced one or more of the three pleasures of life:[2]

- Incontinence: as their pleasure-driven action has arisen from having lost control of their natural appetites and desires;
- Brutishness: as their pleasure-driven action has arisen from attraction to things that repulse the morally healthy soul;
- Malice and Vice: as their pleasure-driven action has risen from their refusing to use reason, humans' most God-like trait (see Alighieri 1993).

The architectural structure of this pornographic and synoptic space is similar to that of the Panopticon popularized by Jeremy Bentham in the late 1700s (Bentham 1995), but also different in important ways. Much like the Panopticon, at the center of this structure lies a rather large and extremely high watchtower, rising as far as the eye can see. I further suggest that this tower oversees a nine-storey building, each floor shaped as a circle, and each circle clearly visible from the central watchtower. Each circle is enormous enough to accommodate as many occupants as one can imagine. While it is impossible from the vantage point of a viewer located inside the central tower to see all inhabitants at the same time, it is possible for such a viewer to see all circles' dwellers over the course of quite some time. In contrast to the Panopticon, however, where guards in the central tower are invisible to the prisoners on each circular floor, in this pornographic Synopticon occupants of the central tower have the option of becoming protagonists themselves to make their presence transparent. They can do so simply by turning the lights and cameras onto themselves, and switching from the role of consumers to that of porn producers.

This simple architectural difference from the Panopticon to the Synopticon belies a radically different set of interaction patterns. In this pornographic Synopticon, power seems to be exercised not through control and repression, but rather through seduction. The denizens of each of the nine circles have chosen to display their aroused and arousing bodies for the voyeuristic pleasure of their peeping viewers, as well as for their own scopophiliac kicks.[3] These are the few—in the Synopticon—the prurient few that the many voyeurs libidinously scope. In fact, in a society based on consumption, power takes more frequently the form of seduction (Bauman 1989). And here the voyeurs have no power but that of consumer choice: the choice of their seducers and the option to become seducers themselves.

Each circle in the Synopticon hosts one or more categories of scopophiliacs that are grouped in relation to the type of pleasure of which they are fond. Table 1 below reports in detail how the residents of the Synopticon are arranged spatially. Categories are meant to illustrate, but are not mutually exclusive or exhausting. The first column indicates the positioning of all circles, ranging from the ground-floor first circle, to the top ninth floor. The second column identifies the category of sin and sinners that Dante established for the structure of his Inferno. I kept Dante's categories unchanged; however, here in the Synopticon, sin is turned into pleasure and the hierarchy of circles is turned upside down with the Ultimate Destroyer reigning supreme at the top (I cannot at this point report on its identity, however). Finally, the third column shows common categories of Internet pornographic pleasure. In my journey through this pornographic Synopticon I was able to virtually meet some of its dwellers, whose stories I will tell. Later, we shall meet the Ultimate Destroyer.

Table 1: The circles of the pornographic Synopticon

| Circle | Circle Dwellers | Some Common Porn Directory Categories |
|--------|----------------|---------------------------------------|
| 1 | Virtuous Pagans Unbaptized Youth | Librarians, Coeds and Teachers, Nurses and Doctors, Teens, Barely Legal, Girls w/ Braces. |
| 2 | The Lustful | FFM, MMF, Groups, Stoners, Smokers, Pissers. |
| 3 | The Gluttons | Suck/Lick, Messy Facials/Bukkake, Fruits and Vegetable Insertions, Rim Jobs, the Drunk, Chubby, Squirts. |
| 4 | The Avaricious | Handjobs, Fingerjobs, FistFucking, Dildo Lovers, Sybian. |

Table continued on next page

Table 1 continued

| 5 | The Angry<br>The Sullen | Army, Police, Gangbangers.<br>Nerds, Bitches, Bikers. |
|---|---|---|
| 6 | The Heretics | Goths, Punks, S&Mers, Nuns, Priests, Bizarre, Pale. |
| 7 | The Violent,<br>Sodomites | Cellophane Wrapping, Extreme, Yacht and Bus-Bangers.<br>Anal, Ass Worship. |
| 8 | Panderers,<br>Seducers | Exhibitionists, Strippers, Panties, Secretaries, Bosses, Waitresses/Waiters, Maids. |
| | Simonists | Free XXX Sites Password Givers. |
| | Fortune Tellers | Blindfolded. |
| | Thieves | Voyeurs. |
| | Sowers of Discord | Massive Cocks, Huge Knockers. |
| | Alchemists | Body-Enhancement Advertisement Sites. |
| | Counterfeiters | Fake Celebrity Porn. |
| | Elemental Natures | Cowgirls, Cowboys, Hirsute. |
| 9 | Traitors to Family | MILFs, Grandparents, Housewives, Pregnant, Twins. |
| | Traitors to Country | Asian, Brazilians, Russians, Dutch, French, Latina/o. |
| | The Ultimate Destroyer | [Unknown to us for now] |

## Some Synopticon Residents

The gluttons, the lustful, virtuous pagans, and unbaptized youth occupy Dante's lower levels of the pornographic Synopticon, where life is often a happy-go-lucky, round-the-clock party. Such virtuous pagans and unbaptized youth appear on the Internet as dormitory students, fraternity and sorority members, and college "sluts" and "studs" who succumb to their sexual desires while trying to cultivate their education. Because here the mind is subjugated to the body, college students easily fall to temptation and wind up fornicating with one or more of the following: substitute teachers and regular teachers (the latter especially for extra credit), lab assistants, sexually frustrated librarians, well-hung custodians, athletic coaches, mean parking lot attendants, furry school mascots, exotic foreign-exchange students, and especially lascivious roommates.

The lustful and the gluttons of circle two and three are seemingly never hungry or sober. Stoners are especially an interesting bunch here. They get high, and take their clothes off, just like that. For instance, in my virtual journey I saw a nun smoking a bong and libidinously punishing a parishioner for his sins. However, the most interesting occupants of this circle seem to be the bukkake buffs. George Kranz, self-proclaimed net sex commentator, sees especially recent derivations of bukkake as a "significant advance in human behavior." He continues:

> The original Japanese films portrayed a highly ritualized sex show where a demure young lass, usually in school girl or corporate uniform kneels in the center of a small room. There is usually some visual prop to emphasize her as the center of attention–velvet ropes hung from brass pedestals forming a fence around her, two or three rows of "security guards" who serve to control access to her. The girl waits patiently, little or no emotion showing on her face as one by one, men who have been masturbating just off camera approach and ejaculate into her face. Often there will be as many, as 75 or 80 men. Sometimes the girl briefly fellates the man of the moment, sometimes not. There is usually no significant sound track (i.e. music or dialogue) other than a few appreciative grunts and groans from the gents. Not to worry though, with characteristic Yanqui ingenuity and resolve, the U.S. porn industry has spotted a good idea, and improved it. The U.S. versions are considerably livelier, almost a party atmosphere. Some of the girls really get into the action, after all they are doing the best thing possible for their complexions–the natural vitamins and proteins in cum have long been known to help condition skin. [In bukkake] her hair is streaked with strands of cum, cum hangs from her chin and occasionally falls to her bare breasts–she is grinning like a she-devil–a good time is had by all.[4]

Circle four houses the avaricious. These indulgent masturbators are never bored. Take the Sybian aficionados, for example. Folks at the fuckingmachines.com website claim that their machines have already been blessed with Internet fame. For instance, in his article "The Information Highway Runs through Her Pussy" Ray Glass (2003) writes:

> [whatever it was…] makes me horny. How will I take care of this boner when I get home? The always-ready standby. Old reliable. The Internet. I'll go online, watch streaming videos of sultry babes getting fucked by robots, crank up my Venus II pneumatic dick-sucking machine to six strokes per second, and get my rocks off like a modern man. I've always harbored a fetish for machine sex, going back so far I don't even wanna tell you. And I've actually created a few such devices, when my feverish excitement could be maintained long enough to construct a proof-of-concept prototype. Consequently, Fuckingmachines.com is a wet dream come-true for mechanical-sex aficionados like me, who crave an assortment of heavy machinery and home appliances used to orgasmic effect on flesh-and-blood cuties.[5]

One of the most popular "fucking machines" is the Sybian, a padded semi-cylinder seat, on which a woman sits with her legs astride, with a changing speed

1200 RPM vibrating dildo-shaped fixture on top that works as a rotating G-spot massager. Other popular machines at fuckingmachines.com include similar contraptions with names like: the intruder, the antique intruder, the double crane, the portafuck, the trespasser, and the goat milker.

On our way to the Ultimate Destroyer on circle nine, we meet the heretics and the violent in circles six and seven. Among the (relatively) violent folks here, yacht-bangers and bus-bangers have recently achieved some popularity. Starting the yacht idea are two chubby middle-aged men cruising around on their boat wearing nothing but their birthday suit and a sailor hat (though they occasionally revert to Viking hats when they take pretend members of the Swedish Bikini Team onboard). Captain Stabbin, a.k.a. the Anal Adventurer, became so popular that those not wealthy enough to "abduct" willing young women on their upscale yacht had to resort to a bus, a van, or lately a Hummer. Even the derivative idea gained success. The idea of the folks at bangbus.com became so popular and so easy to do-it-yourself that "backseat banging" has now become a common category in Internet porn. Among the most creative in circle six we find those who enjoy engaging in bizarre sex. Take for example Dr. Packenwood at packenwood.com—he writes:

> I'm Dr. B. Packenwood a trained hypnotist who has been practicing for over ten years. I recently opened an office downtown and have been handing out flyers all over the place. I've received tons of phone calls from university students asking about the "special student deal" that I was offering. So get this, a hot teen student steps in to my office thinking that hypnosis will cure all her problems. I wave my watch and she's fast asleep and I do whatever I please to her. The best part is she thinks the camera is for her benefit. Little does she know....[6]

Finally, on my way to the highest ring of circle nine where the Ultimate Destroyer resides I run into the MILF Hunters[7] and their prey. There are several MILF Hunters and MILFs on the Internet. MILF is an acronym standing for "Mother I'd Like to Fuck" and refers to women past their twenties who remain attractive enough to be objects of sexual desire "despite" showing signs of aging and their being (presumably) mothers of young children. The MILF hunter at milf-hunter.net is a "man on a mission to trap and sperm moms all across America." On his website he has posted some frequently asked questions:

> *Q: Who is the Milf Hunter?*
> A: The Milf Hunter is a man on a mission, his identity is kept highly secret, so as not to disclose his whereabouts on a hunt. Milfs can sometimes detect his presence, and because they are unsure, it's always best not to disturb them.
> *Q: What does Milf Hunter do?*

A: Milf Hunter traps mature moms with his charm and predatory hunting experience. He hunts during day and night, and can smell his prey from a distance. Once caught, the seduced milf is normally shafted by the hunter.

*Q: What has the Milf Hunter got for us?*

A: Thanks to pack hunting abilities, the Milf Hunter is able to provide us with video footage of his exploits in the field, and in addition, there are many pictures of his trophy catches, with him penetrating the eager milfs for their pleasure.[8]

And yes, the MILF Hunter does actually occasionally wear mimetic makeup and military fatigues.

## The Synoptic Qualities of Internet Pornography

I have portrayed the institution of Internet porn as a synoptic structure and introduced the argument that this pornographic Synopticon differs significantly from a panoptic structure, but what exactly is the significance of these two structures for our discussion of Internet porn? And, what precisely are the differences between the Panopticon and the Synopticon? Let us begin with the Panopticon. For Michel Foucault (1979) the Panopticon serves not only as the model for the operation of body-controlling discursive disciplines but also as the epitome of a top-down social hierarchy with a power structure that revolves around control of many by the few. Yet control is not perennially stable. Forms of discipline and power mutate continuously through time, as discourse changes. Thus the Foucauldian subject is defined by different discourses that dynamically evolve throughout history. An example will serve to illustrate these important concepts. Take any female model portrayed while masturbating with (or perhaps being masturbated by) the Sybian; it is quite in line with Foucault's argument to interpret a fucking *machine* as a technological tool used to discipline a body. Clearly, the type of discipline and power at play here are radically different from the type of power and discipline enforced through, say, a medieval iron maiden, but the relation is similar: power disciplines the body through different technologies, and power depends for its operation on discourse, or knowledge. Discursive knowledge does change through time, but it still operates by defining and controlling its subjects. But let us return to the Panopticon.

In *Discipline and Punish*, Foucault (1979) writes that before the enlightenment punishment of criminals regularly took place in public spaces in order to highlight the awe-inspiring, spectacular properties of discipline. But after the enlightenment, surveillance replaced spectacle as the most common disciplinary technology. Prisoners' bodies would then be separated from other prisoners and confined in individual cells under the threat of constant surveillance of remote guards who remained invisible to the prisoners' view. Foucault argued that the

Panopticon was efficient because prisoners, uncertain of being watched by the guards in the central tower, would ultimately internalize the potential presence of a surveyor and become their own disciplinarians. The Panopticon, Foucault argued, was not simply a model for a prison. All institutions could function in a similar way by controlling the bodies of their subjects through the operation of two related forces. The first force is the force of power operating through discourse; by internalizing the norms of their guardians subjects would discipline their own bodies. The second force is the force of power operating through space; because now authority and the knowledge upon which authority is based are internalized and commonly shared just about everywhere in the Panopticon, the functioning of a panoptic society is assured by the spatial distribution of power among its members. In short, everyone can be both surveyor and surveyed (Foucault 1979, 1980). Once again, one can think of our Sybian models. Arguably, they have internalized the notion that they *must* feel pleasure and therefore they proceed to discipline themselves by pleasuring themselves. Of course herein lies one of the ironies of the pornographic Synopticon: pleasure becomes a duty. Interestingly enough, all this occurs not in a conventional building like structure, but on the Internet.

How then are the Internet and the Panopticon related? According to Winokur (2003):

> Both panopticism and the Internet construct space with a special attention to the subject's internalizing a particular model of space, and a particular notion of how people are distributed throughout space in relation to one another, and with a special attention to the defining of the individual through the space she occupies. Further, both are intensely interested in the construction and distribution of authority over and within the subject.[9]

The point here is that information in the Cyber-Panopticon is used to construct the spaces of consumption that surveyors and surveyed utilize to define their subjectivity vis-à-vis one another. Or, in simpler words, the space of each circle is defined by common practices and common taste. The difference between those who favor the occupants of, say, the innocent "teen" porn circle and those who favor the circle hosting "bizarre" and violent acts is significant. This is, as Winokur (2003) remarks, a form of rhetorical control of our bodies-in-virtual-movement. In fact, as we surf the Internet for porn, much like watchtower guardians, we objectify the circles' occupants (actual individuals portrayed in sexual acts), but at the same time this same gaze constructs their subjectivity. Our gaze accomplishes the latter task because its objects share with us a common discourse and space: that of seduction (Sartre 1943). The scopophiliac object of our gaze is not an inert object; in actuality it becomes a subject through the recognition of erotic desire. Indeed, objects of pornographic representation are fully aware of being watched[10] and as a matter of fact without our gaze they would not exist.

As briefly mentioned earlier, whereas panopticism is based on social stasis, we ought to think of Internet communication as a highly dynamic form of interaction. Not only does the Internet allow us more flexibility in choosing what we wish to survey (whereas film, for example, does not), but it also allows us to become protagonists ourselves. The distinction between surveyors and surveyed in the pornographic Synopticon can become quite blurry when we think of how easily just about anyone with the help of a digital handy-cam or photographic camera can create their own webpage or website. Many forms of sexual exchanges on the Internet are indeed interactive thanks to bidirectional communication technology such as email, IRC, and live feeds (see Waskul 2002). Internet communication best epitomizes what Roland Barthes (1974) called a "writerly" text: text whose meaning is to some degree formed by the reader rather than exclusively by the producer. The decisive argument for synopticism comes from the "widespread desire to consume and be consumed by the product" (Boyne 2000:301), a dynamic typical of seduction. And the latter point should explain why hitherto I have made no distinction whatsoever between professional porn actresses and actors and amateurs. Because the writerly properties of the Internet allow any porn consumer in the central tower to redefine their space and subjectivity by switching the limelight onto themselves and becoming a porn producer, the distinction between pro and amateur porn does not matter. It is no accident that "the most downloaded woman on the Internet"—Cindy Margolis—was a self-starter amateur before her web popularity allowed her to make a living off her pin-up girl appeal. Or think, for example, of all the "backseat bangers" who sprung up on the Internet following the lead of Captain Stabbin. It is not an unrealistic assumption to imagine that these second comers used to be masturbating consumers of Captain Stabbin porn well before becoming producers themselves. Clearly then, what matters is one's success in seducing, and it is to the analysis of this that I now turn.

### Performing the Pornographic Body

Up to this point we have established that we can best describe the social architecture of Internet pornography through the lens of the Synopticon. Whereas panopticism enables control through the separation of space, synopticism facilitates seduction through the fusion of space (Mathiesen 1997). Older communication media, such as film and television, have long been known to allow individuals to gaze into private worlds that mediated representation has turned public (Meyrowitz 1985; Williams 1989). But the Internet, as said, takes this mechanism two steps further. First, the Internet allows us to gaze onto taboo-protected worlds, such as that of machine-enhanced masturbation, which television and film, even in their most liberal moments, could never fully explore (Williams 1989). And second, as said, the Internet allows anyone with web access to turn from the role of surveyor, to that of surveyed. It is then critical for our understanding of virtual pornographic interaction to examine how role transitions such as this can take place.

In contrast to early Foucauldian theory, which is mainly informed by a view of power as control over individuals, Goffmanian dramaturgy (Goffman 1959) places much more emphasis on embodied individual agency. Goffman's central concern is in fact with how bodies actively shape everyday life, and how techniques of body presentation allow individuals to carry out their social roles (Goffman 1959, 1963, 1967, 1969). Let us then go back to one of the fellows we met earlier: Dr. Packenwood. Dr. Packenwood plays the role of a psychotherapist who seduces unwilling and unaware patients and does so effectively by employing certain props and performing context-appropriate scripts. The same logic works for his patients, who play along in looking mesmerized, confused, hazy, and so forth. The very same presentational rules are valid for just about any pornographic category: from teachers and students to cops and speeding drivers, from nurses and doctors to priests and nuns. Or take for example the MILF Hunter. The development of his public character calls for him to be an active predator who "traps" MILFs in places that they presumably frequent: from grocery store parking lots to elementary school playgrounds and "boring" and lonely households. The corollary is that these characters are social actors—whether professional or amateur—by virtue of their playing a role on a specific stage, with appropriate scripts.

There are many roles and parts that people play in the pornographic Synopticon. The body, following Goffman, plays a central role in structuring pornographic encounters. Pornography indeed can hardly transcend the social context of a sexual encounter. A pornographic script is always played within established routines and situations where individuals interact with others; think of the MILF Hunter, Captain Stabbin, and Dr. Packenwood. Even the fantastic realm of pornography they evoke winds up with scripts and performances that occupy places common to everyday life such as the school, the home, the workplace, the car, the doctor's office, the beach, and so on. Hence our *real* everyday erotic fantasies become materialized through our *virtual and mediated* meeting with them, and the success of this encounter depends on the fact that whereas in ordinary communication the rule of civil inattention (Goffman 1963) morally prohibits us from gazing too attentively at others; in virtual pornographic encounters synoptic rules of behavior supersede the norm of civil inattention. In pornography indeed the gaze becomes a stare. But there is also another important component to the synoptic gaze or stare, a component upon which the success of body presentation in pornographic encounters depends heavily. For the analysis of this component we must reflect on morality and embodied subjectivity.

There are no spirits in the Synopticon and there are no truths either, as I said. However, my statement about truth must be qualified. To be precise there are indeed truths in the pornographic Synopticon, but the rules of their formation are different from other contexts. An anecdote will serve to clarify this difficult but important point. Back in my teenage years, one day in class during yet another exasperating hermeneutic pontification over the meanings of Dante's *Inferno* I raised my hand and asked: "Teacher, how is it possible for the *disembodied souls* confined in hell to *feel* the pain inferred upon them through *corporeal* punishment?" Needless to say, I was begging for a non-answer ("Have faith, son!"), but in reflecting on dualism later in my life, I began to wonder whether in order to turn morality on its head all we had to do was *feel with our body rather than think through an oppositional mind*. Thinking through an oppositional mind only results in substituting one morality with another, but ceasing to think at all obliterates morality, as we know it, that is, as an ideology. To understand encounters in the pornographic Synopticon we must then ultimately turn to the rules of stipulation of the Goffmanian order of interaction and the Foucauldian order of discourse.[11] Are these rules stipulated by bodies, by minds, or perhaps by both?

Goffman's social actors in everyday life have to be very careful in choosing the appropriate corporeal rules to come across as credible. Body behavior in structured encounters is governed by notions of what is true, right, and beautiful—or in Goffman's terms by an interaction order that is somehow an autonomous sphere of collective life (Goffman 1983). But body behavior in pornographic encounters between scopophiliacs and voyeurs does not need to rely exclusively on matters of the mind such as logic, ethics, and aesthetics, but rather on rules that the body as well has stipulated. The latter are difficult to understand comprehensively, but we can find an example of how mind and body may operate on separate definitions of what constitutes truth in the pornographic Synopticon in some of the gigs we have examined earlier. Dr. Packenwood, Captain Stabbin, and the MILF Hunter are staging a role for their voyeuristic consumers, but are doing so very poorly (according to the artistic canons of good acting). As a matter of fact, they are acting so poorly that we do laugh at them.

Nevertheless, figures such as these can still satisfy the masturbatory fantasies of their voyeuristic customers as their acting remains in the end peripheral to the "truth" bespoken in porn by an aroused and arousing body.[12] Hence, the order of discourse and interaction in the pornographic Synopticon is a product of the body just as much as it is of the mind. Clearly, this argument partly contradicts Foucault in that it sees the body as playing an agentic role in the construction of sexual meaning, but I believe its utility lies in reapproaching Foucault's thought with Goffman's.

## The Ultimate Destroyer

Throughout my journey across the nine circles I learned that the pornographic Synopticon *can* be a joyous, heavenly space where the surveyors and the surveyed *can* enjoy their bodies freely. But upon visiting the ninth circle I realized that the pornographic Synopticon is no utopian space, for even here we can witness the presence of an element of disharmony and conflict: the Ultimate Destroyer. In Dante's inferno the Ultimate Destroyer is Lucifer, the devil, who through its three wings constantly sends forth blasts of hatred, ignorance, and impotence. Whereas Lucifer's actions *stabilize* the atrocious conditions of hell, in the pornographic Synopticon the actions of the Ultimate Destroyer result in *destabilizing* its social structure. I do not mean to posit that the Ultimate Destroyer renders the idea of synopticism invalid, but rather to suggest that its actions introduce an element of instability within it. The Ultimate Destroyer of the Pornographic Synopticon is the Mind, and what the Mind blasts through the Synopticon are reverberations of objectifying power. Neither the Mind nor the Body ever reaches hegemony within the Synopticon—their balance of forces being directly constitutive of the concept of synopticism. We can understand this dynamic balance by considering, once again, the thought of Goffman and Foucault.

Michel Foucault believed that the human body was produced by discourse and could only exist through discourse (see Shilling 2003). Discourse is irreducible to language but is ultimately dependent on it because language allows discourse to be produced, exchanged, used, and interpreted (Dreyfus and Rabinow 1983). Discourse and language are symbolic properties of the mind, and so is knowledge. People always use knowledge—Foucault believed, following Nietzsche—with a purpose: to gain power over others. And this form of power that the Mind introduces in the pornographic Synopticon is what creates its problematic perennial instability and at the same time its attractiveness! After all, a stable, predictable, and easily accessible sexuality would be simply boring.

First, the Mind destabilizes the free flow of body-governed erotic seduction by reintroducing moral consciousness, which brings some amount of shame back into the Synopticon. As a result, the voyeurs may feel ashamed for masturbating, or ashamed of their perverse taste, or their sexual hysteria, and may feel ashamed to become scopophiliacs themselves or to survey others excessively (see Foucault 1978, 1979). The scopophiliacs, on the other hand may feel shame for uncovering themselves and feeling selfish pleasure. This happens as the reintroduction of the mind in the realm of pornographic sexuality brings back a focus on people's conscious *intentions* while taking away focus from mere bodily actions (see Foucault 1978). The actions of the surveyed may then cease to be purely driven by scopophiliac bodily desire and become instead dictated by the need for public confession. The sin to be confessed here is the futility of the pornographic sexual act, which is futile because it does not lead to reproduction of life. Pornography, after all, is sex for the sake of sex (McNair 2002).

Secondly, the objectifying power of the Mind operates to some extent in the Synopticon "through progressively finer channels, gaining access to individuals themselves [rather than their pornographic representation], to their bodies, their gestures and all their daily actions" (Foucault 1980:151). As a result certain bodies, and more precisely certain body shapes, may become marginalized whereas others assume some controlling power. Namely, the Mind brings history back into the otherwise timeless Synopticon, thus introducing time-contingent regulations on what a beautiful body should look like to appear erotic for others. These cultural forces result in objectifying bodies by controlling them in order to conduce them to an ideal object (Baudrillard 1990).

Thirdly, the Mind reintroduces notions of aesthetics within the "shared vocabularies of body idiom" (Goffman 1963:35) that govern seductive encounters. As a result seduction reverts to a large extent to a highly conventionalized set of "dress, bearing, movements and position, sound level, physical gestures...facial decorations, and broad emotional expressions" (Goffman 1963:33). These shared vocabularies of body idiom reduce the potentially unlimited creativity of sexuality and introduce hierarchy in sexual encounters. Because body idioms are made meaningful by the interaction order existent in a certain society, inequalities between the identity of men and women reemerge. Furthermore, because the vocabulary of bodily idioms is now highly conventionalized, and because body expression is now subjugated to the mind, forms of bodily exploitation return. The body once again becomes to some degree the expressive and instrumental vehicle of expression dictated by a mind that has chosen to disassociate with it, but not fully. The seductiveness of embodied agency and corporeal desire, represented by the sexual fantasies of pornography, continue their emancipatory struggle, and always will—without ever completely prevailing. In the end, the mind and the body coexist disharmoniously in the pornographic Synopticon, and interestingly enough there could be no other way: were there no taboos to break, how could we enjoy being naughty (McNair 2002)?

## Notes

1. I derive the inspiration for the title from Wolfgang Amadeus Mozart (1989). *Così Fan Tutte* tells a story of seduction, sexual desire, and betrayal, and translates literally as "This is the way they all do it." I, however, adopt the gender-neutral *tutti* instead of the feminine *tutte* to indicate that both women and men participate. On the whole, this writing is a mixed-genre essay that derives inspiration from such diverse writers as Dante Alighieri, Jeremy Bentham, Friedrich Nietzsche, Michel Foucault, and Erving Goffman. In particular, I base my idea for the architectural structure of my pornographic Synopticon upon Dante's Inferno (Alighieri 1993), and upon Jeremy Bentham's (1995) Panopticon. I then utilize Nietzschean philosophy and especially Foucauldian and Goffmanian theory to interpret the seductive encounter between consumers and producers of pornographic imagery on the Internet.

2. I ask the reader to notice that I have employed exclusively categories of *legal* pornography. Therefore, even categories such as "teens" used here denote individuals who are fully consenting and legally capable of doing so. Even though I reject most common moral norms employed to condemn pornography I do *not* condone child pornography, bestiality, and portrayals of actual (not simulated) violent acts committed against the will of some of their participants.

3. Scopophilia is the pleasure associated with being looked at. I used the term "scopophiliacs" to refer to those whose sexual acts are reproduced through pornography and the word "voyeurs" to refer to those who consume such imagery.

4. http://www.georgekranz.com/gk/bukkake.htm

5. http://www.spectator.net/1204/pages/1204_f_machines.html

6. http://www.packenwood.com/hypnovictims/malezia/aa-partner03.html

7. This expression was popularized by the recent movie *American Pie*.

8. http://www.milf-hunter.net/

9. http://www.ctheory.net/text_file.asp?pick=371

10. With the possible exclusion of some actual voyeur sites, but these are a small minority. Note that even voyeur sites that promise to capture real sex partners unaware of being photographed or filmed in fact often advertise falsely.

11. There are important differences as well as similarities between Foucault's concept of discursive order and Goffman's concept of interaction order that deserve the full attention of social theorists. Due to my limited space I cannot do so here.

12. This is true for men. Indeed, no man needs to be a good actor to make it in porn—what is needed is the ability to stay erect for some time. Indeed, whereas Hollywood actors need to be good liars, male porn actors need to perform truth. The pornographic Synopticon is and remains mostly a space governed by the male gaze and male desire. Therefore, is the pornographic Synopticon a sexist space? Absolutely, but it does not need to be. See the last page of my chapter for an explanation of this concept.

# References

Alighieri, D. 1993. *The divine comedy*. Oxford, New York, NY: Oxford University Press.

Baudrillard, J. 1990. *Seduction*. New York, NY: St. Martin's Press.

Bauman, Z. 1989. On postmodern uses of sex. In *Love and eroticism*, ed. M. Featherstone. London: Sage.

Barthes, R. 1974. *S/Z*. New York, NY: Hill and Wang.

Bentham, J. 1995. *The panopticon writings*. Edited with an introduction by M. Bozovic. London: Verso.

Boyne, R. 2000. Post-panopticism. *Economy and Society* 29(2):285–307.

Dreyfus, H. and P. Rabinow. 1983. *Michel Foucault: Beyond structuralism and hermeneutics*. Chicago, IL: University of Chicago Press.

Foucault, M. 1980. *Power/knowledge*. New York, NY: Pantheon.

———. 1979. *Discipline and punish: The birth of the prison*. New York, NY: Penguin.

———. 1978. *History of sexuality: An introduction. vol. 1*. New York, NY: Vintage.

Glass, R. 2003. The Information Highway Runs through Her Pussy. *Spectator Magazine,* article 1204. Available online at http://www.spectator.net/1204/pages/1204_f_machines.html

Goffman, E. 1983. The interaction order. *American Sociological Review* 48:1–17.

———. 1969. *Strategic interaction*. Philadelphia: University of Pennsylvania Press.

———. 1967. *Interaction ritual: Essays in face to face behavior*. Chicago: Aldine.

———. 1963. *Behavior in public places: Notes on the social organization of gatherings*. New York: Free Press.

———. 1959. *The presentation of self in everyday life*. Garden City, NY: Doubleday Anchor.

Mathiesen, T. 1997. The viewer society: Michel Foucault's 'panopticon' revisited. *Theoretical Criminology* 1(2):215–234.

Meyrowitz, J. 1985. *No sense of place: The impact of electronic media on social behavior*. New York, NY: Oxford University Press.

McNair, B. 2002. *Striptease culture:Sex, media, and the democratization of desire*. New York, NY: Routledge.

Mozart, W. A. 1989. *Così fan tutte* (Sound Recording). Hamburg, Germany: Deutsche Grammophon.

Nietzsche, F. 1967. *The will to power*. New York, NY: Vintage, Random House.

Sartre, J. P. 1943. The Look, Section IV. In *Being and nothingness: A phenomenological essay on ontology*. pp. 228–78. Secaucus, NJ: The Citadel Press.

Shilling, C. 2003. *The body and social theory, 2nd edition*. London: Sage.

Waskul, D. 2002. The naked self: Being a body in televideo cybersex." *Symbolic Interaction* 25(2):199–227.

Williams, L. 1989. *Hard Core: Power, pleasure, and the "frenzy of the visible."* Los Angeles, CA: University of California Press.

Winokur, M. 2003. The ambiguous Panopticon: Foucault and the codes of cyberspace. *CTheory,* a371.

# Chapter Five

# Way Better Than Real: Manga Sex to Tentacle Hentai

## Joel Powell Dahlquist
## and Lee Garth Vigilant

*Japanese comics and animated cartoons may very well represent one of the most precarious categories of commonly encountered Internet pornography. This unique erotic form—hentai—curiously blends otherwise conflicting images: sex and cartoons, flesh and fantasy, human and alien. Yet hentai is more than a cultural curiosity—it often contains disturbing images of ambiguously gendered characters, less than subtle suggestions of childhood youth, violence, and rape. While much of Internet sex and pornography has been investigated by various social scientists, these cartoon images have largely escaped analysis. In this long overdue investigation Joel Powell Dahlquist and Lee Vigilant provide a layered and nuanced understanding of hentai in a manner that reflects key elements of our contemporary cultural milieu.*

The entry of Japanese comics (manga) and animated cartoons (anime) into Internet markets has not provoked major controversy, but it is a source of consternation for fans and researchers of Japanese popular culture. Some critics portray a devolution of Japanese popular art as it is transplanted to Western markets (Clements 1998a; 1998b; Payne 2003) and assert the importance of history, legend, folklore, and how those imageries guide the intentions of Japanese artists and authors. Others insist that Japanese popular art is an avenue for insights into gender relations (Ogi 2003; Allison 2000; Jones 2003) or law and economics (Kinsella 2000) or even reveals rampant sexual confusion and incest in Japanese culture (see Adams and Hill [1997] for a xenophobic example). But many sense that in diffuse global markets cultural indices have dwindled in favor of the efficient and profitable images associated with Western tastes—action-adventure, science fiction, horror, and even pornography.

Most Americans are acquainted with anime through popular game-related cartoons such as *Pokemon* and *Yu-Gi-Oh*, or the spate of Japanese cartoons on cable television including *Dragon Ball Z, Sailor Moon,* and the American derivations *Samurai Jack* and *Powerpuff Girls*. American parents should be familiar with the successfully exported feature films *Princess Mononoke* and *Spirited*

*Away*. Grandparents remember the black and white *Astro Boy* from 1963 or *Speed Racer* in 1967. The more curious have seen the best of recent feature films such as *Akira* and *Metropolis* (see McCarthy and Clements [2001] for details on all of these productions). Never satisfied with any commentary on manga and anime, American aficionados know the provenance of animated productions and their ancestry in graphic novels, the qualities of many diverse genres within anime, and the rationales for sophisticated storylines.

So everyone in the West is prepared to understand some reference to Japanese cartoons, with dozens of redundant features making anime recognizable to the Western eye. Cheap anime is reminiscent of cheesy American cartoons of the 1960s and 70s where only a generous suspension of disbelief would perceive cartoon figures as "animated." Yet intricate and often beautiful background drawings are combined with bold line figures that preserve the manga tableaus from which most anime descends. Anime has come to *look* Japanese. Androgynous males and outrageously erotic girl-women are drawn with huge, shimmering eyes, ropy hair in colors that do not occur in nature, lipless mouths that form into perfect geometric shapes, and sideways letter vees to represent noses. The best anime features production values inferior to what American audiences have come to expect of movies and television. Formulaic and familiar, anime has become a distinct feature of children's entertainment in the West.

Most of the anime that has become conspicuous in the West is easily perceived as passing and inconsequential children's fare. But in the 1980s American hobby shops began to cater to enduring, adult fan bases for Japanese manga and anime. Japanese popular artists freshened the American markets' genres of superheroes, science fiction, and post-apocalyptic horror, and advanced strange and interesting cultural codes and concerns in romance and adventure. Residing in these popular forms were the comparatively matter-of-fact Japanese standpoint on sexual relations, a good dose of patriarchal values (see Jones 2003), and a glorification of nubile girls as erotic objects for men and heroines for girls and women (see also Poitras 2001). Romance manga were revealed as explicitly sexual, and while graphic novels tended to focus more on relationship stories, erotic videos based on these stories were much simpler. The demands of markets for erotica, of course, were quickly recognized and addressed.

With such a range of forms penetrating markets in many ways, it seems foregone that incarnations of manga and anime would arrive in pornographic domains in the Internet. The path for Japanese comic art is smooth in part because much of virtual erotica from Japan is typified by comic myths about insatiable virgins or by *Love Hina*—the broad comedy about horny, awkward teenagers trying to have intercourse. Transpositions of erotic manga and anime to American retail stores thus seldom require more than some translations or dubbing. The jump to the Internet needs no more than a small web page enterprise, and manga arrives on the Internet in the form of still drawings without much storyline. What is more surprising is that varieties of erotic anime and manga have been marketed so successfully, and that markets continue to expand in diversity and size (so much so that Logan [2001] encourages pornography web masters to quickly diversify into cartoon pornography).

Also located in Japanese anime and manga were expressions of some darker impulses to violence, torture, and domination in sexual contexts. The notorious icon for the hard-core manga and anime of the late eighties and early nineties is *Urotsukidoji*, an incomprehensible phantasmagoria punctuated by teen girls suffering rapes in all available orifices from the tentacle-penises of demons. An entire subgenre of alien rape manga and anime was given life in American and European Internet markets by this feature film and its sequels. Commentators note that tentacles originally skirted Japanese censorship regulations (Clements 1998b; see also Allison [2000] and Kinsella [2000] on other relevant Japanese regulations) and may gamely try to provide historical and cultural explanations for *Urotsukidoji*. In the video retail and hobby shop markets of the 1990s, tentacle anime was often seen as more of a headache than a cultural treasure, and retailers were unhappy at the prospect of dealing in violent pornography and putting customer relations in jeopardy (see Hulse 2001). Internet entrepreneurs, however, have been liberated by large, diffuse markets and can realize the genuine profit potential of violent anime (see also Barron 2000; Fisher 2001).

The landscape of Internet pornography covers three hundred thousand sites, and while growing, the regions represented by cartoon erotica are dwarfed by conventional pornographic offerings. The accessibility, convenience, and speed of the Internet, however, are especially efficient for the sale of pornography and accelerate exposure to all kinds of products. Standard Internet pornography sites often link to hentai (pornographic anime) pages or fold in varieties of drawings and animation along with typical photographic and video pornography. Hentai is presented as a taste, genre, or preference and thus marketed along with other virtual sex products. This means that more and more the curious, determined, or experienced seekers of Internet pornography will encounter animated pornography in the pop-up activity of web surfing.

While long-term fans of manga and anime are prepared for explicitly erotic scenes, first encounters for the uninitiated web surfer must be puzzling. After all, most Internet users and pornography consumers have a typical familiarity with cartoons and consign them to the entertainment worlds of children. Some cartoon pornography sites specialize in spoofing well-known American cartoons and sell rowdy, predictable download shorts of Fred Flintstone copulating with Betty Rubble or Jasmine from the Disney hit *Aladdin* servicing every human and animal character in the story. These sites can be understood as novelties, but will be quickly eclipsed by the many more hentai pages that are jarringly sexual. In the same pop-up arrays of funny sex cartoons, hentai sites offer many of the products expected from conventional pornography pages—thumbnail galleries, streaming and flash videos, GIF's (graphic interfaces for elementary anima-tion)—as well as interactive games and access to whole graphic novels. The smoldering figures in graphic poses are no longer recognizable as crude satires of known cartoon characters, but recapitulate poses and activities found in *photo*graphic and video pornography. As the web surfer clicks along, retrospective (Cicourel 1973; Mehan and Wood 1975) contexts for making sense out of these figures are missing. The conflation of cartoons and explicit erotic sex is initially less coherent than the raunchy teasing of vulgar satire. It embodies many of the same common sense assumptions of photo and video porn pages, but removes illusions of human participants in a sexual encounter.

This leaves a peculiar problem in the sociology of meaning. How did these drawings that have been appropriated out of artistic contexts become rooted as products in the Internet pornography industry? At a microcosmic level, how can cartoon images align with the intensely erotic feelings and masturbatory urges usually associated with other, less virtual pornographic images? Answering these questions begins with understanding how Internet pornography outlets help con-sumers make pornographic sense out of cartoon drawings.

### Indexicality: Making Manga and Anime Pornographic

Sociologists agree that people actively define their situations. Indexicality is a concept that guides investigations into these sense-making activities. Although a complex and nuanced concept in sociology, there is much agreement that indexi-cality refers to the practices that build contexts for establishing the meaning of things (see Leiter 1980; Katovich and Wieting 2000) and that people, rather than texts or artifacts, are the agents of meaning. Garfinkel (1967) argues that estab-lishing meaning is an endless process of tying language acts to contexts, and that contexts themselves are understood in terms of other, encompassing contexts of their own. Anime's immersion in the context of Internet pornography has washed away Japanese cultural footings for understanding. The cultural referents important to understanding anime's chronicle as a medium for popular art are no longer instrumental. Left instead are manifestly prurient references produced by rational marketers who have read their markets and know what objects are likely to sell. Textual and audio-visual cues corral the possible meanings of anime as inherently sexual. Some texts are simple and straightforward: "Uncensored Anime Sex!" or "Sex Galleries!" but presume a contextual familiarity with basic terminology as in "Free thumbnailed hentai and ecchi XXX...Dojin gallery with Streetfighter, Ranma, Evangelion, Sailor Moon..."[1] Other references move genres wholly into the pornographic venue as when pornographic comics are referred to as "manga" regardless of their origin, and regardless of the fact that manga is the Japanese word for comics in general. Likewise, sex is indicated as the encompassing textual referent by the commonly understood but undefined gradations of softcore and hardcore categories applied now to hentai. Finally, hentai web pages will sometimes refer explicitly to consummate masturbation as the purpose of the site visit. "This site is hot! Get out your Kleenex!" "Jack off to this free hardcore hentai anime better than most sex..." "Prefect[2] [sic] masturbation pics..."

The arts of manga and anime have been rendered pornographic through the abbreviation or elimination of cultural and other contextual supports. Like most pornography, hentai expresses sex without the usual linkages between emotions and productive unions (see Tittle and Paternoster 2000) and it has been stripped of culturally meaningful settings that accompany manga stories. Without explanation or situational development, manga and anime girls are posed in unmistakably pornographic activities that show enormous breasts and butts to advantage. School uniforms, torn or in disarray sometimes figure prominently. Coupled with the sartorial demonstrations of innocence are faces that signify youth, helplessness, and inexperience. This Madonna-prostitute complex is amplified by the absence of any hair under the arms or around genitalia.[3] The production of prurient visual indices for manga and anime extends to a variety of subgenres as well. For example, "altered pictures," or figures from other planets, dimensions, or planes of existence have the requisite phalluses, breasts, and orifices that signal sex, and are made more intriguing by their otherwise extra-human forms.

Having cemented the sexual context for manga and hentai, more elements can be meaningfully elaborated for appeal to other preferences in the market. Much of hentai is violent, dominant, and oriented to bondage and rape. Tentacle hentai is the clearest example of this. With the text surrounded by eight color drawings of girls being restrained and raped by tentacles, a typical site declares:

> We are glad to see you and want to represents [sic] hundreds of HQ evil tentacles pictures and movies for your pleasure. Blood, Sperm, Broken Pussies Pain, Nightmare, Tentacle Monsters fucking Innocent teen girls with their many dicks!

Of course, much of the indexical work is already accomplished when consumers arrive at pornography sites prepared to view pornography (see Fisher 2001). But hentai marketers leap over any remaining obstacles by referencing both real worlds and other virtual worlds as inferior to manga and anime. Some claims are diffident. "My friends thought I was crazy to get hot over a comic. But you have to see her!" Others call cartoonish properties to the foreground as the best features of the meaningful experience. "It's way better than real!" crows Ben's Hentai Page. "It's better than photos!" says another. "Better than anything!" Sinful Toons speaks more explicitly to the possibilities represented by the virtual qualities of hentai:

TOON SLUTS CAN SPREAD, OPEN, AND GRIND THEIR WAY INTO POSITIONS THAT NO REAL GIRL CAN. EXPLORE THE LIMITLESS WORLD OF FUCKING AT ITS VERY RAUNCHIEST! YOU'LL ALSO GET TONS OF BONUS EXTRAS . . .

L'il Miss Hentai argues:

HENTAI GIRLS CAN DO ANYTHING! REAL GIRLS COULDN'T BEGIN TO TAKE WHAT THESE GIRLS DO! 6 FOOT TENTACLES, 24 INCH COCKS, DEMONS AND ALIENS . . .

As evocative, titillating and exciting as these advertisements try to be, artistic possibilities of the virtual world are driven most by the rational, pedestrian engines of commercial necessity. So, the standard male fantasies of photo and video porn sites are first recapitulated with a hentai imprimatur. Office girl, school girl, or girl-in-shower are all likely, as is oral sex administered by a hentai girl on giant demon penis. Or the fairy girl, equipped with stubby horns, pointed ears, wings, and serpentine tail along with outlandish breasts, is made trite and standard as fairy-with-insatiable-appetite-for-hard-sex. But the claims on these pages are not only that hentai drawings are adequate for masturbatory fantasy, but that they are better than the less virtual records of photos and videos. Hentai is a commercially viable masturbation aid because it is *more virtual*, expressive of possibilities, and ultimately *more ambiguous* than photos and videos.

In her study of the relatively hot (McLuhan 1964) medium[4] of phone sex, Flowers (1998) argues that the successful interaction with phone sex customers involves constructing a context in which the customer feels desirable. The best fantasies, then, are not about the erotic qualities of the phone sex worker as such, but fuel desire by imaginary responses to the masculinity and appeal of the customer (see also Bordo 1993; Barcan 2002). Similarly, Waskul (Waskul, Douglass, and Edgley, 2000) studying the super hot medium of chat room sex, begins his discussion by noting that the eroticism of physical contact is replaced by detailed, intimate descriptions, and that the appeal emerges from contradictions of sexual form. In the relatively cool media of Internet images, producing fantasy events that can signify the desirability of a viewer is problematic. Photographers can certainly stage competent models in come-hither poses and expressions, videographers can add audio and motion contexts, but a cartoonist can effectively signify many more messages than a model can capture in poses. The bold, gestural lines that indicate the ripe sexuality of perfect breasts and butts, also signify in the simple lines of manga faces that the sexual object is helpless with desire, enthralled by lust, stricken with fear, or swallowed in grief and pleasure. Thus the simplicity of drawings and the elegant possibilities of virtual representations can be meaningfully presented as "better" than real. In the perfect, spectacular depictions of pure sexual availability, and in the signifying potential of crudely drawn faces, hentai has distinguishable, indexical advantages lacking in other virtual sex experiences. While a lower level of involvement is provoked by the cold medium of the Internet proscenium than by chat room or phone encounters that require interaction, more senses are engaged in filling in the gaps left by videos, still pictures, and especially hentai and manga sex drawings.

Paradoxically, the authority of hentai is in this simplicity. Japanese animation often shows limited production values. Even the best films rely on the frozen tableau or still, expressionless figures who move nothing but their mouths when they speak. When the simple drawings are combined with jerky animation the first impressions of hentai anime seem more likely to inspire laughter than arousal. But because the artist communicates simple messages in a cold medium, obstacles to fantasy are reduced. Animation may be limited to a few simple and repetitive motions, for example, but the line drawings of large, erect nipples, tumescent penises, and mouths stretched into large O's effectively mark sexual meanings.

Drawings also eliminate the implied challenges of photos and videos as records of real people and real movement. The conventional absence of pubic hair on manga figures, for example, makes genitalia accessible to the gaze, and also implies virginal excitement that the shaved and photographed model cannot. Drawings can always present flesh to advantage as well. So the seemingly complex and peculiar tentacle hentai makes sense as an erotic convention in part for the simple technical possibilities it represents. Tentacles can be placed to remain out of the viewer's line of sight (see Hwang [1999] for a lively discussion of this; see also Clements [1998b]).

In longer anime productions storylines are simple, and tend to parallel the straightforward paths to sex found in conventional pornographic video. The imponderables of mutual attraction are set aside. In *Love Hina* boy wants girl, girl is irritated at first, but suddenly is amenable to sex. Girl wants girl in *Vampire Princess*, but girl resists because she is not a lesbian. Suddenly, she is overcome with desire. A maid is sent to the room by her master to provide sex for a guest. A nurse can't resist a patient. Of course in the bondage and rape fantasies that are shot through hentai even simple wooing is unnecessary. The challenges of feeling desirable are obliterated by simple domination scenarios that do not provide the thinnest excuses for why characters are having sex in the first place. The appeal of rape and domination fantasies is in this barbaric simplicity. Perhaps this is why so much of hentai is indexed as "hard core" and is likely to signify some combination of domination, bondage, and rape.

### Distance: Phenomenal Contradictions of Hentai Experience

In his discussions of multiple, subjective realities, Schutz (1967) spoke to the mundane, the sublime, and the fantastic. Daily life, work, science, dreams, and fantasies all share the status of real because they have subjective meanings, and exist "in a certain relationship to ourselves" (1967:207). Schutz's multiple realities explain how hentai pornography can simultaneously function as an object of aesthetic and pornographic consumption: art for commercial sake *and* pornography for masturbatory urges. In essence, the world of cybernetic hentai, although purporting no reference to the "real" world of pornographic actors in simulated sex acts, still manages to align itself with intensely erotic feelings for the adult patrons of the thousands of Internet sites catering to this sexual genre. Hentai appeals both to the aesthetic world of everyday artistic creations, and the world of erotic phantasms. But how is it possible for a cartoon image, with all of its incompatibilities to the *real* world of simulated sex acts by *real* sex workers, to arouse adult consumers in their worlds of erotic phantasms?

Phenomenally, the pornographic experience of cybernetic hentai for masturbatory or erotic consumption is largely an experience in the world of phantasms, but one with some serious projection problems to overcome. For one, the masturbatory experience with ordinary erotica does not enjoin a radical *suspension of disbelief* as does the experience of cybernetic hentai. Ostensibly, the consumer of simulated pornography involving "real" actors need only, for masturbatory aims, project upon him/herself the fantasy of the "live sex act." He/she might fancy him/herself in a "live sex act" with a very "real" pornographic actor on screen. However, cybernetic hentai does not afford the same opportunity. It rather poses a quandary. It requires more than mere fantasy to accomplish masturbatory aims; it requires a radical suspension of doubt and bodily projection into manga for successful interplay. Ultimately, there are two choices: the reification of the manga to stand in place for, or completely substitute, human form; or, the reification of one's own corporeality into manga in order to masturbate over hentai. It is necessary to suspend doubt in the *obvious* logical incompatibilities between the *real* body, existing in the world of daily life, and the erotic, yet fully cybernetic Hentai image, existing in the world of phantasm.

Schutz recognized the limits of the world of phantasm when he suggested, "within the realm of imaginary merely factual, *but not* logical incompatibilities can be overcome" (1967:238, emphasis added). Yet the "logical incompatibility" between the corporeal and the erotic-cybernetic does not pose a problem, at least for masturbatory or erotic stimulation, for multitudes of hentai consumers the world over. Why not? In the fantasy world of postcorporeal, indexical, cybernetic sex, there is no resistance to overcome. Fantasies free the subject from "objective" spaces and standard temporal frames (as does sex in general—see Davis 1983). "No longer are we confined within the limits of our actual, restorable, or attainable reach. What occurs in the outer world no longer imposes upon us issues between which we have to choose nor does it put a limit on our possible accomplishments" (Schutz 1967:234). Or, in a modern, cybernetic echo of Schutz, Waskul (2002:206) contends "…the dislocated and disembodied nature of computer-mediated communications makes cybersex an experience that potentially expresses a sexuality separate from and transgressive of the person, the body, and everyday life." In the lonely confines of fantasy, between corporeal individuals and cybernetic-hentai bodies, lies freedom to assume any role, or "even vary my bodily appearance," or play with possibilities unfathomable in the *real* worlds of daily life and work (1967:239). This is the appeal of cybernetic and telegenetic escapism, an appeal that promises an experience way better than real.

Hentai is pure simulacrum. It does not claim to be a simulation of a "simulation of the real" things of human pornographic sex acts. It does not copy or affirm the "real" video and photographic simulations of "real" bodies acting out "real sex" acts. Instead, hentai is presented as a better unreal experience than the other unreal experiences. Hentai, especially in tentacle sex, its most extreme and uncommon version, has "no relation to any reality whatsoever; it is its own simulacrum" (Baudrillard 1994:6). Tentacle sex/rape of nubile girl-women isn't doubling back on any reference in the real world. There is no real thing to simulate. It exists for its own purpose as an erotic phantasm of the strange and teratological.

The experience of hentai is morally distancing. Tentacle hentai offers the telegenetic signs of the most perverse and debased sexualities. It opens for fantastic examination a sexuality that transgresses all "simulated" moralities of the "real" world, where tentacle sex between nubile girl-women and cloned boy-men monsters are the order of the day—a monstrous sex-feast of the most abnormal acts: pedophilic bestiality, sex with machines, sex with cyborgs, sex with dangerous protruding tentacles, and, of course, an endless stream of the most debasing, brutal, and humiliating rape images. How is this possible as a pornographic artifact? It is made so by a phenomenological distancing from other "real" photographic images. *A "real" porn actress would never survive a beating like that. A "real" porn actress would never survive teratological tentacle sex—in all orifices.* Even violent pornography that purports to be more real than "snuff films" (such as those produced by Extreme Associates) has natural limits. While deploying actors "just" acting, this violent video and photographic porn at least simulates "real" scenes of "real" victims. Hentai makes no such claims. This level of simulacrum references nothing "real," yet it is profoundly real *per se* as sounds, texts, and pictures in consumer markets around the world.

Ultimately, manga sex and tentacle hentai, with their omnipresent nubile girl-women, in barely postpubescent bodies, more than obliquely reference child molestation, domination and bondage fantasies, and sadomasochistic rape without shame or reproach. After all, manga sex and tentacle hentai are just cartoon fantasies where demons and aliens with tentacles are dominating—in the most vicious ways—other *cartoons*. They are not *real*.

Thus, the distance of manga sex and tentacle hentai from the "real" mitigate the most shameful responses—encouraging both rapt engrossment in the fantasy and cold distance from acts of violence, domination, molestation, rape, bondage, and torture. The cybernetic experience of watching a virtual rape of a girl-woman by a tentacle monster enhances a forbidden sexual fantasy while assuaging the shame of masturbating over grossly violent cartoon signs. The moral distance afforded by tentacle hentai and manga also fosters an emotional distancing. Because this genre is cartoon, it prevents reflexive empathy with, or sympathy for, the horrific violation of girl-women or boy-men. There is never a thought that this "porn star" is someone's daughter or son, sister or brother. This is pure seduction in the animated images of high school lovers, but absolute domination in images of uninhibited violence and ultimate transgression. Hentai and manga sex lack the accompaniments of moral and emotional strains (See also Evans-DeCicco and Cowan [2001] for a comparison to attitudes on real porn actors).

### Conclusion: Hentai as a Postmodern Pornography

A rational quality of markets is that they diversify in order to grow and perpetuate themselves. Internet pornography markets have diversified and grown in staggering proportion. The consumption of virtual men and women is now accomplished in hundreds of thousands of pornography sites that seem to exhaust sexual possibilities. The cynical and calculated appropriation of Japanese anime into this industry illustrates a crisis marked by what Baudrillard (1993) refers to as "after the orgy" of modernity's liberation of all aspects of life. *"After the orgy, then, a masked ball. After the demise of desire, a pell-mell diffusion of erotic simulacra in every guise, of transsexual kitsch in all its glory. A postmodern pornography, if you will, where sexuality is lost in the theatrical excess of its ambiguity."* (1993:22, italics added). Hentai works by promising its audience a break from merely modern pornography and its mundane drudgery and boredom of a "real," precybernetic, sexuality (see also Nagel [2002] on the routine nature of pornography consumption).

Cyber-porn, in hentai form, is a postmodern sexuality that stresses ambiguity: "Is she a girl or a woman?" "Is he a boy or a man?" "Is it a man, or a machine, or a cyborg?" This is an ambiguity that invites the indexing of perfect fantasies. It is, as Baudrillard might suggest, a "liberated sexuality" because there are no boundaries fencing the deviant and impossible, or the normative and possible. Hentai thrives on ambiguity, difference, and nomadic identities. But hentai is a postmodern pornography for another reason. Once "real" sexuality is liberated, the liberation process itself, embodied in experimentations and transsexualities (both cybernetic and corporeal), imposes limits on the omnipresent quest for a sex that is *new, bold,* and *"cutting edge."* Everything *"real"* and possible has been tried in corporeal form (1993). What's next is inevitable: a sexuality, or cybernetic simulacrum, that simulates the limitless boundaries of nothing. There are no limits to the possibilities, and this is why hentai sex, in its crude, empty scribbling, is more real—and better than real.

## Acknowledgments

Thanks to the staff at Paradox Comics and Cards in Fargo, North Dakota, for their help in understanding Manga, Anime, and Hentai. Thanks to Mark Hansel and Deborah White for their comments on this essay.

## Notes

1.  Thumbnail galleries are sets of pictures that can be enlarged individually with a left click of the mouse. Ecchi is a term not commonly used in Internet pornography sites to refer to softcore Japanese animated erotica. Dojin is the appropriation of known cartoon characters for animated and still sexual art. So the Ranma, Evangelion, and Sailor Moon here will be pictured in a variety of sexual contexts and activities.

2. Misspellings are common. See web pages most consulted by the authors: Adult Hentai Reactor, Anime Girls, Avsluts, Banzai Hentai, Beautiful Japanese Hentai, Ben's Hentai, Bohemian Hentai, Fucking Toons, Hardcore Toons, Hentai Kitty, Hentai Playground, Hentaiseeker, Hentai Station, Hentai Studio, Hentai Toonami, Hentopia, Just Toons, L'il Miss Hentai, Puki Anime Porn, Sinful Toons, Tentacle-Hentai, Violent-Comix.

3. Cultural critics insist that leaving manga and hentai figures hairless is in response to Japanese censorship regulations. However, these conventions persist after Japanese laws have been relaxed and persist in Internet venues where the laws are inapplicable or unenforceable.

4. Sociologists appreciate McLuhan's metaphor of hot and cold media because it unites the interpretive actions and experiences of people with the limitations of media objects. Thus, for example, information flow is restricted to words and verbal cues on the telephone (a hot medium) requiring that speakers and listeners concentrate on messages and take in sparsely contextualized information, while users of television (in contrast a cold medium) fill in the many informational and contextual gaps themselves. Compare this with Mehan's views that all mediated language acts are indexical in that fringes of context are constantly being filled by actors making sense out of messages.

## References

Adams, K. A., and L. Hill, Jr. 1997. The phallic female in Japanese group-fantasy. *The Journal of Psychohistory* 25:33–66.

Allison, A. 2000. *Permitted and prohibited desires: Mothers, comics, and censorship in Japan.* Berkeley, CA: University of California Press.

Barcan, R. 2002. In the raw: 'Homemade' porn and reality genres. *Journal of Mundane Behavior* 3. Retrieved from www.mundanebehavior.or/issues/v3n1/barcan.htm

Barron, M. 2000. Sexual violence in three pornographic media: Toward a sociological explanation. *Journal of Sex Research* 37:161–68.

Baudrillard, J. 1994. *Simulacra and simulation.* Ann Arbor, MI: University of Michigan Press.

———. 1993. *The transparency of evil: Essays on extreme phenomena.* New York, NY: Verso.

Bordo, S. 1993. Reading the male body. *Michigan Quarterly Review* 32:696–735

Cicourel, A. V. 1973. *Cognitive sociology.* London: Macmillan and Co.

Clements, J. 1998a. View from the inside: The mechanics of anime pornography. In *The erotic anime movie guide,* ed. H. McCarthy and J. Clements. pp. 16–21. New York, NY: Overview Press.

———. 1998b. Tits and tentacles: Sex, horror, and the overfiend. In *The erotic anime movie guide,* ed. H. McCarthy and J. Clements. pp. 58–81. New York, NY: Overview Press.

Davis, M. 1983. *Smut: Erotic reality/obscene ideology.* Chicago, IL: University of Chicago Press.

Evans-DeCicco, J. A., and G. Cowan. 2001. Attitudes toward pornography and the characteristics attributed to pornography actors. *Sex Roles: A Journal of Research* 44:351–61.

Fisher, W. A. 2001. Internet pornography: A social psychological perspective on internet sexuality. *Journal of Sex Research* 38:312–23.

Flowers, A. 1998. *The fantasy factory: An insider's view of the phone sex industry.* Philadelphia, PA: University of Pennsylvania Press.

Garfinkel, H. 1967. *Studies in ethnomethodology.* Englewood Cliffs, NJ: Prentice Hall.

Hulse, E. 2001. Anime Extreme. *Video Business* 35:35–38.

Hwang, R. W. 1999. Hentai anime: What's up with the tentacles? *Hardboiled* April:2, 4.

Jones, S. 2003. Oriental Lolitas. *New Statesman.* February 3:38–40.

Katovich M. A., and S. G. Wieting. 2000. Evil as indexical: The implicit objective status of guns and illegal drugs. *Symbolic Interaction* 23:161–82.

Kinsella, S. 2000. *Adult manga: Culture and power in contemporary Japan.* Honolulu, HI: University of Hawaii Press.

Leiter, K. 1980. *A primer on ethnomethodology.* New York, NY. Oxford University Press.

Logan, M. 2001. Hentai 101—A primer on Japan's amazing cartoon porn. AVN Online. Retrieved from www.avonline.com/issues/200109/

McCarthy, H., and J. Clements. 2001. *The anime encyclopedia: A guide to Japanese animation since 1917.* Berkeley, CA: Stone Bridge Press.

McLuhan, M. 1964. *Understanding media: The extensions of man.* Cambridge, MA: MIT Press.

Mehan, H., and H. Wood. 1975. *The reality of ethnomethodology.* New York, NY: John Wiley and Sons.

Nagel, C. 2002. Pornographic experience. *Journal of Mundane Behavior* 3. Retrieved from www.mundanebehavior.org/issues/v3n1/nagel3-1.htm

Ogi, F. 2003. Female subjectivity and shoujou (girls) manga (Japanese comics): Shoujou in ladies' comics and young ladies' comics. *Journal of Popular Culture* 36:280–304.

Payne, P. 2003. Hentai anime serves up some dark fantasy, tentacles, violation. *Oregon Daily Emerald Online Edition.* February 27. Retrieved from www.dailyemerald.com

Poitras, G. 2001. *Anime essentials.* Berkeley, CA: Stone Bridge Press.

Schutz, A. 1967. *Collected papers I: The problem of social reality.* The Hague, Netherlands: Martinus Nijhoff.

Tittle, C. R., and R. Paternoster. 2000. *Social deviance and crime.* Los Angeles, CA: Roxbury.

Vigilant, L. G. and J. B.Williamson. 2003. Symbolic immortality and social theory: The relevance of an underutilized concept. In *Handbook of death and dying*, ed. C. D. Bryant. pp. 173–82. Thousand Oaks, CA: Sage.

Waskul, D. 2002. The naked self: Being a body in televideo cybersex. *Symbolic Interaction* 25(2):199–227.

Waskul, D., M. Douglass, and C. Edgley. 2000. Cybersex: Outercourse and the enselfment of the body. *Symbolic Interaction* 23(4):375–97.

## ❖ Part Three
# Problems, Deviance, and Ethics

In academic literatures and popular culture, understandings of Internet sex have largely ensued from the presumption of problems and deviance. These are among the most common stories of Internet sex; stories that concern Internet addiction (Young 1998; 2001), cybersex compulsivity (Cooper 2000; 2002), virtual infidelity (Schneider and Weiss 2001), and various other forms of misuse, victimization, and abuse. The sheer volume of these troublesome tales and the ease with which they circulate in popular culture clearly illustrate a moral bias that continues to color understandings of the intersection of sex and technology.

The therapeutically oriented and psychiatric minded have been quick to pronounce epidemic tales about "something sinister going on in cyberspace" (Young 1998: 3)—particularly with regard to sex and pornography. Described with such ominous words as the "Dark Side" (Cooper 2000; Young 1998:12), a "Drug of Choice" (Delmonico, Griffin, and Moriarty 2001:147), and "A Millennial Addiction" (Young 1998:28), these kinds of frightening words have received ample press. Clearly, the tendency to contextualize Internet sex within clinical and therapeutic frameworks may be more or less valid. However, this book seeks to provide an alternative: in *addition* to clinical frameworks, Internet sex can be contextualized within society, culture, and history.

More than just another contemporary psychosocial disorder, Internet sex is a social, cultural, and historical phenomenon. Yet, this is not to dismiss the presence of real problems. Sex and pornography on the Internet have posed challenges for law enforcement, expanded the potential for sexual victimization, created communicative environments for legitimizing deviant sexual identities, and brought about numerous potential difficulties for various social institutions. The readings in Part Three address many of these problems of deviance and ethics.

Undoubtedly, the Internet has expanded access to sex and pornography. As Donna Hughes describes, the Internet has also expanded the potential for sexual exploitation of women and children. Sexual predators are more able to harm or exploit women and children with efficiency and anonymity. Pimps and child pornographers are better able to traffic the images and bodies of women and children. The global nature of the Internet has created new problems for law enforcement that often require a sorely lacking structure of international cooperation. Hughes's words are a sobering reminder of how new communication technologies may be appropriated for exploitation and victimization just as easily as they may be appropriated for legitimate exploration and empowerment.

Keith Durkin's extensive research on Internet pedophiles is highly regarded and widely cited. Here Durkin expands his investigations to include not only pedophiles but also zoophiles, with a special focus on how the Internet is used to validate these deviant sexual identities and manipulate the stigma of deviance. Unfairly stigmatized people such as gays, lesbians, bisexuals, and transsexuals have found the Internet an important resource for information, networking, support, and the management of stigma. As Durkin details, sexual deviants may exploit the same resources to the same ends.

Apprehension about the effects of Internet sex on marriage and committed relationships have been widely expressed in popular and academic circles. Some authors have suggested alarming concerns about "virtual infidelity" and its capacity to undermine committed relationships (see Schneider and Weiss 1999). As Jim Thomas suggests, these concerns are nothing new. Indeed, in the process of unpacking the ethics of Internet sex, Thomas reminds us that expressed views "are as much about discourse as about intercourse." Indeed, as Thomas clearly illustrates, "So much of sex-talk isn't about sex, and sorting through all the nuance agendas gets a bit confusing." Consequently, it is exceedingly difficult to pronounce absolute and universal ethical principles of Internet sex—even when narrowly examined in the context of committed relationships.

Internet sex is often an experience of transgression. Thus, it should be no surprise that the experience is seasoned with deviance and potential for deviant activity. For the very same reason, it is also no surprise that Internet sex is an explosive terrain for various issues of morality and ethics. Since we are essentially talking about sex and pornography, these issues ought to be anticipated, if not downright predictable: regardless of its context or means of expression, sex and pornography has always been a steamy caldron of deviance, morality, and ethics. While Internet sex has clearly introduced new dynamics, the Internet did not create the sexual deviant, the unfaithful lover, the abuser, or the victimizer. Indeed, as the readings in Part Three illustrate perhaps most clearly of all, the Internet presents a new context for addressing old problems that are often troubling, frequently contentious, and sometimes quite ambiguous.

## References

Cooper, A. 2002. *Sex and the Internet: A guidebook for clinicians.* New York, NY: Brunner-Routledge.

————. 2000. Cybersex and sexual compulsivity: The dark side of the force. *Sexual Addiction and Compulsivity* 7:1–3.

Delmonico, D., E. Griffin, and J. Moriarty. 2001. *Cybersex unhooked. A workbook for breaking free of compulsive online sexual behavior.* Arizona: Gentle Path Press.

Schneider, J., and R. Weiss. 2001. *Cybersex exposed: Simple fantasy or obsession?* Center City, MN: Hazelden.

Young, K. 2001. *Cybersex: The secret world of Internet sex.* London: Carlton.

————. 1998. *Caught in the net: How to recognize the signs of Internet addiction and a winning strategy for recovery.* New York, NY: John Wiley & Sons.

## ❖ Chapter Six

# The Use of New Communications and Information Technologies for Sexual Exploitation of Women and Children

## Donna M. Hughes[*]

*The Internet has created new opportunities for sex and sexual expression. However, not all of these new "opportunities" are within the confines of the law. Donna Hughes points out various ways new communications technologies have expanded the potential for sexual exploitation of women and children. New technologies have increased both the volume and accessibility of sex—in legal and illicit forms—while also creating conditions that are difficult to police.*

### Introduction

New communications and information technologies have created a global revolution in communications, access to information, and media delivery. These new communications and information technologies are facilitating the sexual exploitation of women and girls locally, nationally, and transnationally. The sexual exploitation of women and children is a global human rights crisis that is being escalated by the use of new technologies.[1] Using new technologies, sexual predators and pimps stalk women and children. New technical innovations facilitate the sexual exploitation of women and children because they enable people to easily buy, sell, and exchange millions of images and videos of sexual exploitation of women and children.

These technologies enable sexual predators to harm or exploit women and children efficiently and anonymously. The affordability and access to global

[*] Hughes, Donna M. 2002. "The Use of New Communications and Information Technologies for Sexual Exploitation of Women and Children. *Hastings Women's Law Journal* 13 (Winter): 129–148.

communications technologies allow users to carry out these activities in the privacy of their home.

The increase of types of media, media formats, and applications diversifies the means by which sexual predators can reach their victims. This paper will not attempt to categorize all the types and uses of this new technology. However, this paper will describe the most common and newest of these technologies and how they are used for the sexual exploitation of women and children.[2]

### New and Old Technologies Combined

Older technologies like television and cable are now combined with modern technologies to create new ways of delivering information, news, and entertainment.[3] Web TV combines the television with the Internet.[4] New cable networks use satellite transmission to deliver hundreds of channels, and pay-per-view delivers content on demand.[5]

Presently, there is a high demand for pornographic videos through mainstream communication networks such as cable TV.[6] Only one of eight major cable companies in the United States does not offer pornographic movies.[7] Satellite and cable companies say that the more sexually explicit the content the greater the demand.[8] *Adult Video News* reports that pornography offerings on TV by satellite or cable are increasing video store sales and rentals, not decreasing them, as might be expected.[9] The explanation is that pornography on TV is advertising pornography and finding new buyers.[10] The mainstreaming of pornography is increasing the exploitation or abuse of women and children used in making pornography.[11] According to Paul Fishbein, owner of *Adult Video News,* anything sells:

> There are so many outlets [for the videos] that even if you spend just $15,000 and two days—and put in some plot and good-looking people and decent sex—you can get satellite and cable sales. There are so many companies, and they rarely go out of business. You have to be really stupid or greedy to fail.[12]

Another producer said:

> [A]nyone with a video camera can be a director—there are countless bottom feeders selling nasty loops on used tape. Whatever the quality or origin of a product, it can at the very least be exhibited on one of the 70,000 adult pay Web sites, about a quarter of which are owned by a few privately held companies that slice and dice the same content under different brands.[13]

As a result of the huge market on the Web for pornography and the competition among sites, the pornographic images have become rougher, more violent, and degrading.[14] One producer claimed that there were "no coerced" performances in pornography videos, although she immediately acknowledged that "there are little pipsqueaks who get their disgusting little (misogynistic) videos out there."[15] The "misogynistic porn" this producer refers to involves degrading images, such as ejaculation on the woman's face, real pain, and violence against women that results in physical and emotional injuries.[16]

In the last ten years, some American and European pornography producers have moved to places such as Budapest, Hungary, because of the availability of cheap actors from Eastern and Central Europe.[17] Budapest is a destination and transit city for women trafficked from Ukraine, Moldova, Russia, Romania, and Yugoslavia.[18] There are hundreds of pornographic films and videos produced each year in Budapest.[19] Budapest is now the biggest center for pornography production in Europe, eclipsing rivals such as Amsterdam and Copenhagen.[20] Most Western European producers of sex videos use Eastern European actors whenever possible.[21] An executive at Germany's Silwa production company explained: "They cost less and do more. Even excruciating or humiliating acts usually cost only two or three hundred dollars."[22]

The postal service, traditionally the most anonymous and popular way to transmit pornography, is still used by collectors and producers of child pornography to distribute the pornography.[23] Now, sending materials through the mail is combined with Internet technology.[24] Raymond Smith, U.S. Postal Inspection Service, who handles hundreds of cases of child pornography, has found that the rise in Internet use by sexual predators has also increased their use of the U.S. mail.[25] He said that from the time they first started investigating child pornography in the early 1980s until five years ago, they had almost eliminated the distribution of child pornography.[26] But since the Internet became publicly available, the number of cases connected to the Internet has steadily increased.[27] In 1998, 32 percent of cases were related to Internet.[28] In 1999, 47 percent were Internet related, and in 2000, 77 percent of the child pornography cases were Internet related.[29]

Producers of child pornography advertise their videos on the Internet and distribute them through the mail.[30] Men in chat rooms trade small files, still images and short movie clips on the Internet, but longer movies are sent by mail.[31] Stalkers talk to children in chat rooms, ask them to take pictures of themselves, and send them through the mail.[32] When stalkers convince children to travel to meet them, they send them bus and plane tickets through the mail.[33]

Scanners and video digitizers are used to turn old pornographic images, films, and videos into electronic formats that can be uploaded to the Internet.[34] About half of the child pornography online is old images from films and magazines produced in the 1960s and the 70s.[35] Digital cameras and recorders enable the creation of images that do not need professional processing, thereby eliminating the risk of detection.[36] These new types of equipment also make it technically easier for people to become producers of pornography.[37] Digital media formats are not static or independent.[38] One format can be quickly converted into another.[39] Videos are still the primary production medium for child pornography, and the still images for the Internet are produced from video captured images.[40] From one video, 200–300 still images can be captured, and then uploaded to a newsgroup or to a web site.[41] According to the COPINE (Combating Paedophile Information Networks in Europe) Project, production of child pornography still combines older methods of production, while using new Internet technologies for distribution.[42]

> It is safe to say that the number of manufactures [producers of child pornography] has increased over the years with the availability of new medium. Home development of black and white 35MM film, self-developing Polaroid film, video cameras, camcorders, computer scanners, CUseeme technology [live video and audio transmission] and now computer cameras (including video) have made child pornography easier and easier to produce and reproduce.[43]

One police analyst noted that prior to the Internet the majority of collectors of child pornography were not distributors because duplication technology was not readily available.[44] Now, making copies of image files "involves a few clicks of any computer mouse allowing for effortless distribution."[45] Therefore, collectors of child pornography have quickly and easily become distributors.

### New Technologies for Sexual Exploitation

**Digital Video Disk**

One new technology is Digital Video Disk (DVD), which provides high-quality videos and interactive capabilities for the viewer.[46] While making the videos, scenes can be shot from multiple angles, and all points of view can be added to a CD ROM.[47] The viewer can then choose the version, point of view, or camera angle he/she prefers.[48] Viewers can watch the movie in chronological order, moving from one character to the next, or watch the movie from one character's point of view.[49] Viewers can interact with DVD movies in much the same way they do with video games, giving them a more active role.[50] According to one producer:

> If a viewer wants something different, we give it to him. The viewer can go inside the head of the person having sex with [name deleted], male or female. He can choose which character to follow. He can re-edit the movie. It's a great technology.[51]

The following is a description of a recent pornographic movie recorded on DVD:

> Chasing Stacy from VCA Labs, is a choose-your-own-adventure flick that follows Stacy the porn star as she signs autographs, drinks coffee, works out at the gym and takes a shower. At various points, a small green icon appears in the corner of the screen and Stacy looks straight at the camera. That's when viewers get the chance to ask Stacy out on a virtual date by pressing the Enter button on the DVD remote control. The date scenes are filmed so that the viewer feels like he's sitting directly across a glass table from Stacy, who provides insights into her personal life. Later, the viewer can select whether to take Stacy back to her house, to her office, or to another locale for a tryst. With the remote control, the details can be chosen as the action unfolds.[52]

The pornography producer, VCA, released this DVD in July 2000 and sold more than 12,000 copies by January 2001, making it the fastest selling title they have.[53]

Although technologies like this have many applications and enable creativity and interactivity, when used in pornographic films, these raise the question of the impact on people, their relationships, and expectations about relationships. A portion of men who use pornography and seek out women in prostitution do so because either their lack of social skills or their misogynistic attitudes prevent them from establishing relationships with their peers.[54] Technology such as this may further distance and alienate some men from meaningful and realistic relationships.[55]

There are a number of venues and media formats with different technologies for the transfer of files and communications, including Usenet newsgroups, World Wide Web, e-mail, live synchronous communication (text and voice chat), bulletin or message boards, Web cams for live transmission of images or videos, live video conferencing (live video chat), streaming video, peer to peer servers, and file sharing programs.[56] All forums and applications offer ways to engage in the sexual exploitation of women and children.[57]

How each is used for sexual exploitation depends on the legality of the activity, which varies from country to country; the techniques adopted by the sex industry or individual users; and the level of privacy or secrecy attempted by the users.[58] Perpetrators have taken advantage of new technologies and applications to stalk victims, transmit illegal materials, and avoid detection by law enforcement.[59] According to one official: "If it can be done, they're doing it."[60]

## News Groups

Usenet newsgroups are still popular sites for the exchange of information on how to find women and children for sexual exploitation.[61] Although much media attention is given to child pornography rings and cases that use sophisticated technologies to keep their activities secret, such as the Wonderland Club that used a Soviet KGB code to encrypt all its communications, the older public newsgroups are still commonly used to upload and download child pornography.[62] The COPINE Project reports that over 1000 child pornographic images are posted on newsgroups each week.[63]

## Web Sites

Web sites are used in various ways to assist in the sexual exploitation of women and children. Web sites are the most popular venue for the distribution of pornography online. Large legal sex industry businesses have sophisticated Web sites with subscription fees that bring in millions of dollars per year.[64] There are also tens of thousands of free pornography sites that are maintained by amateurs or someone making a relatively small amount of money from advertising banners for larger sites and businesses.[65] Web sites offer streaming videos that can be viewed with web browser plug-ins.[66] The most recent versions of Web browsers (e.g. Internet Explorer, Netscape) come packaged with these plug-ins.[67]

Pimps and traffickers use the Web to advertise the availability of women and children for use in making pornography.[68] One example includes prostitution tourists and Western producers of pornography who have been traveling to Latvia since the early 1990s to find vulnerable children and young adults to sexually exploit in their videos.[69] In August 1999, the Vice Police in Latvia initiated criminal proceedings against the owners of Logo Center, a "modeling agency," for production of pornography and the use of minors in the production of pornography.[70] The two managers of the Logo Center provided women and children to foreign prostitution tourists and foreign pornography producers.[71] They had several Web sites[72] with pornography, information about minors, and photographs of their "models" in different sex acts.[73] During the time these pimps operated they exploited approximately 2000 women, men, girls, and boys, resulting in 174 juveniles relying on prostitution for their basic livelihood.[74]

The Logo Center supplied women and children for pornography production in other countries. In one case they supplied "porno models" to a Swedish pornography producer who made videos in Finland.[75] The Logo Center Web site had links to other sites with bestiality and child pornography.[76] After being arrested, the two owners were charged with distribution of child pornography.[77]

Pimps also use Web sites to advertise their brothels or escort services directly to men.[78] These sites are often used to attract foreign businessmen or tourists.[79] The following is from a Web site in Prague, Czech Republic:

> Would you like to spend an exciting night in Prague with a beautiful young girl? She will do everything for your pleasure. She will make you happy with kissing you on your mouth, French sex and sexual intercourse. During your stay, you can visit the "Golden City" with your girl. The girls are pupils and students, who are financing their education.[80]

Increasingly, prostitution Web sites include photographs of the women, sometimes nude.[81] This practice exposes women, identifying them to the public as prostitutes.[82] Many of the photographs look like modeling photographs, and the women may never have intended for those photographs to be used to advertise them as prostitutes.[83] Some of the women may not even know their photographs are on Web sites. Women suffer from the stigma placed on them for being in prostitution.[84] This public display and labeling further harms women in prostitution.[85]

Web based message boards and bulletin boards are increasingly popular for an exchange of information by perpetrators of sexual exploitation.[86] They are used in much the same way as newsgroups, but can be private and protected by passwords.[87] Using these applications, men can book sex tours and "appointments" with women through the Web, e-mail and chat rooms.[88]

Message boards on brothels' Web sites enable men to post "reviews" of the women for other men, and communicate with pimps about the women's appearances and "performances."[89] On sites where the women's photos are displayed, men can evaluate the women:[90]

> Alina's new photos indicate that she has gained some extra weight!! Please advise what is her weight currently. Thanks and regards. ...[91]

Another example includes:

> Dear Milla:
> What happened to Alina? She seems that she gained some weight since the last time she was with you. She must not be 52Kg as written on her page. Please advise her exact weight.[92]

Men use message boards to make reservations for their upcoming visits.[93] A Web site for a brothel in Prague, Czech Republic, had the following message and request:

> Hallo Mila! I found your page on the Internet.
> I'm going to Prague this summer and probably will visit your establishment. How long time before do one have to make reservations? Could you please put out som more photos of the girls. Is there also possible to have analsex with the girls if you stay overnight? See you! /Peter[94]

Another posting included:

> I understand from our talk, by telephone you have, 6 girls our more, ATT the time, girls are from Ukraine. I will be in Praha, late August 2000, So I will arrive to Praha, late at night, if I remember rite, me flights is from Iceland to Copenhagen and from Copenhagen to Praha. do you have some taxi our pick up from the airport? I wold like to stay in your house the first 2 nights when I am testing your girls after that I will know which of your girls I like. I will chosen one of them to stay in me hotel four 2 nights, so I will have one of your girls, one hour at the time in your house before I chosen which one I chosen to stay with me in me hotel, is that ok with you? I understand you have 6 girls, I wold prefer to have sex with all of them, and then chosen one of the to stay in me hotel four 2 night after thatch, is thatch ok with you? Are your girls shaved? Ragnar . . . .[95]

Web sites are also used to market images and videos of rape and torture.[96] Slave Farm, a Web site registered in Denmark, claims to have the "world's largest collection of real life amateur slaves."[97] Men are encouraged to "submit a slave to the picture farm." The images include women being subjected to sexual torture, bondage, and fetish sadism.[98] Description of images include: "needle torture," "hot wax," "extreme hogtie," "hanging bondage," "tits nailed to board," "drunk from the toilet," and "pregnant bondage."[99] Live chat is available where men can "command the bitches."[100] A number of images are available free, but full access requires payment of a subscription fee.[101] The women in the images and videos are visibly injured, with cuts, burns, bruises, welts, and bleeding wounds.[102]

Another Web site registered in Moscow, Russia, advertises itself as "the best and most violent rape site on earth."[103] It claims to have "Several Hunders [sic] of rape pics."[104] Subscribers are offered 30,000 hard-core porn images, 500 online video channels, and 100 long, high-quality videos.[105] There are images and videos of "violent rapes, ass rapes, mouth rapes, gang rapes, nigger rapes, torn vaginas, and tortured clits."[106] A free 13 MB video and audio movie can be downloaded in twelve segments, each about 1 MB.[107] The film shows a hooded perpetrator raping a woman in an office.[108]

Previously, few people had access to such extreme material.[109] As one consultant explained,

> [f]ormerly men used to have to remove themselves from their community by three levels [to find extreme, violent pornography]. First, they had to go somewhere, physically, then know where to go, and then know how to find it. The Web makes it very easy to get that far removed very quickly."[110]

The resurgence of child pornography through the Internet is a priority for some law enforcement agencies, resulting in unparalleled international cooperation to break up the rings.[111] In contrast, the pornography of adults and postadolescent teens has been ignored.[112] In the United States and Europe, there are very few cases of prosecution of producers of adult and postadolescent teen pornography.

A lot of the pornography is extremely misogynistic, with women portrayed as seeking and enjoying every type of humiliation, degradation, and painful sex act imaginable.[113] Women and children are harmed physically, sexually, and emotionally in the making of pornography.[114] Although, there is less information about women in pornography, it is likely that many women are coerced into making pornography just as they are coerced into prostitution. In addition, by filming the violence and sex crimes against women and postadolescent teens, thereby turning it into pornography, images of these violent crimes can be distributed publicly on the Internet with no consequences to the perpetrators.[115]

The percentage of degrading, violent, misogynistic pornography continues to increase, and the images and videos become more readily available.[116] However, there doesn't seem to be anything new in the content of pornography; perpetrators have always raped and tortured women and children in the making of pornography.[117] What is new is the volume of pornography produced and the fact that an average person with a computer, modem, and search engine can find violent, degrading images within minutes, a search that could have taken a lifetime, just fifteen years ago. The increase in video clips with audio and streaming video makes the action and harm come alive.[118] New techniques, such as shockwave flash movies, enable the creation of animated videos.[119] Skilled amateurs can create snuff films for distribution on the Web.[120] One person I interviewed said that "[w]ith virtual film, it is possible to produce a snuff film from animation, but very difficult to tell it is not real. Now, we are limited only by our imaginations. There is nothing that can't happen on the Web." [121]

## Chat Rooms

Real-time synchronous communication, or "chat," is a popular means of communication on the Internet.[122] Chat is available through Internet Relay Chat (IRC) channels, Instant Messaging such as ICQ, Web-based chat sites that are accessed through browsers, Multi-User Dimension (MUD), or Multi-User Simulated or Share Hallucination (MUSH) programs.[123] There are over 100,000 chat rooms available to users worldwide.[124] Some of these formats and the "rooms" users create are open to the public, some are private and require passwords, and others are used for one-to-one communication.[125] No messages are archived or stored and no log files are maintained, as is done with e-mails or Web accesses, so stalkers use them to look for victims without the danger of being traced by law enforcement authorities.[126] There have been numerous cases in the United States and the United Kingdom where predators contact children for both online and physical meetings.[127] Often, during these meetings, the children are emotionally and sexually abused.[128] There have also been numerous cases of online stalking of adults that began with conversations in chat rooms, which led to physical meetings that turned into sexual assaults.[129]

In chat rooms, perpetrators engage children in sexual conversation or expose them to sexual material, including adult and child pornography.[130] Predators sexually exploit children online through this sexual talk.[131] Perpetrators ask children to send them pictures or sexual images of themselves or their friends.[132] They may encourage the children to perform sex acts on themselves or friends for the stalker's sexual satisfaction.[133] Stalkers use these activities as part of a grooming process to entice children into more direct contact, such as telephone conversations and eventual physical meetings.[134]

When the child stalkers use voice chat the predators and stalkers encourage the children to get headphones to reduce the risk of someone else in the house hearing the voices.[135] They suggest that children get Web cameras for their computers and move their computers to their bedrooms where the stalker can encourage sexual touching and masturbation while they watch via a Web cam.[136]

A typical ruse employed by paedophiles is when the predator asks the victim what she is wearing. This is usually followed by asking her to take something off such as her underwear. The more cunning paedophile will say something more innocuous like "do you enjoy taking showers," swiftly followed by "do you touch yourself in the bath?" It is also commonplace to ask the girl if she has pubic hair in order to build up a mental picture of her level of physical maturity. The intention of most paedophiles is to engage the girl in cybersex activities.[137]

In one transnational case, Franz Konstantin Baehring, a thirty-seven-year-old German man living in Greece, contacted a fourteen-year-old girl from Florida in a chat room.[138] He followed his Internet communication with letters by mail and telephone calls.[139] After a year of corresponding, he convinced the girl to run away from home and travel to Greece.[140] To assist the girl in leaving her home, Baehring contacted a woman at a mobile phone store and convinced her to assist an "abused girl in leaving home."[141] The woman met the fourteen-year-old, gave her a programmed cell phone and drove her to a local airport.[142] The girl flew to Ohio, where Robert Arnder, a convicted child pornographer and one of Baehring's contacts, assisted the girl in getting a passport and leaving the United States: Baehring paid Arnder $2000 dollars for his assistance.[143] Police were able to trace the girl's travels and her contacts by examining the e-mail messages left on her computer at home.[144]

Upon investigation of Robert Arnder, who assisted the girl in Ohio, they found that Arnder had pornographic images and videos of his own thirteen- and seventeen-year-old daughters on his home computer.[145] He had sexually abused his daughters for at least five years.[146] Arnder has since been indicted on 147 counts of rape, 145 counts of sexual battery, two counts of compelling prostitution, six counts of pandering obscenity involving a minor, four counts of pandering sexually oriented material involving a minor, three counts of child endangerment, and one count of interference with custody.[147]

In Greece, Baehring kept the fourteen-year-old girl under control by locking her in an apartment in Thessaloniki.[148] She was not permitted to answer the phone or the door.[149] The girl's friends received e-mail messages sent from Internet cafés in Athens and Thessaloniki saying that she was happy.[150] Baehring told his mother that he felt pity for her because she suffered from leukemia and he was trying to make her happy.[151] He told the girl that he was a child psychologist who specialized in hypnotherapy and ran a youth center.[152]

When authorities found Baehring, he was charged with abduction of a minor with malicious intent, sexual assault, and exposing a minor to improper material.[153] Investigation of Baehring's home revealed child pornography of other girls.[154] He is suspected of involvement with pornography rings on the Internet.[155] The girl suspects that Baehring may have had other girls under his control and used them in making pornography.[156]

The international effort to find the missing girl involved the Polk County Sheriff's Office in Florida, the U.S. State Department, the U.S. Customs Department, U.S. Postal Inspectors, the FBI, Interpol, the U.S. Embassy in Greece, the Greek Consulate, and the police in Greece.[157] The international cooperation has been praised, but the intensity of these efforts also highlights the resources needed to find one girl, and there are thousands of girls missing each year from parts of the world where such resources and cooperation don't exist.[158]

## File Transfer Protocol

Although File Transfer Protocol (hereinafter FTP) is one of the oldest ways of exchanging files on the Internet, it is still popular with child pornography collectors for one-to-one exchange of child pornography.[159] FTP allows users to have direct access to another person's computer hard drive to upload and download files.[160] This technique of file exchange is more likely to occur between child pornography collectors who have met in other venues and have come to trust each other.[161]

## Live Video Chat

Every venue on the Internet is used to transmit images of sexual exploitation. The number of video clips is increasing and streaming video is available for those with high-speed Internet connections.[162] Live Web broadcasts have become common.[163]

In 2000, a case of human smuggling and trafficking was uncovered in Hawaii, U.S.A., in which Japanese women were trafficked into Honolulu to perform live on the Internet for audiences in Japan.[164] Due to more restrictive laws concerning pornography in Japan, the men decided to operate their Web site from Hawaii and broadcast the live shows back to Japan.[165] The Japanese men in Hawaii placed ads in Japan for "nude models."[166] Upon their arrival in Hawaii, the women were used to make pornographic films and perform live Internet sex shows.[167] The entire operation was aimed at a Japanese audience.[168] The Web site was written in Japanese.[168] The women performed strip shows by Web cam and responded to requests from men watching in Japan.[170] They used wireless keyboards for live sex chat with the men at a rate of $1 per minute.[171] The Japanese men, operating as Aloha Data, used digital cameras to capture the live video chat, then transmitted it to a server in California run by a "not respectable, but not illegal" Internet service provider called Lucy's Tiger Den.[172] Japanese viewers accessed the performance through the California server.[173]

The U.S. Immigration and Naturalization Service pursued the case, not because of the pornographic content of the broadcast or the sexual exploitation of the women, but because of immigration violations.[174] This case offers some twists in crime, human smuggling or trafficking, and new technologies.[175] James Chaparro, Director of the Anti-Smuggling and Trafficking Unit, U.S. Immigration and Naturalization Service, characterized the case in this way: "The Japanese men violated U.S. immigration law by smuggling/trafficking Japanese women into the U.S. in order to circumvent the Japanese law against pornography."[176] Omer Poirier, U.S. Attorney in Honolulu, who handled the case described it in this way: "Japanese men were smuggling women into the U.S. from Japan to provide services for men in Japan."[177]

## Peer-to-Peer Networks and File-Swapping Programs

In the last two years, a new technology was developed and released as freeware that can create a network of peer computers.[178] The result is an open, decentralized, peer-to-peer system.[179] File-swapping programs are used to find files on the network.[180] Using the program, the user designates one directory on his/her computer that will be open to the public and another for downloaded files.[181] When the user logs on to the Internet, he/she will be automatically connected to all other people running the same program.[182] All available files are indexed into a large searchable database.[183] When keywords are entered, the request moves from one computer to the next returning links to files.[184] At that point, the program can download the requested files from other members' network computers.[185] It is touted as a revolution in how computers and people communicate with each other on the Internet. Examples of these peer-to-peer networks include: Napster, Scour Exchange, Gnutella, Freenet, Imesh.[186]

These programs create a decentralized system, meaning there is no central server through which all communications pass.[187] Consequently, there are no logs of transmissions, and transmissions are not traceable because each site can only trace the connection back one level.[188] You can enter the public network or create a private one of your own.[189] These features make this new information technology very attractive to perpetrators.[190]

> [S]oftware that turn[s] your PC into both a client and a server. They'll create a true Web by allowing users to easily connect directly to each other. ...Download Gnutella and you can trade any type of file, pirated or not, with anybody else on the Gnutella network in virtual anonymity. [191]

Gnutella has a monitoring feature that allows users to monitor the searches of others to see what people are searching for.[192] According to Glenn Nick, U.S. Customs Cyber Smuggling Center "most searches on these networks are for adult and child pornography."[193]

## Technologies for Anonymity and Disguise

For those engaging in criminal activity or sexual exploitation, anonymity and disguise are critical. Criminals in general are using new communications technologies, such as mobile phones, to avoid police tracing of their phone calls.[194] Mobile phone services often offer free or cheap phones for signing up for their services.[195] Criminals use these phones for a week, and then discard them.[196] Prepaid phone cards enable anonymous use of landline telephone systems.[197] Users of cellular and satellite phones can be located far away from their home bases and still be able to use their phones.[198] Mobile phones can be programmed to transmit false identification.[199] Those engaging in international sexual exploitation use new technologies for ease of communication and to avoid detection.[200] Criminals can avoid being traced by sending their communication through a series of carriers, each using different communication technologies, such as local telephone companies, long distance telephone companies, Internet service providers, wireless networks, and satellite networks.[201] They can send the communication through a number of different countries in different time zones.[202] This complicated routing of communication makes it difficult to trace the perpetrator.[203]

In addition, criminals can avoid identification by transmitting their messages over the Internet through a series of anonymous remailers that strip off identifying headers and replace them with new ones.[204] One remailer service removes identifying features from the header, holds all incoming message until five minutes after the hour, and then resends them in random order to make tracing an individual message more difficult.[205] Messages can pass through up to twenty other remailer services, with at least one located in a country known for its lack of cooperation with the global community and law enforcement.[206]

Perpetrators can also utilize technologies that do not save incriminating evidence. New technologies like Web TV, in which Web communications are displayed on a TV, do not have a file cache, like browsers installed on a computer.[207] Therefore, illegal material is not accidentally left in the cache to be discovered by the police.[208]

Encryption is a technology used to disguise the content of either text or graphics files. Currently, there is a debate among lawmakers around the world about whether law enforcement agencies should be provided with encryption keys so they can decode messages if there is evidence of its use in committing a crime.[209] Several law enforcement officials in the United Kingdom and the United States have indicated that at this point the capabilities and threat of encryption seem to be talked about more than they used to for cases of trafficking and sexual exploitation.[210] Encryption programs are not easy to use, and other methods of hiding activity or content are more popular and easier to manage.[211]

## Technologies of Cyber Hijacking

The sex industry uses techniques such as "page jacking" to misdirect or trap people on pornographic Web sites as page after page of pornography opens up. Page jacking is a technique the sex industry uses to misdirect users so they mistakenly come to their Web sites.[212] The Web sites include false key word-descriptions so that the search index will bring these individuals on to pornographic Web sites.[213] The users will then click on the link of their chosen topic, only to find themselves on a pornographic Web site.[214]

Another technique used by the sex industry is called "Mouse trapping." "Mouse trapping" occurs when the sex industry Web page designers disable browser commands, such as "back" or "close," so that viewers cannot leave a pornographic site.[215] Once intended or unintended viewers are on pornographic sites, they are trapped on the pornographic sites because the "back" or "close" buttons/icons are disabled so that when clicked, another pornographic Web site opens up, resulting in an endless number of Web pages opening up on the viewer's screen.[216] In addition, pornographic Web sites can change the default homepage setting on a Web browser, so the next time the user opens the browser he/she is taken directly to the pornographic site.[217] Furthermore, the sex industry has no idea who they are trapping on their Web sites, whether they are children or adults who fervently do not want to view pornography.[218]

Pornographers are very aggressive about using popular current events and search subjects to misdirect viewers.[219] The sex industry has exploited just about any topic on the Web to trap people onto its Web sites.[220] Pornographers will even exploit the arrests of other pornographers.[221] For example, when a research assistant performed a computer search for news reports about the breakup of a child pornography ring in Russia, she found that entering the case-related keywords directed her to Web sites with child pornography.[222]

## Conclusion

The use of new communication and information technologies for the sexual exploitation of women and children is creating a crisis for women and children's status, rights, and dignity all over the world. Pimps, traffickers, stalkers, and users of pornography and women and children in prostitution have adopted new technologies to further their abuse and exploitation of women and children.

The use of new communications and information technologies in the sexual exploitation of women and children continues to grow with the increased number of users on the Internet. Internationally, there have been governmental and law enforcement responses to distribution of child pornography, and in the U.S. and U.K. official responses to child stalkers in chat rooms. However, there is little governmental intervention to stop the sexual exploitation of adult women.

## Notes

1.  For the purpose of this paper, I use the term "sexual exploitation" to refer to trafficking for purposes of sexual exploitation; commercial sex acts, such as prostitution, pornography, and live sex shows; stalking for purposes of sexual assault or abuse; and all forms of child sexual abuse.

2.  This paper is not about strict legal definitions, nor is it about the law. In fact, many experiences of women and children fall into gray areas, rather than conform to existing definitions. Also, much of the research on sexual exploitation and the Internet focuses on images, and the people in the images are rarely available for interviews to describe their experiences, their consent or coercion, their freedom or slavery. The extent to which the experiences of these women and children meet existing legal criteria for crimes is beyond the scope of this article.

3.  Donna M. Hughes, *The Impact of the Use of New Communications and Information Technologies on Trafficking in Human Beings for the Sexual Exploitation: A Study of the Users* (report submitted to the Group of Specialists on the Impact of the Use of New Information Technologies on Trafficking in Human Beings for the Purpose of Sexual Exploitation, Committee for Equality Between Women and Men, The Council of Europe, May 2001).

4.  *Id.*

5.  *Id.*

6.  Kenneth Li, Silicone Valley: Porn Goes Public, The Industry Standard, Nov. 6, 2000, *at* http://www.thestandard.com/article/display/0,1151,19696,00.html (last visited Mar. 22, 2002).

7.  Frank Rich, Naked Capitalists, *N.Y. Times Magazine*, May 20, 2001, at 51.

8.  *Id.*

9.  *Id.*

10. *Id.*

11. *Id.*

12. *Id.*

13. Rich, *supra* note 7.

14. *Id.*

15. *Id.*

16. Martin Amis, *A Rough Trade, Guardian Unlimited,* Mar. 17, 2001, *at* http://www.guardian.co.uk/Archive/Article/0,4273,4153718,00.html (discussing the high-risk, increasingly violent world of the pornography industry) (last visited Mar. 22, 2002).

17. Natasha Singer, *Blue Danube, at* http://www.nerve.com/Photography/Plachy/BlueDanube/ (last visited Feb. 25, 2001) (on file with author).

18. Fedor Lukyanov, "Alive Goods" Is Flow from the East, *Rossiyskaya Gazeta, at* http://www.rg.ru/english/eco_soyuz/03_11_1.htm (last visited Mar. 23, 2002).

19. Singer, *supra* note 17.

20. To Its Buyers and Sellers, the Sex Trade Is Just Another Busine$$, *at* http://www.pirko.de/Englisch/lustig/Sex.html (last visited Mar. 23, 2002).

21. The Sex Industry: Giving the Customer What He Wants, *The Economist,* Feb. 14, 1998, at 21.

22. *Id.*

23. Interview with Raymond Smith, Fraud, Child Exploitation and Asset Forfeiture Group, Office of Criminal Investigations, U.S. Postal Inspection Service (May 7, 2001).

24. *Id.*

25. *Id.*

26. *Id.*

27. *Id.*

28. *Id.*

29. Interview with Raymond Smith, *supra* note 23.

30. *Id.*

31. *Id.*

32. *Id.*

33. *Id.*

34. James F. McLaughlin, *Cyber Child Sex Offender Typology* (2000), *at* http://www.ci.keene.nh.us/police/Typology.html.

35. *Id.*

36. *Id.*

37. Donna M. Hughes, *Pimps and Predators on the Internet—Globalizing Sexual Exploitation of Women and Children* (Apr. 1999), *available at* http://www.uri.edu/artsci/wms/hughes/pprep.htm.

38. *Id.*

39. *Id.*

40. Max Taylor, et al., Child Pornography, the Internet and Offending, *Isuma: Can. J. Poly'y Res.,* Summer 2001, at 94.

41. *Id.*

42. *Id.*

43. McLaughlin, *supra* note 34.

44. *Id.*

45. *Id.*

46. Karen Kaplan, Pushing Porn On DVDs, *L.A. Times,* L.A. Jan. 9, 2001, at A1.

47. *Id.*

48. *Id.*

49. *Id.*

50. *Id.*

51. Rich, *supra* note 7.

52. Kaplan, *supra* note 46.

53. *Id.*

54. Joe Parker, *How Prostitution Works*, *at* http://www.prostitutionresearch.com/parkerhow. Html (last visited Mar. 23, 2002).

55. Hughes, *supra* note 3.

56. *Id.*

57. *Id.*

58. Hughes, *supra* note 37.

59.  *Id.*

60.  Interview with Glenn Nick, U.S. Customs Smuggling Ctr. (May 17, 2001).

61.  Taylor, et al., *supra* note 40.

62.  Stuart Miller, Technological Level of Wonderland Network Shocked All Investigators, *Irish Times,* Sept. 3, 1998, at 15.

63.  Taylor, et. al. *supra* note 40.

64.  Donna M. Hughes, The Internet and Sex Industries: Partners in Global Sexual Exploitation, *IEEE Technology & Society Magazine,* Spring 2000, at 35.

65.  *Id.*

66.  *Id.*

67.  Hughes, *supra* note 3.

68.  Hughes, *supra* note 37.

69.  Personal Communication with Valdis Pumpurs, Head of the Criminal Police of Latvia (May 2001).

70.  *Id.*

71.  *Id.*

72.  Web site urls: logosagensy.com, pronorussian.nu, marige.nu, and logosagensy.nu. (These web sites are no longer available on the Internet) (on file with author).

73.  Personal Communication with Valdis Pumpurs, *supra* note 69.

74.  *Id.*

75.  *Id.*

76.  *Id.*

77.  *Id.*

78.  Hughes, *supra* note 37.

79.  *Id.*

80.  *Milas Holiday and Escort Service in Prague,* http://www.prag-girls.de/framehallo.htm, (last visited Apr. 21, 2001, Web site no longer available online) (on file with author).

81.  Hughes, *supra* note 37.

82.  *Id.*

83.  Hughes, *supra* note 3.

84.  See generally *Coalition Against Trafficking in Women, Making the Harm Visible: The Global Exploitation of Women and Girls* (Donna M. Hughes & Claire M. Roche eds., Feb. 1999).

85.  Hughes, *supra* note 37.

86.  Hughes, *supra* note 3.

87.  *Id.*

88.  *Id.*

89.  *Milas Holiday and Escort Service in Prague, supra* note 80

90.  *Id.*

91.  *Id.*

92.  *Id.*

93.  *Id.*

94.  *Id.*

95.  *Id*

96.  Hughes, *supra* note 37.

97.  *Slave Farm,* at http://www.slavefarm.com (last visited Mar. 19, 2002) ("the world's largest amateur BDSM site").

98. *Id.*

99. *Id.*

100. *Id.*

101. *Id.*

102. *Id.*

103. http://www.borov.com (last visited Feb. 26, 2001; Web-site no longer links to this material) (on file with author).

104. *Id.*

105. *Id.*

106. *Id.*

107. *Id.*

108. *Id.*

109. Interview with Jeff Middleton, Computer Focus (May 17, 2001).

110. *Id.*

111. Hughes, *supra* note 3.

112. *Id.*

113. *Id.*

114. Liz Kelly & Dianne Butterworth, Address at the Journal of Information Law and Technology's event entitled, Policing the Internet: First European Conference on Combating Pornography and Violence on the Internet (Feb. 14, 1999) (for a description, see Yaman Akdeniz, *Policing the Internet – Conference Report*, 1 J. Info. L. & Tech (1999), *at* http://elj.warwick.ac.uk/jilt/Confs/97_1pol/akdeniz.doc); *In Harms's Way: The Pornography Civil Rights Hearings 39–199* (Catharine A. MacKinnon & Andrea Dworkin eds., 1998) [hereinafter *In Harm's Way*].

115. Hughes, *supra* note 3.

116. See generally *In Harm's Way*, *supra* note 113.

117. Hughes, *supra* note 3.

118. *Id.*

119. Interview with Jeff Middleton, *supra* note 109.

120. *Id.*

121. *Id.*

122. *Internet Crime Forum, Internet Relay Chat Sub-Group, Chat Wise, Street Wise: Children and Internet Chat Services* (Mar. 2001), *at* http://www. Internetcrimeforum.org.uk/chatwise_street wise.html (last visited Mar. 23, 2002) [hereinafter *Internet Crime Forum*].

123. *Id.*

124. *Id.*

125. *Id.*

126. *Id.*

127. *Id.*

128. *Internet Crime Forum*, *supra* note 122.

129. Karamjit Kaur, More Internet Date Rapes, *Straits Times* (Singapore), Feb. 28, 2001; Tom Gardner, *Associated Press*, Feb. 19, 2001; Conal Urquhart, Killerspreadhi's Rape Fantasies on the Internet, *The Times* (London), Oct. 4, 2000.

130. *Internet Crime Forum*, *supra* note 122.

131. *Id.*

132. *Id.*

133. *Id.*

134. *Id.*

135. *Id.*

136. *Internet Crime Forum, supra* note 122.

137. *Id.*

138. Interview with April Hindin, Postal Inspector, Tampa, Fla. (May 15, 2001).

139. *Id.*

140. *Id.*

141. *Id.*

142. *Id.*

143. *Id.*

144. Interview with April Hindin, *supra* note 138.

145. Man faces 308-Count Indictment Related to Alleged Sex Acts with Teens, *Associated Press,* Jan. 24, 2001.

146. *Id.*

147. *Id.*

148. Jill King Greenwood, Missing-Girl Case Points to Greece; 2 Suspects Charged, *Tampa Trib.,* Jan. 27, 2001, at 12.

149. *Id.*

150. *Id.*

151. Missing Teen Found, Says She Doesn't Want to Go Home, *Athens News,* Feb. 2, 2001 [hereinafter *Missing Teen Found*].

152. *Id.*

153. German Man Charged with Luring Florida Girl Overseas, *Associated Press,* Feb. 3, 2001.

154. *Id.*

155. German Suspected of Links with Pornography Rings, Athens News, Feb. 6, 2001.

156. *Missing Teen Found, supra* note 151.

157. Hughes, *supra* note 3.

158. *Id.*

159. *Id.*

160. *Id.*

161. *Id.*

162. *Id.*

163. Hughes, *supra* note 3.

164. Immigration Raid Closes Internet Porn Site, *Associated Press,* Jan. 15, 2000.

165. Interview with Omer Poirier, U.S. Attorney, Honolulu, HI (May 1, 2001).

166. *Id.*

167. *Id.*

168. *Id.*

169. *Id.*

170. *Id.*

171. Interview with Omer Poirier, *supra* note 165.

172. *Id.*

173. *Id.*

174. Hughes, *supra* note 3.

175. *Id.*

176. Interview with James M. Chaparro, Director of the Anti-Smuggling and Trafficking Unit, U.S. Immigration and Naturalization Service (May 1, 2001).

177. Interview with Omer Poirier, *supra* note 165.

178. Hughes, *supra* note 3.

179. *Id.*

180. *Id.*

181. *Id.*

182. *Id.*

183. *Id.*

184. *Id.*

185. See generally *Gnutella,* http://welcome.to/gnutella (last visited May 1, 2001).

186. Hughes, *supra* note 3.

187. *Id.*

188. *Id.*

189. Ron Harris, Gnutella Gives Copyright Holders Headaches, *Associated Press,* Apr. 10, 2000.

190. Hughes, *supra* note 3.

191. Jesse Berst, How Napster and Friends Will Turn the Web Inside Out, *ZDNet,* Apr. 24, 2000, *at* http://www.zdnet.com/anchordesk/stories/story/0,10738,2554369,00.html.

192. *Id.*

193. Interview with Glenn Nick, U.S. Customs Cyber Smuggling Center (May 17, 2001).

194. Richard Davis, New Technology: What Impact Will This Have on How Criminals Manage Their Business?, Address at the Wilton Park Conference entitled Organised Crime: The Dynamics of Illegal Markets, West Sussex, UK (Mar. 1, 2000).

195. *Id.*

196. *Id.*

197. *Id.*

198. *Id.*

199. *Id.*

200. Hughes, *supra* note 3.

201. *See generally* President's Working Group on Unlawful Conduct on the Internet, The Electronic Frontier: The Challenge of Unlawful Conduct Involving the Use of the Internet (Mar. 2000), *at* http://www.usdoj.gov/criminal/cybercrime/unlawful.htm

202. *Id.*

203. *Id.*

204. Hughes, *supra* note 37.

205. Dorothy E. Denning & William E. Baugh, Jr., *Hiding Crimes in Cyberspace,* Infor., Comm. & Soc'y, Sept 1, 1999, at 251–76

206. *Id.*

207. Taylor et. al., *supra* note 40.

208. Hughes, *supra* note 3.

209. Denning & Baugh, *supra* note 205.

210. Hughes, *supra* note 205.

211. *Id.*

212. Hughes, *supra* note 3.

213. *Id.*

214. *Id*

215. *Id.*
216. Hughes, *supra* note 3.
217. *Id.*
218. Hughes, *supra* note 37.
219. *Id.*
220. *Id.*
221. Personal communication with Amy Potenza, Research Assistant, University of Rhode Island (May 24, 2001).
222. *Id.*

# Chapter Seven

# The Internet as a Milieu for the Management of a Stigmatized Sexual Identity

## Keith F. Durkin

*Steve Silberman (1994–1997) once wrote a brief but impassioned article, largely about JohnTeen—an adolescent who discovered the Internet as an important means for managing the stigma of homosexuality, networking with others in similar situations, sharing hardships, expressing anger, and finding support. JohnTeen is not alone; many have discovered the Internet as a place of solace from the brutalities of intolerance. However, the same networking resources valued by JohnTeen are also used by sexual deviants to justify activities that many consider loathsome, if not criminal. Keith F. Durkin explores these dynamics among pedophiles and zoophiles on the Internet.*

One of the most sociologically significant aspects of the Internet is its capability to bring together geographically dispersed individuals. Rheingold (1993) noted that computer-mediated communication can support ties between people, and such relationships between computer users can constitute virtual communities. The concept of virtual community suggests "an assemblage of people being virtually in a community rather than being a real community in the nostalgic sense" (Fernback and Thompson 1995:14). While many scholars acknowledge that there are a number of significant differences between on-line and face-to-face communities, they maintain these on-line groups are communities nonetheless (Song 2002). For instance, Internet relationships frequently are highly segmented and tend to be "based on shared interests rather than holistic relationships based on family, neighborhood, or work relationships" (Driskell and Lyon 2002: 382). In these virtual communities, users can meet people of similar interests and exchange social support (Walther and Boyd 2002). For instance, some virtual communities are orientated to providing support for those dealing with physical illnesses and diseases such as cancer, multiple sclerosis, HIV/AIDS, and chronic fatigue syndrome. Others focus on emotional and behavioral difficulties such as anxiety, depression, eating disorders, alcoholism, and drug addiction.

Through the Internet, people with socially disvalued sexual orientations or predilections "can correspond with persons who share similar interests and identities throughout the world" (Durkin 2001a:63). Accordingly, there are virtual communities that seek to provide support for individuals with disvalued sexual identities (Hegland and Nelson 2002; Walther and Boyd 2002). For instance, traditionally isolated and disenfranchised individuals such as gays, lesbians, bisexuals, and transgendered persons have formed a large number of virtual communities (Cooper, McLoughlin, and Campbell 2000). Yet members of the aforementioned groups are arguably gaining an increased degree of acceptance in the wider society. However, the most extremely disvalued forms of sexual deviance, such as apotemnophilia, bestiality, necrophillia, pedophilia, and urolinga also have an Internet presence (Durkin and Bryant 1995; Gossett and Byrne 2002). The purpose of this current undertaking is to examine how virtual communities for pedophiles and zoophiles may facilitate the management of the stigma associated with those identities. While this research focuses on two of the most extreme forms of sexual deviance, the finding can contribute to our understanding of the identity management strategies of less severely stigmatized individuals, such as gays, lesbians, bisexuals, and the transgendered.

### Stigma Management and Deviant Identities

There is frequently a stigma associated with engaging in deviant behavior or possessing a deviant identity (Goffman 1963). Stigma is a social stain which serves as "an indicator that one has been singled out as a shameful, morally discredited human being" (Goode 1994:104). Sexual orientation is an excellent example of a stigmatized identity (Chrobot-Mason, Button, and DiClementi 2002). On a social level, interaction is frequently difficult for the stigmatized individual since they have an attribute that tends to evoke negative or punitive responses from others (Susman 1994). This stigma "effects the very identity of those to which the negative attribute is ascribed" (Schulze and Angermeyer 2003:299). On the individual level, those possessing a stigmatized identity experience negative self-attitudes (Kaplan 2001) such as a diminished self-concept (Gardner 2001).

Because of the stigma associated with deviance, this "stigma becomes a characteristic to be managed" (Gardner 2001:402). While individuals who posses a deviant identity must confront some difficult issues, the protection of their self-image from possible destruction is arguably the foremost concern (Kelly 1996). Consequently, persons with a deviant identity may use a variety of strategies to circumvent or at least partially alleviate this stigma. Sociologists have advanced a number of theories and concepts to address this phenomenon. Some examples include: vocabularies of motive (Mills 1940); techniques of neutralization (Sykes and Matza 1957); deviance disavowal (Davis 1961; McCaghy 1968; Durkin and Bucklin 2001); accounts (Scott and Lyman 1968; Lyman 2001); deviance avowal (Turner 1972; Durkin and Bucklin 2001); vocabularies of adjustment (Cressey 1973); disclaimers (Hewitt and Stokes 1975); and tertiary deviation (Kitsuse 1980).

There has been a great deal of research conducted on the management of a deviant identity. Sociologists have investigated the identity management strategies of a wide assortment of people whose behavior or beliefs are considered deviant, including convicted child molesters (McCaghy 1968), dishonest shoe salespersons (Friedman 1974), motorists who are suspected of driving while intoxicated (Warren and Phillips 1976), participants in singles dances (Berk 1977), taxi-dancers (Hong and Duff 1977), a hit man (Levi 1981), convicted rapists (Scully and Marolla 1984), college students who miss class (Kalab 1987), convicted murderers (Ray and Simons 1987), participants in chain letters (Boles and Myers 1988), pedophile organizations (de Young 1988, 1989), obese persons (Hughes and Degher 1993), police officers who work in internal affairs departments (Mulchahy 1995), female bodybuilders (Duff and Hong 1996), unemployed professionals (Letkemann 2002) and voluntary childless individuals (Park 2002).

## Virtual Communities for Two Stigmatized Sexual Identities

Adults who have sexual contact with children, or posses such an orientation, are among the most stigmatized individuals in our society. In their national study of sexual behavior and attitudes, Janus and Janus (1993) found that none of their 2,753 respondents believed that it was acceptable for adults to have sexual contact with children. There is an "overwhelming abhorrence" among members of the general public regarding pedophiles and their behavior (Robinson 2001:221). The mere prospect of adults engaging in sexual activity with children "inspires an innate disgust" in most people (Finkelhor 1979:693), and pedophiles are "considered to be among the most degenerate" of deviant categories (Bryant 1982:332).

Pedophiles use the Internet for a variety of purposes, including contacting children, obtaining pornography, and communicating with other pedophiles (Durkin 1997). There are a variety of websites, chat room/channels, newsgroups, and discussion forums for these individuals. These outlets allow pedophiles to develop ongoing relationships with others (Quayle and Taylor 2002). One example would be the Usenet newsgroup alt.support.boy-lovers. Many participants in that forum are avowed pedophiles (Durkin and Bryant 1999). Furthermore, pedophile organizations such as NAMBLA (the North American Man/Boy Love Association) also have a strong Internet presence (Durkin 1997).

Although many academics (e.g., Peretti and Rowan 1982) use the terms interchangeably, bestiality normally refers to "sexual activities with animals," and zoophilia normally refers to a "sexual preference for animals as a sex object" (Walton 2001:19). In any case, a serious social stigma is attached to both the activity and orientation. In the United States, only a few states have explicit laws forbidding human-animal sexual contact (Fleming, Jory, and Burton 2002). In England and Wales however, the maximum penalty for a person having sexual intercourse with an animal is life in prison (Duffield, Hassiostis, and Vizard 1998). Currently, some observes classify acts of bestiality as cruelty to animals (Walton 2001). Criminologist Peirs Beirne (1997) has described this behavior as a form of sexual assault.

Similar to pedophiles, zoophiles have a noticeable presence on the Internet. There are a large number of websites and discussion forums for bestiality enthusiasts (Walton 2001). Some contain extremely graphic visual portrayals of human-animal sexual contact, while others focus on discussion and writings. Apparently one of the historically popular discussion groups "began as a joke but soon attracted a sincere and dedicated following of persons with a genuine interest" (Durkin and Bryant 1995:192). There are also zoophilia advocacy groups on the Internet (Schneider 2001). One example is ZOO (the Zoophiliac Outreach Organization).

The data for this study were derived from websites, newsgroups, and other discussion forums. While some of this material was obtained from the author's files, which represent more than ten years of investigating sexual deviance on the Internet, other material was collected especially for this project. Content analysis of websites and other computer-mediated communication has been used in a number of previous studies (e.g., Durkin 1997; Durkin and Bryant 1999; Gosset and Byrne 2002; Hegland and Nelson 2002). The central research question was, "How might virtual communities of pedophiles and zoophiles contribute to the management of these stigmatized identities?" There appears to be four types of stigma management techniques present: (1) validation; (2) accounts; (3) semantic manipulation of the deviant label; and (4) deviance disavowal.

## Stigma Management Techniques

### Validation

One way in which virtual communities facilitate the management of stigma is by providing validation for the disvalued sexual identity. Hegland and Nelson (2002:14) noted

> The virtual world of the Internet provides a safe and anonymous place that allows those individuals who live on the fringes of society to reflect on their own paths, meet others, and offer or receive advice and support without risking public condemnation or persecution.

On the Internet, "an individual with a deviant sexual identity can receive reinforcement and affirmation" (Durkin 2001a:63). Virtual communities are a place where someone can be assured that they are not alone since there are others with the same identity (Song 2002). The realization of others who have similar thoughts and desires can result in a sense of liberation for the individual (Leiblum 1997).

It appears that validation plays a major role in the virtual communities for pedophiles. Some posts to discussion boards involve responses to individuals who indicated that they were struggling in coming to terms with their sexual orientation. The following is a typical example of this type of posting.

> I deduce that what you've found over these years exactly the same as I have. Peculiar sexuality? Nonsense. I congratulate you on being one of us lucky people who truly appreciate the beauty of the younger man.

Other messages take the form of pleas for help and support. The following example is illustrative of such a posting.

> I am afraid that I can no longer go on if I don't have anyone with whom I can speak freely. You are the only ones I can be open with about my life. ...I have to be able to speak with people who understand me and don't condemn me. ...I just lost a relationship, and now the thoughts of ending it all are coming back to me. I don't know if I can stop them without someone I can talk to. I only have one place left to turn, and that is you.

Other postings involved providing validation to pedophiles that were facing personal problems because of their orientation or behavior. An example of this phenomenon is a posting offered in response to a pedophile who was forbidden to see the boy he was "involved with" by the boy's parents:

> I guess, every boy lover knows the pain (in various ways) in which you have been and in which you will be again, also everyone of us knows everyone tells you the opposite than what you feel is alright, and the only people who share your opinions are out there in cyberspace. There are ups and downs that spread above our lives—it's also out of the reason that we never fully can control our relations together with the boys we love, but have to accept the fact that there are third parties who have the legal right to tell us what to do and what not. ...Get your head up, there are people thinking of you, and perhaps a special boy waiting for you.

The validation of a stigmatized identity is also commonplace in virtual communities for zoophiles, or the "zoo community" as members call it. Schneider (2001:80) speculated that a person who finds a zoophilia group on the Internet "can interpret his or her erotic feelings towards animals" and be provided with "self-esteem" by identifying with the group. This appears to be the case. For instance, one posting about a zoophile organization that has been widely disseminated on the Internet claims:

> We have all shared the experience of relief when we discovered that there were others like us and none of us were slavering degenerates.

A new user to one discussion forum posted the following message regarding his discover of the group.

> Just two days ago I was living in darkness! Now a beam of light has broken the shadows and come to me.

In fact, providing validation appears to be an expectation for some zoophiles. For instance, one message contained the following suggestion for veteran group members:

> Take a newbie under your wing and mentor him. It's a dirty job but someone has to do it. Do it well and it will be a quick job with benefit to all.

## Accounts

Scott and Lyman (1968:46) defined an account as "a linguistic device that is employed whenever an action is subjected to a valuative inquiry." Accounts are a type of exculpatory mechanism used by individuals to explain deviant behavior (Durkin 2001b). They constitute an effort by the individual "to minimize the damage to his or her identity" (Higginson 1999:26). There are two major categories of accounts. The first category, excuses, consists of "socially approved vocabularies for mitigating or relieving responsibility when conduct is questioned"

(Scott and Lyman 1968:47). Types of excuses include an appeal to defensibility, an appeal to accident, an appeal to biological drives, and scapegoating. The second category of accounts, justifications, acknowledges responsibility for the act in question, but denies the wrongfulness of it (Lyman 2001).

There are several types of justifications, including denial of injury, denial of victim, condemnation of the condemners, appeal to loyalties, the sad tale, BIRGing, claim of benefit, and a claim of self-fulfillment. Accounts can be given orally or in written form (Lyman 2001). Accordingly, computer-mediated communications "provide a perfect medium for the use and dissemination" of accounts (Quayle and Taylor 2001:897).

There are three main types of accounts, all justifications, which are used by pedophiles and zoophiles in their virtual communities. The first is denial of injury. When using this account, the individual attempts to justify the behavior in question "by redefining the activity in such a way as to negate its negative quality, such as injury, harm, or wrong" (Pogrebin, Poole, and Martinez 1992:244). For pedophiles, this normally appears to involve denying the widely held belief that sexual contact with an adult is harmfully to children. For example, one pedophile wrote in a posting:

> A child is a sexual being. Therefore, children should have the right to explore any aspect of sexuality they desire to engage in. There is no doubt that children can and do have the ability to decide for themselves what they want. ...Children that are sexually active should be left to themselves to decide who should be the sex partner. ...Consensual sex is justified in all forms, so there should not be a tag of criminal placed on intergenerational sex.

For zoophiles, this type of account usually attempts to deny that a human having sexual contact with an animal is a form of abuse. In a posting that recently appeared on a zoophilia discussion forum, one participant argued:

> The simple fact is, once an animal reaches sexual maturity, he or she is aware of what sex is and how it works, and therefore capable of consenting to or denying sexual contact...zoo sex is consensual, and therefore not abuse.

A second type of account that is used by these individuals is condemnation of condemners. The deviant who uses this type of account attempts to shift the focus from their behavior to the alleged transgressions of those who condemn them. In the case of pedophiles, this is normally police, social workers, and parents. In a message that appeared on one Internet newsgroup a pedophile wrote:

> Our children are in danger. There are predators loose in the world who, in the guise of "protecting" children are, in fact, profiting immensely—meantime destroying the very ones they pretend to protect. Throughout history, one group of people or another has been singled out for attack by the "mainstream" population. Now, another group is under attack—directly putting our children at risk. ...Thousands of children a year are being "brainwashed" by supposedly well-meaning psychiatrists and psychologists, as well as "child protection agencies," who all...derive 100% of their profit from perpetuating the lie that a person who loves a child is a "child molester".

For zoophiles, animal rights advocates tend to be the recipients of this condemnation. For instance, in a discussion group, one zoophile wrote:

> Let the haters of my love of animals poison themselves with the bile of their contempt. Let them drown in their self-righteous indignity. And let them burn in the self-ignited and eternal fire of their hypocrisy. ...I'm usually a pleasant fellow, but right now I feel rather torqued at two "animal rights" bigots.

The final type of account used by these individuals is BIRGing (basking in the reflected glory of related others). This involves "publicly trumpeting some connection with successful others" (Richardson and Cialdini 1981:41). This technique is commonly used by individuals, such as deviants, who are in need of interpersonal prestige (Richardson and Cialdini 1981). A posting that appeared on one newsgroup frequented by pedophiles contained the following statement.

> Some of the more famous lovers of boys throughout history include the following: Alexander the Great. The Greek philosophers Socrates and Plato. Plato was 13 when the two met. The Greek poets Anacreon, Alcaeus, Meleager, Strato, and many others far too numerous to mention. ...Oscar Wilde, commonly thought to be the "father of the modern gay movement." In fact, he loved boys, not men. Allan Ginsberg, the beatnik poet of the '60s, and his literary guru William S. Burroughs (of "Naked Lunch" fame).

An informational posting about a zoophile organization that has been widely distributed on the Internet contained the following information.

> Those who continue animal contacts long or often enough to be considered full-blown zoophiles tend to be well educated and above average intelligence. ...[Most] tend to be white-collar people with greater than high school education...they include independent businessmen, engineers, government employees, farmers, ranchers, etc...

## Semantic Manipulation of the Deviant Label

Another way in which individuals can attempt to manage stigma is through semantic manipulation of the deviant label. This would appear to be a major mechanism for both public and self-image enhancement (Durkin and Bryant 1999). Individuals in marginally stigmatized occupations have employed this technique. Thompson and Harred (1992) noted that trash collectors call themselves sanitational engineers, undertakers called themselves funeral directors, and dogcatchers use the term animal control officer in a self-descriptive fashion. Additionally, car salespeople now advertise "used cars" as "previously owned automobiles."

Salamon (1989) found several examples of this phenomenon in a study of a homosexual escort agency. First, the customers seemed to be more comfortable with using the term "date" for the services they purchased rather than "homosexual" contact. Second, the owner of the agency insisted that he provided an "introduction service" rather than promoting "prostitution." Third, and perhaps most importantly, several of the escorts referred to themselves as "masseurs." Salamon (1989:9) noted:

> While the masseur may be assumed to be a sexual deviant as the result of his profession...it may be thought to offer a professional title with relative respectability.

In the context of the larger society, pedophiles are referred to with such pejorative appellations as "child molesters," "perverts," "sexual predators," and "baby rapers." However, this is not the case in the virtual communities for pedophiles. In these settings, pedophiles refer to themselves as "boy lovers." In fact, a widely circulated document on the Internet is called "The Boylove Manifesto." This type of language is also used by the largest pro-pedophile organization in the United States, NAMBLA, a group that has a significant Internet presence (see Durkin 1997). Additionally, the children that pedophiles have contact with are never referred to as "victims" in the context of these virtual communities, instead, they are sometimes called "loved boys." Through this type of semantic manipulation, pedophiles may be able to conceptualize themselves as adults who simply have a "romantic" interest in boys.

Individuals who are sexually attracted to animals or have sexual contact with animals are frequently labeled "perverted" or "mentally ill" in our society (Walton 2001). However, in virtual communities, zoophiles go to great lengths to distance themselves from the term "bestiality." In a newsgroup posting, one user wrote:

> Bestiality generally refers to the use of an animal strictly for sexual relief, usually only a few times. A bestialist merely uses an animal as a release of sexual tension when no other outlet is available. Most zoophiles, on the other hand, prefer a non-human sexual partner. The relationship goes beyond the mere physical and becomes an emotional partnership.

Members of these virtual communities always appear to refer to themselves as zoophiles or "zoos." Recently, some members have begun to use the term zoosexuality. According to one website:

> Because of the negative connotations applied to the term zoophilia, the term zoosexuality was coined a number of years ago to help distance zoos from any more negative light than already exists.

Much like pedophiles, it would appear that the zoophiles wish to conceive of themselves as individuals with a "romantic" interest in animals, rather than someone with disordered sexual inclinations or desires.

## Deviance Disavowal

Another way in which stigma appears to be managed in these virtual communities is through the use of deviance disavowal. This is a technique in which "the deviator attempts to sustain a normal definition of his or her person" (Durkin and Bucklin 2001:86). This involves attempts on the part of deviants to "deny to themselves as well as others that the deviation is their essential character" (Schur 1979:28). This concept was introduced by Davis (1961) to describe the process by which the visually disabled attempt to present themselves as being "normal." By conceiving of himself or herself as a normal person, the deviator's self-concept is protected (McCaghy 1968).

The pedophiles and zoophiles that use this strategy in virtual communities seek to deny the most negative aspects of their identities—specifically, the actual or desired sexual contacts with children and animals. These thoughts and actions are presented as being of peripheral importance, and not an indicator of these individuals' "true being." Instead, pedophiles and zoophiles who use this technique present themselves as possessing socially approved attributes—a genuine concern for children or animals. While this can be theoretically accomplished to a limited extent with semantic manipulation of the deviant label, deviance disavowal goes a step beyond mere linguistics.

A common theme in the deviance disavowal of pedophiles is the expression of concern for the general welfare and betterment of youth. One poster to a newsgroup for pedophiles attempted to put this disavowal in a historical framework:

> [T]hroughout the history of the world [pedophiles] have played a vital role in the shaping of societies. A group of people who in many cultures held positions of prominence and prestige. For thousands of years, these people have been reaching out...to lead, instruct, and see to the general welfare of our youths.

Although the "concern" for young people is presented as the most salient aspect of the pedophiliac identity, the sexual aspect is marginalized. An excellent example of this strategy appeared in another post to an Internet newsgroup:

> Although one's sexuality is a very important facet of one's life, for a boy lover...being sexually attracted to boys itself is not a critical feeling. ...What is most important is the way in which the boy lover feels emotionally, and this almost always determines how he will act toward boys. He discovers that not only do boys have a special, almost romantic place in his heart, but that he has very few problems communicating with boys if the opportunity presents itself. Boy lovers make the best teachers and child care workers due to the fact that they are most sensitive to boys' needs.

Deviance disavowal also plays a pivotal role in the virtual communities of zoophiles. As is the case with pedophiles, the sexual aspects of the identity are minimized. For example, one poster to a Yahoo group recently remarked, "There is more to being a zoo than animal intimacy." Some zoophiles appear to make conscious efforts to present themselves as "normal" people. On a website, one wrote:

> Almost all zoos can and do have successful relationships with humans. Most zoos have sex with humans as well as animals. Many enjoy long term relationships, including marriage. Many who are zoo-exclusive still have human friends and occasionally have to discourage humans who find them attractive.

Additionally, these zoophiles actively seek to present themselves as advocates for animals and animal-related causes. Many participants in these virtual communities claim to be active in pro-animal causes and report volunteering at animal shelters. Speaking of his caring for a blind horse, one zoophile wrote:

> This then, is what it means for me to be a zoophile. I have accepted the care of one who has need beyond my experience, beyond my material want, need or existence. She shall never want for food, for shelter, for medical care. It is in giving that I am made whole; in sacrifice of self that I live; in service that I am made free.

## Discussion

Virtual communities focus on any conceivable interest, avocation, or identity. As such, the Internet would seem to provide an unprecedented source of social support for individuals with extremely stigmatized sexual identities. It was traditionally assumed that pedophiles were relatively isolated individuals with little or no contact with persons of similar proclivities (Durkin 1997). Likewise, it was taken for granted that practitioners of bestiality were secretive due to the serious social stigma associated with such activity (Fleming et al. 2002). However, because of the anonymity of the Internet and the fact that it transcends geography, pedophiles and zoophiles can correspond with others in a nonthreatening and supportive environment.

An examination of the various websites, newsgroups, and other forums that comprise these virtual communities suggest that these groups may facilitate the management of deviant sexual identities. While stigma management is normally a concern for anyone with a deviant identity, it is even more of a consideration for pedophiles and zoophiles, given the strong public disapproval these individuals face. Such a strong stigma posses a serious threat to these individuals' self-concept. On the most basic level, this stigma may be partially ameliorated through the validation one may receive when they discover these virtual communities. They may come to the realization that there are others who share the disvalued identity. At times, this validation involves users actually exchanging messages of support and affirmation.

A particularly prominent stigma management strategy in these virtual communities is the use of accounts. All of the accounts that were observed took the form of justifications; none were excuses. If pedophiles and zoophiles were to offer excuses, this would be tantamount to admitting they were deviant, immoral, or even pathological. In essence, they would be accepting the stigmatized label. Accounts can serve an exculpatory function (Scott and Lyman 1968; Lyman 2001). When an individual offers a justification for an act or identity, they "seek to assert its positive value" (Lyman 2001:58). With justifications, pedophiles and zoophiles can define their sexuality as "acceptable," and thus maintain a positive self-image.

The other two stigma management strategies, semantic manipulation of the deviant label and deviance disavowal, also seek to redefine the typical public conception of these identities. The larger society describes pedophiles and zoophiles with negative labels such as "pervert," "degenerate," "sick," "sex offender," and "mentally ill." However, these individuals choose to refer to themselves as "boy lovers," "zoos," or "zoosexuals" in the context of these virtual communities. Similarly, they attempt to minimize the significance of sexual activity to their identities through deviance disavowal. The desire for sexual contact with children or animals is presented as a minor and limited aspect of their identity. Instead, it is argued that the most salient aspect of their "true being" is a genuine concern for the welfare of children and animals. The use of these two particular strategies lends support to those who criticize labeling theorists for portraying the deviant "as the prototypical vulnerable and helpless victim" of social reaction and stigmatization (Kitsuse 1980:8). Instead, deviants can reject or modify the label, thus attempting to negotiate their identity (Durkin and Bucklin 2001).

There appears to be very little, if any, possibility that these virtual communities will change public perceptions of pedophiles and zoophiles. In terms of the rhetoric of pedophile organizations such as NAMBLA, Robinson (2001:233) observed:

> Regardless of how the behavior is defined and rationalized by pedophiles, the majority of individuals within American society do not advocate sexual relations between adults and children.

The assertions made by pedophiles in virtual communities are unlikely to be accepted by members of the public. For instance, the claim made by one pedophile that "boy lovers" make the best teachers and childcare workers would be met with scorn, contempt, and ridicule. Likewise, members of the public in general, and animal rights groups in particular, will not approve of humans engaging in sexual activities with animals regardless of any statements made in virtual communities. However, these stigma management strategies are clearly for the benefit of other pedophiles and zoophiles. Bryant (1982:18) noted that some forms of sexual deviance "may be viewed and understood differently by participants" and members of the public. Accordingly, these stigma management efforts may help enhance the self-concept of these pedophiles and zoophiles.

However, there is a certain amount of transparency, if not hypocrisy, associated with some of these stigma-management attempts. This is especially true for the deviance disavowal strategy. While the significance of the sexual act to the identity may be disavowed, it is nonetheless present in these virtual communities. For example, in the pedophile communities there were a few instances of individuals seeking to trade pictures. Also, there were a number of links to and advertisements for "erotic literature" for "boy lovers." This inconsistency is much more prominent in the virtual communities for zoophiles. Some of the websites that contained examples of stigma management techniques also had links to bestiality pornography sites as well as explicit banner advertisements for "animal sex" sites. There were also readily accessible "how to guides" that provided information on the mechanics of engaging in sex with a variety of animals species including dogs, horses, and pigs.

While the current study focused on the identity management strategies of pedophiles and zoophiles, the results have applicability that extends far beyond these individuals. Pedophiles and zoophiles face an extreme amount of social disvaluement. However, all individuals who possess a stigmatized identity have to manage this stigma (Gardner 2001; Kelly 1996). Accordingly, some of the same strategies used by zoophiles and pedophiles can be used by gays, lesbians, the transgendered, and other individuals who have a stigma (albeit less severe) attached to their sexuality.

An important and intriguing question for future research is whether the information contained in these virtual communities is merely a form of intellectual graffiti (see Durkin and Bryant 1995), or does it have the capacity to initiate, encourage, and sustain deviant behavior? While there has yet to be a major empirical investigation of this question, it seems reasonable to speculate that the latter may be true. These virtual communities provide an unprecedented source of support for sexual deviants. As Song (2002:43) opined:

> [T]hrough computer technology, it has become quite easy to offer support to those conducting sexual relations that the current moral order deems illicit or inappropriate.

In turn, these social relations can help sexual deviants to "normalize their activities" (Quayle and Taylor 2002:355). Theoretically, at least, the virtual communities documented in this current undertaking may function in a manner similar to more traditional deviant organizations. Becker (1963:38–39) noted that such organizations provide the deviant with rationales that:

> neutralize the conventional attitudes that the deviant may still find in themselves toward their own behavior. …The deviant who quiets his own doubts by adopting the rationale moves into a more principled and consistent kind of deviance.

There have already been anecdotal reports of pedophiles who participate in virtual communities attempting to engage in sexual contact with children (see Durkin 1997; Quayle and Taylor 2001). However, there is a compelling need for studies specifically designed to investigate this possible relationship.

## References

Becker, H. 1963. *Outsiders: Studies in the sociology of deviance.* New York, NY: Free Press.

Beirne, P. 1997. Rethinking bestiality: Towards a concept of interspecies sexual assault. *Theoretical Criminology* 1:317–340.

Berk, B. 1977. Face saving at the singles dance. *Social Problems* 24:530–544.

Boles, J., and L. Myers. 1988. Chain letters: Players and their accounts. *Deviant Behavior* 9:241–257.

Bryant, C. 1982. *Social deviancy and social proscription: The social context of carnal behavior.* New York, NY: Human Sciences Press.

Chrobot-Mason, D., S. Button, and J. D. DiClementi. 2002. Sexual identity management strategies: An exploration of antecedents and consequences. *Sex Roles* 45:321–336.

Cooper, A., I. P. McLoughlin, and K. M. Campbell. 2000. Sexuality in cyberspace: Update for the 21st Century. *CyberPsychology & Behavior* 3:521–536.

Cressey, D. R. 1973. *Other people's money: A study in the social psychology of embezzlement*, 2nd ed. Montclair, NJ: Patterson Smith.

Davis, F. 1961. Deviance disavowal: The management of strained interaction by the visibly handicapped. *Social Problems* 9:120–132.

de Young, M. 1989. The world according to NAMBLA: Accounting for deviance. *Journal of Sociology and Social Welfare* 16:111–126.

———. 1988. The indignant page: Techniques of neutralization in the publications of pedophile organizations. *Child Abuse and Neglect* 12:583–591.

Driskell, R. B., and L. Lyon. 2002. Are virtual communities real communities?: Examining the environments and elements of community. *City and Community* 1:373–390

Duff, R. W., and L. K. Hong. 1996. Management of a deviant identity among competitive women bodybuilders. In *Deviant behavior: A text reader in the sociology of deviance*, 5th ed., ed. D. H. Kelly, pp. 555–567. New York, NY: St. Martin's Press.

Duffield, G., A. Hassiotis, and E. Vizard. 1998. Zoophilia in young sexual abusers. *The Journal of Forensic Psychiatry* 9:294–304.

Durkin, K. F. 2001a. Cyberporn and computer sex. In *Encyclopedia of criminology and deviant behavior, volume IV: Sexual deviance*. C. D. Bryant, ed. pp. 62–66. Philadelphia, PA: Brunner-Routledge.

———. 2001b. Accounts: Recent trends and developments. In *Encyclopedia of criminology and deviant behavior, volume I: Historical, conceptual, and theoretical issues*, ed. C. D. Bryant. pp. 4–6. Philadelphia, PA: Brunner-Routledge.

———. 1997. Misuse of the Internet by pedophiles: Implications for law enforcement and probation practice. *Federal Probation*. 61(3):14–18.

Durkin, K. F., and C. D. Bryant. 1999. Propagandizing pederasty: A Thematic analysis of the on-line exculpatory accounts of unrepentant pedophiles. *Deviant Behavior* 20:103-127.

———. 1995. Log on to sex: Some notes on the carnal computer and erotic cyberspace as an emerging research frontier. *Deviant Behavior* 16:179–200.

Durkin, K. F., and A. M. Bucklin. 2001. Deviance avowal and disavowal. In *Encyclopedia of criminology and deviant behavior, volume I: Historical, conceptual, and theoretical issues*, ed. C. D. Bryant. pp. 85–87. Philadelphia, PA: Brunner-Routledge.

Fernback, J. and B. Thompson. 1995. Virtual communities: Abort, retry, failure? A paper presented at the annual meeting of the International Communication Association, Albuquerque, NM, May.

Finkelhor, D. 1979. What's wrong with sex between children and adults? *Journal of Orthopsychiatry* 49:692–697.

Fleming, W. M., B. Jory, and D. L. Burton. 2002. Characteristics of juvenile offenders admitting to sexual activity with nonhuman animals. *Society & Animals* 10:31–45.

Friedman, N. L. 1974. Cookies and contests: Notes on ordinary occupational deviance and its neutralization. *Sociological Symposium* 11:1–9.

Gardner, C. B. 2001. Stigma, concept of. In *Encyclopedia of criminology and deviant behavior, volume I: Historical, conceptual, and theoretical issues*, ed. C. D. Bryant. pp. 402–404. Philadelphia, PA: Brunner-Routledge.

Goffman, E. 1963. *Behavior in public places: Notes on the social organization of gatherings.* New York, NY: Free Press.

Goode, E.1996. Gender and courtship entitlement: Responses to personal ads. *Sex Roles* 34(3–4):141–169.

———. 1994. *Deviant behavior*, 4th ed. Englewood Cliffs, NJ: Prentice–Hall.

Gossett, J. L., and S. Byrne. 2002. Click here: A content analysis of Internet rape sites. *Gender & Society* 16:689–709

Hegland, J. E., and N. J. Nelson. 2002. Cross-dressers in cyberspace: Exploring the Internet as a tool for expressing gender identity. *International Journal of Sexuality and Gender Studies* 7:139–161.

Hewitt, J. P., and R. Stokes. 1975. Disclaimers. *American Sociological Review* 40:1–11.

Higginson, J. G. 1999 Defining, excusing, and justifying deviance: Teen mothers' accounts for statutory rape. *Symbolic Interaction* 22:25–44.

Hong, L. K., and R. W. Duff. 1977. Becoming a taxi-dancer: The significance of neutralization in a semi-deviant occupation. *Sociology of Work and Occupations* 4:327–342.

Hughes, G., and D. Degher. 1993. Coping with a deviant identity. *Deviant Behavior* 14:297–315.

Janus, S., and C. Janus. 1993. *The Janus report on sexual behavior.* New York, NY: Wiley.

Kalab, K. A. 1987. Student vocabularies of motive: Accounts for absence. *Symbolic Interaction* 10:71–83.

Kaplan, H. B. 2001. Deviant identity and self attitudes. In *Encyclopedia of criminology and deviant behavior, volume I: Historical, conceptual, and theoretical issues*, ed. C. D. Bryant. pp. 109–114. Philadelphia, PA: Brunner-Routledge.

Kelly, D. H. 1996. *Deviant behavior: A text reader in the sociology of deviance*, 5th ed. New York, NY: St. Martin's Press.

Kitsuse, J. I. 1980. Coming out all over: Deviants and the politics of social problems. *Social Problems* 28:1–13.

Leiblum, S. G. 1997. Sex and the net: Clinical implications. *Journal of Sex Education Therapy* 22:21–27.

Letkemann, P. 2002. Unemployed professionals: Stigma management and derivative stigma. *Work, Employment, and Society* 16:511–522.

Levi, K. 1981. Becoming a hit man: Neutralization in a very deviant career. *Urban Life* 10:47–63.

Lyman, S. M. 2001. Accounts: Roots and foundations. In *Encyclopedia of criminology and deviant behavior, volume I: Historical, conceptual, and theoretical issues*, ed. C. D. Bryant. pp. 7–13. Philadelphia, PA: Brunner-Routledge.

McCaghy, C. H. 1968. Drinking and deviance disavowal: The case of child molesters. *Social Problems* 16:43–49.

Mills, C. W. 1940. Situated actions and vocabularies of motive. *American Sociological Review* 5:904–913.

Mulchahy, A. 1995. Headhunter or real cop?: Identity in the world of internal affairs officers. *Journal of Contemporary Ethnography* 24:99–130.

Park, K. 2002. Stigma management among the voluntary childless. *Sociological Perspectives* 45:21–45.

Peretti, P. O., and M. Rowan. 1982. Variables associated with male and female chronic zoophilia. *Social Behavior and Personality* 10:83–87.

Pogrebin, M. R., E. D. Poole, and A. Martinez. 1992. Accounts of professional misdeeds: Sexual exploitation of clients by psychotherapists. *Deviant Behavior* 13:229–252.

Quayle, E., and M. Taylor. 2001. Child seduction and self representation on the Internet. *CyberPsychology & Behavior* 4:597–608.

———. 2002. Child pornography and the Internet: Perpetuating a cycle of abuse. *Deviant Behavior* 23:331–361.

Ray, M., and R. L. Simons. 1987. Convicted murderers' accounts of their crimes: A study of homicide in small communities. *Symbolic Interaction* 10:57–70.

Rheingold, H. 1993. *The virtual community.* Reading, MA: Addison-Wesley.

Richardson, K. D., and R. B. Cialdini. 1981. Basking and blasting: Tactics of indirect self-presentation. In *Impression management theory and social psychological research,* ed. J. T. Tedeschi. pp. 41–53. New York, NY: Academic Press.

Robinson, D. M. 2001. Pedophiliac organizations. In *Encyclopedia of criminology and deviant behavior, volume IV: Sexual deviance,* ed. C. D. Bryant. pp. 221–223. Philadelphia, PA: Brunner-Routledge.

Salamon, E. 1989. The homosexual escort agency: Deviance disavowal. *British Journal of Sociology* 40:1–21.

Schneider, A. 2001. Deviance advocacy groups. In *Encyclopedia of criminology and deviant behavior, volume I: Historical, conceptual, and theoretical issues,* ed. C. D. Bryant. pp. 80–84. Philadelphia, PA: Brunner-Routledge.

Schulze, B., and M. C. Angermeyer. 2003. Subjective experiences of stigma: A focus group study of schizophrenic patients, their relatives, and mental health professionals. *Social Science and Medicine* 56:299–312.

Schur, E. M. 1979. *Interpreting deviance: A sociological introduction.* New York, NY: Harper and Row.

Scott, M. B., and S. Lyman. 1968. Accounts. *American Sociological Review* 31:46–62.

Scully, D., and J. Marolla. 1984. Convicted rapists' vocabulary of motive: Excuses and justifications. *Social Problems* 31:530–544.

Silberman, S. 1994–1997. "We're Teen, We're Queer, and We've Got E-Mail." *Wired 2.11.* Wired Magazine Group, Inc.

Song, F. W. 2002. Virtual communities in a therapeutic age. *Society* 39 (2):39–45.

Susman, J. 1994. Disability, stigma, and deviance. *Social Science and Medicine* 38:15–22.

Sykes, G., and D. Matza. 1957. Techniques of neutralization: A theory of delinquency. *American Sociological Review* 22:664–670.

Thompson, W. E., and J. L. Harred. 1992. Topless dancers: Managing stigma in a deviant occupation. *Deviant Behavior* 13:291–311.

Turner, R. 1972. Deviance avowal as neutralization of commitment. *Social Problems* 19:308–321.

Walther, J. B., and S. Boyd. 2002. Attraction to computer mediated social support. In *Communication technology and society: Audience adoption and uses,* eds. C. A. Lin and D. Atkin. pp. 153–188. Cresskill, NJ: Hampton Press.

Walton, C. E. 2001. Bestiality. In *Encyclopedia of criminology and deviant behavior, volume IV: Sexual deviance,* ed. C. D. Bryant. pp. 19–22. Philadelphia, PA: Brunner-Routledge.

Warren, C. and S. Phillips. 1976. Stigma negotiation: Expression games, accounts, and the drunken Driver. *Urban Life* 5:53–74.

# Chapter Eight

# Cyberpoaching behind the Keyboard: Uncoupling the Ethics of "Virtual Infidelity"

## Jim Thomas

*Much has been written about the effects of Internet sex on marriage and committed rela-tionships. Problems of "virtual infidelity" have received considerable press and raised predictable concerns. The issue, however, is far from clear; the very concept of "virtual infidelity" is not without critics. Jim Thomas investigates the ethics of Internet sex, largely in the context of committed relationships. As Thomas discovers, Internet sex ex-poses sometimes conflicting and frequently ambiguous dilemmas that make it difficult to pronounce concise, absolute, and universal ethical principles.*

There ain't no sin, and there ain't no virtue. There's just stuff people do. It's all part of the same thing. And some things folks do is nice, and some ain't so nice, but that's as far as any man got a right to say

> —Jim Casy to Tom Joad. Steinbeck, *Grapes of Wrath* 1939/1991:32.

Cliff Stoll (1995:234) once observed that computer networks, like cars and tele-visions, confer a most seductive freedom, the "freedom to." It's not surprising, then, that the freedom to explore Internet sex and pursue online coupling has become a tempting, and growing, pastime for many adults already coupled to somebody else offline. Some estimates suggest that up to 10 percent of adult Internet surfers become hooked on cybersex (infidelitycheck 2002).

For me, though, Internet sex has never held any great fascination. After all, I'm more or less an absolutely monogamous, fidelity-unchallenged, reasonably happily married male. Until I met Natasha. And her Russian sisters. They must have read my online writing and seen my manly homepage bio-jpegs. Or some-thing. Why else would these three lovely nubile women send me, a virtual stranger, email and nude pictures and sexy promises? Before I knew it, I was exchanging emails and pictures and stories and chatting online and typing with one hand while looking at their pictures and reading their real-time chat-promptings. Was I being unfaithful to my partner?

Nope. Because I'm making this up. There was no exchange of pictures, no chatrooms, and no temptation to accept Natasha's prurient offers. In fact, there was no Natasha. Not because I'm prudish, reserved, or judgmental about such things—I'm far too jaded to judge Netporn as an ethical lapse. So why would I not be attracted to all those Natashas spamming my email account? After all, this wouldn't really be sex. What actually disinclines me toward these libidinally laden come-ons is that, if there were a Natasha, and had I succumbed to her allures, I'd have to 'fess up to my Internet partner, with whom I'm open and honest and totally committed.

Now, nobody knows about my Internet partner. Not my friends, not my priest, and especially not my wife. Nor does her husband know about me. Although we've never met face-to-face, we swap pictures and speak together on the phone about once every two weeks. We met on an online academic listserve in 1999, exchanged some emails, and over the next two years gradually became friends as we increasingly shared information. It began slowly, first by swapping research notes and bibliographies, then sharing drafts of papers, and finally we began sharing summaries of our day's events, personal problems, and deepest joys and fears. We made each other laugh, cry, and grow, as we shared intimate parts of our day. Could it be we were in love? Was I being unfaithful to my wife?

Nope. I'm making this up too. Every word. No Internet partner, no Internet intimacies, and absolutely no Internet sex. I'm not even Catholic.

The closest I've ever come to displaying e-infidelity was an errant, flirtatious email, totally innocent, intended for a female friend I inadvertently misdirected to my wife, who, of course, being unamused, assumed the worst. The very worst. No, I'm not making this up, and everything from here on is true. The "e-oops" (that's what we call embarrassing misdirected missives) happened. And, complicated by some past non-virtual peccadillos, it took considerable explaining. A faux-flirtatious interaction, even if innocent, wasn't, if that's what was going on, appropriate. And if it wasn't going on, and it wasn't, then it better not go on in the future. So, no untoward e-coupling was happening. Remember, everything from here on is true.

But, what if I were not making up these stories? What's wrong with online sex or coupling between partners who are attached to other partners in presumably offline monogamous relationships? Who do such things hurt? Swapping precious ASCII is hardly the same as sharing precious bodily fluids, and surely safe hex is more benign than safe sex. Would an E-involvement with another woman (or man) constitute infidelity? Even if it didn't, would it still count as unethical behavior? Are Net romances a serious social problem that creates a "monogamy myth" that risks corrupting the relationships of future generations (Vaughn

1989) or indicative of a potential underlying pathology (Schneider and Weiss 2001)? There are certainly legal, therapeutic, interpersonal, domestic, and societal ramifications. After all, an estimated 20 percent of wives and 25 percent of husbands are estimated to have had extramarital affairs, and the numbers nearly double when non-physical, but intensely emotional, affairs are added (Harris 2003). In challenging the "monogamy myth," Vaughn (2003) argues that the figures might be as high as 60 percent for men and 40 percent for women. Some scholars argue that up to one-third of divorce litigation is triggered by online affairs (infidelitycheck 2002).

This paper is only partially about online sexual activity. It's mostly about how we socially construct, code, talk about, and impute value judgments to "cybersex," especially when participants are partnered to others offline. Some observers argue that the Internet provides a unique new way of interacting that challenges conventional definitions of sexuality and requires new ethical rules as well. I'm not so sure; perhaps we too hastily reduce cyber-romance to issues of ethics and character.

The proliferation of imprecise terms to describe online romantic or sexual activity creates confusion when discussing sexual activity. Netsex, the broadest label, is an umbrella term that generally refers to any online activity of a sexual nature that involves titillation, varying from an exchange of provocative ASCII texts to viewing pornography. "Cybersex" and "Netsex" tend to be synonyms, applied to both sexually stimulating activities as well as to more complex online relationships that sometimes emerge. A subset of Netsex behaviors includes behaviors in which participants may not directly engage in overt onanistic behaviors while online, but nonetheless become "cybercoupled." Here, I use the terms "cybercoupling" and the corollary "cyberinfidelity" to refer to online activities in which two people who have not previously met offline become, through an exchange of electronic communications, emotionally involved (cybercoupling). Cyberinfidelity is the issue raised when one or both online partners are also coupled with an offline partner.

In this paper, I explore the complexities of Netsex by focusing primarily on online dyads in which at least one participant is coupled to a different offline partner. My assumption is that cybercoupling is the most extreme form of Net sexual activity because it is interactive, occurs over an extended time, includes fantasizing and role playing, and involves an emotional bonding. The concept of cybercoupling thus becomes a lens for unpacking the ethics of broader online sexual activity by exploring the question of what really counts as sex and infidelity. All interaction and social statuses entail rights, obligations, expectations, and a sense of what the costs are for violations. In Western culture, aside from life

and death issues, matters of sex carry some of the heavier prescriptions and proscriptions delimiting what we ought or ought not do, say, see, or hear. The concepts of romantic coupling and the ideal of monogamy are among the most
enduring and cherished bonds. "Till death do us part," and all that. Waskul
(2003) observed that the gray area of "good and evil" may reflect whether we
view online behavior as an extension of real life or something all together different:

> Many people presume that Internet activities are not bound by the same codes; others
> suggest just the opposite—it's a classic bifurcation and most of us are very uncertain
> about this "black and white" characterization.

My goal here is to elaborate Waskul's insights and extend the gray areas
surrounding the ethics of online sex and romance, coupling, and infidelity on a
sliding scale of involvement, acceptability, and blame. Cybercoupling becomes
an icon—a symbolic signpost—for a broad range of Netsex interactions. While
this reproduces some of the conceptual ambiguity surrounding most discussions
of Netsex, I suggest that part of the definitional problem is inevitable because of
the ambiguity of the meanings of the "sex" itself. I argue that, while the same
broader ethical standards apply both online and off, there is a sliding scale of
ethical accountability shaped by the context of the interaction, the expectations
of partners, and the consequences of the behaviors.

## Mapping the Terrain

Moral certitude is rarely as certain as it seems. Jim Casy, the jaded former rever-
end in John Steinbeck's *Grapes of Wrath*, routinely found his spiritual status as a
moral sage a useful tool for post-sermon sexual seductions. He tried to explain
his shift from moral absolutism to cynical realism. His inability to reconcile his
sexual appetites with his moral sensitivities shattered his belief in absolute ethical imperatives, despite his occasional honoring of the symbols of rectitude
when it was for immediate self-gratification. Through Casy, Steinbeck was attempting to describe the intricate and dialectical dance between good and evil,
the Gordian knot created as the two intertwine.

Most of us recognize, or would like to think we recognize, the necessity for
fairly fundamental social principles of good and evil. We accept that preying on
others is a bad thing; injustice isn't nice; and the sexual improprieties of our
partners are quite unacceptable. Yet, on this latter point, the definitions of "sexual," "improper," and "unacceptable" generally depend on what your own definitions are. It's not that most people accept nonmonogamy when presumably

committed to one partner. Instead, something so seemingly unambiguous in the abstract becomes murky when participants are confronted with competing interpretations and conflicting meanings of the same facts in their personal behavior. Even more so than in the real world, the blurred line between acceptable interaction and actions less so tend to muddy the ethical territory of cyberspace. Cyberspace is no longer an invisible, unsettled "electronic frontier." It has grown into a populated and still-evolving world community. Although figures vary, in 1995, there were 16–26 million people online worldwide, with about 18 million of those computers users being online in the United States. In 2002, this had surged to over 580 million worldwide users online, with over 165 million of them in the United States (NUA 2002a, 2002b). This provides a rather large pool of potentially harvestable sexmates. The dramatic increase in online activity brought a corresponding awareness of cyberinfidelty, leaving some observers, moral entrepreneurs and—not surprisingly—marriage counselors to cluck as if this were a suddenly new and rampant phenomenon. It's not, and an understanding of the social context of cybersex requires grounding in a brief history of its origins.

### News Flash: "Cybersex in Cyberspace"

The term "cyberspace" is now a bit hackneyed, and most of us recognize that cyberspace is not really a place. It is something that happens with people using computers. Cyberspace connotes interaction with others by means of a personal computer and a modem connection that allows access to users at other computers. The term, originally coined by William Gibson, refers to something that happens in the mind:

> A consensual hallucination experienced daily by billions of legitimate operators, in every nation, by children being taught mathematical concepts...A graphic representation of data abstracted from the banks of every computer in the human system. Unthinkable complexity. Lines of light ranged in the nonspace of the mind, clusters and constellations of data. Like city lights, receding..." (Gibson 1984:51)

As we sit at the computer keyboard and magically etch our ASCII for others to see, we feel as if we leave it somewhere, and that "somewhere," cyberspace, is simply a metaphoric way of identifying the experience of electronic communication. Cyberspace offers marvelous resources. It also offers activities, such as electronic mail, public access systems, and chat rooms, where people meet, flirt, argue, heal, carouse, or fall in and out of love.

Concerns about cybersex and infidelity have received increased media attention in the new millennium from a combination of media stories (e.g., Edwards

2002; Esposito 1999; Kampert 2002), counselors or therapists (Dr. Phil 2003; Glass 2003; Maheu and Subotnik 2001; Vaughn 2003), alarmists (Schneider and Weiss 2001), and rigorous scholars (Mileham 2003; Waskul 2003, 2002, 2004; Waskul, Douglass, and Edgley, 2000). Judging from some of the media hyperbole and sensationalism that subverted the gravitas of Mileham's groundbreaking work on chatroom interaction and Net infidelity, it would seem that the issues of Netsex and cybercoupling have only recently emerged. However, recent accounts seem unaware that these and the related issues of "fidelity," ethics, and sexual interaction emerged full-scale at least as early as the 1980s. Then, as now, the same motivations that drove people to explore sexual gratification offline also motivated them online.

Netsex didn't emerge de novo in a vacuum or overnight. It has coevolved at the same speed, and with the same trajectory, as other computer changes since the 1970s. Historically, 25 years is barely a generation. In Net time, however, a quarter of a century constitutes quantum changes in computer-mediated communication. Two major technological breakthroughs occurred in the mid 1970s that provided the medium for cybersex: Inexpensive personal computers (PCs) and PC modems.

PCs, as we know them today, emerged out of the microcomputer revolution of 1975–76. The first publicly marketed viable desktop computers went on the market in the mid 1970s. Although these originally had little utility for the average person, techno-junkies were exploring the possibilities for games, work, and especially communication. Commercial digital modems were marketed as early as 1965 as a means of transferring data between mainframes. When PC modems became commercially available with the development of the mass-produced standard Hayes PC modem in 1979, which allowed users to send information between their system and another, it began a digital revolution that included the Golden Age of hacking (Thomas 2004), the Internet, and, of course, Netsex.

The development of inexpensive modems led to the invention of Bulletin Board Systems (BBSes) that allowed PC users to communicate with other users over telephone lines. As curious youth began to discover that PCs were fun, adults were also exploring their potential for communication. In 1978, Computerized Bulletin Board System (CBBS), the first BBS in the country, went online and allowed PC users to communicate with other users by dialing into a central PC that hosted the BBS. There, users could exchange information in public or private forums and download and upload text files and programs. They could also exchange graphics, such as pictures. BBSes provided public and private forums for sexually oriented synchronous and asynchronous ASCII conversations, downloading sexually enticing text and graphic files, and engaging in fantasy role playing, all in the privacy of one's room. Some BBSes, such as Event Horizons and Amateur Action, were early purveyors of explicit sexual material in the early 1980s.

The territory for virtual sexuality was born.

As the virtual world of the BBS evolved, so too did more sophisticated systems that allowed users to communicate faster and more directly using networked computers accessed through mainframes or other shared servers. Bitnet, a short-lived early network of computer-mediated communication common at educational institutions, was a primitive, yet effective, introduction into the world of email and newsgroups for university students and staff who found the new medium a novel and often addictive pastime for communicating, meeting new people, and engaging in the occasional fantasy with online strangers. "Bitsex," the term for casual flirting and provocative one-on-one email or discussion list sexual stimulation, provided a forum for students and others to sexually stimulate a partner or develop clandestine relationships.

The Internet, a vast connection of internetworked worldwide computer systems able to communicate with each, publicly emerged in the 1980s, and became the primary conduit for computer-mediated communication by the early 1990s. Stimulated especially by the needs of scholars and students at academic institutions, the Internet provided the backbone for an array of PC communication tools that facilitated the growth of online coupling. Many of these services offered a libidinal outlet for curious explorers. Usenet, an asynchronous text messaging system, enticed users with forums such as alt.sex, alt.sex.bondage, sex.strip-clubs, and alt.sex.spanking, in addition to forums for the exchange of graphics ranging from mildly lewd to extreme hardcore. Before the popular instant messaging now common on the Net, Unix operating software provided commands such as "talk," "ytalk," and "chat," that allowed two or more users to communicate privately.

Public access systems, such as The Well (1985), Compuserve, and America Online (1989/1991), provided a new type of virtual community for users to come together and interact with millions of others. Although Compuserve was established in 1969 as a computer-sharing service, it wasn't until a decade later that it emerged as a significant cyber-presence, becoming the first online service provider to offer its subscribers email and real-time chat, a precursor to AOL's now infamous chatrooms and, later, instant messaging, both of which became fertile cybersex playground for everything from felons trolling for illegal sex to gender-bending role playing. MUDs (multi-user domains) and MOOs (object-oriented), text-based software that allowed for the creation of real-time virtual communities, usually of fantasy role-playing games, occasionally included highly sexual scenarios.

By the early 1990s, virtual sexuality attracted media attention in part because of male predators bilking women with whom they became involved in online romances, or "cyber Lotharios" such as the man on Sausalito's The Well, who romanced and exploited five female members simultaneously, both online and off, apparently not realizing that, even online, one ought never forget the adage, "women talk." His involvement drew considerable media attention both for his online seduction and for his offline interactions that included monetary and other exploitation.

Also in 1993, the provocative issue of online rape arose in a fantasy game on LambdaMOO. If fantasized cybersex is considered sex, or at least infidelity, what should we call an online fantasy rape? Dibble's (1996) provocative essay raised an intriguing issue: How should an online community respond to an AS-CII sexual assault? What social meaning, pejorative or otherwise, should we impute to a MOO character who compels others in the fantasy game to unwillingly service him sexually?

The sexual escapades emerging on BBSes, in chatrooms, and on the then new Internet in the mid 1980s seem rather quaint in the 21st century. Today, with over 60 percent of the United States. online, and with growing awareness of accessability to online communities, the omnipresence of email, the ease of instant messaging and file sharing, and the comfort level in which a casual message can contain the subtextual seeds—wittingly or not—for something more, both the opportunity for, intensity of, and prevalence of Internet relationships continues to increase dramatically. So too does its visibility, fueled by media stories and moral entrepreneurs who are certain that, even without physical contact, cybersex counts as "sex."

The question of what counts as "sex," however, is less simple than it seems, and raises issues that aren't immediately obvious.

### What's Online Sex, Anyway? Cybercoupling and Infidelity

Even in the tactile, corporeal world, what counts as sex varies. Glass (2003) rejects the view that without sexual contact, infidelity does not exist. She acknowledges that gender differences temper this judgment to the extent that women tend to see emotional attachment as the primary criterion for infidelity. Men, by contrast, view sexual intercourse as the definitive factor, and only 46 percent of males judge online sexual activity to constitute infidelity (infidelitycheck 2002). But, Glass argues, the emotional damage even of noncontact interaction, such as Internet affairs, is sufficiently damaging to constitute infidelity.

On the other hand, when former President Bill Clinton claimed, "I never had sex with that woman, Ms. Lewinsky," he reminded us that online or off, not all people share the same definition of "sex" all the time. Christina G. (1997:3) underscores the uncertainty of what seems, to some, so certain. In describing her youthful promiscuity, she initially kept score, taking pride in the number of her many sexual partners. As the years passed, she realized that she was counting fewer of them, not because partners didn't physically enter her, normally a *sine qua non* of "real sex," which they may or not have done, but because her meaning of sex was shifting:

> The problem was, as I kept doing more kinds of sexual things, the line between SEX and NOT-SEX kept getting hazy and more indistinct. As I brought more into my sexual experience, things were showing up on the dividing line demanding my attention. It wasn't just that the territory I labeled SEX was expanding. The line itself had swollen, dilated, been transformed into a vast gray region. It had become less like a border and more like a demilitarized zone (Christina G. 1997:5).

Another question complicates the definition: Is "sex" something that can be defined or excluded by fiat? If, for example, sexual relations are a necessary criterion for adultery, redefining "sex" by excluding some sex acts normally seen as the primary criterion would be one way to reduce the incidence of adulterous affairs. After all: no sex, no adultery. Another would be to redefine "sexual relations." Had Ken Starr conducted his investigation of President Clinton in Thailand, it might have been far shorter:

> A group of Thai judges gave a definition to conjugal infidelity. From now on, oral sex isn't adultery at all, and it isn't classified as "sex."…Forty-five of the sixty judges and consultants said that sex is only when partners have genital contact. The rest of the judges insisted that sex was any kind of contact when genitals of at least one partner were involved. However, the majority dominated in the dispute, and oral sex was referred to the category of an innocent pastime no longer forbidden (Pravda 2002).

The credibility of Pravda notwithstanding, this illustrates the ease by which the socially constructed meaning of sex could be changed by fiat. A recent case in the United States refined the meaning of sex when the definition of "sexual intercourse" required to sustain an accusation of adultery was dramatically narrowed by the New Hampshire Supreme Court:

> If a married woman has sex with another woman, it isn't adultery, a narrowly divided state Supreme Court decided yesterday. Adultery, three justices ruled, only occurs when the sexual relations between a married person and another could fertilize an egg (Vos 2003).

If the demarcation lines between sex and nonsex are foggy face-to-face (as it were), they are even murkier online. Cybersex and Netsex remain common terms that include activities ranging from accessing computer-mediated sexually explicit material, interactive games, and other forms of sexually stimulating images. However, as Waskul (2002:110) observes, cybersex is only marginally related to pornography, which tends to be passive, onanistic, and primarily a male-oriented activity. The term reduces the complexities of highly nuanced online sexually related interactions to something one-dimensional and partial. Waskul. Douglass, and Edgley (2000:17) also note that many scholars adopt definitions of cybersex, such as "any form of sexual expression accessed through the computer or the Internet," that range from naive to self-servingly inaccurate. Many of these definitions come from pop psychologists, marriage counselors, and moral entrepreneurs who have built a career out of perceived sexual pathologies. Netsex becomes one more pathology to be treated or judged:

> Cyber-infidelity is defined as the act of engaging in acts of a romantic or sexual nature with an individual or individuals through electronic or virtual communities, i.e., as established through dating websites, email discussion lists, interactive games, chat rooms or newsgroups. Cyber-infidelity can easily lead to a cyber-affair, which involves the emotional investment of time and energy into an individual, group, or community (Maheu 1999).

Maheu's definition of cybersex was focused to fit a therapeutic clinical model:

> Cyber-sex occurs when people use computerized content (text, sounds, or images obtained from software or the Internet) for sexual stimulation. They usually start by typing provocative and sometimes erotic words to each other. They might also send voice files to one another, describe their fantasies, or show each other pictures or videos of themselves or other people. Whichever technology they use, the individuals create a shared sexual excitement and usually end with masturbation (Maheu and Subotnik 2001:12).

Such unnuanced definitions lead to conflation of types, motivations, and processes of Internet interpretations of sexuality and romance. As an antidote, Waskul draws from those who have experienced online sex to refine the definition, adding both an interactive and synchronous component:

> In fact, among participants, cybersex is a word that strictly refers to real-time erotic communications between people, usually through typed text, digital cameras, or both (Waskul 2004:17).

While the distinctions in these competing definitions might seem overly subtle, Waskul's conceptualization rightly recognizes that "having sex," online or off, is more dynamic and interactive than passive. But, whether cybersex need be synchronous also seems debatable. Would two letters by postal mail exchanging sexually stimulating words or images, or by post-it notes, be "memo sex?" Would reciprocal and interactive faxing of titillating text or images constitute fa(u)x-sex?

Further illustrating the complexity of cybersex, some scholars contend that cybersex is accelerated because Internet communication is the most disembodied of all forms of interaction. Yet, is sharing ASCII and audio-video files to create an online history with a partner any more disembodied than the more limited bandwidth of a hardcopy letter, a phone call, or even yelling to somebody unseen in another room? Perhaps the perception of disembodiment contributes to the judgment that cybersexual attachments "aren't real," which some scholars suggest tends to surprise participants (Turkel 1995:21). But, there is a corporeal and emotional component not easily dismissed:

> Netsex, tinysex, virtual sex—however you name it, in real-life reality it's nothing more than a 900-line encounter stripped of even the vestigial physicality of the voice. And yet as any but the most inhibited of newbies can tell you, it's possibly the headiest experience the very heady world of MUDs has to offer. Amid flurries of even the most cursorily described caresses, sighs, and penetrations, the glands do engage, and often as throbbingly as they would in a real-life assignation—sometimes even more so, given the combined power of anonymity and textual suggestiveness to unshackle deep-seated fantasies. And if the virtual setting and the interplayer vibes are right, who knows? The heart may engage as well, stirring up passions as strong as many that bind lovers who observe the formality of thrusting in the flesh (Dibble 1996:381).

One difficulty in trying to establish a clear, invariant definition of cybersex is that the varieties of all sexual activity are too broad and nuanced to make a single, simple, definition possible. Therefore, while recognizing the ambiguous and vague shadings of Netsex as including a variety of nuanced, fluid, and pliable behaviors, this paper emphasizes the variant of Netsex termed cybercoupling as a way of teasing out a range of behaviors and ethical judgments imputed to them. These behaviors range from relatively harmless flirtations and virtual stimulation between casually paired couples, to something more intense, as occurs when two people meet online, forge an escalating relationship, and establish a bond of commitment and intense emotional attachment, even though one or both may be coupled to an offline partner. The question posed here: Is cybercoupling unethical? The answer depends on how we perceive the context of offline partners who are "poached" by online counterparts.

## Cyberpoachability and Infidelity

The concepts of adultery and infidelity, while intertwined, are not synonyms. Adultery, with its historical roots in religion and later in law, has shifted in meanings over the millennia, as the Oxford English Dictionary lists the original intent as describing an act of making a marriage impure. The definition was clear: Intercourse was required for adultery, and adulterers were punished by death. The King James version of of the Bible, Matthew, chapter V (27–28), expands the act to thought:

> 5:27 Ye have heard that it was said by them of old time, Thou shalt not commit adultery:
> 5:28 But I say unto you, That whosoever looketh on a woman to lust after her hath committed adultery with her already in his heart.

Shifting the definition from the bed to the head caused some embarrassment for presidential candidate Jimmy Carter in his November 1976 interview in *Playboy* magazine, even while hinting at a gray area of "guilt":

> I've looked on a lot of women with lust. I've committed adultery in my heart many times. This is something that God recognizes I will do—and I have done it—and God forgives me for it. But that doesn't mean that I condemn someone who not only looks on a woman with lust but who leaves his wife and shacks up with somebody out of wedlock. Christ says, Don't consider yourself better than someone else because one guy screws a whole bunch of women while the other guy is loyal to his wife (Sheer 1976:86).

Although the intense opprobrium and its punishment shifted over the centuries, the term still applied only to married partners. The term "infidelity" is both broader and more vague. It applies both to married and nonmarried partners, and also includes behaviors other than sexual intercourse. Infidelity generally falls in the category of "doing the wrong thing," which would seem to make it unethical. Ethics, after all, is about doing the right thing, not necessarily about thinking the wrong thing. But, ethics connotes choice. In criminology, we call this *mens rea*, which simply means that we intentionally did bad, and we should be held accountable.

However, like the definitions of adultery and infidelity, intentionality, too, can be unclear. Glass (2003) argues that in the current "new infidelity" of contemporary online and offline culture, couples do not intentionally begin an affair with a conscious decision. Instead, they drift into it as they unwittingly forge a relationship that gradually crosses the line from the platonic safe area, through the gray area, then well into the red zone of committed emotional attachment. Especially with online involvements, the "crept-up" factor plays a major role.

Participants may not intend to romantically pursue another person, and the small choices made may not be unethical either individually or even in the aggregate. Only when the realization that a coupling relationship has developed do the issues of ethics grow murky. There may not have been original intent to betray a partner or act unethically. Instead, there was a gradual drift in initially indiscernible and incremental steps whose choices were, perhaps, even noble. Although not cyber-based, one example of the subtle and well-intended process by which noble intents led to unanticipated outcomes involved at least eight New York firefighters who left their wives and families to start new lives with the widows of coworkers who were victims of 9/11 (CBSNEWS 2003). They did not begin their new relationships intending to stray. The original intent was highly ethical. They were assigned to comfort the widows, but comfort incrementally turned to intense passion and intimacy:

> This is the essence of the new crisis of infidelity: friendships, work relationships, and Internet liaisons have become the latest threat to marriages. As these opportunities for intimate relationships increase, the boundaries between platonic and romantic feelings blur and become easier to cross (Glass 2003:1).

In addition to the "crept-up" factor, several additional factors complicate issues of *mens rea*. First is naiveté. While electronic communication has been common for a decade, even experienced users may not recognize the signs of growing involvement, as attachments slowly creep up on the participants. Most of us have had years of experience dealing with the face-to-face "boy-girl" dynamics in the initiation or discouragement of flirtation, romance, and "something more." Although ASCII is simpler, perhaps because of the very fact that it *appears* simpler, we often lack the sophistication to recognize how simple words can nurture growing emotional attachment to and passion for the online conversational partner.

Second, and a corollary to naiveté, is the "invisible poaching" factor. Poachable, a term that circulated among San Francisco bartenders in the early 1970s, refers to the public cues that a coupled person gives off that signal accessibility for sexual involvement with a person other than the established partner. As bartenders, accurately reading poachability cues were an asset in facilitating the needs of customers. It was also a skill useful for defusing conflicts when customers misread the cues. Schmitt and Buss (2001:894) converted the term into a serious scholarly concept to analyze behaviors intended to attract another person who is already in a romantic relationship, or to signal accessibility to others, even though already in a coupled relationship. Their conceptualization describes the physical cues that one gives off to enhance attractiveness or to symbolize sexually proceptive behaviors such as prolonged eye contact (Schmitt and Buss 2001:913).

Accessibility cues online are much more difficult to exhibit or inhibit than in face-to-face interaction. There are no cues such as body posture, eye contact, or other audio-visual tips to alert us to the intents of others or to the impact our ASCII may have on them. Granted, as in bars, some coupled individuals are constantly "on the make" and cruise online for targets, coupled or otherwise. Others frequent chatrooms or IRC channels where consensual surreptitious pairings readily occur. But, the question at hand isn't whether one "meets" somebody online, even if some flirtation occurs. It's how the value judgments we make about the next steps become translated into categorical ethical statements based on imperatives of "right and wrong" when ASCII cues develop into something beyond flirtation that evolve into what Waskul (2000; 2002) has labeled outercourse or altersexuality. These terms refer to the gray area of sexually laden interaction that may not, on the surface, conform to conventional definitions of "sex" or whose initial cues escape a person's radar in initial stages of a potential relationship's development. This is the invisibility factor in which the poaching cues that we may recognize face-to-face may be less obvious in ASCII. In ASCII, as conversational partners negotiate emotional space and distance, they also subtlety renegotiate accessibility barriers as they use simple monologic discourse to expand a rich dialogic partnership that can bring them closer with neither recognizing it.

An additional factor in online interaction is that the normal barriers to poaching, such as mate-guarding by the offline partner or snooping by offline friends, dissolve behind the keyboard. The relative solitude and ability to create barriers between our external environment and the world behind the screen excludes partners who, in face-to-face settings, may be physically present to send off barrier cues (such as threatening looks to a potential poacher or paying increased attention to the mate). It also excludes other cues such as wedding rings, pictures of children on the desk or in the wallet, and other artifacts of possession or attachment.

Another way to signify poachability is by the silences we leave and what we do not reveal to others that might make us a potential tryst magnet. In ASCII, we can filter mate barrier cues by avoiding talk about domestic life, children, and topics that invoke images of a partner. Collectively, poachabilty cues in ASCII are far more complex, nuanced, and subtle than in face-to-face interactions, making judgments of intents all the more difficult.

A final poachability factor, one that can reduce the culpability of some participants in online coupling relationships, is the unique nature of the computer medium to create a preliminary *tabula rasa:* We cannot initially judge the conversational partner on the other end on the basis of audio-visual cues as we do face to face. For some, physicality in real life was not optimal for attracting others. Offline attributes that might be perceived as less desirable face-to-face can be replaced with more alluring online personas, as Net sage Michael Godwin (1994) observed:

> In, uh, "face-to-face mode," these two people might never have broken the ice. But online they revealed their deepest secrets to each other, and each discovered a kindred spirit. Even the often-disappointing first meetings of would-be online lovers tell you something of the power of text—it's those face-to-face distractions (his weight problem, say, or her acne) that prevent the union of those who otherwise might be soulmates."

Of course, none of the factors that mitigate display of or acting on accessibility cues necessarily absolves online couplers from accountability. But, they do suggest that the imputation of ethical "guilt" on the basis of the outcome of the actions glosses over the primary doctrine of guilt assessment, *mens rea*. This raises the issue: On what grounds can we judge online coupling as ethical or unethical?

### Discourse from the Trenches

In an attempt to examine how experienced Net surfers judged the issues of Netsex, cyberinfidelity, and poaching, from October through December, 2003, I initiated a discussion in two online forums in which the participants were currently, or had been recently, involved in a committed offline relationship. The first group was two classes of college sociology students. The issues of online coupling were raised in class offline as an introduction, and then brought to the class online conferencing board. The discussion generated about 65 posts from 28 posters. The second discussions occurred on a public access system frequented by technologically sophisticated professionals and others, all of whom had considerable online experience, including in cybercoupling. This produced 60 responses from 23 posters. The selections below are unedited, except for formatting. The goal was not to produce a survey or body of data to allow generalization of opinions. Instead, it was to identify forms of discourse and how definitions and judgments of cybercoupling, cybersex, and cyberinfidelity were interpreted.

The input from both groups provided thoughtful commentary and illustrated the breadth of perspectives underlying individual judgments. Despite the online experience of the commentators, neither the definition nor the meaning of cybersex in any of its variants became clearer. Although the posts do not allow significant systematic generalizations, not surprisingly, the gender differences broke along lines predictable by existing research: women tended to weigh cybersex and poaching as an emotional violation, while men tended to judge it as infidelity only if there was extreme physical contact of a sexual nature.

The primary problem in mapping out the issues was defining basic terms, on which there was considerable divergence (e.g., "cybersex," "infidelity," "betrayal"), and the context of interaction and the relationship between the offline couples was the key factor in defining cybersex for some respondents:

Source: online community (male)
Date: December, 2003

It depends on the relationship, the nature of the questionable interaction, the extent of the interaction, etc. I would think the extent to which the technology was material would only depend in some instances. So, the question would not be is looking at porn on the internet infidelity, but is looking at porn in any context infidelity? looking at porn now and then, or spending most waking hours looking at it? What if it wasn't a romantic e-relationship, but an intense personally intimate relationship with a stranger, but sex was never mentioned? If someone goes to a strip club, is that infidelity? If they get a lap dance? A conversation with a stripper in a strip club? Is this conversation different than chat with a stranger? is masturbating some sort of infidelity? What about sex fantasies? What about having sex with your partner, but thinking about someone else?

Ultimately, the core issue is what is fidelity. Once this has been defined, then you can look at infidelity. What is fidelity, besides being highly personal, is also not so easy to pin down, I feel.

However, those who saw cybersexuality as cheating cast it in terms of "mate possession" and an encroachment on the offline dyad. Both males and females tended to cast their discourse not so much as an ethical violation, but rather as a tort, a personal wrong, and a challenge to the offline bond. Some described the primary problem as a subversion of trust:

Topic: INTERNET SEX!! WHO CARES?!?
From: Student discussion list (female)
Date: October, 2003

Internet sex is cheating or infidelity. Even though you're just talking or emailing, it's with someone else other than your significant other. That's a form of emotional cheating. Sending pictures clothed is not right either. You should be having these discussions or whatever with the person you're with, that's why you're with them.

Others framed cybersex as an unambiguous issue of replacing the offline partner who laid claim to exclusivity with a surrogate:

Topic:          INTERNET SEX!! WHO CARES?!?
From:          Student discussion list (female)
Date:          October, 2003

My personal opinion as an engaged individual is that "internet sex" and sex are one in the same. If my partner was to engage in either activity with an individual other than me, I would consider it infidelity. For me personally, there is no sliding scale of acceptability. It is my opinion that all forms of computer sex are gross and if I found out that my mate was engaging in this type of behavior—He couldn't pack his bags fast enough to avoid the mental pain I'd inflict. The idea of a person choosing to whack off to an e-mail or pictures as opposed to getting the real thing is baffling. Why, why, why????

Sometimes, past experiences with online romances shape the context and provide a recognition of the very real possibility of cyber interactions evolving into something much deeper, which extinguishes the line between cyber and offline life:

Source: online community (female)
Date: December, 2003

As someone who married a man I met online, I'd take it pretty seriously. Not viewing porn, mind you, but being involved in cyber-flirtations or cyber-sex. It's as real a relationship as any, though different, and if you have a monogamy agreement it's a violation. Not everyone is monogamous of course, and couples all have their own lines of what's acceptable. But cyber counts as well as RL counts, as far as I'm concerned.

The impact of alternative online sexual encounters on an offline partnership also raises the issue of replacement of or withdrawal from offline sexuality:

Source: online community (female)
Date: November, 2003

The big thing for me is not what you do with your body parts, so much as whether a relationship is taking your emotional focus out of the marriage I can see online sex going either way. Is it *replacing* marital sex, or removing the incentive for marital sex? Is it a casual thing like watching a single porn video might be, or is the person shutting down from the marriage and anticipating their nights with someone else? (Not saying those are the only two possibilities).

The structure of some discourse raised the issue that an intimacy that was once special is now shared:

Topic: INTERNET SEX!! WHO CARES?!?
From: Student discussion group (female)
Date: October, 2003

I believe that all forms of internet sex should be constituted as cheating. Whether you're dating/engaged/married, whatever it is, the fact of the matter that you are looking elsewhere for feelings of comfort and belonging instead of the relationship that you are committed to. If you're only online to look for a friend, then you might as well go out to the bars, because that's a better place to find friendship. There are so many pedophiles, perverts, rapists out there that search for their next victims online, that the internet is the last place you should look for some type of "alternative" sexual pleasure. I'm sorry, I know a lot of people may think that I'm being petty but come on. I wouldn't want my boyfriend talking dirty and exchanging sexual fantasies with anyone other than me. If he is looking elsewhere for sexual pleasure then that obviously means that something is missing in our relationship and that "we" not "he" needs to work things out together!!

Some discourse reflected a sliding scale of acceptability, and implied that it could be a diagnostic cue for problems in the relationship rather than simply an ethical flaw:

Topic:          INTERNET SEX!! WHO CARES?!?
From:           Student discussion list (male)
Date:           October, 2003

In my opinion, virtual sex is not necessarily conducted in a chat room. I feel that you should have some visual contact, whether it is over a web cam or something. If 2 people are just chatting in a chat room, I do not see anything wrong with that. If you take it to the next level, then you might be crossing a boundary. In my opinion, infidelity is when you do engage in a sexual encounter with someone else while in a relationship. Does this mean if you are watching porn, is that infidelity? Is there a difference in chat rooms and 900 numbers? I feel that it is OK to flirt. It makes everyone feel good (generally). If someone is married and engaging in such activities, what does that say for the marriage? Is something missing to make that partner look elsewhere?

The sliding scale and escalating involvement might not be a "sex" or an "ethical" issue, but rather signs of problems in the relationship that could be the occasion for generating dialogue with the offline partner:

Conf: SEX SEX SEX SEX (on the internet?)
From: Student discussion list (male)
Date: October, 2003

While there are potential problems with establishing relationships online, I don't think that someone who has observed their significant other having conversations in an internet sex chat room should up and end the relationship. I admit that there are lines that should not be crossed with internet talks (i.e. sending provocative pictures, meeting, dating, etc.), simply talking to someone should not be taken as seriously as some people in class are saying it should. I recall a person in class stating that she would end her relationship with her husband if she caught him having internet sex without allowing him to explain, I think this is extremely harsh. If a person is having internet sex, he/she should be comfortable enough with his/her partner that they could talk about it in advance to see if there would be a problem. If the person is going behind their partner's back, I think that the relationship has underlying problems to begin with and that internet sex may be the least of the couple's worries. In sum, simply talking to someone about sex on line is no different than going to a bar and flirting. While many women consider internet sex infidelity, they would also consider a partner who forbids them from flirting a "control freak" or "possessive". I fail to see a difference.

Physical sexual contact might be the necessary condition to constitute "cheating," but cybersex likely fulfills an offline vacuum that reflects not so much infidelity, but lack of communication:

Conf: SEX SEX SEX SEX (on the internet?)
From: Class discussion group (female)
Date: October, 2003

I'm not really sure if internet sex is considered cheating. For one I think that in order to be cheating you need to be with that person physically and have so called sex on the internet you're not with them physically. Secondly, sex is an intimate relationship and how intimate can you be on the computer? However, I do feel that it is wrong that your partner is talking to others on the computer because that shows a lack of communication between the two of you. There is obviously something missing

While some accepted that online "romances" or heavily sex-laden chat or flirtation may not constitute infidelity, or even be unethical, it would be personally harmful to the offline partner and relationship, because the outcomes risk the social harms of pain and distrust:

Topic:       INTERNET SEX!! WHO CARES?!
From:       Student discussion list (male)
Date:        October, 2003

I don't like the term infidelity. It's loaded, and it starts us thinking in the wrong direction. How about the term "acceptable?" I'm not about to play semantics. There are some things I might not like that might be acceptable in a broader sense, but if he's doing things that bother me, or would hurt me, I think I have a right to know. I'd object. This isn't really about ethics, is it? Isn't it really about how relationships are formed and preserved? How that's done can't easily be measured against a standard of right or wrong.

Regardless of whether online poaching could be readily defined, the outcomes, not the intents or even the acts themselves, constituted the definitive characteristic for some:

Topic:          INTERNET SEX!! WHO CARES?!?
From:           Student discussion list (male)
Date:           October, 2003

Internet sex? What does that mean? Infidelity? What does THAT mean? Let's define our terms, OK? Let's define "unethical." If we judge a behavior to be wrong, does that make it unethical?

For me, sex means something physical, not something mental, and as long as it happens in ASCII, it remains mental. Is forming mental sexual images of somebody while masturbating infidelity? If so, how about fantasizing about somebody else while you're making love with your partner? (c'mon. Don't say you've never done it!).

If online chat escalates to email, then to phone calls, then to physical contact, yes, I'd have a problem with that. If I caught my partner escalating, we would have some fundamental issues. In fact, if I caught my partner fantasizing about anybody else (I admit a double standard), I would be hurt, angry, and confrontational. But I'm not sure that I would call it an ethical issue.

We're back to definitions.

The personal pain it would cause if one's own offline partner became involved can temper abstract tolerance or ambivalence for cyber involvements:

INTERNET SEX!! WHO CARES?!?
From: Student discussion group (female)
Date: October, 2003

I think that this is a hard hard issue. I know that I would be really upset if I saw that my boyfriend or husband was doing something like this, but at the same time I don't think it is infidelity. They are not physically doing anything with the other person so I guess it is not as bad as it could be. Unless, they took it far enough to actually see them on the side. I think that it is naturally for people to fantasize about things like this and if this is the way that they want to express themselves, I don't think there is anything wrong with it. There is obviously something missing in that relationship if your spouse is talking to others on the internet.

Sometimes, activities in cybercoupling reflect neither an ethical judgment nor conventional views of monogamy. Instead, the involvement of an offline partner could lead to internalization of blame when the coupling was discovered:

Topic: INTERNET SEX!! WHO CARES?!?
From: Student discussion group (female)
Date: October, 2003

When I thought about this question I had to think how would I feel if my boyfriend was engaging in internet sex or coupling and frankly I would be really hurt. I would feel like I am not giving him what he needs, and instead of telling me about it he ran out and found someone else. True there may be no physical contact, but I still think it is cheating. Try to think about it this way, which is worse a drunken mistake or an emotional relationship created over time. Both are bad but which is worse.

For some, cybersex reflects not only a personal violation, but also a broader challenge to the social fabric resulting from irresponsible individualism and the violation of conventional values:

Topic:        INTERNET SEX!! WHO CARES?!?
From:        Student discussion group (female)
Date:         October, 2003

When this topic was brought up in class and I said I would be so hurt if I found out that my spouse was doing this sex thing over the internet. It would be a violation of the emotional bond that is shared between a husband and wife. If the spouse is communicating to someone else to begin with then the relationship was already in serious trouble. I think lack of communication is one of the main reasons why marriages fail. More and more we are becoming individuals rather than communities, so people are just doing what ever the heck they want and not worrying how the other person is violated. I have many friends that have lost their spouses because they have met someone else on line. I don't blame the internet because I think if you are making time for each other, doing things together, then there is not a lot of time to be chatting on the net. My friend who is an executive for SBC told me a story of a guy who was on company time (at work) and was busted looking at porno. He had 23 years with the company and was going to be able to retire in 2 years. Instead, he was fired that day, lost all of his benefits, and had to explain to his wife. Well on that note, the internet could change your life at a click of a mouse.

Even those attempting to sort things through the ethical issues found no clarity:

Topic:        INTERNET SEX!! WHO CARES?!?
From:        Student discussion list (male)
Date:         October, 2003

I think everybody here is bringing up valid points. Unfortunately, this issue seems to break down into personal opinions and feelings. If I caught my spouse engaging in Internet sex, sure I'd care. I would probably be confused and confront her on it. I would not consider it cheating. I don't think it would be a relationship ender, just a small problem that could be repaired.

> I discussed this issue with my fiancé. She says that this type of activity is definitely cheating and it would end the relationship. We seem to reflect the general conflict between genders here.

Ethics, however, is another story:

> Being a deontologist myself, I would feel that my duty would be to not upset my relationship. If an action of mine, such as engaging in Internet sex, caused this upset, I would be acting in an unethical manner.

Finally, sometimes the issues entail complex questions for which there are simply no simple answers:

> Source: online community (female)
> Date: November, 2003
>
> Which situation would you *least* want to be in?
>
> 1) Your spouse has a specific sexual need which you do not meet, which he satisfies with pornography and/or visits to paid specialists?
>
> 2) Your spouse engages in sexual activity to orgasm with another human online?
>
> 3) Your spouse engages in sexual activity ditto with another human IRL?
>
> 4) Your spouse is physically faithful but is for many years in love with another person and unable to give that person up for any length of time, and that relationship, while it takes place mostly online, is nonetheless emotionally intimate?

These commentaries are not simply a collection of isolated posts. In the aggregate, they reflect a variety of meanings, interpretations, and variations not so much on cybersex, but about sexuality. What sense, then, can we make of these various narratives above that reflect an array of feelings, judgments, perspectives, and images?

So much of sex-talk isn't about sex, and sorting through all the nuanced agendas gets a bit confusing. Three broad categories of responses emerge from the commentaries. First is ethical absolutism. Online couplings and alternative sexual gratification are wrong by their nature, regardless of motive or consequence. Online couplings, by definition, subvert trust and the expectation of monogamy. Second, ethical ambivalence reflects uncertainly about whether the acts are, of themselves, wrong, but context, motive, and outcome become primary factors to consider. Third, interactional instrumentalism characterized the view that online interactions should be judged not by rule violations, but by consequences. The primary criterion was on the pain, on the distrust, and on the potential creation of instability in the offline partnership.

Views of cybercoupling are as much about discourse as about intercourse. The varieties of defending, resisting, judging, and imaging the issues reflect more than views about sex. They reflect hidden values that shape how we frame the talk, boxing us in from a more critical view of the cultural location of cybercoupling in the context of monogamy and social control. In short, "it depends."

### Ethics, Sex, and the Rashomon Effect

We tend to think of ethics as absolute, or at least as containing some transcendent "truth." Yet, isolating ethical judgments as if the behaviors or incidents occurred as discrete events to be weighed against a single standard creates several problems. First, behaviors do not occur in a vacuum, and second, there is rarely a single ethical standard against which to assess behaviors that are embedded within sociocultural, ideological, and other socially constructed foundations.

Because of the difficulty of defining cybersex or cyberinfidelity, judging the ethics is no easier. The lack of a clear definition of what counts as an offense exacerbates the problem of assessing both intent and "guilt." Another complicating problem is that of sorting through the competing ethical frameworks that might not be shared. Whether we judge an act as unethical may depend on our rhetorical skills and our competence at weaving narratives into compelling accounts that describe, justify, or condemn the behaviors.

In Akira Kurosawa's stunningly challenging film *Rashomon*, four participants in a heinous crime are later called to account for what they saw. Each weaves the same facts into a narrative that both coincides with and contradicts the narratives of the others. Painstaking elaboration of the factual chronology of events by each fails to produce a "true" judgment of accountability. The perspectives and intents of each narrator shaped their individual perspectives, and it was impossible to know where fabrication and deception ended and good-faith differences in standpoint began. Kurosawa's simple message: "truth" is a social construct, not absolute, and like all social constructs, it becomes distorted through the prisms through which we view it and by selective distortions of the audience who hears it. Neither the teller of a tale nor an audience can ever be truly sure of the "reality" of what is ultimately heard.

The Rashomon effect penetrates the interpretations of online sexually related activity in several ways. First, as the previous section illustrated, "sex" is not necessarily a definable act, and making scholarly attempts to create an invariate and finite meaning is neither possible nor desirable. Our perspective, our agendas, and our cultural standpoint may shift over time or place, or we may even hold different meanings simultaneously. "One man's blowjob is another man's perk of office." Perhaps the best we can hope for is a working definition that provides broad parameters for the discourse at hand.

Second, the Rashomon effect challenges any absolute, invariant, and universal set of "ought" principles or ethical framework on which to comfortably pass judgment on online couplings. The underlying philosophical foundations of ethical principles vary, and multiple observers can readily arrive at competing or contradictory interpretations of the same event. The view that cyberinfidelity reflects unethical behavior also reflects competing value systems based on two different ethical perspectives. Although a bit oversimplified, the following overview helps to illustrate the ethical ambiguity.

We can divide ethical perspectives into two broad philosophical perspectives. The first, the deontological position, is based on "rule following" and proceeds from formally specified precepts that guide how we ought to behave. An example would be that breaking into other people's houses or coveting our neighbor's partner is wrong. Deontological positions are further subdivided into act-deontological and rule-deontological. In the former, basic judgments of value are particularistic or situational, drawing on shared principles of, for example, "justice" to establish the proper course of action in a given situation. In the latter, behavior is guided by concrete, universal rules, such as "thou shalt never lie, because lying leads to nasty outcomes."

Second is the teleological perspective, associated with, but not exclusive to, utilitarianism. Teleological perspectives operate from the premise that ethical behavior is determined by the consequences of an act. The goal or end of an act should be weighed with a calculus that, on balance, results in the greatest social good or the least social harm. Utilitarianism, the most common form of teleological theories, is also divided into two variants: Act-utilitarianism and rule-utilitarianism.

Act-utilitarianism holds that correct actions are contingent upon the nature of the particular situation, and the guiding principle is the degree to which the specific act will maximize the greatest balance of "good." Rule-utilitarianism, associated with John Stuart Mill, emphasizes the primacy of general rules of conduct, but these rules are derived from the principle of the greatest universal utility, which is:

> ...that pleasure and freedom from pain are the only things desirable as ends; and that all desirable things (which are as numerous in the utilitarian as in any other scheme) are desirable either for pleasure inherent in themselves or as means to the promotion of pleasure and the prevention of pain (Mill 1863/1957:10–11).

"Happiness" in this perspective is neither a hedonistic nor an indolently selfish concept, but based instead on the cultivation of the "public good" and the utility of the act as a means toward that end. Unlike teleologists, utilitarians argue that their position avoids becoming entrapped in normative or contradictory rules and potentially relativistic duty-imposing obligations.

Consider a married partner who vowed to love and honor the mate "until death do us part," or at least as long as they remain in a mutually consensual committed relationship. But, the partner becomes cyber-romantically involved with another, with whom an intense pairing occurs. The involvement, the straying partner notices, reduces personal stress, increases happiness, increases attentiveness and sensitivity to others (including the mated partner), and generally improves quality of life. In this case, cyberinvolvment is, on balance, more beneficial than harmful. Of course, this would be an empirical judgment, but that's the point: an ethical judgment, in this view, requires context, and the context—not an a priori rule—guides judgment.

In the above commentaries from online posters, whether expressions of online sexuality were ethical or not ranged from the Kantian categorical imperative of "thou shalt not, period" to the more utilitarian "whom does it hurt?" This not only illustrates the difficulty of ethical assessment, but also emphasizes a significant point: whether cybercoupling constitutes an ethical lapse depends.

### Sexuality and Control Narratives

Like *Rashomon*, how we frame our judgments about cyberpoaching reflects our biographies, our ideologies, and both our individual and social standpoints that provide the lens through which we view and talk about the topic. Rather than attempt to come to an absolute conclusion about definitions or culpability, we can recast the question as a critique of sex, gender, and power. We can also view the varieties of discourse as reflecting various control narratives that contain the conceptual machinery, or ideology, of appropriate expressions of sexuality.

Maines (1993) refers to narratives as types of stories that take past events and transform them into story elements by using types of plots and settings that confer structure, meaning, and context. The stories possess a logical and temporal ordering to provide a coherent accounting. Control narratives are stories that channel perception, cognition, and action in preferred ways and limit them in others. Maines's (2001:193–196) analysis of incest narratives illustrates how control narratives are rhetorically and politically managed by those best able to manipulate the discourses that convey them. Those with the best narrative skills have more power than those who do not, and when narrative power is coupled

with the cultural power of images of "right and wrong," control narratives become a significant resource to control preferred views of normative behavior,
rather than to challenge them.

Power, status, and identity narratives are embedded in discourses. Discourses are sets of symbols that we use to communicate who we are, or who we
think we are, the context in which our existence is located, and how we intend
ourselves to be understood as well as how we understand (Schwalbe et. al.,
2000:435). Discourses are ways of talking and writing. To regulate discourse is
to compose a set of formal or informal rules about what can be said, how it can
be said, and who can say what to whom (Schwalbe, et. al., 2000:435). Discourses embody opportunity structures that frame how we talk and are shaped by
ideological and other powerful sociocultural forces. As Ferree (2003) observes
in her analysis of the rhetoric of abortion debates, discursive opportunity structures are inherently selective, and ways of expressing ideas and issues in one
way simultaneously restrict it from moving in other directions.

In an ideal world of symmetrical power, emotional security, and a high self-
concept of our physicality, the opportunity structures of discourses on sexually
tinged interactions and on discussions about such discussions might be less relevant. But we all confront a variety of personal demons ranging from possessive-
ness, insecurity, and doubts about physical characteristics and (sexual)
performance. No, we can't control thoughts or fantasies, and fantasizing might
be natural. Unfortunately, the polysemous nature of sexuality in our culture pre-
cludes talk of polyamory. The contemporary framing of sexuality in intellectual
discourse doesn't reduce the pain, anger, or jealousy of a partner who might
(even wrongly) suspect us of lusting (after others) in our hearts, especially when
our focus should be centered on the partner who believes he/she does not share a
partner's intimate fantasies, words, or feelings with potential rivals.

But we need not fall back on moral relativism or nihilism to reflect on
Nietzsche's (1889/1972:55) observation:

> Moral judgment has this in common with religious judgment that it believes in realities
> which do not exist. Morality is only an interpretation of certain phenomena, more pre-
> cisely, a MISinterpretation. Moral judgment belongs, as does religious judgment, to a
> level of ignorance at which even the concept of the real, the distinction between the real
> and the imaginary, is lacking; so that at such a level "truth" denotes nothing but things
> which we today call "imaginings."

The transition from a society based primarily on face-to-face interactions to
one shaped by ASCII has created new symbols, metaphors and behaviors, but on
which we impute ethical judgments based on Old Testament images of gender

possession and control. Baudrillard (1987:15) observed that our private sphere now ceases to be the stage where the drama of subjects at odds with their objects and with their image is played out, and we no longer exist as playwrights or actors, but as terminals of multiple networks. The public space of the social arena is reduced to the private space of the computer desk, in which alternative forms of existence can be explored and developed in the head, not the bed.

## Conclusion

To participate in cyber relationships is to engage in what Baudrillard (1987:15) describes as private telematics, in which individuals, to extend Baudrillard's fantasy metaphor, are transported from their mundane computer system to the controls of a hypothetical reality, isolated in a position of perfect sovereignty, at an infinite distance from the original universe. There, identity is created through symbolic strategies and collective beliefs (Bordieu, cited in Wacquant, 1989:35). This allows for the recreation of experiences that serve simultaneously to challenge existing forms of interaction while also recreating online alternatives. That which cannot easily be done offline becomes more realistic online.

At root, however, we may be addressing the wrong issues. Rather than attempt to clarify the ethics of sexuality, online or off, we might better examine conventional conflicts of the meaning of such behaviors in the context of changing views of sexual power, cultural discourse, and the ways that control narratives operate. Being nice is nice, causing pain is not nice, but transgressions are not necessarily immoral, as Baudrillard (1987) observed. Perhaps the appropriate questions involve the modernist religion-based conceptions of intimacy, possession, and the quest for personal satisfaction in the context of competing obligations. None of this should be interpreted as a justification to cause others pain, but rather as an attempt to expand the lessons of cyber involvements to the broader issues of sexual control in ways that increase, not strengthen, the bonds of communication, trust, and commitment between partners in a changing postmodern society.

## References

Baudrillard, J. 1987. *The Ecstasy of Communication*. New York, NY: Semiotext(e).

CBSNEWS. 2003. The early show: Firemen divorce for 9/11 widows. December 2. http://www.cbsnews.com/stories/2003/12/02/earlyshow/living/main586338.shtml

Dibble, J. 1996. A rape in cyberspace; Or how an evil clown, a Haitian trickster spirit, two wizards, and a cast of dozens turned a database into a society. In *High noon on the electronic frontier*, P. Ludlow, ed. pp. 775–395. Cambridge, MA: MIT Press.

Dr. Phil. 2003. Relationships/Sex: "Infidelity." http://www.drphil.com/advice/advice.jhtml?contentI d=090302_relationships_internetporn.xml&section=Relationships/Sex&subsection=Infidelity

Edwards, E. 2002. E-mail courtship: The dating game with a safety net. *The Chicago Tribune.* June 20:6

Esposito, S. 1999. Tri-city couples have love-hate relationship with Internet. *Tri-City Herald.* May 8. http://www.tri-cityherald.com/news/1999/0508.html

Ferree, M. M. 2003. Resonance and radicalism: Feminist framing in the abortion debates of the United States and Germany. *American Journal of Sociology.* 109(September):302–344.

Christina, G. 1997. Are we having sex now or what? In *The philosophy of sex: Contemporary readings,* A. Soble, ed. pp. 3–8. Landham, MD: Rowman and Littlefield.

Gibson, W. 1984. *Neuromancer.* New York, NY: Ace.

Glass, S. P. 2003. *Not just friends.* New York, NY: The Free Press.

Godwin, M. 1994. ASCII is too intimate. *Wired Online* 2(April). http://www.wired.com/wired/archive/2.04/idees.fortes1.html

Harris, L. 2003. Emotional affairs: Not just sex. *Microsoft News.* http://women.msn.com/106091.armxinfidelitycheck. 2002. http://infidelitycheck.org/

Kampert, P. 2002. Virtual infidelity: In causing pain, it's the real thing. *The Chicago Tribune.* Feb 3:1

Maheu, M. M. 1999. Women's Internet behavior: Providing psychotherapy offline and online for cyber-infidelity. http://telehealth.net/articles/women_internet.html

Maheu, M. M., and R. B. Subotnik. 2001. *Infidelity on the Internet: Virtual relationships and real betrayal.* Naperville, IL: Sourcebooks.

Maines, D. R. 1993. Narrative's moment and sociology's phenomena: Toward a narrative sociology. *The Sociological Quarterly.* 34(1):17–37.

_____. 2001. *The Faultline of Consciousness: A View of Interactionism in Sociology.* New York, NY: Aldine de Gruyter.

Mileham, B. L. A. 2003. Online infidelity in Internet chat rooms: An ethnographic exploration. Unpublished doctoral dissertation, University of Florida, Gainesville.

Mill, J. S. 1863/1957. *Utilitarianism.* New York, NY: Bobbs-Merrill.

Nietzsche, F. 1889/1972. *Twilight of the idols and the anti-Christ.* Harmondsworth (Eng.): Penguin.

NUA Internet Surveys. 2002a. How many online. http://www.nua.ie/surveys/how_many_online/world.html

———. 2002b. How many online (U.S. and Canada). http://www.nua.ie/surveys/how_many_online/n_america.html

Pravda. 2002. The law: Oral sex innocent fun for all. November 15. http://english.pravda.ru/fun/2002/11/15/39571.html.

Schmitt, D. P., and D. M. Buss. 2001. Human mate poaching: Tactics and temptations for infiltrating existing mateships. *Journal of Personality and Social Psychology.* 80(6):894–917.

Schneider, J. and R. Weiss. 2001. *Cybersex exposed: Simple fantasy or obsession?* Center City, MN: Hazelden.

Scheer, Robert. 1976. Interview: Jimmie Carter. *Playboy.* 23(November):63, 64, 66, 68–71, 74, 77, 81, 86.

Schwalbe, M., S. Godwin, D. Holden, D. Schrock, S. Thompson, and M. Wolkomir. 2000. Generic processes in the reproduction of inequality: An interactionist analysis. *Social Forces.* 79(2):419–452.

Steinbeck, John. 1939/1991. *The Grapes of Wrath.* New York, NY: Penguin Books.

Stoll, C. 1995. *Silicon snake oil: Second thoughts on the information highway.* New York, NY: Doubleday.

Thomas, J. 2004 (Forthcoming). The moral ambiguity of social control in cyberspace: A Retro-assessment of the "golden age" of hacking. *New Media and Society.*

Turkel, S. 1995. *Life on the screen: Identity in the age of the Internet.* New York, NY: Simon and Schuster.

Vaughn, P. 2003. The monogamy myth: Introduction – the myth and the reality. http://dearpeggy.co m/myth.html

————. 1989. *The monogamy myth. A new understanding of affairs and how to survive them.* New York, NY: New Market Press.

Vos, Sarah C. 2003. Gay sex can't be adultery. Concord (N.H.) Online Monitor. November 8.http://www.concordmonitor.com/stories/crime/2003/0c0c26e2_2003.shtml

Wacquant, Loic J. D. 1989. Towards a reflexive sociology: A workshop with Pierre Bordieu. *Sociological Theory.* 7(Spring):26–63.

Waskul, D. 2004. Ekstasis and the Internet: Liminality and Computer-Mediated Communication. *New Media & Society.* [forthcoming]

————. 2003. *Self-games and body-play: Personhood in online chat and cybersex.* New York, NY: Peter Lang.

————. 2002. The naked self: Being a body in televideo cybersex. *Symbolic Interaction.* 25(2):199–227.

Waskul, D., M. Douglass, and C. Edgley. 2000. Cybersex: Outercourse and the enselfment of the body. *Symbolic Interaction.* 23(4):375–397.

# Part Four

# Gender, Race, and Internet Sex

Most of us rest assured that people are what they appear to be; in any encounter it only takes a few routine moments to assess key physical variables such as gender, race, ethnicity, age, and physical attractiveness. We seldom think much of it; we seldom question if people are as they appear. Certainly, everyone knows that deception is everywhere; things are not always what they seem. The appearance of age, gender, physical attractiveness—even race and ethnicity—can be temporarily or permanently altered through surgery, pharmaceuticals, cosmetics, fashion, diet, and exercise. However, these kinds of more-or-less normative tactics of appearance fraud are seldom very upsetting; the art of illusion is not the same as the deceit of the con—even though both mystify and mislead.

On the Internet people must decide what and how to communicate in a process where people, places, and things are *re*presented—*made* to exist—in an environment where they are not "there" otherwise; on the Internet every person, place, or thing is an unknown possibility lurking invisibly in an unseen background until the decisive moment when communication occurs (Waskul 2004, forthcoming). Consequently, it is not surprising that Internet environments often exaggerate the illusions and deceits of normative everyday life. As we have already learned, the Internet allows people to literally *re*present age, gender, physical attractiveness, race, ethnicity, and all other defining characteristics of personhood. Qualities of personhood are literally *re*presented in words and images that allow unprecedented power to redefine. Perhaps nowhere are these dynamics more salient than in the case of gender, race, and ethnicity.

However, as earlier readings have also illustrated, constructions of personhood on the Internet do not materialize from thin air—they are fashioned from symbolic resources of society and culture. Likewise, earlier readings have further demonstrated how these constructions also reflect upon society and culture. In Part Four we examine these same constructions and reflections in the specific contexts of gender and race. How are gender, race, and ethnicity constructed in Internet sex and what do those constructions reveal about society and culture?

In the case of gender, Naomi McCormick and John Leonard provide one of the more common accounts of Internet environments, as a communicative space where "we are free to experiment with gender and our sexualities, freed at last from our physical bodies and the sound of the human voice." McCormick and Leonard are quick to point out various ways the Internet defies the common rhetoric of gender utopia—sexism and sexual harassment are as common on the Internet as in everyday life (if not more so). Nevertheless, McCormick and Leonard are hopeful about the prospects of sexuality and gender on the Internet.

Lauren Langman's analysis of gender in Internet pornography obliterates McCormick and Leonard's optimism. However, cynicism must be tempered: McCormick and Leonard examine the Internet as a means for connectivity and personal expression; Langman examines the unsavory ways that women are portrayed as a pornographic commodity. Indeed, Langman examines something quite different from McCormick and Leonard: the marketing of gender by entrepreneurs of Internet pornography. Here, unlike either everyday life or Internet environments where people communicate directly with one another, the *re*presentations of gender come in overtly prepackaged forms—mostly images that people consume as opposed to symbolic representations that people interactively fashion. Langman's disturbing analysis of the carnival of grotesque degradation surrounding the portrayal of women in Internet pornography is more than provocative. Langman reveals a gendered hostility that has roots in society, culture, the economy, and history.

There are very few studies examining race and ethnicity in Internet sex. This is unfortunate given the obvious ways race and ethnicity intersect with erotic imagery on the Internet—especially with regard to Asians and Africans. Erica Owens's study provides a rare glimpse into the ways that race is defined and interpreted in the context of the even less examined phenomena of Internet dating services. Granted, unlike most of the readings that comprise this book, Owens explores how people use the Internet for the purposes of real-life romantic and sexual interests; Owens does not explore romantic and sexual relationships *on* the Internet. Even so, people who use the Internet in the hopes of making a real-life love-connection must *still re*present themselves in overt ways. In this case, Owens closely examines relationships between race and sexual attractiveness in Internet personal advertisements.

These readings illustrate various ways that gender, race, and ethnicity are constructed in Internet sex and what these constructions indicate about society and culture. The indications are not always clear and are sometimes conflicting. However, one thing is for certain: Internet sex conclusively reveals how the 1996 MCI advertisement—"There is no race. There is no gender. There is no age. There are no infirmities. There are only minds. Is this utopia? No, the Internet"—is patently untrue.

# Chapter Nine

# Gender and Sexuality in the Cyberspace Frontier

## Naomi McCormick and John Leonard[*]

*On the Internet, gender frequently assumes traditional sexist forms. Likewise, interactions between men and women on the Internet often become another of many examples of male dominance and female harassment. Naomi McCormick and John Leonard illustrate these realities. However, as McCormick and Leonard also point out, the Internet can also be an important tool for sexual and gender empowerment. Consequently, McCormick and Leonard suggest some tempered enthusiasm for the nature of gender and Internet sex.*

Cyberspace has been touted as the new frontier, the wave of the future ungoverned by cultural expectations and physical realm. Here…we are free to experiment with gender and our sexualities, freed at last from our physical bodies and the sound of the human voice (c.f. Lemonick, 1996; McCorduck, 1996; Stone, 1993). Or, are we so free?

Think for a moment about the gendered, heterosexualized, male-dominant discourse relayed in this example of cybersex.

> Julie told him things…she had never shared. …After a while, Tony said simply, "I want to make love to you." …Julie followed Tony's instructions. …She sat naked at the computer. …While Julie rubbed her own clitoris, it seemed to her that the pressure was coming from Tony's tongue. …[Tony wrote]: "Tell me when you want me to enter you." …[Julie answered]: …"I'm inside" [Tony replied]. …She felt totally opened up. Suddenly she had an orgasm. …(Afterwards, glancing at the terminal, she saw the words]: "Good night beautiful lady." Tony had logged off (Lewis & Lewis, 1986, pp. 32–33)

We believe that computerized interactions, while allowing for experimentation are not yet unrestrained by patriarchal culture. Discussing our own empirical research and that of others, adding the insights of science journalists, we will indicate who inhabits cyberspace and how it feels to live there. This article touches on women's negative experiences, including sexual harassment, but also suggests the feminist possibilities of the Internet. Our criticism of the "boy's

[*] McCormick, Naomi and John Leonard. 1996. "Gender and Sexuality in the Cyberspace Frontier." *Women and Therapy.* 19(4):109–119.

club" atmosphere is tempered by a description of "woman space" on the Net, the possibility of bending or dissembling gender, electronic resources for lesbians and other women, the saga of cyber-guerrilla girls who beat male chauvinist hackers at their own game, and of course, all about cybersex—from flirting to "adultery." The article ends with a description of the implications of our work for feminist activists and therapists.

## Gender Census, Gender-Roles, and Male Dominance

...Women who use computers at work are just as likely to have home computers as their male colleagues; nearly four out of ten employees who use computers at work also use them at home (Coates, 1995). However, estimates of the number of women using the Internet and commercial services like America Online, Prodigy, and CompuServe vary wildly. ...Although women are the fastest growing group of initiates to the Internet, cyberspace remains a man's world. ...Not only do white, heterosexual men outnumber other groups in cyberspace, they dominate it as well. Even preschool boys have been observed taking over school computers and video games, refusing access to girls (Kiesler, Sproull, & Eccles, 1985).

In some cases, male-dominance takes on chivalrous overtones. In our interactive investigation of a MUD (Multi-User Dungeon, role-playing game on the Internet), experienced players offered significantly more help if we presented ourselves as a female novice than if we pretended to be male. Interestingly, players offered our female character substantially more assistance than her male counterpart, even when she was depicted as physically unattractive and frowning, her messy hair suggesting that it has been a while since her last shower.

Masking gender, ethnicity, age, sexual orientation, social status, physical disability, or appearance, the textual communication of cyberspace, some argue, could eliminate sexism and prejudice—making total equality possible for the first time in history. Yet, gender role-playing persists (Cobb, 1995). After all, Net users were socialized differently. As girls, women were taught to be "nice" or submissive and pleasing. Since boyhood, in contrast, men learned to be independent, assertive, and willing to engage in conflict. Linguists claim that "Netiquette," the social rules governing interactions on the Internet, is gendered. In cyberspace, too, men talk like men, confident and confrontational, and women talk like women, seeking consensus and approval. Reflecting their subordinate status, women who go online send fewer and shorter messages than men and are more likely to be "lurkers," reading what others say rather than sharing their personal convictions.

Contributing to a "boy's club" atmosphere, computer-mediated communication is disinhibiting (Maier 1995a, 1995b; Siegal, Dubrovsky, Kiesler, & McGuire, 1986). Reduced social context and the possibility of anonymity contributes to *flaming* or outrageous discourse, with a tendency for men and boys to be flamers and women and girls to be flamees (Cobb, 1995; Shea, 1995). Computer users, compared to persons engaged in face-to-face and telephone conversations, are especially likely to communicate informally and inappropriately—swearing and voicing opinionated and extreme positions (Kiesler, 1987; VanGelder, 1996). Here are examples of hypermasculine, homohating flaming from our content analysis of undergraduates' electronic mail:

> I would rather be a fucker than a hose-head buddy! [Neal] you suck big harry dicks.
> ...Rip off your head and shit down your neck rectum scab!!! ...You are truly the
> scum of the earth. (McCormick & McCormick, 1992, pp. 389–390)

Examples of sexist, adolescent discourse from the same study follows: "Hey [Sue] Wanna Take a Shower!" "Wee Wee I want your body!!!" "Will you cum over tonight?" (p. 390).

## Sexual Harassment

Publishing in the feminist periodical *Ms.*, Aliza Sherman (1996) writes these surprising words:

> The media have portrayed cyberspace as a very menacing place for women, glee-
> fully recounting the various types of harassment. ...Women are being excluded from
> the next domain of power and information, with the familiar excuse that they need
> protection. I have been online for more than eight years, and I have not been har-
> assed once. (p. 27)

In contrast with Sherman's dismissal of women's fears, several journalists report that sexual harassment and sexualized discourse on the Net are so widespread that some women adapt gender-neutral screen names to avoid inquiries regarding their physical appearance and sexual desires (Cobb, 1995; "High-Tech Harassment," 1993; Jensen, 1995; Kantrowitz, Rosenberg, Tanner, & Hacket, 1994; Maier, 1995a, 1995b; Rigdon, 1994; Shea, 1995; Sheppard, 1995). These reports are strongly supported by our research. In a field experiment in which we presented ourselves as a female or male novice seeking assistance from more experienced players on a MUD or Internet game, only the female novice was sexually harassed. In four such instances, other players disclosed that they were giving our female character "a long passionate kiss in the mouth," were looking up her "skirt to see her well proportioned figure," and wanted to take a shower with us. An earlier observational study yielded complementary findings. About 14% of the electronic mail transmitted locally by undergraduates at one college was coded either as *crude flirtation,* e.g., "Did you know that you have a really cute ass!!!," or as including sexualized *humor and symbolic content,* e.g., "Mr. Beast, I am extremely sorry for not return addressing you, however, I have not had the time as I was busy exploring your girlfriend" (McCormick & McCormick, 1992, pp. 390–391).

## Woman Space and Lesbian Space on the Net

Prompted by sexual harassment and their exasperation with the "boys club" locker-room atmosphere of cyberspace, women and some men began establishing "woman space" on the Net in the early 1990s, assessing the likely gender of would-be subscribers via telephone voice verification. Women-oriented online services include ECHO (East Coast Hang Out) and Women on the WELL (Whole Earth 'Lectronic Link), both of which carry men subscribers but offer private conferences restricted to women, Women's WIRE, which claims that 90% of its subscribers are female, and Systers, a feminist consciousness-raising group for women employed in computer science. Of special interest to those desiring respite from cyberspace's heterosexualized discourse, there are numerous lesbian and queer studies resource sites on the Word Wide Web.

...Woman-oriented and lesbian and gay-oriented cyberspace provides valuable services. Here, women of all sexual orientations can discuss sensitive sexual and health concerns freely when their friends or therapists are unavailable for consultation. Here, too, isolated lesbian and gay teenagers and young adults can find emotional support for "coming out" (Lewis & Lewis, 1986) and mature persons can enlarge their circle of lesbian and gay friends.

## Gender Neutrality and Disguise

In cyberspace, computer users are free to choose an online name or "handle" that has no relationship to their real names or gender (Maier, 1995b; Stone, 1993). "A 43-year-old Bostonian who thought he was having a hot fling with a 23-year-old woman discovered to his dismay that *she* was an 80-year-old man in a Miami nursing home" (Toufexis, 1996, p. 53).

Their ability to disguise being female in cyberspace can help some women leave sexism behind, the content of their ideas no longer ignored by the patriarchal types who automatically tune out women's voices (Shea, 1995). For women, gender neutrality or deception reduces the possibility of sexual harassment and increases the chances of being taken seriously.

Men who mask or dissemble online gender may gain an invaluable opportunity to experience how women are treated in a male-dominant world. For example, the second author of this article had a major feminist consciousness-raising experience after he first presented himself as a woman new to the world of MUD Internet games. Prevented from taking risks which were necessary to build skills as a player because he was "a woman," his female persona was stalked by another player who followed him in virtual reality from room to room against his will. This cyber-stalking incident left him more determined than ever to work for women's rights. The possibility for a man to disguise himself as a woman does not always serve feminist interests, however. As Sandy Stone (1993) explains, female impersonation on the Net betrays women's trust that we/they are truly interacting with other women.

## Cyber Guerilla Girls

The possibilities of discovering the benefits and costs of male privilege are not limited to those women who adopt gender neutral and masculine handles or online names. According to Romero (1995), a growing minority of female hackers use their expertise as career "computer-geeks" to be assertive and aggressive in ways denied them in the "real" world, where men's greater physical strength overwhelms women's superior intellectual powers.

> I think the online world can be a boot camp for girls, [says one female hacker]. ...They're not in physical danger so they can be combative in effective ways. (Romero, 1995, p. E6)

> If someone challenges me, I can do anything, [says another female hacker]. ...For example, there's someone who's begging for trouble. He's harassing people, saying...[we women] aren't real hackers. I have his full name, his Social Security number, his bank account, his real address. ...I can't refuse a dare. (Romero, 1995, p. E6)

The underground and occasionally criminal world of hackers is hardly the best place for most women to celebrate their potential power in virtual reality. Still, we confess to being somewhat exhilarated by learning of the exploits of women like Tankgirl who gets even with on-line "dip-s" who persist in asking her out on dates despite her repeated refusals by "flood[ing] the living daylights out of their system and filling their in-boxes" with unwanted email (Romero, 1995, p. E6).

## Flirting and Cybersex

Chat forums, especially those which give commercial Internet users an opportunity to flirt and talk about sex, are extremely popular (Maier, 1995a; 1995b). Lewis and Lewis (1986) suggest that electronic sexual encounters are appealing for three reasons. First, anyone and everyone can present themselves as sexy on the computer, regardless of age, disability, or physical appearance. Second, people may feel freer to express unusual sexual feelings and fantasies on the computer than in "real life," where they fear others would reject them. Third, computer romance knows no physical, boundaries. Text-driven electronic love affairs can intensify rapidly; the lack of actual physical contacts soothes anxieties about sexual performance, and the electronic lover's seemingly telepathic communication skills create an illusion of instant and complete accessibility.

Electronic love affairs, however beguiling, are not free of problems. Like romances outside of cyberspace, they may sour or be "discovered" by jealous mates. In 1993, two women who used an electronic bulletin board to comfort one another after being rejected, learned that they had simultaneously been involved with and jilted by the same cyber lover (Gregory & Cole, 1993; Schwartz, 1993). Eventually, the women exposed the "cyber scam-artist" publicly to other computer list members who put him on trial for his alleged misbehavior. Admitting that he "didn't think the same concerns about fidelity [that were expected of]...physical relationships applied here in cyberspace," the man, whose privacy had been violated, felt pressured into resigning from his electronic discussion group (Gregory & Cole, 1993). More recently, a New Jersey man sued his wife for divorce after she had a steamy onscreen affair with "The Weasel," a married man from North Carolina who provided her with cybersex but no actual physical contact (Toufexis, 1996; "The Wired and the Restless," 1996).

Unlike commercially purchased erotica, cyber-romance requires another human being, whose words—sincere or not—move the individual sexually and emotionally. In addition, computer-mediated communication provides "real life" lovers with an opportunity to meet the person of their dreams physically or work on improving an existing romantic relationship. To illustrate, here are some examples of actual romantic discourse, complete with typographical errors, from our study of undergraduates' electronic mail.

Hi there, Pretty Lady, I realize that we don't know each other, but how does dinner and a movies sound to remedy that situation? ...You probably think this is a joke, but I really would It. Thine evermore. (example of *refined flirtation* from McCormick & McCormick, 1992, p. 395)

I just wanted to say I had a great weekend and I Love YOu very Very Much. I can't wait to see you again. ...I'm sorry for all the problems we've had and I hope they never come back. LEt's make every weekend like the last one O.K.! (example of a *work on relationship and love message* from McCormick & McCormick, 1992, p. 396)

Obviously, cybersex does not expose lovers to physical harm, unwanted pregnancy, or sexually transmitted disease. But true, too, it cannot protect them from emotional pain. Cybersex enables the timid to take sexual risks and eliminates anxieties about physical appearance. Cybersex, like the love letters of old, enables individuals to present themselves carefully, choosing just the words and phrasing they think will have the greatest impact. This advantage is not cost-free. For those who first meet and fall in love online, an actual physical encounter may be disillusioning. The mental magic of cyber-intimacy, where so many positive characteristics can be projected onto the beloved, cannot readily be recaptured in "real time" in the "real" world.

### Implications for Feminist Therapists and Activists

Women who have been sexually harassed or subjected to the "boy's club," locker room atmosphere of much online discourse may feel discouraged by cyberspace. Yet, it would be a shame for women to avoid a place so rich in resources. "The online world is brimming over with information to satisfy any curiosity or interest" (Sherman, 1996, p. 27). If navigated with care, the information highway gives women quick access to resources that would once have required years of research to find.

The Internet is a[n] excellent place for feminist therapists and scholars to touch base with one another and be more accessible to clients in crisis. It is also an ideal site for feminist and lesbian activism. Computer-mediated communication is especially beneficial to women who are physically disabled. Online, chronically ill and disabled women can support one another, learn more about self-care and health, work together for improved services and legislation, and enjoy intimacy and good company without ever needing to leave their homes.

In the world of cyberspace, no one can judge us solely by our physical appearance, gender, age, ethnicity, or health status. Here, too, women can explore what it might feel like to try new ways of interacting, assume desired interpersonal risks, and even experience what it is like to shed the traditional female role by passing ourselves off as gender neutral or male. Eventually, this experimentation may inspire new and more assertive strategies for handling "real" problems and situations.

The cyberspace community can be a support group for women between therapy sessions or when friends are unavailable. It may also be a place to check out information about sex or share fantasies with someone else. For women exploring their sexuality, cyberspace can be a place to experiment with and create fresh and better ways of being intimate and finding pleasure without the risk of disease, pregnancy, or physical harm. It also may be a healing space within which to discuss prior experiences with sexual coercion and abuse with sisters or seek advice on handling a current romantic relationship or problem.

Cyberspace provides lesbians and bisexual women with innumerable opportunities to network and meet potential partners and friends. These opportunities will be especially prized by young people who are first coming to terms with their sexual orientation and by rural and suburban individuals who live at considerable distance from urban lesbian and gay communities. Last but not least, cyberspace provides opportunities for feminist therapists to take a walk on the wild side, meeting and conversing with a variety of persons who can enrich our understanding of women's sexual desires and potential.

## References

Coates, J. 1995. "Sea change: Cyberspace No Longer a Guy Space." *Chicago Tribune*. February 12, Section 7:p. 5.

Cobb, N. 1995. "Gender Wars in Cyberspace!" *Boston Globe*. March 8, pp. 29, 32.

Gregory, S., and Cole, W. 1993. Heartbreak in cyberspace. *Time*. July 18:142, 53.

High-Tech Harassment. 1993. *Futurist*. 27 (November–December):5

Jensen, K. 1995. "A Woman's Place? In Cyberspace!" *Atlanta Journal Constitution*. January 8:G 1–G2.

Kantrowitz, B., Rosenberg, D., Tannen, D., and Hackett, G. 1994. "Men, Women, and Computers." *Newsweek*. May 16:48–55.

Kiesler, S. B. 1987. "Social Aspects of Computer Environments." *Social Science*. 72(1):23–28.

Kiesler, S., Sproull, L., and Eccles, J. S. 1985. "Pool Halls, Chips, and Wargames: Women in the Culture of Computing." *Psychology of Women Quarterly*. 9:451–462.

Lemonick, M.D. 1996. "The Net's Strange Days." *Time*. February 19:47, 55.

Lewis, H. R., & Lewis, M. E. 1986. *The Electronic Confessional: A Sex Book of the 80s*. New York, NY: M. Evans and Company, Inc.

Maier, F. 1995a. "Cyberspace: Where the Women Aren't." *San Francisco Chronicle.* February 19:B5–B6.

———. 1995b. "Woman.Not@CyberWorld: In the Computer Age, Guess Who Isn't On-line?" *Washington Post.* April 16:C1, C3.

McCorduck, P. 1996. "Sex, Lies, and Avatars: Sherry Turkle Knows What Role-Playing in Cyberspace Really Means." *Wired.* 4 (4):106–110, 158–165.

McCormick, N. B., and McCormick, J. W. 1992. "Computer Friends and Foes: Content of Undergraduates' Electronic Mail." *Computers in Human Behavior.* 8(3):1–27.

Rigdon, J. 1994. "Now Women in Cyberspace Can Be Themselves." *Wall Street Journal.* March 18:223, pp. B1, B5.

Romero, D. 1995. "A New Force Lurks Amid the Cyber Shadows." *Los Angeles Times.* December 1:pp. E1, E6.

Schwartz, J. 1993. "On-line Lothario's Antics Prompt Debate on Cyberage Ethics." *The Washington Post.* July 11:pp. A1, A8.

Shea, V. 1995. "Not Afraid to Flame." *Computerworld.* August 21 (29):81–82.

Sheppard, N. 1995. "Women Teaming Verbal Thugs Travel Internet." *Chicago Tribune,* February 8:pp. 1, 14.

Sherman, A. 1996. "Claiming Cyberspace: Five Myths That Are Keeping Women Offline." *Ms.* July–August (6):26–28.

Siegel, J., V. Dubrovsky, S. Kiesler, and T. McGuire. 1986. "Group Processes in Computer-Mediated Communication." *Organizational Behavior and Human Decision Processes.* 37:157–187.

Stone, A.R. 1993. *Violation and Virtuality: Two Cases of Physical and Psychological Boundary Transgression and their Implications.* Available on the World Wide Web URL: http//www.en.utexas.edu/~slatin/opera. At website, see Sandy Stone's home page.

"The Wired and the Restless." 1996. *Time.* February 12(147): 24.

Toufexis, A. 1996. "Romancing the Computer." *Time.* February 19 (147): 53.

Van Gelder, L. 1996. "Virtual Sisterhood." *CompuServe Magazine.* February (15):30–33.

# Chapter Ten

# Grotesque Degradation: Globalization, Carnivalization, and Cyberporn

## Lauren Langman

*Portrayals of women in Internet pornography are often less than flattering. In fact, Internet pornography is sometimes downright grotesque. Lauren Langman examines the tendency to carnivalize the grotesque in Internet pornography and entertains social and cultural implications of these extreme expressions. How are we to understand these unsavory and sometimes hostile expressions? Langman provides clues.*

Depictions of the human body in general, and sexuality in particular, long preceded modern civilization. Early carvings, pottery, statuary, paintings, and even architectural ornaments of antiquity have long celebrated the human body and sexuality. So too has sexuality been a common, if not universal, topic of folk tales, jokes, music, poetry, literature, and, with the advent of philosophy, speculative thought. Plato reserved leadership for older men, freed of sexual passions—and then came Viagra. In some societies, the sexual, the passionate, and the Dionysian were extolled—as, for example, in temple prostitution; a clever means of ensuring folks came to church. In Apollonian societies, desire in general and sexuality in particular was repressed in the name of harmony and order, typically as a means of suppression by which the elites maintained control over the disciplined bodies of the masses (still practiced in societies where premarital and extra-marital sex is punishable by death[1]).

Yet, as Durkheim (1893) would suggest, even in a society of saints there must be sinners to uphold the norms; the very existence of norms creates pressures toward deviance. In addition, most societies necessarily sustain as least some measure of liminality—in-between zones where experiences of inversion, transgression, and resistance are tolerated if not celebrated (Turner 1969). It is, perhaps, for all these reasons (among others) that portrayals of the body and sexuality—especially as challenge and resistance to dominant norms—have long been points where policed boundaries of acceptability have faced contestation, resistance, and transgression. It is precisely at these liminal spaces of transgression that one finds moral and political debates over what is "beautiful" and "acceptable," what is "grotesque" and "obscene," what "should" be encouraged and what "must" be controlled (if not eliminated). In one case we can talk about erotica as an art form for museums and galleries and wax eloquent; conversely, we can label those same depictions as immoral, pornographic, vile, vulgar, disgusting and mobilize efforts to erase such smut from society. Needless to say, repressive efforts have proven largely ineffective and, indeed, the force of repression often intensifies the very deviance it seeks to suppress. For example, nineteenth-century Victorianism witnessed flourishing bordellos and pornography. Meanwhile, Freud (1989 [1917]) taught us how repression might manifest in symptoms, dreams, fantasies, or combinations thereof.

Two points are evident from the examples above. First, as genres of cultural expression, depictions of people engaged in sexual acts (whether we call it "erotica," "pornography," or both) have always been articulated through specific forms of media. Secondly, like any other forms of cultural expression, meaning and interpretation is historically situated. Even so, as a long tradition of media/culture studies has argued, the *form* of the media—oral, scribal, print, radio, television, and now Internet—has consequences *independent* of its content (McLuhan 1964). Thus, in this essay I intend to explore cyberporn as an Internet-dependent media and interrogate the impacts of globalization on computer-mediated communication in relation to pornography.

It is well known that pornography is one of the most profitable aspects of e-commerce, with estimates of over 80,000 adult websites. Collectively, adult e-commerce reveals a predictable range and diversity. Many adult sites are small and relatively low profile. Some are extremely large and highly publicized—such as the well-known Danni's Hard Drive, or the much larger Cybererotica (by any standard, *the* pioneer of the Internet porn industry). Other sites claim to offer bonafide amateurs who live in webcam-wired apartments, dorm rooms, homes, and just about anywhere else a voyeur would pay to peep. Many, perhaps most, representations and acts found in cyberporn are hardly new. What makes cyberporn different is less the content than the access, affordability, and anonymity, which allows many otherwise "respectable" citizens opportunities to easily and cheaply gaze on the transgressive (Cooper 1998). The use of the Internet, with its endless range of seemingly enormous choice, gives the viewer a vast spectrum of artistic, commercial, and intellectual sites—all with apparent varieties of cyberporn abundance. Thus, the Internet itself provides a realm of audio-visual pleasures granting seeming empowerment and choice (Williams 1989).

In the short space of a single paper, one can say little about the wide gamut of pornography in general, or about cyberporn in particular. Rather, I will attempt to suggest that the rise of cyberporn has been associated with the growing popularity of a particular genre that can be termed "grotesque degradation." This degradation is *not* simply a variant of traditional bondage-domination (B/D) or sado-masochism (S/M). However "deviant," transgressive or inverted, BDSM practices reveal truths about sexuality, suggest a relationship, and mutual pleasure, in that the masochist may well find pleasure in submission. Rather, "grotesque degradation" will be seen as moment of global capital, whose "truths" are embedded in one of the major cultural trends of our age, what can be called the "carnivalization of society."

## Reading Cyberporn

Scholarly interest in cyberporn is scant at best, a surprising fact considering its apparent widespread popularity. But the highly charged nature of sex in general, and the marginal status of pornography—complete with unflattering stereotyped images of men in black (as in raincoats) masturbating in seedy theaters—deters many from serious consideration of cyberporn as genre of cultural expression. To the social critic, however, the huge market for the many kinds of cyberporn is evident and, accordingly, there is an equally evident multiplicity of interpretations by a variety of academics, moral critics, and the aficionados themselves. Most of the viewers are male, but increasingly couples enjoy watching others copulate, sodomize, or whatever. Of course the most typical depictions are heterosexual, but there is an increasingly wide range of combinations, situations, body textures, and particular acts available for consumption in the marketplace of Internet pornography. Thus one might choose to find racialized Others engaged in typical oral, genital, or anal penetrations. Or, perhaps, differentiations by particular age groups, young women—including implications of virginity (as some sites claim conspicuous words like, "tight virgin pussy getting fucked")—or, maybe, "more experienced," often-horny women ("neglected housewives looking for cock"), even older "grannies" that have not, apparently, lost their zest for sex. These men and women vary by specific physical attributes—often breast and penis size, ranging from tiny to enormous. Equally varied is overall body shape—ranging, once again, from tiny to enormous. There is also a predictable range of choices in sexual combinations, practices, and fetishes: men with men, women with women, men with women, men alone, women alone, ménages à trois, group sex, multiple penetrations, fetish wear, S/M, B/D, sex toys, vegetable insertions, animal sex, and so on.

There are numerous proposed ways to understand the plethora of cyberporn, ranging from moralists convictions that would condemn the exposure of a bare breast to the libertarians who celebrate unfettered free speech and artistic expressions that challenge the boundaries of acceptability. Perhaps the most fundamental scholarly critique of cyberporn is the classical feminist view of pornography as patriarchal (if not misogynist) representations of women that degrade, objectify, and render women complacent (if not submissive) objects of male lust that are reified by the male "gaze." Moreover, it is often argued, from this point of view, that pornography encourages rape and denigration of women. These kinds of feminist-inspired antipornography arguments have received ample criticism. For example, the moralism of Dworkin (1974) and Mackinnon (1987) was countered by Paglia (1990). In contrast, Paglia argued that pornography, exotic dancing, and prostitution are sites of female empowerment; they are sites of feminine agenic guardianship of the realms of sexual secrets. Paglia's views notwithstanding, *both* moralistic positions are dependent on essentialist notions of women, sexuality, and desire. As will be argued, given the vast ranges of genres of cyberporn, there is no one reading. Yes, some of pornography (on the Internet or elsewhere) aims to degrade but, at the same time, it can celebrate the erotic, challenge dominant and often repressive sexual codes, and even reveal truths of the larger society. Indeed, as will be seen, I am not suggesting *all* porn is degrading. Finally, as I will also argue, the unconscious gratifications of viewing simulated degradation can stabilize the conscious life of some males.

Following Kipnis (1999), Williams (1989), and Lillie (2002), I suggest that pornography in general, and cyberporn in particular, can be understood as cultural *productions* and *discourses* that both *construct* and *interpret* sexuality—they are discourses about sexuality that interrogate cultural understandings. Thus, cyberporn can be read (or decoded) as cultural texts concerning sexuality, but, even more, by deconstructing the processes of coding and decoding, we can illuminate society as a whole and the nature of cultural constructions of gender identity. Thus, various traditions of literary, cultural, and film critique, rooted in Sade (1987), Freud (1930), Foucault (1978), and others may reveal more about the cultural meanings of cyberporn than debates that concern issues of morality.

As a sociologist, I would suggest that cultural forms, from pottery to pornography, cannot be understood apart from historically specific social context. Within this framework, I also suggest we must start with the nature of the economic system—both how it produces goods and services and the distributions of wealth. From this point of view, there are at least three dominant trends that contextualize our present age: globalization, feminism, and the carnivalization of culture.

Globalization, the economic reality of the present age, can be understood as the emergence of an integrated world market that is dominated by deterritorialized economic actors and transnational corporations that are decoupled from nation states. Globalized economic enterprises employ the most advanced technologies of design and production, which has radically altered the nature of work, politics, and culture. More specifically, when anything can be made and shipped anywhere in the world, often by automation, there has been a massive restructuring of work in which traditionally well-paid manufacturing jobs have declined and lower-paying service jobs have proliferated. Moreover, with the global restructuring of work and technological change, we often see many of the more educated and heretofore privileged workers face problematic futures. Thus, globalization has fostered a growing inequality in the distribution of wealth and income alongside growing insecurities about economic prospects. As will be argued, one of the most salient aspects of these new economic realities has been the erosion of job security and expectations of a stable, linear career. Marx's (1972) discussion of the alienation of workers understood powerlessness, dehumanization, and meaninglessness. And, as will be argued, cyberporn, like religion, can be both a wail of genuine suffering and a palliative—an opiate—for some of the people.

One of the most significant changes of the past few decades has been the rise of feminism and, in turn, the massive entry of women into the paid labor force—especially in the higher echelons. Today, women comprise almost half of the students in law, medicine, architecture, and graduate programs in arts and sciences. Feminism has challenged traditional gender roles and norms that present men as the breadwinner, authority figure, and a crass character who prefers violent games and submissive women. While glass ceilings still exist, they are slowly but surely being shattered; income disparities are waning, cultural definitions are shifting, and women are gaining ever more political office.

Along with newly found economic and political power, women have become more independent in a wide range of activities—from buying homes and cars to taking increasing control over their bodies and sexuality. But these changes in women's roles, seemingly through usurpation of male prerogatives, have also fostered (or at least encouraged) changes in male behavior. Traditional male assertiveness and independence is no longer as functional as it once was. One might also note the important role of Hugh Hefner and *Playboy* in challenging definitions of masculinity, femininity, and sexual morality. As Bordo (1993) has suggested, Hefner was as much a part of the sex and gender revolutions as was Betty Friedan's (1964) *The Feminine Mystique*. While some feminists claimed Hefner objectified sexuality and constructed women as passive, compliant dispensers of sexual favors, Gloria Steinem (1963) noted that the Playmate was not a "fallen woman" or "evil temptress," but the "girl next door." And,

Helen Gurley Brown (1962) announced it was OK for "nice girls" to be sexual and enjoy it without shame or guilt. Thus, for both men and women, traditional sexual norms and moral values were interrogated. The early groundwork for normalizing female sexuality would pave the way for female agency in a number of realms, not the least of which include higher education and work.

Today, many men face increasing conflicts between traditional notions of male dominance and privilege and differing norms and expectations in school and on the job. Thus, we can see, beside the economic factors noted above, there are also growing feminist challenges to traditional masculine power and identities that have led to an increasing degree of uncertainty and anxiety over what constitutes "manhood" in an era when men's bathrooms increasingly come equipped with infant changing tables.

Faced with what many men see as challenges to their traditional male gender roles—powerful, agentic, and deserving of deference—there have been numerous responses, including the embrace of conservative religions with essentialist notions of gender that enshrine and sacralize male power. Various moments of popular culture encourage, at least in the imaginary, portrayals of "real men" as assertive individuals who "do what real men gotta do" to salvage masculinity. This might include rather chauvinist and misogynist forms of popular culture such as the celebratory *Man Show*, Howard Stern's *Locker Room,* or, as will be illustrated, escapes to the erotic imaginaries of cyberporn where real men are studs with large and powerful genitalia, and women are "sluts," "whores," and "cunts" whose primary role is subordinated sexual service—and masculinity is never interrogated.[2]

Informed by psychoanalytic film theorists such as Mulvey (1989), I will suggest that economic insecurity on the one hand, and more assertive women on the other, has aroused both castration anxiety and assaults to male narcissism that certain forms of pornography assuage by reinscribing an active assertive male vis-à-vis the passive, compliant, and, most of all, subordinated females. Seeing a naked vagina (but a mouth or anus will do), providing a direct or scopophilic gratification, affirms that the male has the penis and the power and she, the castrated one, is powerless. But further, in what will be called "grotesque degradation," she is not only constructed as inferior, but is systematically degraded and punished for having challenged the power of the penis. Like a dream, such desires are fulfilled in the imaginary, and they stabilize the quotidian. Much like symbolic violence reduces actual violence, certain pornographic imagery makes actual life easier—it is a "time out" that usurps actual sexuality. But as will be argued, "grotesque degradation" is also a central moment of commodified pleasures of the transgressive carnivals provided by the contemporary "culture industries."

## Carnivalization

The carnivalization of society, one of the major cultural trends of our age, has been a development in which culture industries have revived the medieval carnival and transformed it into a commodity. More specifically, we have seen a variety of emergent subcultures and mass mediated entertainment genres (from shock-jocks to shock-rock to professional wrestling) that each, in their own way, valorize the grotesque and celebrate transgression. While also, for example, goth, punk, or extreme body modification subcultures may well appear grotesque, various patterns of sexuality, drug use, or fashions express resistance against the dominant values and standards of the society. As a result of carnivalization, with transgression as a form of resistance, the moral center of society has shifted downward to embrace what is vile, vulgar, and disgusting—currently, a highly profitable sector of global capital. Thus, moral distance between what is acceptable and what is pornographic has narrowed, and cyberporn can be considered a moment of this carnivalization.

For Bakhtin (1968), the medieval carnival was a popular celebration that stood in opposition to the official feasts and tournaments that celebrated and secured the power of the aristocratic elites.[3] Carnival was a lucid critique of the elites, their culture, lifestyle, and values. Typical patterns of hierarchy, deference, and demeanor were ignored (Bakhtin 1968). The carnival was a liminal site of transgression that included reversals of the quotidian and inversions of the dominant norms and standards of propriety. Restraints of everyday life waned; all forms of the prohibited were valorized. Moral boundaries of "decency" from the political to the erotic were transgressed—especially those that concern the body, bodily indulgence, orifices, excreta, the profane, the vulgar, and the obscene. Carnivals expressed the Dionysian that Nietzsche claimed was suppressed by restrictive Apollonian domination. Celebrations often involved bodily excreta and secreta; much of the critique of elite power took scatological forms.

The carnival, as a site of resistance apart from everyday life and subservience to the elite landowners and clergy, celebrated the disgusting and grotesque. Transgression, as resistance to elite power, rejected dominant authority and its morals. Typical practices included parody, mockery, satire, humiliation, and hectoring of kings and queens, priests, and bishops. Above all, laughter stood as a rebuke to the elites. But, however transgressive the carnival may have been—whatever hope and freedom it provided as a form of cultural resistance in lieu of political action—the carnival served to sustain the structural arrangements in which land owning dynasties were legitimated by the clerical elites. Similarly, a central moment of contemporary mass culture has been the resurrection of the carnival. The "culture industries" have packaged the grotesque and commodified the transgressive to secure huge profits and at the same time, insure the reproduction of the system.

## The Grotesque

The grotesque stood in direct opposition to medieval forms of high art and literature. It was a realm of freedom that spoke truths of the system. The grotesque stood as critiques of the dominant order—often embodied in masks or representations of faces with greatly exaggerated and distorted features and shapes such as bulging eyes and/or protruding nose. These forms of resistance repudiated elite domination, norms, values, and practices. For Bakhtin (1968), one of the most important aspects of "grotesque realism" is its function of degradation: bringing something or someone down to earth to create something better. As Bakhtin (1968:21) explains:

> To degrade is to bury, to sow, and to kill simultaneously, in order to bring forth something more and better. To degrade also means to concern oneself with the lower stratum of the body, the life of the belly and the reproductive organs; it therefore relates to acts of defecation and copulation, conception, pregnancy, and birth. Degradation digs a bodily grave for a new birth; it has not only a destructive, negative aspect, but also a regenerating one. To degrade an object does not imply merely hurling it into the void of nonexistence, into absolute destruction, but to hurl it down to the reproductive lower stratum, the zone in which conception and a new birth take place. Grotesque realism knows no other lower level; it is the fruitful earth and the womb. It is always conceiving.

The grotesque—that which was vile, vulgar, and disgusting—stood as a challenge to the dominant social order and a critique of its lifestyles and values. The grotesque stood as an inversion, a reversal that revealed truths about the elite class and their system. "Grotesque degradation" not only reveals truths about sexuality, but stands as a critique of global capital that produces alienation in a manner that denies agency and dignity. As will be argued, "grotesque degradation," as a genre of cyberporn, serves similar compensatory functions. The reduction of the person to a naked sexual being defined by his or her genitalia fosters a migration of subjectivity from political economy and the problematic nature of work to an erotic imaginary wherein "grotesque degradation" provides highly pleasurable gratifications absent from other arenas of social life.

## Cyberporn, the Carnivalesque, and Degradation

For Freud (1915), the "vicissitudes of instincts" means desire can be articulated in "disguised" ways; it could assume other symbolic forms of expression. Sexual desire might, therefore, take nonsexual forms such as slips of the tongue, dream symbols, or pathological symptoms. Repression could cloak desire within sublimated forms of aesthetic production. At the same time, the plasticity of desire was such that sexuality itself might serve other functions such as power, domination, narcissism, self-abasement, and so on. Thus, certain genres of pornography that I would label "grotesque degradation" can serve similar compensatory functions—providing encapsulated realms for securing particular forms of traditional masculine identities and/or easing transitions to new forms of masculine identity in the face of economic factors and the expansion of feminism. The transgressive eroticism of "grotesque degradation" is much like Freud's (1912) observations on "psychic impotence," where [male] sexual potency requires "debasement in the act of love." Freud's analysis was based on the difficulty of fusing affection and respect (of the idealized object) with lust and passionate sexuality—as it was only with a "debased" sex object, either the whore or his denigration of his partner, that the man could overcome psychic impotence and find complete satisfaction. While Freud's theory is grounded in Oedipal dynamics, in a very similar way, if the conditions of political economy render the man occupationally impotent and his agency attenuated, then transgressive sexuality with a debased Other—a "slut," "whore," "bitch," or "cunt"—restores his "potency." In this way, venues such as cyberporn render erotic satisfactions through affirmations of agency that potentially degrade the Other. Indeed, Linda Williams (1989:163) argues:

> that contemporary pornography offers compensatory fantasies designed to make up in the domain of sexuality the power that is denied men in their work and political lives. ...the contemporary increase in pornographic consumption can be accounted for by male loss of power in the wake of feminism and women's new unwillingness to accommodate their pleasures to those of men.

Williams (1989:154–5) further suggests that pornography can be seen as a sign of men giving up the struggle for real economic and/or erotic power and, instead, finding symbolic alternatives in an erotic imaginary.

> In cinematic hard core we encounter a profoundly "escapist" genre that distracts audiences from the deeper social or political causes of the disturbed relations between the sexes; and yet paradoxically, if it is to distract effectively, a popular genre must address some of the real experiences and needs of its audience.

More specifically, I am arguing that the growth of "grotesque degradation"—of cyberporn as a central moment of the carnivalization of society—reveals a fundamental truth of advanced capital. It both disempowers and humiliates many men who are long accustomed to the rewards of patriarchy. At the same time, it reveals how the "erotic culture industries" provide various genres of cyberporn that would symbolically assuage pain and humiliation through the degradation, disempowerment, and dehumanization of someone even lower in the social hierarchy. Indeed the "sluts," "whores," and "cunts" are not even located in those hierarchies. Cyberspace potentially offers commodified sexual utopias, dream worlds of erotic gratification for those who may live in real worlds of deprivation and insecurity. Nevertheless, these commodified gratifications and ersatz identities move discontent from the political economy to the cultural, where discontent is neutralized and hegemony is secured—reproducing the conditions of its own genesis.

In face of macroeconomic changes due to globalization—that directly impinge on work roles, economic security, and the transformations of everyday life in which changing gender norms and expectations have challenged traditional notions of masculinity—"grotesque degradation" provides fantasy realms of hypermasculinity in which women are not simply objects of male lust, but are systematically degraded in retaliation for their assertiveness.[4] Identities are not simply self-referential narratives or scripts of subjectivity, but deeply held essential moments of self. Therefore, challenges to identity foster a great deal of stress, strain, and intense emotions—from fear to anxiety. More specifically, assaults to identities that can be regarded as shameful and/or humiliating, yet denied or unacknowledged, can dispose anger and rage (Scheff 1994). This anger can be neutralized through expressions of fantasy, and thus, "grotesque degradation" provides fantastic realms of empowered male identities who find agency in aggressive degradation and humiliation of the female Other. In the medieval carnivals, the elites were the objects of parody and degradation. Today, however, the "culture industries" insure that degradation is transmitted downward for those men rendered insecure by global capital, ashamed of their economic fragility, and humiliated by the challenges of new forms of gender identities and relationships.

In classical studies of authoritarianism, those who were subject to authority from above demanded deference and respect from those below. Degradation is psychologically similar; those who feel degraded, indeed "screwed," may find recompense in controlling, degrading, and "screwing" someone beneath them—someone weak and powerless. Who better to fill that role than a woman? Or, at least, the compliant woman who seeks, enjoys, and "deserves" her degradation for usurping the power of the male. The castrating "bitch" gets what she deserves. As we shall see, her comeuppance is a mouthful of cum, giant cock in her ass, urine or feces on her body, or invasions of her privacy. Notwithstanding the commodification of transgression in general and the mass marketing of cyberporn, for the typically male viewer there is an interweaving of "pleasure, desire, and [compensatory] identity produced through relations of power and mechanisms of this technology of sexuality" (Lillie 2002: 8). In other words, the production of cyberporn can be seen as the means by which a technology of power—the computer and Internet—creates discourses that discipline the erotic body. Meanwhile, the identity of viewer, constructed through his (and it is mostly his) gaze, reaps pleasure in viewing the erotic body, which becomes integrated into a number of fantasies and fantasized gratifications that are less erotic, per se, but provide alternative realms of dignity, respect, and agency (see Sennett and Cobb 1972, 2003).

For example, consider the readership of *Hustler* compared to *Playboy*. *Hustler* readers are more likely blue-collar, while *Playboy* readers are more upwardly mobile, and upper middle class. Surely, male blue-collar workers have perceived their economic insecurities due to "women taking their jobs"—when, in fact, the jobs have been exported or automated. Now, even educated and affluent workers face economic insecurities and, while more open to feminism, at the same time they too face the ambiguities of gender norms. In both cases, for some people, certain kinds of cyberporn not only put women in their place, but "fuck them hard"—which secures and repairs, in fantasy, eroding concepts of masculinity (much the same can be said about audiences of Howard Stern or Rush Limbaugh; no matter how different in ideology, they share a common misogynist stance).

Fundamentalism is a common means of preserving "traditional" identities in the face of rapidly changing social and economic realities of the present age—especially fundamentalist forms that celebrate the biologically based essentialisms of male power and instrumentality as opposed to female submission and affectivity. Thus, ironically, the same social factors that can sometimes lead to radically conservative religious fundamentalism, can also lead to the consumption of the "grotesque degradation" of cyberporn.

Psychoanalytic theory—noting the central role of sexual desire, as well as the repression that attempts to keep it in check—charted the many ways the ego defended itself against impulses, the demands of reality, and a demanding superego. At the same time, the impulses often took disguised forms to "sneak" past the ego and find gratification. Among these defenses were projection and disavowal: the capacity to deny that one has a particular desire and, at the same time, find gratification of that desire by identifying with another person who does gain that gratification. This insight has been central to psychoanalytic film theory. People flock to cinema, watch television, and/or log on to the Internet to find symbolic gratifications through viewing another. Love for the lonely, power for the powerless, adventure for the bored, aggression for the meek, and recognition for the ignored—all can be found on one screen or another. (This is not to ignore the unique aspects of the Internet, not the least of which are the vast ranges of choice, the anonymity, and seeming empowerment.)

Thus, visual media provide unique fascinations. "Part of the fascination then, comes from the fact that while it allows for the temporary loss of ego (the spectator becomes someone else) it simultaneously reinforces the ego. In a sense, the film viewer both loses him/herself and refinds him/herself—over and over—by continually reenacting the first fictive moment of identification and establishment of identity" (Flitterman-Lewis 1992:214). Therefore, insofar as the fantastic realms of cyberporn exist as encapsulated worlds of erotic imaginary that realize aspects of selfhood—real or imagined—"we are what we view." We might well enjoy the carnivalesque, especially "grotesque degradation," in ways that stabilize and "repair" the self. Much like a joke that allows an aggressive or erotic impulse gratification in symbolic form, viewing cyberporn allows the construction of a moment of selfhood, through identification with the representations, where the unpleasant or otherwise denied could be both acknowledged and repudiated. As such, cyberporn, like much of popular culture, allows one means for displacement of anger and resentment toward global capital and its neutralization. Similarly, insofar as women today may be seen as threatening male identities and/or demanding new patterns of interaction, their "grotesque degradation" in cyberporn serves to enable a splitting of the ambivalence and so neutralize resentment. The ephemeral self that is constructed in cyberporn—momentary, episodic, and encapsulated articulations—serves to sustain other, more typical, normative, and much more public expressions of self.

Based on the previous arguments, I will briefly analyze five basic ideal typical expressions of carnivalized cyberporn—each represent expressions of "grotesque degradation" in which a wounded male identity can find imaginary repair and solace in the erotic imaginaries that stand apart from the realities and insecurities of a global economy with its many assaults on dignity and respect. These basic ideal typical expressions include, but are not limited to, "cum guzzling sluts," "painful anal," "giant cocks," "shit on me," and the "intrusive gaze."

## "Cum Guzzling Sluts"

Various sites that feature "cum guzzling sluts" are among the most obvious examples of "grotesque degradation" in cyberporn. The visible expression of the man's pleasure—his ejaculation, "the money shot"—has become a central moment of modern pornography (Williams 1989). And, as previously noted, the excreta and secreta of the body—especially the lower body—was also a central moment of the medieval carnival. As a basic form of "grotesque degradation" in cyberporn, portrayals of "cum guzzling sluts" are not much different. The basic theme of the "cum guzzler" is that she swallows the male ejaculate (either directly, or from a glass that may well be overflowing from the contributions of many men). In one variation, a Japanese practice called *bukkake*, a large number of men ejaculate upon the woman's naked body. In another variation, the man (often many men) ejaculates on the woman's face (what is called a "facial") or on her neck/breasts (called a "pearl necklace").

This is not the place for an extensive examination of oral sex practices between lovers. Oral sex tends to be a matter of personal taste. Certainly, oral sex is a common practice. Furthermore, whether or not the fellator swallows depends on the quality of the relationship (among other things), the meaning of swallowing (acceptance of the other, more polite than spitting, etc), and the extent to which the fellator accepts/enjoys the taste of semen. However, in the cyberpornotopias of "grotesque degradation," with total anonymity of participants, there is no relationship; she is degraded, disempowered, and dehumanized—much as Marx described the alienation of the wage laborer.

Most often, the male ejaculates as a result of his masturbation—though there may have been intercourse or fellatio prior to his orgasm. Either way, her very selfhood is erased as her face (or any other portion of her body) is covered with his "manhood." Her body is a receptacle for ejaculate. The whole of the woman's identity is equated with what is between her legs. At best, she is a vagina, and only a vagina. At worst, she is little more than a towel or Kleenex. Her only function is to bring him to orgasm through her degradation. Moreover, not only does she bear first hand witness to his ecstatic pleasure, she receives in return only his taste or stain.

### Painful Anal

Anal sex is often (mistakenly) equated with sodomy—the so-called "crime against nature"—an abomination that some have (mistakenly) suggested led to the biblical destruction of Sodom.[5] But regardless of one's perspective or personal sexual preferences, anal penetration is ipso facto transgressive by most religious codes and much popular sentiment. Anal sex is transgressive because, like oral sex, it is a purely erotic practice—an act that cannot lead to conception and serves no known procreative function.[6] Furthermore, anal sex typically assumes the penetrator as the empowered agent, and the recipient as passive instrument—although, in many cases, recipients quite enjoy anal eroticism and might even initiate anal intercourse.

The relationship of anal penetration to the penis and male power has a long history, clearly dating to at least the Greco-Roman eras. As Freidman (2001:28–29) notes:

> The penis was so much the symbol of Roman strength and power that some believe the architectural centerpiece of the Empire, the Forum of Augustus, may have been designed to resemble one. Though the building has never been fully excavated, a surviving blueprint shows a long hall flanked at the bottom by two hemispheres. When viewed from above, this plan suggests the grandest *fascinum* ever built. This seems fitting, considering the rites of power and masculinity that took place there. It was at the Forum that Roman males came to exchange the robe of boyhood, the *toga praetexta*, with its purple stripe and *bulla* (the locket containing a replica of an erect penis) for the all-white *toga virilis*. The Forum was where emperors set up their tribunals, where the Senate declared war, and where triumphant generals dedicated their victories to the god Mars. The Forum of Augustus was a monument to masculinity, a proving ground and place of honor for powerful men of penetrating vision. Why wouldn't it be designed as a penis?

Insofar as the typical mode of anal intercourse assumes the recipient is bent over, standing on his/her knees, turning her backside to the penetrator, s/he is in a universal position of subordination among primates. Thus anal sex connotes transgression as well as the submissiveness and passivity of the one who is penetrated and thusly degraded. Again returning to the Romans, "[A Roman's] idea of manhood was measured by the power dynamic of sex. A Roman penetrated others with his penis; he was never penetrated by someone else's penis. A man who allowed that to happen endured *muliebria pati*, 'a woman's experience.' That man was no longer a real man" (Friedman 2001:24–25).

While many people enjoy anal sex—with adequate lubrication and relaxation—in "grotesquely degraded" form, anal sex is assumed to inflict pain upon the recipient who is "ripped wide open," and whose "asshole is fucked raw." As such, I have termed the genre "painful anal." A typical caption might read: "these sluts will moan with pain as they are ripped apart," or "our whores will take you up their asses and then lick the shit off your dick" (a variant of cum guzzlers above and excreta below). The important trope is that those who are passive get "fucked up the ass"; a most apt metaphor of how global capital has rendered people hurt, economically passive, and politically enfeebled. The victims of neo-liberal capital, whose jobs, benefits, pensions, and insurance are now all problematic, they are, indeed, getting "fucked up the ass." The symbolism of male masochism is blatant. The viewer, in the guise of the agent who penetrates, who is in the superior position of standing and penetrating, gains pleasure; yet at the same time, part of the viewer is identified with the penetrated and attempting to disguise or deny (through disavowal) his passivity vis-à-vis global capital. Psychoanalytically, this can be seen as an attempt to transform passivity into activity rather than an experience of powerlessness and/or shame. Thus, the anger to the "butt-fucked bitch" is a displacement from the economy and, in turn, disavows one's own denigrated, "butt-fucked" self.

## Giant Cocks

Size matters in the erotic imaginary of cyberporn—especially favored are large breasts and "giant cocks." As Friedman (2001:28) already suggested, "A large penis was Roman power become flesh: it was respected, sometimes feared, always coveted." Similarly, in the imaginary of cyberporn, size matters insofar as it is both a sign of masculine power and a theoretical indication of the capacity to provide greater sexual pleasure—notwithstanding the fact that penis size, especially length, is marginally related to the physical experience of sexual pleasure. In short, the giant penis is symbolic—a visual marker of male empowerment. An erect protrusion is clearly visible and dramatically marks male differentiation from females who are "castrated," lacking an external sex organ, and powerless. (Conversely, her breasts become the complimentary visible marker of a difference that is valorized as subordinate.) In a world where the social aspects of gender are ever more ambiguous, the massive protruding penis as well as the large (if not grotesquely huge) protruding breasts are evident visual signs of valorized difference.[7]

"Giant cocks," as grotesque and exaggerated elements of male fantasy, demonstrate and celebrate phallic power as compensatory masculinity. For those threatened by economic insecurities, possession of anatomical masculinity is a fallback position of agentic power verses castration and impotence. Those who receive giant cocks are portrayed as either wildly orgasmic and appreciative, or writhing with excruciating pain. To the erotic imaginary of cyberporn, what matters is not her (and it is mostly her) response be it pleasure or pain, but that there is a powerful response—a granting of recognition and, hence, a validation of the power of the man who possesses the giant penis. The giant cock calls forth the woman's acknowledgement of male superiority and power. Much like the struggle for recognition between the master and the slave, his selfhood, masculine self-consciousness, and narcissism requires the subordinate to respond and recognize him in order for him to see himself as powerful. In this case, it matters not whether her response is ecstatic orgasm or unbearable agony; what matters is that "powerful manhood" is recognized and deferred to—at least in the erotic imaginary, if not found in the quotidian of work and family (see Hegel 1807).

This mechanism, the appeal to symbolic patriarchal power with the penis as its emblem, long antedates cyberporn. From the architecture and mentality of Rome to the teeming slums of many inner cities, when few males have decent jobs, the compensating stance is machismo—especially as evidenced in large numbers of sexual partners and even larger numbers of children. Lower-class men gain status and prestige through plural seductions. In an adversarial world of lawyers, DNA evidence, and sympathetic juries, the realities of macho-masculinity face limits—especially for the better educated. But in the cyberporn imaginary, the possessor of a grotesque giant cock elicits a strong response from the degraded; he finds agency and recognition; he disavows his passivity and humiliation by projecting it to the one who gets "fucked." In other words, in psychoanalytic terms the possessor of the giant cock turns passivity into activity.

**Shit on me**

"They treat us like shit in this place." Almost any sociologist who conducts occupational research has heard this statement repetitively. Save for well-paid corporate elites and/or highly skilled professionals in exceedingly marketable occupations, people of many professions complain of mistreatment: overworked, underpaid, little appreciated, and easily discarded. Furthermore, as was earlier noted, for Bakhtin (1969) central elements of carnivalesque grotesque and transgression included bodily excreta and secreta. Indeed, much of the degradation and parody of the elites took highly scatological forms. A similar parallel among the cyberpornotopias are sites of scatological "grotesque degradation," where the primary feature is urination and/or defecation. Although some of these scatological sites shade into the next category (voyeurism), the essential theme is the degradation of being urinated or defecated upon, consuming urine or feces, and/or covering herself with urine or feces. While such behaviors can be easily understood psychoanalytically from the victim's point of view (e.g., a need for debasement, punishment, and even a call for attention if not rescue), what might the viewer gain from viewing this? As I have argued, certain segments of cyberporn articulate in symbolic eroticism the real or imagined degradation that people experience. But this humiliation is disavowed—it is not part of the self but is projected to the subordinated woman. As she is degraded by excreta, she displaces the shame and anger of the workplace from the self to the "not me."

Meanwhile, otherwise denied agency, empowerment, and dignity is experienced through identification with the male fellatee with a giant cock, who also anally penetrates. So, too, may he defecate or urinate upon the women—an almost universal expression of disdain and humiliation—as is mooning, a necessary prelude to defecation. The dynamic of "shit on me" is quite similar to "painful anal." It is possible that "shit on me" is a less literal and more symbolic form of what is unambiguously portrayed in "painful anal." Indeed, from one point of view, "shit on me" is something of a synthesis of "cum guzzling sluts" and "painful anal." In "painful anal" she is fucked in the ass; in "shit on me" she is wiped with his ass (and likes it).

### The "Intrusive Gaze"—Peek-a-Boo, I See You

In most cyberporn, performers are clearly performing in front of a camera for an intended audience. Many of these self-presentations unambiguously suggest the model enjoys showing off his or her body and demonstrating his or her sexuality to the camera—if not, ultimately, to the viewers. Similarly, there are numerous sites where the viewers are "invited" to watch what "really happens" in certain places that are typically highly privatized. Various spam invitations may read, "I'm Angela [or Christy, Dawn, or even Lauren], cum and watch me and my friends get real nasty." In sites such as VoyeurDorms, the participants know they are being observed: viewers have the "privilege" of entering a private realm and watching a "show," seemingly performed just for the viewer. Indeed, in some websites, the subscriber can enter commands for performer(s) to enact.

But, in other cases, the observer is hidden and the gaze intrudes into private realms. Safe from scrutiny, were it not for the placement of a webcam, the "panopticon of cyberspace" disciplines the observed and, perhaps, the observer as well. There are myriad places and situations where the viewer can gain "special" access to the "backstages" of the personal and sexual life of others. This might include bathrooms watching women pee (perhaps viewed from webcams placed in the toilet bowl), shower, or change tampons; dressing rooms where they change clothes; bedrooms or coed dorms where people may be having sex; or doctor's offices (a subgenre is gyniporn where webcams are inserted in the vagina). Webcams are sometimes even placed in floors to catch "upskirt" shots of women. In one variant, *"Street Blowjobs,"* a webcam is supposedly hidden in the fellatee's eyeglasses to catch a "bird's eye" view of the action. A closely related genre of cyber-voyeurism consists of celebrities in the buff—for example Jennifer Lopez, Britney Spears, Pamela Anderson, Angelina Jolie, Nicole Kidman, Christina Aguilera, and so on—and gives the viewer a privileged "gaze" that de-privileges the "star" (or at least the star's image) by revealing just who and what she is when naked or having sex (the Pamela and Tommy Lee tape is infamous). To paraphrase Adorno, the "stars come down to earth." To which we add: "and seemingly elevate the viewer."

What is the appeal of the "intrusive gaze" when, as some might argue, there is an element of voyeurism in all cyberpornography? For Freud, voyeurism was a sexually gratifying form of scopophilia found in the act of gazing at people who cannot look back or don't know they're being watched. The "intrusive gaze" is more specific in that it typically involves seeing nudity and/or body functions (from elimination to sexual activity, from masturbation to group sex). The fundamental point is not so much what is seen; indeed, the naked body and sexuality revealed by the "intrusive gaze" differs litte from other cyberporn. Rather, the viewer is seemingly unbeknownst to the observed and, as such, violating her privacy and destroying her dignity. Degrading the observed empowers the observer.

To understand this, we must first note that privacy and its relation to sexuality is a historical construction that emerged with the rise of market society. As Aries (1962), Elias (1978) or Zaretsky (1976) have argued, the construction of the individualistic, autonomous, self-controlled Western notion of subjectivity was dependent on the prior emergence of privacy—a relatively unique cultural moment of freedom. We recall that in the late French courts, official business was often conducted while the king was either in bed—the *leve* (morning) or *couche* (night time), or upon his chamberpot. Following the separation of the household from the economy, and the creation of "private realms," the modern bourgeois self emerged as its body functions (from elimination to bathing to masturbation to sexuality) were made shameful and shielded from an uninvited gaze. Indeed there is a reason genitalia are often called "privates" or "private parts," as the socialization of shame shields them from view.

Slowly but surely, with the "civilizing process" and the "invention of childhood," came the inculcation and development of a sense of shame over exposure of the body's "private parts," excretory functions, and/or sexual activities. Thus, for modern people, to have one's privacy invaded or intruded upon is a violation—a disempowering assault upon one's dignity and the integrity of self.

What, then, is the appeal of the "the intrusive gaze"? The simple answer has already been noted: as a form of "grotesque degradation" it grants the viewer a sense of empowerment. This empowerment takes place at both structural and personal levels. In his classical analysis of the "look," Sartre (1943) noted how the Other captured his facticity by his glance. The "look" rendered the self a powerless subject, constructed by the gaze of the Other. Similarly, for Foucault, the move from public torture to private incarceration—ever subject to the warden's gaze—"subject-ed" the prisoner, inscribed his/her subjectivity, and disciplined the soul; surveillance itself enabled "discursive power" the ability to control by defining the person observed. The prisoner never knew when he was being observed from the panopticon; he might be sleeping, using his chamber pot, picking his nose, or masturbating—but at no time did he have privacy as a realm of personal freedom, agency, and choice of action. Thus, the power of the gaze disempowered the person observed though, in this case, for the sake of reforming his/her soul.

In the "backstage" of personal life one may prepare and rehearse self-presentations or hide other aspects of self from assault and critique. Goffman refers to some of these realms as "stalls"—the implication of bathrooms is evident. There is freedom, safety, and an authenticity in spaces where one's actions are spontaneously given rather than given off to an audience for an intended reason. The erasure of the boundaries of privacy, where one is protected from assaults to the self, destroys one's dignity and defiles subjectivity. The "intrusive gaze" does not allow the Other to manage his or her impressions—his or her "secrets" are exposed, he or she is degraded, his or her "dignity" assaulted, and he or she is rendered powerless. When the private realm is exposed, and the difference between authenticity and presentation is evident, if not discrepant, the person is subject to degradation, shame, humiliation, and must undergo reparations—such as self-denigrations—that elevate the status of the observer. Thus, for example, in the inverted worlds of the cyberpornotopias, pornography actress "Huston" boasts with great pride how she consecutively took on 620 guys and invites the viewer to watch the action—for a fee. But when the "intrusive gaze" of the webcam shows the "girl next door" masturbating, fornicating, or defecating, her status wanes, her dignity is rent, and the viewer is empowered.

The long history of psychoanalysis has explored the unconscious dynamics of voyeurism—how desire can be aroused and fulfilled though seeing others in erotic ways, undressed, partially dressed (especially in underwear), or engaged in sex acts—but in the case of voyeur porn, however, the gratifications are not only erotic, but also involve the creation of a "desiring self." Unlike a dream where the erotic is "hidden from the self," "grotesque degradation," is more narcissistic than erotic, the "hidden" disavowed self of the viewer is realized in seeing what is typically "private." The intrusion empowers the subjectivity of the viewer/voyeur by eroding the boundaries of privacy, assaulting, and degrading the Other, who is seen in compromising ways and powerless to negotiate her impressions.

## Conclusions

Before the modern age, feudal societies were ruled by dynastic elites whose authority claims were based on God's will, or so the elite bishops told the people. How did they deal with their domination and subjugation? Following Bakhtin (1968), we noted how the carnival emerged as a liminal site where transgression, inversion, and reversals of norms were celebrated; where the grotesque, especially the grotesque body and/or the lower body and its excreta and secreta, were valorized as a repudiation of the elites, who were ridiculed, parodied, and hectored. But the grotesque was not just repugnant; it revealed a truth about a society in which the wealthy enjoyed comfort while peasant life was short, nasty, and brutish. During the carnival, for people otherwise dominated, resistance expressed as symbolic degradations of the elites (often in scatological forms), provided encapsulated realms of agency, empowerment, dignity, recognition, and respect.

In much the same way, pornography in general, and cyberporn in particular, are more than displays of bodies often involved in various sexual acts. For many people, there is genuine enjoyment of the "polymorphous perversity" that Freud so disdained. While it may be many things—an alternative to loneliness, an explorations of ones' sexuality, or even a shared activity—for the present purposes, as transgression, such portrayals reveal much about society, its hypocrisies, and the repressions that Freud, Weber, and Elias suggest maintain Western civilization. To which we note, following Reich and Marcuse, civilization was equated with its capitalist form in which repression at the level of the psychic economy served to maintain the political economy, albeit at the cost of personal pain and suffering. For some people, pornography and the erotic cyberpornotopias alleviate some of that suffering. Thus "polymorphous perversion" has an emancipatory moment, as both a critique of capital and a challenge to repressive norms of sexual life.

But this essay is not concerned with cyberporn in general, only the genres of "grotesque degradation" that Bakhtin saw as essential elements of the carnival of critique and resistance. "Grotesque degradation" reveals truths about the hidden side of neoliberal globalization. While the grotesque degradation of cyberporn may be a critique of the ways workers are treated, as a commodity, it assuages a damaged (male) self, and provides escape and distraction that serves to sustain larger systems of domination. Williams (1989:154–5) notes, "In cinematic hard core we encounter a profoundly 'escapist' genre that distracts audiences from the deeper social or political causes of the disturbed relations between the sexes; and yet paradoxically, if it is to distract effectively, a popular genre must address some of the real experiences and needs of its audience." In pornography genres that qualify as "grotesque degradation," it is not "the powers that be"—the elites of global capital—who are degraded, but the sex "partners" (sex objects) who are rendered "sluts," "whores," and "cunts" who serve as little more than orifices and bodies to be watched.

In "grotesque degradation," the "sluts" do not find such pleasure: there is nothing but pain, shame, suffering, and degradation. They are commodified symbolic representations of subordination located between the nodules of globalization and the cyberpornotopian fantasies of the Internet, where they function as erotized scapegoats. Such cyperpornographic representations of degradation provide realms of compensatory masculinity, granting symbolic empowerment and recognition apart from the "real world" of economic anxiety and insecurity. Insofar as the symbolic representations of exploitation take place in the erotic imaginary, they foster and reward the migration of consciousness from the political economy to a cultural site where privatized hedonism neutralizes political action. Almost 40 years ago, Marcuse (1964) termed this "repressive desublimation."

It is, of course, ironic that the same technologies of production and control that have so adversely impacted working conditions and job security (among the white-collar as well as blue-collar workers) also mediates the ameliorations for insecurities, anxieties, and anger. The same technologies provide alternative compensations to wounded egos through the degradation of the Other and/or grotesque expressions of masculinity. While cyberporn in general uses technologies of Internet power to construct subjects, it also constructs and/or affirms the identities of the viewer. "Grotesque degradation" provides and sustains compensatory masculinity in encapsulated realms where submissive, degraded, masochistic women—"deserving" of pain and humiliation—allow the viewer to split and project his own pains, humiliations, and degradations. In identifying with the degraded, pained woman, he can both experience and deny his own humiliation and indirectly acknowledge his masochism. The "cum guzzling slut," painfully split open by a giant cock in her ass, and pissed and shat upon, is indeed the everyman in a global society. But, at the same time, in the privacy of his own home, with the anonymity of the screen, the viewer can find a space for a simulated masculine identity that provides performative agency, dignity, and respect otherwise denied.

As was argued, between globalization and the erosion of job stability and promises of a stable secure career, together with feminist challenges to traditional male identities—for segments of the population—the reaction has been both shame-engendered rage and disavowed masochism. As Uebel (2000) put it:

> Cyberporn offers nothing less than a fantasy scene for self-flagellation, wherein men, having internalized, however partially or imperfectly, feminist modes of recognition, try to defeat their own aggressive impulses. Cyberpornographic masochism is thus an expression of eroticized historical and social guilt. The question here is: what has happened to men that they feel compelled to behave in non threatening, even nonheroic, ways? ...I would suggest provisionally that it has to do with an ideal image of masculinity to which men feel constant pressure to measure up and from which they feel increasingly alienated. It also involves an ideal image many men experience as imperiled by the punitive regime of techno capitalism. ...These masochistic mentalities are accommodated in cyberporn, as nowhere else on a mass-cultural scale. Men exposed to 30 or so years of the discourse and political effects of feminism are men who, for one reason or another, know it is unacceptable to evince the outright patriarchalism that was part and parcel of American social life until feminism asserted itself. What results is a tension between the "enlightened" consciousness of the American male at the end of the 20th century and a patriarchal sedimentation so old it is indissoluble. This tension is then reconciled fantasmically through a masochism that, on the face of it, seems to involve a forfeiture of dominance, but that in fact is nothing other than a compensatory mechanism, one that, at the level of fantasy, allows for the restoration and consolidation of masculine power.

Carnivalization in general and, in particular, contemporary genres of carnivalesque cyberporn that celebrate "grotesque degradation" sustain domination by letting off male steam (if not semen), and serve to reproduce the social order. But at the same time, there is, in cyberpornotopias, a moment that functions as bulwark against the general conservative trends of the present and confronts the established norms, codes, and images of a world of erotic pleasure in face of domination. Is cyberporn a form of "repressive desublimation" that secures domination, or do the polymorphous perversions of grotesque degradation stand as a critique, a call to arms and a vision of a truly emancipated society where gender hierarchies are absent and cyberporn is not needed as a compensatory balm, but rather becomes a catalyst that allows humanity to realize thwarted pleasures?

### Acknowledgments

The author wishes to express a great deal of thanks to Dennis Waskul for his help in developing this paper, his suggestions have been invaluable. Further,

Gary Fine's comments on parts of the manuscript are much appreciated. Meghan Burke's editorial help was indispensable.

## Notes

1.  This was, of course, Freud's (1930) argument. Civilization was founded on repression. Similarly, Reich (1970) would argue that it was capitalism, not civilization per se that demanded such suppression, an argument later developed by Marcuse (1964).
2.  This needs qualification, there are some works of pornography (or perhaps sexually explicit mainstream productions) in which questions are raised about the nature of gender identities in a changing world. Perhaps the best example might be the classic *Wanda Does Wall Street* where the intelligent, ambitious secretary—using her seductive charms—manages to rise in the hierarchy to become CEO of a Wall Street brokerage house. While this may reinforce the image of the woman who screws her way to the top, nevertheless, she does assert her agency through sexuality—much as men have done since the dawn of civilization.
3.  Surely we might trace its roots earlier to the cults of Dionysus or the Saturnalia.
4.  This is often a common theme in other genres as well. Consider horror movies: the strong, assertive women are typically the victims. The moral is that a woman ought to stay home and be compliant or she may have her throat slit.
5.  Jewish tradition, including the prophets, does not refer to the sexuality of Sodom, but to its cruelty, xenophobia, or perhaps gang rape. God never mentions homosexual sex. See http://www.uahc.org/ask/homosexuality.shtml
6.  In some cultures/subcultures, the value of virginity is so strong that couples often practice anything but, which means primarily butt.
7.  I have elsewhere argued that the popularity of professional football can be seen as a celebration of masculinity, in which the highly angled and muscled male players are juxtaposed with rounded, female cheerleaders whose choreography serves to foster bouncing breasts. And if they are not easily noticed, pom-poms become their symbolic exaggerated representation. (See Langman, 2003)

## References

Aries, P. 1962 . *Centuries of childhood*. New York, NY: Vintage Books.

Bakhtin, M. 1968. *Rabelais and his world*. Cambridge, MA: MIT Press.

Bordo, S. 1993. Reading the male body. *Michigan Quarterly Review*. 32:696–735.

Brown, H.G 1962. *Sex and the Single Girl*. New York, NY: Random House

Cooper, A. 1998. Sexuality and the Internet: Surfing into the new millennium. *Cyber-Psychology & Behavior*. 1(2):24–28.

Durkheim, E. [1893] 1984. *The division of labor in society*. New York, NY: The Free Press.

Dworkin, A. 1974. *Pornography: Men possessing women*. E.P. Dutton, reprint.

Elias, N. 1978. *The civilizing process*. Cambridge, MA: Blackwell.

Flitterman-Lewis, S. 1992. Psychoanalysis, film, and television. In *Channels of discourse: Television & contemporary criticism* (2nd ed.). R. C. Allen, ed. Chapel Hill, NC: University of North Carolina Press.

Foucault, M. 1978. *History of sexuality: An introduction vol. 1.* New York, NY: Vintage.

Freud, S. 1930. *Civilization and its discontents.* New York, NY: WW Norton & Company.

_____. [1917]. 1989 *Introductory Lectures on Psychoanalysis,* New York, NY: Norton.

———. [1915] 1974. Instincts and their vicissitudes. In *The standard edition of the complete psychological works of Sigmund Freud, vol. 14.* J. Strachey, ed. and trans. London: Hogarth Press

———. [1912] 1974. On the universal tendency to debasement in the sphere of love. In *The standard edition of the complete psychological works of Sigmund Freud, vol. 11,* J. Strachey, ed. and trans. London: Hogarth Press.

Friedan, B. 1964. *The feminine mystique.* New York, NY: Norton.

Friedman, D. 2001. *A mind of its own: A cultural history of the penis.* New York, NY: Penguin Books.

Hegel, G. F. [1807] 1967. *The phenomenology of the mind.* New York, NY: Harper and Row.

Kipnis, L. 1999. *Bound and gagged.* Durham, NC: Duke University Press.

Langman, L. 2003. Culture, identity, and hegemony: The body in a global age. *International Sociology.* 18(4).

Lillie, J. 2002. Sexuality and cyberporn: Toward a new agenda for research. *Journal of Sexuality Culture.* Spring.

MacKinnon, C. 1987. *Feminism unmodified.* Cambridge, MA: Harvard University Press.

Marcuse, H. [1964] 1992. *One-dimensional man : Studies in the ideology of advanced industrial society.* Boston, MA: Beacon Press.

Marx, K. 1972. The economic and philosophic manuscripts of 1844. In *The Marx-Engles reader,* Tucker, ed. New York, NY: W. W. Tucker and Co.

McLuhan, M. 1964. *Understanding media: The extensions of man.* Cambridge, MA: MIT Press.

Mulvey, L. 1989. *Visual and other pleasure.* Bloomington, IN: Indiana University Press.

Paglia, C. 1990. *Sexual personae: Art and decadence from Nefertiti to Emily Dickinson.* New Haven, CT: Yale University Press.

Reich, W 1970. *The mass psychology of fascism.* New York, NY: Farrar, Straus & Giroux.

Sade, M. 1987. *The 120 days of Sodom and other works.* New York, NY: Grove Press

Sartre, J. P. [1943] 1956/1974. The look, section IV. In *Being and nothingness: A phenomenological essay on ontology.* pp. 228–278. Secaucus, NJ: The Citadel Press.

Scheff, T. 1994. *Bloody revenge: Emotions, nationalism, and war.* Boulder, CO: Westview Press.

Sennett, R. 2003. *Respect in a world of inequality.* New York, NY: Norton.

Sennett, R., and J. Cobb. 1972. *The hidden injuries of class.* New York, NY: Knopf.

Stienem, G. 1963. "I Was a Playboy Bunny," reprinted in *Outrageous Acts and Everyday Rebellions.* New York, NY: Henry Holt and Co.

Turner, V. 1969. *The ritual process: Structure and anti-structure.* Ithaca, NY: Cornell University Press.

Uebel, M. 2000. Toward a symptomatology of pornography. http://muse.jhu.edu/ journals/theory _&_ event/toc/tae3.4.html

Williams, L. 1989. *Hard core: Power, pleasure, and the "frenzy of the visible."* Berkeley, CA: University of California Press.

Zaretsky, E. 1976. *Capitalism, the family and personal life:* New York, NY: Harper and Row.

# Chapter Eleven

# Race, Sexual Attractiveness, and Internet Personal Advertisements

## Erica Owens

*Much has been written about gender on the Internet. With a few notable exceptions comparatively little has been written about race, ethnicity, and new media technologies—especially with regard to sex and pornography on the Internet. Erica Owens provides one of the few accounts of how Internet users—in this case people who use the Internet for personal advertisements—construct race and ethnicity in the context of sexual attractiveness.*

When considering the topic of racism, whites' perceptions of the racial dimensions of sexuality and sexual attractiveness must also be taken into consideration. Failure to do so ignores the many links between racist acts—occurring from the time of slavery until the present—that stem from white fears of miscegenation, or "race mixing" (Russell 1998). The link between racism and fear of nonwhite sexuality is reciprocal. Fear of the sexuality of African Americans, most notably of black men, has been used as justification for the control of black bodies both during and after segregation (Feagin and Vera 1995).

White fear of the sexuality of persons of color runs extremely deep, and can be seen as a mixture of antipathy and longing. According to Roediger (1991), whites' stereotyping of black freedom, including sexuality, is a symptom of the loss of freedom felt by whites following Industrialization. To these newly constrained whites, blackness in all of its perceived sensuousness stood for all they had lost. This conceptualization of black sexuality as something unfettered, animalistic, and dangerous has long been used as justification for exploitation and control of the black body by white persons. The discursive use of the concept of sexual threat allowed whites to sanction blacks, especially black males, for any perceived action that challenged the socially understood "place" of each. For instance, Russell (1998:21) notes that "the stated rationale for lynching was to protect the sanctity of the White female from the Black man," yet fewer than one-third of all lynchings involved allegations of interracial sexual assault. The sense that blackness, and especially black sexuality, is a dangerous and dirty thing is by no means just a historical artifact, however. More recent research shows that even among "tolerant" whites, the idea of a family member dating a person of another race is met with a strong and violently negative response (Feagin and Vera 1995). When it comes to sexual expression, whiteness is seen as appropriate, and anything that deviates from this norm is characterized as dirty, immoral, or perverse.

To more fully understand the depth and irrationality of whites' racial fears, it is necessary to consider the racial dimensions of perceived sexual attractiveness as it pertains to whites' understandings of self. Sexual attraction never occurs without some sort of Other, whether as an image or in person. But, this Other is held in relation to the viewer—each individual weighs what he or she brings to the table with what the potential partner is offering to see if there is a basis for exchange (Goode 1996). It is the viewer's perception of this Other that leads to sexual attraction. One woman's prince is, as the saying goes, another woman's frog. To assume that this weighing does not include racial capital is a notable oversight.

Frankenberg (1993), one of the first researchers to conduct detailed work on white conceptions of race, shows that white women's perceptions of sexual actions and propriety have a distinctively racial dimension. Frankenberg shows several patterns: white men are supposed to protect white women from the threat of black male sexuality, white women who engage in interracial sexual contact are considered deviant and severely stigmatized, and nonwhite sexuality (especially the sexuality of black men) is exaggerated as "hypersexual." It is not only black Americans who are stigmatized in this manner. Asian women also suffer from whites' stereotypical perceptions of their attractiveness, generally either as an exotically seductive "dragon lady" or a submissive and meek "china doll" (Hsia 1997).

While we are beginning to understand more about what white people think about black sexuality and interracial relationships, we do not know much about how these perceptions affect definitions of white sexuality or sexual desirability. This study attempts to partly address this gap in the literature by examining the racial dimensions of sexual attractiveness presented by white people in Internet personal ads used to find romantic partners. These ads represent a microcosm of individual understanding of sexual worth and attractiveness, or an efficient way to distill what an individual considers his or her most marketable qualities and what qualities he or she requires in a partner (Goode 1996). Based on this assumption, I explore whites' perceptions of the racial dimension of sexual attractiveness by considering the language in ads placed by both whites who seek other whites specifically and those who seek partners of another race.

This distinction is key. There are few studies on personal ads, and studies that explore race through the use of personal ads often ignore "white seeking white" ads. As a result, social scientists are left with a quandary: the topic of race is investigated, but only by examining people of color. White people are not seen as having race unless it is in foil to the "Othered" race of a nonwhite person (Russell 1998).

Almost nothing has been written on the use of personal ads to find partners of another race (for a rare exception, see Yancey & Yancey, 1998). No studies comparing personals use among and between groups of whites with differing levels of racial tolerance and involvement were found. Thus the question remains: how do ideas about sexual attractiveness display whites' attitudes about race—toward both nonwhite and whites alike? And how do these attitudes about race intersect with racial "tolerance," itself a problematic term suggesting that the white majority only grudgingly accepts the nonwhite other.

On one end, white supremacists that seek a racially pure mate are expected to represent the most extremely negative view of nonwhite sexuality, and are also expected to base their own ideas of sexual attractiveness (self and partner) on race and racial ideology. At the other end, whites actively seeking interracial relationships are expected to have a positive view of the sexual attractiveness of people of other races and a neutral-to-positive view of the sexual attractiveness of whites. As a comparison group, whites who are seeking partners without specifying race are included to see if similar patterns exist outside of the portrayal of the racial dimension of sexuality of the partner, although it is acknowledged that there is some danger that these advertisers have not specified partner race because whiteness, as an often-assumed default category, may be expected of partners without such specification (see Russell 1998).

## Method

In total, one hundred and fifty personals placed on Internet dating service pages were analyzed.[1] Fifty subjects (25 women, 25 men) were taken from each of three groups: white supremacist seeking same, nonsupremacist white, and white seeking interracial relationship. White supremacists were chosen on the basis of their specifically designating themselves as such by participating in a supremacist dating service. Nonsupremacist whites were defined as those whites who did not mention any form of racially charged rhetoric in their ads (i.e., no "white power" or "proud to be white") and who did not specify that their partners had to be either white or nonwhite. Whites seeking interracial relationships were defined as those who specified that their desired partner should be a member of a different racial or ethnic group, including African-Americans, Latinos, Asians, Native Americans, and Pacific Islanders.

In all cases, subjects self-identified themselves as white or Caucasian. Potential subjects who listed their race as primarily white or Caucasian were excluded if they also listed black or African American, Latino, Native American, or Asian. These exclusions were made to help ensure that subjects would perceive themselves as white (both through self-identification and the Others' identification of them), as the perception of whiteness and what it means to be white or nonwhite is critical to this analysis. Because of space and time constraints, my sample excludes gay and lesbian whites seeking mates. It is likely that including this group as well would have necessitated analyses of gender and class positions that are beyond the scope of this paper.

## Analysis

White supremacist ads were analyzed first, using Frankenberg's (1993) material as a conceptual framework. These ads were coded first for patterns related to this framework: white male as protector of white women, white women as deviant if desiring interracial sexual contact, white women as virtuous if "true" to her race. Other patterns were coded as they emerged from the data.

Ads posted by whites seeking interracial relationships were analyzed next. These ads were coded to check whether whites seeking interracial relationships were less overtly racist than other whites.[2] As a comparison group, nonsupremacist whites' ads were then analyzed. These ads were coded to see if any of the patterns found in the previous two analysis groups also held in this group as well. Finally, content frequency was recorded for nonsupremacist whites and whites seeking interracial relationships, using categories that had emerged from initial findings from preliminary analysis of white supremacist ad content.

### The Color of Sexual Attractiveness

When white persons specifically consider race in looking for a sexual partner, racial stereotypes of nonwhite bodies, sexualities, and character traits are prominent. Surprisingly, this pattern was found in both the white supremacist group as well as the group of whites seeking nonwhite partners. In each of these cases, the nonwhite Other's racial status serves as the dominant consideration for partner choice—whether through attraction to, or avoidance of, perceived characteristics of the Other. It is only when race is notably absent from the text that we see a shift in the main focus to core issues of compatibility such as hobbies or (non-racialized) personality traits.[3]

**White Supremacists**

As might be expected, white supremacists strongly portrayed sexual attractiveness as a matter of racial purity. This was accomplished through stressing one's own and one's desired partner's whiteness and white ideology, and also through portraying people of other racial or ethnic groups as deviant or dangerous.

White supremacist women showed a strong tendency toward constructing the attractive partner as someone who would protect them and serve as a hero to the race:

> I have never wanted kids to tell the truth because I have been afraid of how they would turn out in the way the world is today. However, I am sure if I have a strong white man along with me that we could accomplish anything. Like I said, I have no children now and have never been married. I am looking for a strong white male to come and save me. Please help. (White Supremacist Female 3—WS/F003)

> I am looking for an Aryan man who knows how to be a leader and will take charge. He must love animals and children, especially White children. He must be ambitious and use his talents to improve racial awareness and advance the White cause. (WS/F006)

> I am looking for a single white male to take me away from this liberal state. (WS/F007)

> Personal philosophies and spirituality are not an issue with me as long as you fight everyday to uphold the core belief of the 14 Words—WE MUST SECURE THE EXISTENCE OF OUR RACE AND A FUTURE FOR WHITE CHILDREN. (WS/F011)

In extending this argument, white women in need of a protector or champion must be seen in terms of extremely traditional gender norms that are intimately linked with racism. In this case, white women are unable to protect themselves from the threat posed by black men or other men of color. While this is not explicitly stated in the above narratives, considering the narratives of the white "protectors" sheds additional light. Women who engage in interracial sexual contact are extremely stigmatized. To be considered "decent," a white woman must remain "true" to the white race:

> I just got out of the Army (after 3 years) and I'm back home now and it seems as though the girls have all turned into race traitor psycho sluts since I've been gone. But I know that somewhere out there in Sacramento there have to be some decent Aryan girls left. (WS/M002)

> Most Americans haven't any idea about what is actually taking place in this world...the future of this world depends on the survival of the race of people who have created civilization after civilization. I truly believe that we will eventually overcome the adver-

sity...in order to pull through these trials we must all make certain that we form strong
bonds with those who are of solely European heritage and are also racially aware. I could
never date or marry a woman who is not determined to be true to her race.

I'm looking for a long term relationship with a decent girl. I'm not looking for tattooed
skins, just a nice racially conscious girl that's looking for a decent, hard working guy.
(WS/M012)

The construction of decency does not stop at women who are loyal to the
white race, however. Racial prejudice combines with expectations of traditional
womanhood to form a picture of supremacist femininity. In this area, many supremacist men are outspoken about their desire for a very traditional mate:

I am looking for a decent old-fashioned woman of the same age or close to mine.
(WS/M006)

I am looking for a proud white Aryan woman...a strong woman to help raise my child
the proper way. (WS/M005)

I am searching for someone who has the same views as myself and also knows what it
takes to raise a decent white family. (WS/M004)

The attractive white supremacist woman is a traditionally feminine mother
figure, capable of teaching her children racial ideology and decency. Again, this
is clearly a marker for separatist living, as "decency" is serving here as a code
for "whites who do not have contact with persons of other racial or ethnic heritage." Looking at supremacist women's idealization of the white mother, the
separatist nature of the role is underscored:

My kids will be respectful and polite, and I don't think I can accomplish that when
they're around black and Mexican gangs. (WS/F001)

I believe in teaching my future children history and knowledge as it should have been
taught, without Zionist influence. (WS/F005)

In both of these statements, it is striking not only that the women believe
that their children must be kept safe from people of other racial or ethnic heritage, but also that they believe it is their own personal responsibility to ensure
that separation occurs. Both of these women complain of undue negative influence on their children, but frame it in such a way that they underscore their own
role in raising the "decent" (separatist) white child. The first woman fears that
she will not be able to "accomplish" proper child rearing if her kids are around

"gangs" of people of other races (i.e., not kept separate), and the second fears exposing her children to the school system, which she considers biased.

Supremacist women's desire to be considered attractive as the traditional wife and mother-protector of white children extends into their reports of labor force participation. An extremely striking feature of these women's ads is the rejection of career or education unless it is directly linked in some way to furthering supremacist goals:

> I have a bachelors of education degree in secondary education and have taught several years but had to give up my job because I refused to teach the mongrelized, heathen anti-Christian curriculum in the public schools. (WS/F009)

> I plan to join the Klan in the near future, and my only career goal right now is to be married with children, and have fellowship with like minded men and women. (WS/F001)

> I am a student majoring in Human Biology, and plan to obtain an M.D./Ph.D. My political affiliation is National Socialist. I intend to use my medical knowledge for the purposes of advancing the Aryan race. My research interests include genetic technology, race differences, and the Nature/nurture debate. (WS/F004)

The first two statements specifically rejecting employment in favor of supporting white supremacist ideals also support a very traditional, stay-at-home housewife ideal of women's place in the family. In both cases the women also support their feminine purity through the device of separatism. "Decent" women don't have contact with "mongrelized" ideas, but rather exchange ideas with those who are of "like mind," meaning white supremacist. The final statement above is a striking contrast, and stands as the only example of a woman discussing plans or desire to work. Unlike the women who need protecting through separatism, this woman stands on the front as a "white warrior" dedicated to the cause of white power. Here, again, separatism is quite notable. This woman's career goals will not only conform to a separatist ideal, but will help to enforce this ideal through medical knowledge and "genetic technology." The bottom line of separatism has now been reached: not only must the races not mix socially or sexually, but also through the application of modern science and genetics people of other racial or ethnic origin may be stigmatized still further. Although not obviously stated, the potential use of this woman's future knowledge for eugenics in support of white power is frighteningly real.

These two extreme stances represent a key factor in white supremacists' perception of sexual attractiveness. Contrary to what is generally expected, partners do not try to maximize their options by stressing professional competence or financial security. Of the fifty ads analyzed, only three mentioned either money or professionalism in their self-description, and only two mentioned these traits in relation to a desired partner. The common denominator of racist ideology seemed to drive these inclusions, as has been illustrated above. Employment or income only factors into perceptions of attractiveness among white supremacists when it serves to support or potentially contradict the ideal of separatism. It was expected that these findings would stand in contrast to findings in the other two groups, where professionalism and income would have a greater value as a marker of attractiveness to a potential mate.

Descriptions of physical attributes also do not follow what might be expected based on current literature on dating and attractiveness. Generally, people are assumed to maximize their own attractiveness in personal ads (often slightly exaggerating) while not over inflating it to the point of risking rejection when a face-to-face meeting occurs (Goode 1996). The goal is to present the most attractive package possible, as physical attractiveness is an important criterion in mate selection. White supremacists do mention physical characteristics, but not as often as might be expected (35 of 50 list no physical characteristics of desired partner). When characteristics of self or desired partner are mentioned, they tend to be described in relation to supremacist ideals of lineage and separatism.

Lineage seems to have two components: physical soundness and racial purity. Both of these mark an individual specifically as attractive and as "good physical stock." The stock-type references, as well as the desire for a "pedigree" or family history of race and soundness, strongly suggests that the physically attractive white supremacist is one whose body won't betray the white race by producing children who are "less than whole" or "less than white":

> I come from pure stock, my teeth are totally straight, my eyes can focus and I have all my limbs, and I can assure you that there has been no inbreeding. He he! I am looking for a man with similar traits who hopes to raise a big white Aryan (perfect) race, but who also has the $$ to support us all. (WS/F003)

> Looking for females to correspond with who enjoy metal music and are proud of their heritage. I am of complete Irish descent, and I will respond to all. (WS/M014)

> I'm a Hiberno-Saxon who is seeking another intelligent and politically active Celt with either red or fair hair. ...Please respond if you're a clean and sober non-smoker with absolutely NO trace of non-white ancestry and NO family history of genetic birth defects. (WS/M001)

The other marker of the physically attractive white supremacist is the use of symbols that signify white power ideology and separatism. While less common than the requirement of appropriate lineage, this aspect is still quite notable.

Body markings or fashions that are European seem to be especially favored, as are fashions that have been identified with neo-Nazi movements such as shorn hair and certain clothing brands:

> To the right are photos of me (I'm not miss photogenic). I normally dress rather casual, jeans, shirt, and Doc Martins. ...[partner's looks] Tattoos and some piercings are fine. I prefer men with a slightly stocky or muscular build, short or shaved hair, 5'7" or taller. (WS/F017)

> I like very short hair, goatee beards and tattoos (I have several Celtic tattoos myself). (WS/F005)

> I would love to meet a guy that is into the oi punk scene...into Dr. Martins, suspenders...and does not have long hair!!! The lesser hair, the better. (WS/F020)

Fuller understanding of the racial dimension of perceived sexual attractiveness among these extremists can be had through distilling most desired characteristics down to their corollary ideological component in the white power belief system. Employment or education is mentioned, if it pertains somehow to white supremacist beliefs. Gender roles are clearly paramount, but only in relation to the understood meaning of and threats to whiteness. Physical attractiveness is nearly completely driven by factors that will help support the ongoing drive for racial purity and strength of representation. Most notably of all, nearly one-fifth (9 out of 50) of white supremacists sampled listed *no desired physical, personality, or interest characteristics expected of partners at all* save that they be dedicated to the ideals of the white power or white supremacy movement.

## Whites Seeking Interracial Relationships

If white supremacists represent one extreme in the continuum of acceptance of persons of other racial or ethnic origins, whites that are interested in nonwhite persons sexually are commonly held to represent the other end of the spectrum. This seems to be supported by findings that even tolerant whites who do not consider themselves racist will react negatively and strongly to the idea of someone in their family having an interracial relationship (Feagin and Vera 1995). It seems the idea of interracial sexual contact is the breaking point for many "tolerant" whites' facades of acceptance of people of color. If this is the case, it would also seem natural to assume that those who were not only tolerant but desirous of an interracial relationship would be much less racist in their perceptions of the racial dimensions of sexual attractiveness.

According to my data, this was not the case. I analyzed this group of 50 ads using Frankenberg's (1993) framework where relevant (there was no group, for example, of white women to be protected by white men), and supplemented this with Roediger's (1991) discussion of whites' desiring of the "sexually free" Other as a cloaked desire for freedom lost to themselves. Patterns found supported both Frankenberg's and Roediger's analyses of the sexual aspect of interracial relations. Whites seeking interracial relationships were found to engage in the following practices: assumptions of hypersexuality of desired partner, assumptions of "exotic" nature of desired partner, objectification of desired partner, desire for appropriation of partner's culture, and assumptions of racially determined personality characteristics.

When characterizing the desired partner, many whites who were seeking interracial relationships stressed sexuality in such a manner that it was tied to the prospective partner's race. Generally, when passion and sexuality are mentioned as important characteristics, they are placed front and center of the description of the desired partner and are not framed as merely one of a number of desired traits:

> And that Amazon within you if not already awakened will!...Tell me baby if you could be any animal you choose to be during mating season, which would you pick and why? (White Male WM seeking Black Female BF104)

> I am seeking a sexually aggressive Asian female, looks, weight and height are unimportant. (WM seeking Asian Female AF 116)

> (Headline: Hot sexy beautiful woman seeks black male for freaky times) I like to get down and get freaky and kinky. I'll [do] almost anything to please my man. I love to suck on things. My dream is to find a black male who likes big girls and will wanna get with this big girl to do some exploring and to get real freaky. (WF seeking BM 106)

> (Headline: Blond lady looking for BLK male to fulfill fantasies) I am an adventuresome 26 year old lady who has a few more fantasies to fulfill. I wish to fulfill them with a local adventuresome attractive black male (not the stereotypical white girl fantasies, much more sophisticated). (WF seeking BM 124)

Less overt examples include tagging the term "passionate" to the racial characteristic of the desired partner, or the term "lover," as in "Passionate Asian Lover Strongly Desired" (headline text).

A less blatant version of the assumption of sexual naughtiness is found when whites seeking interracial relationships talk about the exotic nature of their desired partner:

(Headline): Looking for that exotic Asian beauty. (WM seeking AF 110)

I have a good job, and am basically happy...just lacking the Spanish spice to complete the picture. (WM seeking Latina Female LF 111)

(Headline): Looking for a Latin heartthrob to light up my life. (WF seeking LM 105)

I'm an attractive single woman (very long blond hair, clear blue eyes and cute) that's looking to share an awakening with a sensual black man. (WF seeking BM 108)

Most strikingly, often the characterization of desired black partners takes on a consumption aspect. Black partners, and *only* black partners, are frequently objectified in terms of food. All of the following examples are taken from the headlines these white advertisers use to attract their potential black mates:

SWM seeks SBF for chocolate vanilla swirl. (WM seeking BF 102)

White knight seeks chocolate kiss. (WM seeking BF 107)

White Brotha lookin for that sweet redbone. (WM seeking BF 109)

Cup of cream looking for some dark coffee to warm up with. (WM seeking BF 118)

Vanilla looking for some brown sugar. (WF seeking BM 116)

I love dark meat unless you are serving chicken or turkey. (WF seeking BM 120)

These images are extremely important for three reasons. First, although they might seem cute or playful, they in fact characterize black sexuality as a commodity to feed white desire. Food is necessary yet transitory. Once eaten, it is absorbed into the body of the consumer and has no remaining existence separate from what it provides to the consumer. Secondly, the characterization of black sexuality as feeding white desire is common to both white men and women in these examples. It cannot be written off as a gendered artifact of sexism or patriarchy—quite the opposite, as the only example that blatantly characterizes the black body as "meat" comes from a white woman's ad. Finally, white people in search of partners who are not white but also are not black do not use similar imagery. This is not an example of white sexual desire as consuming of the "Other." These images are a portrayal of white sexual desire as destructive hunger *when considered in the context of black sexual attractiveness only.* More research on this phenomenon is needed to make a definitive connection, but there is enough evidence to suggest that white sexuality and the white self take on distinct characteristics when the desired body is black.

Whites who are looking for interracial relationships also seem to want to appropriate the culture of their desired mate. This typically takes two forms. The white person supports his or her fit with the person of color by stressing prior experience in interracial dating situations, or mentions specific aspects of the desired partner's background that fit with or interest them:

I do like Asian culture and I always have. (WM seeking AF 110)

I love Latin culture and want to find a pretty Latina who will help me continue to learn Spanish, and share her culture with me. ...I want to travel and enjoy Latin cultures sometime soon. (WM seeking LF 111)

I play ole timey banjo just like the slave did 150 years ago who brought the banjo from Africa. I sing also. (WM seeking BF 114)

I like Thai food especially "Tom Yum Kung" and "Phat Thai." I like many things about the Thai culture. I speak Thai a little bit, but I am sure I will learn more. (WM seeking AF 121)

I am not looking for a jungle fever fling, and I have dated outside of my race before, once seriously. (WM seeking BF 122)

He is most likely a black man, since I have an interest in Africa and its people. (WF seeking BM 113)

In these examples, the white person seeking an interracial relationship presents him- or herself as a sort of tourist. It is important to remember that these ads are venues for white people to explain to potential partners (white or not) why they would make a good match. By stressing the cultural aspects of their attraction, white advertisers may be intending to characterize themselves as people who "understand" the cultures of the mates they desire. But, in each case, the examples given serve as a petty reduction of the world of a marginalized person. Banjo playing is seen as a link to black culture, complete with the appropriation of slave history; ethnic food tastes or the desire for language lessons are stated as a basis for common understanding; interest in a continent full of different nations and peoples becomes a reason to look for a black mate, despite the fact that some black men in the U.S. are ethnically from other areas such as Latin America or the Caribbean.

In addition to cultural capital, whites endow potential partners who are not white with special personality traits linked to their race. Here again, reductionistic thinking is clearly evident. A black woman does not have the freedom to come into the relationship as an individual with quirks of her own, but is expected to have a specific attitude:

> 30 something looking for a black woman because they have an "attitude" I enjoy so much. (WM seeking BF 118)

> I can't explain the attraction, I just know how I feel. When people ask, I tell them that Black women don't play games (well, at least that sounds good). ...You see, in general most white girls are nice. But I don't do nice. To put it bluntly, nice people suck. ...I'd rather deal with a difficult person who has nice moods than a nice person with nasty moods. Call me crazy but I don't like surprises. So, in a nutshell, I'm seeking a good-hearted Black woman who doesn't take any shit. (WM seeking BF 125)

Black women are seen as sharing a characteristic of having some sort of attitude, either unstated (and considered universal enough to be readily understood) or characterized as negative. In both cases, the white men searching for the black woman with attitude portray themselves as unusual for wanting a black woman, and provide the expected "attitude" as justification for their desire, as presumably this attitude cannot be found with a partner who is not black.

Other common personality assumptions include women of color as either more docile and easygoing, or more intense:

> I would like to meet a sweet Thai lady, to spend the rest of my life with. She should not smoke or drink, and have traditional Thai values. (WM seeking AF 121)

> During my several business trips to Central and South America I had occasion to notice how beautiful and passionate Latin women are. This is why I decided that my future wife: MUST BE A LATINA. (WM seeking LF 124)

> I've always believed African-American women have more common sense than Caucasian women, and are also more physically attractive and passionate. (WM seeking BF 101)

> I would like to meet an Asian woman, because I believe (through experience) that they are the most loving and faithful of most women. (WM seeking AF 108)

> I know in my heart that a woman of color is best suited for my easy going personality. (WM seeking BF or LF 114)

All of the statements made by white men in search of interracial relationships are doubly illustrative. Most obviously, they serve as examples of how whites perceive people of color. Ironically because all of these statements come from ads which are designed to bring a response from a potential partner, these are characterizations that white people think are overwhelmingly *positive* and will please the very people being stereotyped. In comparison with ads posted by white supremacists, ads posted by whites who are seeking interracial relationships are not markedly free from racist images. In both groups, interracial sex is a transgression. For white supremacists, it is a choice to be condemned, and for interracial partners, to be justified through still more sexually and culturally contentious images.

Another dimension of these ads can be found in what is unstated. When white men and women provide descriptions of their ideal interracial partner, they are both describing the goal of their search and justifying their interracial choice. As such, these descriptions are mirror images—what is especially prized in the partner of another race is what cannot be found with a white partner. The desire for an interracial relationship in these cases provides a rare window into the aspects of white sexual attractiveness that whites themselves find lacking.

## Comparison with Nonsupremacist Whites as Control

Nonsupremacist whites tended to be much more descriptive of themselves in their ads than whites in the other two groups studied. While in nearly all ads the advertiser provided a "thumbnail sketch" of his or her looks, nonsupremacist whites went to great lengths to describe personal attributes and minutiae:

> I am 5'7", I have short blond hair and blue eyes. ...I am 27 years old. ...I am a Certified Nursing Assistant, and a Phlebotomist, but currently I am driving for UPS. I am a student who is working on my nursing degree. ...I am an outdoors type of person, but I also like to cuddle up in front of a nice fire, or a good movie. I also like to meet new people. (Nonsupremacist White Male NWM 201)

> Here are things that I enjoy (in no particular order): quiet; visual art (i.e. Cadillac Ranch, Christo, Leonardo); music (classical, R&R, and various ethnic); gardening (vegetable, ornamental, bonsai); all animals (including the "creepy" ones); history; travel by car and foot; football; opera; swimming; plastic bubble wrap; dreaming; concepts; archaeology. (NWM 204)

> I have many interests, which music, dancing, sports, movies and kids are a great part of. I coach youth basketball for the YMCA and I work in purchasing for an oil and gas equipment company. I am 5'7" tall and have an athletic figure with long legs, brown hair and big brown eyes. ...I love carnivals and amusement parks...and yes all the scary rides too!...Some of the things I don't like are snobs, people who hurt children or animals, controlling possessive mates, dishonesty, Chinese food, and snakes!! (NWF 210)

These ads may seem hokey or crowded, but they are not atypical of this group's efforts. The second example above totaled four printed pages when downloaded, and included the titles of his 20 favorite movies among other descriptions. Overall, nonsupremacist whites seemed to want to provide a global description of "who they are," including as many tastes, quirks, hobbies, interests, and credentials as possible.

Another unusual pattern found in these ads that was not present in the ads from the previous two groups is the tendency to challenge gender stereotypes as a mark of one's own attractiveness. For men, this was accomplished by talk of domestic capabilities and "feminine sides":

> Just for those ladies that don't believe it, men can take care of themselves. I cook (8 years as my job), I know how to iron and separate colors (5 years in the military), but I don't do windows. (NWM 201)

> I am strong, yet sensitive, masculine, but still in touch with my feminine side. I do not see that women are the weaker sex, but that they are an intriguing, complex, fascinating work of art. (NWM 207)

> I can cook, I can sew, do laundry, clean house and do all the things necessary to sustain life. (NWM 224)

Women who challenged traditional gender expectations tended to stress professional accomplishment, in stark contrast to white supremacist women who disavowed career ambitions:

> I am a well traveled trilingual Ph.D. historian working in the fashion and beauty industry. ...I live internationally, travel on a whim. (NWF 204)

> Not into barefoot and pregnant? Great! I am tall, empathic, former family counselor, three professional degrees, in Marquis' Who's Who in the World, value love above wealth, self employed. Founded a shelter for victims of domestic violence at a time and in a country where male political and religious leaders did not want it. Was once fired from a top 5 U.S. retailer for refusing to steal utilities. (NWF 207)

> I used to be a pilot, a nurse, a college instructor; now I'm an attorney who is lonely with only her cat to keep her warm. (NWF 220)

These comparisons need to be taken as quantitative differences rather than just qualitative ones. Some of the whites who were seeking interracial relationships listed a hobby or two, or personal interests, but it was not a distinct pattern in the way that it can be consistently seen in this third group. Similarly, some of the women in the second group mentioned jobs (and some of the men mentioned nurturing activities), but gender challenges were not focal points or large chunks of the narrative as they are for nonsupremacist whites.

Potential partners were not typically described in extremely sexual ways in this group. Nor were potential partners described as exotic, capable of providing needed cultural capital, or fundamentally passionate or retiring. In no case did a nonsupremacist white man or woman describe a potential mate as a food item, although objectification of self and other as animals (kittens, teddy bears) was not uncommon. White men and women who did not include a specific racial or ethnic background in their list of partner requirements do not seem to have the same loaded expectations of their potential mates as do those who are looking for a person from another racial or ethnic group. Rather, they seem to be presenting themselves as uniquely as possible in the effort to find a custom fit with a person who shares many of the same individual interests and hobbies.

When children were mentioned in the third group of ads, it was a form of disclosure or a promise of future potential rather than an imperative:

> I am not looking for a woman with children, although I would like to have them eventually (children that is...LOL [laugh out loud]). (NWM 201)

> I also enjoy going bowling, wrestling with my 10 year old son and seven year old daughter whom I see often. (NWM 212)

> I have two beautiful, blond haired, blue eyed, boys who look just like their dad (very cute, so they say.) (NWM 225)

> I have an effervescent personality, love people, children (although I have none of my own). (NWF 201)

> He needs to be honest, loving caring, romantic. Must like children, animals, the ocean, outdoors and inside equally. (NWF 219)

## Discussion

Global comparisons between this third group of ads and the other two groups were difficult to make because of the vastly different tone and content of the text. Generally, nonsupremacist men and women were more likely to want an individual suited to them because they wanted a partner in their life. There was no one "type" of person sought, and no major category of "sexuality," or even of "personality." Most ads mentioned more subjective traits such as "caring," "honest," and "attractive" rather than the expectation of a certain look or way of acting. This marked a notable departure from both white supremacist whites and whites who were in search of partners of a different racial or ethnic background.

In contrast, white supremacist men and women wanted a partner who would fit the needs of their racist belief system. The attractive partner in these ads was much more rigidly defined, and followed very traditional gender norms. Employment or financial security was a nonissue among members of this group (3 mentions in relation to self, 2 in relation to desired partner) compared to nonsupremacist whites (20 in relation to self, 3 in relation to other) and whites seeking partners of another race (19 in relation to self, 14 in relation to other). Interestingly, specific physical attributes of the desired partner were mentioned in supremacist ads (15) and nonsupremacist ads (11) much less often than in ads by whites seeking an interracial relationship (23).

These frequency comparisons taken together with the textual analysis describe a situation where whites choosing dating partners from either social extreme (white supremacy, or the desire for interracial relationships only) have a much more strongly defined set of expectations for potential partners. Although the issue seems at first to be one of preference based on skin color alone, taking a wider view shows that each group's choices are constrained by perceptions of what race itself means and where this meaning intersects with ideals of sexual attractiveness. For supremacist whites, the desirable partner is the supremacist of the opposite sex. All other characteristics are secondary, and none can supplant this fundamental requirement. Oddly enough, whites who are seeking a mate of another race also have a form of racial tunnel vision, and tend to see the attractive mate mainly in terms of characteristics that are seen as an extension of not being white. In neither case is there room for the potential partner to be considered as an individual.

This is not a plea for "color-blindness," or the polite form of racism that pretends that skin color does not matter and therefore racism will just magically go away if everyone would start "ignoring" race (see Carr 1997). Rather, it is a call for recognition that whites' perceptions of the racial dimensions of sexual attractiveness constrain behavior to some extent so long as there is the recognition that race *is* a factor in partner choice. It could further be argued that, whether or not whites are aware of its presence, race is *always* a factor in partner choice, if only because the current system of institutional racism in the United States prevents many white people from considering interracial relationships as an option.

## Notes

1.  Supremacist subjects were found on a dating page designed to match up partners with similar "Aryan" characteristics and views. Subjects from the other two groups were found through an Internet dating page clearinghouse, which posts ads from numerous other sites. General dating ads were chosen at this clearinghouse page as opposed to ads designed for people wanting casual sex partners or platonic friendships. Nonsupremacist whites were chosen at random by scrolling down each page and pulling the ad that the cursor landed on when scrolling stopped.

Whites seeking interracial relationships were more difficult to find. This search required reading through the headlines on each page and pulling those that either stated directly a desire for a partner of another race or hinted at the possibility of this desire by using words that indicated a search for difference or adventure: "looking for something different" or "feeling adventurous and want some spice." Only those ads that specified the desire for a partner of another race in either the headline or in the body of the text were used. Ads were pulled during three separate searches, approximately two to three weeks apart, to help provide a more diverse pool of subjects to choose from.

2.  To test this assumption, certain patterns related to Frankenberg's (1993) and Roediger's (1991) work on white assumptions of nonwhite persons were coded: assumption of sexual excess or hypersexuality, desire for cultural appropriation, assumption of racially determined personality traits, and perception of other as "exotic." Objectification of the desired nonwhite partner was also coded.

3.  This should not be read as a suggestion that all white persons who are attracted to persons of color are only interested in the prospective partner's race, nor am I arguing that interracial relationships cannot be based on true affection and compatibility. It is likely that seeking an anonymous partner online, rather than beginning a dating relationship with a person one has met before, makes consideration of specific personality traits difficult. It is also possible that personal ads used for this purpose reflect a search for sex rather than an effort to find lasting companionship, despite my efforts to weed out "sex only" sites from consideration.

## References

Carr, L. G. 1997. *"Color-blind" racism.* Thousand Oaks, CA: Sage.

Feagin, J. R., and H. Vera. 1995. *White racism.* New York, NY: Routledge.

Frankenberg, R. 1993. *White women, race matters: The social construction of whiteness.* Minneapolis, MN: University of Minnesota Press.

Goode, E. 1996. Gender and courtship entitlement: Responses to personal ads. *Sex Roles* 34(3–4): 141–169.

Hsia, H. C. 1997. Selfing and othering in the "foreign bride" phenomenon: A study of class, gender and ethnicity in the transnational marriages between Taiwanese men and Indonesian women. Unpublished doctoral dissertation, University of Florida.

Roediger, D. R. 1991. *The wages of whiteness: Race and the making of the American working class.* London: Verso.

Russell, K. K. 1998. *The color of crime: Racial hoaxes, white fear, black protectionism, police harassment, and other macroaggressions.* New York, NY: New York University Press.

Yancey, G. and S. Yancey 1998. Interracial dating: Evidence from personal advertisements. *Journal of Family Issues* 19(3):334–349.

# Part Five

# The Internet Pornography Industry

The pornography industry is undeniably large and extremely profitable, although estimations of both vary widely. Even the lowest calculations are staggering: if the American pornography industry reaps a mere 3 billion dollars a year, that's still more than live sporting events and music combined (and the pornography industry is undoubtedly *much* larger, at least financially). More liberal estimates place the pornography industry at about 15 billion a year (and some suggest it is even more profitable than that). Any way you cut it, pornography is big business with revenues measured in the billions.

The pornography industry is important, not merely due to the substantial money involved, but also because the industry reflects society's uneasy relationship with sex, magnifies changing definitions of obscenity, is an intense arena for political struggles between various entrenched interests, and exemplifies shifting norms of social and sexual relationships. In addition, the pornography industry vividly illustrates the varied ways that technology intersects with society and culture. Indeed, relationships between technology and pornography are direct: the pornography industry has always been among the first to effectively exploit new technologies for creation of lucrative products and the opening of new markets—in both respects, pornography has a history of challenging the boundaries of existing social institutions and cultural norms.

For all practical purposes, technology gave birth to the pornography industry—the printing press, photograph, film, video—each medium a resource by which pornography has built empires. Since at least Johannes Gutenberg's printing press (1436), technological innovation has vastly expanded the capacity to create and distribute words and images and, along the way, various entrepreneurs have always found sexually explicit materials to have ready markets of eager consumers. From the printing press, to the photograph, to the VCR to the Internet—the history of these kinds of technological innovations is intimately woven into the fabric of pornography (see Lane 2000). Furthermore, the pornography industry is typically on the cutting edge of these technologies. The Internet has been no different—"the pornography industry is once again at the forefront of technological innovation and change" (Lane 2000:xxii)—the pornography industry pioneered the most sophisticated of Internet technologies, all but invented e-commerce, and still, to this day, if one wants to see the most refined of Internet technologies, one *must* peruse the porn sites.

The readings in Part Five explore the ways the Internet has continued to epitomize pornography's close relationship with technology, create new opportunities for entrepreneurs and, in the process, challenge the boundaries of social institutions. Taylor Marsh opens with an account of her experiences working for Danni's Hard Drive—a major Internet pornography corporation. Like many early entrepreneurs of Internet pornography, former exotic dancer Danni Ashe bootstrapped a small financial endeavor that grew rapidly and, along the way, confronted the successes and failures of that growth. Marsh tells us about these struggles, the people that work behind the scenes of Internet pornography, the nature of their work, and the precarious circumstances encountered. In the end, Marsh also explains how the ethics of the pornography industry can cause difficult personal conflicts—enough to end her career with Danni's Hard Drive.

Perhaps most people understand that pornography has shaped the Internet from the very beginning. Even so, few are aware of the enormous pioneering role the pornography industry really played. Lewis Perdue details this significant influence, gives a provocative account of just how large the Internet pornography industry is, why e-commerce has much to learn from the successes of pornographic ventures, and how everyone who uses the Internet is in debt to the entrepreneurs of e-porn.

All these innovations have posed serious challenges to state and federal law. Stephen Roberds traces the development of obscenity law, detailing how and why the Supreme Court has emerged at the forefront of First Amendment issues and what this means for the present and future of the Internet pornography industry. Like many contemporary social institutions, the Internet has profoundly influenced legal structures; the inherent challenges of the Internet pornography industry to legal definitions of obscenity vividly illustrate this relationship.

These readings all magnify one central theme: whether viewed as a source of opportunity, innovation, or challenge, the Internet pornography industry represents a precariously significant technological, cultural, and social development. The short history of the Internet pornography industry has already proven this significance; one can only wonder what is in store for the future.

## References

Lane, F. 2000. *Obscene profits: The entrepreneurs of pornography in the cyber age.* New York, NY: Routledge.

# Chapter Twelve

# My Year in Smut: Inside Danni's Hard Drive

Taylor Marsh[*]

*For the most part, investigations into the sex industry have been from a distance—the voices of sex workers are seldom heard. The silence is even more deafening for the Internet sex industry; we know little about what goes on behind the scenes of pornography entrepreneurs and sex-service providers on the Internet. Taylor Marsh provides a rare glimpse into the inner workings of a major Internet pornography corporation—Danni's Hard Drive—telling about the people who work in the company, the nature of their vocation, and the difficult circumstances they encountered.*

...This drama is about the people and the absurd situations that pervade porn specifically seen though the year I spent as managing editor...of a neophyte entrepreneurial Internet company, Danni's Hard Drive, which is run by a woman. The story that will unfold is partly about Danni Ashe, a woman who started off by stripping for a living, but who eventually landed on the World Wide Web, leaving her very first job behind to take on her second job, president and head porn Diva of her own multi-million dollar Internet and video smut company. On the other side of the story sits a strong and sassy authority-bucking female writer (me) who, while accomplishing a lot for her boss, would ultimately become the sequin studded g-string that cut just a little too tight up Danni's derriere.

This story is about people in an industry with the motive to make money using a very low standard by which to choose online content, which hardly fazes the millions of surfers who just want to see as many topless or naked women as they can. It's about an industrious former stripper who created and founded the "number one subscription site on the Web," and the gal that she hired to assemble a creative and technical team, recreate and reorganize her content, as well as perform the tasks of managing editor at what was undoubtedly the first and most critical "strategic inflection point" in her company's history[.] ...Andrew Grove, Chairman of Intel, has spoken about the strategic inflection point for years. Basi-

[*] Marsh, Taylor. 2000. *My Year in Smut: The Internet Escapades Inside Danni's Hard Drive.* Bloomington, IN: 1st Books. Pages xv–xix, 4–17, 18–20, 21–31, 36–38, 40, 41–45, 59, 75–76, 77, 80–85, 87–91, 130–131, 134–138, 144, 155–157, 160–161.

cally, it's a point in corporate time when something radical impedes a business's standard way of operating so that a radical change in procedures must be implemented in order for the company to continue to prosper.

In July 1997, Danni's Hard Drive, www.danni.com, was going through such a strategic inflection point, turning the business away from ad hoc amateur practices into a serious money making machine. Danni's contract with the people who provided all of her pictorial and written content, The Score Group, was about to end. When it did, The Score Group was coming online and about to become her number one competitor. If Danni didn't make it through this critical corporate juncture the future of her company was in serious jeopardy. It was the most emotionally charged, unprofessional period of my long creative career. To say I was unprepared for the combustible atmosphere at Danni's Hard Drive is a profound understatement.

...My conclusions are many, but one in particular rests uncomfortably with me. Whether speaking of Alfred Kinsey, Hugh Hefner, or Larry Flynt, and regardless of whether you approve, agree, or can stomach their products, along with their capitalistic ambitions, these men also had political passions, purpose, and philosophies that each of them believed in and staked their lives on. ...The current generation of techno smut peddlers hasn't the conscience, the heart, or the soul of any of their political and philosophically oriented predecessors.

### Online Smut

...Why do men, who still make up the majority of smut surfers, go searching online for pictorial porn? In an article in the *London Guardian,* May 1998, Danni Ashe gave the answer on which most porn sites are launched: Because most men masturbate. That's the obvious answer, which doesn't tell the whole story, if it can be told at all.

Porn is a black-and-white issue with little gray area. You either enjoy participating in the act of voyeurism or you don't; are aroused by seeing naked bodies overtly exposed or you aren't; find viewing human beings locked in a game of sexual power titillating or you don't. It's the utter fascination most of us have with the physical, peeking into another's private, intimate world to see what someone is like when they are unmasked and completely vulnerable. Capturing the animalism in a person's humanity when they're stripped down, naked, and exposed to the bone is an enthralling spectacle to behold for many, regardless of gender.

...When designing types of pornography, there are several terms that are most often used: erotica, soft-core, and hard-core. Mr. Hugh Hefner, of Playboy

Enterprises, considers his pictorial content to be strictly erotica, which is a fairly honest claim[.] ...Danni Ashe is strictly soft-core because she doesn't perform in male-female sexual duos or allow anything that appears under the heading of her corporation to involve dildos, toys, or penetration. In fact, Danni doesn't even like to consider what she does for a living pornography[.] ...However, though Danni doesn't allow anything produced by DHD [Danni's Hard Drive] to be of a hard-core nature, she has no compunction whatsoever about making money off of the XXX-rated video feeds she supplies on her subscription site [HotBOX], or featuring hard-core porn stars or buying material from other sources that are hard-core.

...There is also a bit of "class-ism" that comes with the labeling of pornography. Soft-core is often labeled the "clean" pornography; a title Danni Ashe and her soft-core porn compatriots hang on to as a sort of shield of erotic respectability. Hard-core pornography is the "dirty" stuff. The hypocrisy of such erotic snobbery is stupefying, but I must admit that I used this type of rationalization when I decided to work for Danni Ashe.

...The look of Danni's site was very appealing to me and obviously to many others as well. One reason is that DHD doesn't make you feel ashamed or dirty to log on and participate in the delicious voyeurism it offers. The minute you log on to the site you are greeted by a clean white background displaying visuals of topless women in playful poses. The light-hearted attitude of the site is another advantage, featuring jokes, pictures of the day, and silly bloopers of naked porn stars, which are often out-takes of photo sessions that are quite funny. But the fact that the naked porn Divas are directly involved in promoting themselves on DHD/HotBOX gives the surfers something very unique—permission to look. ...This is a decidedly different approach from that of the other large smut sites on the Web, because they simply offer salacious pictorial spreads without any real voice coming from the porn stars they are featuring.

...The amount of content on Danni's Hard Drive is staggering[.] ...The only way you can manage a site like DHD/HotBOX is to be an A-type personality with a tendency towards anal retentiveness. The checking and rechecking of links and pages was fierce, comprising a good portion of each and every day. ...Danni's Hard Drive, the free site, is filled with topless pictures of the porn Divas, which are meant to be a teaser for what is offered in HotBOX, and is arguably the largest free side porn outlet on the Web. HotBOX offers voluminous porn pictorials complete with sopping spread shots and the ever-present and necessary "pink shots." Pink shots are close-ups of female genitalia. In 1998, DHD/HotBOX featured over 250 nude models, strippers, and porn actresses, and by fall 1999, HotBOX had over 50,000 lewd, smutty, and salacious pictorials archived, with these numbers multiplying monthly. After my arrival, DHD began offering males showing off their exposed, raging erections in our erotic stories, but women are the true stars of DHD/HotBOX. ...There are many different sections of DHD/HotBOX, including one that exclusively stars Danni Ashe. As of fall 1999, HotBOX offered over 1,800 of her nude shots, pink shot pictorials, as well as her available pornographic videos.

...In...January of 1998, Danni's contract with The Score Group, the magazine group that supplied all of her porn content and allowed her to archive all of their back issues, would expire, and Danni would have to begin providing the content for her site herself. If this didn't qualify as a strategic inflection point, I don't know what does.

The Score Group's four magazines that Danni had contracted to publish online, which included scads of sensational spread shot pictorials, which were also available in her HotBOX archives were: *Naughty Neighbors,* which is an amateur magazine that is tremendously popular; *Leg Show,* which is, in my opinion, one of the best fetish publications in print; *Score,* a strictly huge boob extravaganza; and *Voluptuous,* featuring humongous hooters brought to you by nature not modern medicine. What makes The Score Group so successful and most of their ventures lucrative is that they have easy access to prime porn photographers; a good reputation among the most popular big-breast models, porn stars, and strippers; and a huge database of loyal, paying magazine subscribers that have been with them for years. ...But they weren't online yet, so taking advantage of Danni's early entry into online porn was a good deal for everyone involved. But all this was about to change and with it the business reality at Danni's Hard Drive/HotBOX.

The challenge of changing out the site's content and removing four very popular print magazines from the subscription portion of DHD/HotBOX was incredibly difficult. ...This meant that if Danni Ashe wanted to keep her site supplied with new material, she would have to find and purchase original photos that hadn't had Internet exposure yet. She'd always given her HotBOX subscribers pictures that couldn't be found anywhere else on the Web, and Danni wasn't about to change that guarantee now. Next she would have to secure contracts with long-term publishing rights, obtain model releases and age verifications, then edit the pictorials that would appear in unique online magazines that had yet to be created.

...We had decided to produce four electronic magazines: a big-bust E-zine, a pretty girl, an amateur, and a fetish. We went through all sorts of names before we decided on what to call our E-zines. Some names we wanted to use were already registered, which is a big problem now that so many people in porn are online. Names like sex kitten, all amateur, fetish.com, and others were not available. So our E-zine names became: Nippleodeon, CyberBeauties, NaughtyNewbies, and NetFetish, though our fetish e-zine was not very satisfying, due to Danni's soft-core company policy. It was discontinued soon after I left. We'd planned to create and continually add new E-zines as photographs became available to DHD. "Sexual Prime" was in the works, which featured porn pictorials of women from ages thirty to fifty, and would be launched in late 1998.

...We all worked like crazed fools preparing the four new E-zines[.] ...DHD definitely lost subscribers, but that couldn't be helped. The contract was over and her competitors were coming online, creating a site entitled scoreland.com. And since they had easier access to all the naturally big-breasted models than anyone else in the world, all we could hope for was that these print pornographers wouldn't understand the Web culture for about six months, which would give DHD time to build up our original content. That's exactly what happened.

...Danni Ashe had a couple of content rules that I was responsible for enforcing. The first-person narrative is used throughout the site to make it seem more welcoming and intimate, though as large as this site is it's impossible to imagine that anyone really thought of it as an intimate site. There was a link for "Danni's Diary," and underneath it was a teaser for the reader to come see what "I've" been doing lately. The other rule was that the site...was to be "fun and light." There could never be anything negative in tone heard coming from the Divas or appearing anywhere else on the site. The best possible spin was always put on the Diva's porn bios, making them appear like the girl next door, even if that was a huge stretch of the imagination.

...In addition to the new content we were creating, the new E-zines were to have two celebrity columnists in each one. The columnists were not to be professional writers or even individuals who had any writing experience at all. These columnists were to be nude models or porn stars that would provide a column along with a roll of film of them in the buff that went along with the column's topic for the month. The more arousing, titillating, and provoking the columns and their accompanying pictures were the better. Danni took complete responsibility in choosing the columnists, making certain that each lady was significantly saucy and spicy enough to satisfy her HotBOX subscriber's appetites. After Danni had chosen the columnist, they would then be handed off to me so that we could discuss the subject matter, hopefully matching the woman and her "writing" with the E-zines for which she'd been chosen.

...The Editor's Desk was the first serious content ever seen on DHD/HotBOX. ...The Editor's Desk included an opinion section, which featured editorials on anything from Ken Starr's investigations to President Clinton's involvement with Paula Jones and Monica Lewinsky, and articles about potential privacy and sexual equality.

Being the editor for the eight revolving DHD columnists was nothing short of an utter nightmare. The women had no clue what was involved in writing a column, let alone any idea of what the word "deadline" meant. ...The other fact that made my job as editor so difficult, especially with regard to columnists, was that I had no authority, in actuality. All of these women were acquaintances of Danni's, and she needed these girls in order to make her subscription site profitable. ...Though trying to stay out of my job, Danni would usually assert her authority, which was ultimate, making my job of handling the columnists in any professional manner near to impossible. ...It is very daunting as an editor to come into a personality-driven Internet site and try to absorb the intent and voice of the personality.

...There was one issue in particular regarding content, which involved one of Danni's pictures of the week, that turned into a major cause of irritation, embarrassment, and disgust for me. One of my team came into my office one day to deliver that week's picture, laughing as he did so. I looked at it and couldn't believe my eyes. It was a picture taken at a local erotica convention with Danni Ashe standing next to a T-shirt that had written on it, "Even God Loves Pussy." I was appalled. The look on my face said it all. I replied, "Don't even think of bringing that into me again." A couple of weeks went by and this loathsome photo made it back around to my office once again, with the instructions that it was to go up. Danni even commented to me that she thought it was funny.

My reply was the exact opposite. Her reaction to my adamant disapproval being, "Well, I guess each person has their own ideas about what's funny."

Danni vetoed my decision not to publish it, and the picture went up. It lasted three days. When we got more cancellations and I had DHD staffers coming into my office complaining about it, as well as others questioning my judgment via email, that was it. ...So, instructing my team to pull the picture and expunge it from our archives forever, I then set about writing Danni a long memo about my decision. It was one of the many times that I thought I could get fired, due to the fact that Danni didn't condone being overruled for any reason[.] ...Continual content clashes were only one recurring aspect of the challenges I faced as managing editor of Danni's Hard Drive. The biggest obstacle I faced was my boss, who as it turned out, had no intention of letting me do the job she'd hired me to do.

### The Land of Estrogen

Everyone in the office had an alias or web persona, to which all of the individuals in this story will be referred. Because of the nature of our work online, as well as the work in which the gals in the adult entertainment business engage, real identities are guarded rather closely, which is understandable. ...The stigma behind working in porn remains large.

Danni Ashe started her Internet corporation with the help of her girlfriends. One such friend was Shannon. Danni relied solely on the technical and design skills of this young woman to help her get what would become Danni's Hard Drive and HotBOX up and running. Shannon lived with Danni in those days, as they spent mega-hours in their pajamas hashing out what DHD would look like and what would be the feel of the site. Shannon did all the graphics, as Danni directed her on each and every detail of the website she was creating.

Shannon started in the adult entertainment industry as a topless dancer in a men's club in Houston, Texas, at the age of nineteen. From there she went to the well-known New York club, Stringfellows, but eventually tired of the exotic dancer life, returning to Texas to get a degree in technical design from the University of Texas. Beyond the site's graphics, Shannon pretty much ran the site for Danni in the beginning, while also offering DHD fans some sexy soft-core views of herself. ...Webmistresses were not the norm in the Internet industry in the mid 1990s, and especially rare in the Web porn biz. It was even more unlikely to see a good-looking blonde who posed as a topless webmaster. The guys ate it up.

To originally create the site, Danni coaxed her stripper girlfriends and porn actress friends to give her pictures of them so that she could create a model's directory, which was filled with more big-bust models, strippers, and porn stars than any other site on the Web at the time. ...The gals jumped at what Danni was offering. It was a great deal for the women, who knew nothing of the Internet at this point in time, because it gave them more exposure to surfers who were starving for more nude babes. ...To accompany their topless shots, Danni wrote a short bio about the gals, many of whom she knew personally. The bios weren't literary, but they were written by someone who knew or had heard stories about the gal she was writing about. They were effective and satisfying, however thin in substance, also making the reader feel they were getting to know their favorite porn star, stripper, or nude model. ...The writing was crude and basic, but that actually made the biographies even more endearing.

...I met Danni Ashe on a Saturday afternoon in July, 1997. Her offices, at the time, were in a professional office park. As I walked up to the door, I noticed that only their suite number was etched on the glass. There was little fanfare about the occupants of this particular space, for obvious reasons. I rang the buzzer, and once I identified myself, an attractive woman of color let me in. Her name was Cre.

Cre is a single mother who has an adorable daughter. ...Cre is a church-going mom who has absolutely no interest in porn outside of her work. There is no one that I met at DHD who was nicer or more flexible in doing whatever job she was asked to do. We always enjoyed talking about the Lakers, because Cre is one of their biggest fans. Cre handled most of the customer service and email orders that were placed for HotBOX items.

...The DHD offices were painted a bright white, the walls adorned with paintings and a few articles featuring Danni. In time, there would be wall to wall framed press clippings so that anyone walking into the office would be aware that they'd entered the domain of a major player in porn. The good thing about the offices was that you didn't feel like you were in a smut shop, but just a regular place of work.

When I went to work for Danni her company was all-female, except for one male who managed HotBOX. That's a lot of estrogen all cramped up together. Danni did all the marketing, finances, company managing, while also handling creative and content issues, including recruiting the models for her models' directory, as well as all of the merchandising. She would eventually turn certain areas over to others, but everything was completely and totally controlled by her, with all decisions funneled through her at all times. No decision was ever made in her company without her knowledge and expressed approval. To do otherwise would mean certain and swift reprimand.

One of the gals that was a major figure in the company when I was at DHD was Allison. She did the books for Danni, including the day-to-day managing of the accounting and merchandising. ...She and I would often laugh about pictorials, dismayed that certain women had the nerve to pose when they were so out of shape, overly obese, or not very attractive in looks or physicality. ...Allison had a live-in fiancé and children and was expecting another child. Her life outside the office had no connection to the porn biz whatsoever.

...Allison loved looking at all the smut that came in to DHD[.] ...There was a bulletin board in Allison's office that took up over half of the wall space. It was filled to overflowing with fan letters and pictures that had been sent to Danni from guys from all over the world. Most of the snapshots were nudes or at least partial nudes of men showing their masculinity in full, erect glory. It was a massive collage. A few guys also sent in pubic hair or body fluids, which were quickly discarded. Most were heartfelt and some were hysterically funny. One such letter came in from a guy who was pictured fully clothed and smiling broadly, who was masculine and handsome, with a very wholesome, collegiate-type look. The contents of his letter detailed with great pride, abandon, and explicitness the delicious aroma of his farts. This included written descriptions of the sounds he made as he admitted farting throughout this entire letter-writing session. To date, it is my one and only experience hearing about the pleasures of having a fart fetish.

...Eve is a gal who worked at DHD, who is incredibly bright, motivated, and sort of a hippy-type, though she's far too young to have been born at the height of that era. She's also college educated. ...Eve helped me compile the statistics for my Editor's Desk surveys, like the one I did regarding what our fans believed to constitute a sexual relationship. This survey was done when the Bill Clinton/Monica Lewinsky scandal was in the news. I asked which of the following acts constituted the *minimum* requirements for a sexual relationship to have occurred: penetration, oral sex without penetration, kissing and fondling, heavy petting, cybersex, phone sex; with a final choice of all of the above. Forty percent of my readers stated that any of the preceding acts would constitute a sexual relationship in their opinion. Twenty-two percent said oral sex without penetration constituted a sexual relationship. Fifteen percent said only penetration constituted a sexual relationship.

...Chun was the only male presence at DHD when I first arrived. He was in charge of HotBOX while I was at DHD. Chun is a very quiet, college educated man who kept to himself during the day, but who was forever available to help out the company[.]

...There were no set business hours when I arrived, which I immediately found odd, notwithstanding the nature of the Internet, which is a twenty-four-hour-a-day, seven-days-a-week operation. Still, you never knew when anyone was going to be in the office. People would come and go as they pleased. ...When I arrived at Danni's Hard Drive, chaos was in full swing.

Danni and Shannon were very good friends, but when business started rolling at DHD and the stakes got higher, it was quickly becoming apparent that Shannon wasn't going to be able to handle the growing amount of work and the expanse Danni was planning. Unfortunately, her personal life was also taking its toll[.] ...Most of Shannon's day in the office was spent on the phone attempting to sort out her personal life. The only person who was really present every day, but who wasn't a creative type, was Danni's assistant, Madison. This young woman was willing to work very hard, but was far too inexperienced to take on what was beginning to happen at DHD.

Madison was Danni's assistant when I arrived, and was also responsible for the company's public relations. Part of her job was to coordinate company charity events, something that would eventually become her undoing. ...Madison is a short, petite, very attractive young woman with a BS in Biology and a Minor in Early Childhood Education. Madison, Danni, and Shannon were very close to one another in the beginning.

...When Danni arrived on the Internet her timing couldn't have been better, because the sex industry was just beginning to be noticed online. ...Internet porn companies became headline news, especially if they were run by women, because porn was (and still is) a male-dominated industry. At the time, DHD had an extra selling point with the media because the entire company, minus one male employee, was all women. Even after Danni hired me, and I began to hire testosterone to balance all the estrogen in the company, Danni would encourage the guys to pick female aliases to use as their online and email names so that she could continue hyping the image of an all-female porn company.

...Danni, once called "boss lady" by the office gals, is a good-looking, sexy, big-busted, blonde ex-stripper who has an all-natural figure that only God could have created. She is a young woman who is ruthlessly determined, prone to avoiding anything that hints of substance, and one of the shrewdest, most intuitive Internet porn entrepreneurs around, who made her first million before she was thirty. ...Danni, having held only the jobs of stripper and adult porn actress before becoming president of her own Internet porn company, has never had any professional business experience. She's learned it all on the job.

...My life has been spent in the entertainment business, being a union performer, employee and self-employed[.] ...I guess the only thing that Danni and I had in common was that I had been Miss Missouri, and she a stripper, both of us using our looks to get us somewhere else, although my body was never really my strong suit. Beyond that, there was also the fact that we were both involved in exploring sex, though in very different ways and for very different reasons.

...Originally from Seattle, Washington, Danni began her adventures as a stripper on her home turf at the age of seventeen, though her bio now states that she started when she was eighteen. She had begun building her fan club through producing porn videos of herself, her ambitions growing in direct proportion to the fans she was seducing. Danni found herself with the opportunity to "feature" dance on the road in Florida. A feature dancer is like a "guest star" at a local club, a woman who has often performed in pornographic videos or been seen in adult men's magazines. ...Well, the night she was readying herself to perform in Florida, no one had bothered to tell her about certain zoning restrictions that applied to the club where she was to perform. ...So when Danni began her strip tease, or as the *Los Angeles Business Journal* reported in February 1997, "...a table dance that crossed local decency regulations," the local Florida police appeared, arresting her as they raided the strip joint. It was this event that was the real catalyst for Danni's transformation from stripper to computer enthusiast to multi-millionaire pornographer and Webpreneur. Viewing her husband's corporate website might have excited her and put the notion of the Internet into her head, but only after she'd had her jail experience in Florida.

...Danni and I needed each other from a purely business standpoint. She was at a critical business point in her company, the outcome of which would determine her professional future. It didn't matter that we would never be friends, as long as we both got what we wanted from one another and out of the experience. The goal of our partnership was to make DHD/HotBOX the hottest porn site on the Web. That is exactly what happened.

...Although I didn't join the company until her site was off and running, Danni's vision of what she wanted her site to be has remained clear, if somewhat multi layered. My interpretation of what she wants her site to be is a place of enjoyment, pleasure, and release. Thinking isn't forbidden, but it's not exactly encouraged.

At the time I was working for Danni Ashe her philosophy about pornography was, as I've intimated, complex. There were no insertion pictorials...including pictorials featuring the use of dildos. A woman can have a dildo in her hand, but she can't be seen putting it inside herself. A man and a woman can be pictured or seen getting ready to have sex, with a woman holding the man's penis; but the woman can never insert the penis into her or take it into her mouth. In fact, in Danni's hundreds of personal porn pictorials, never did she use sex toys, insert anything into herself, or ever have anything to do with boy/girl penetration scenarios. You can view Danni exposing herself fully through wide sopping spread shots; see pictures of her in bondage scenarios or in fetish wear; even enjoy numerous bisexual rompings with Danni and her gal-pal porn playmates as they carnally devour one another from breast to buttocks, but she refuses to participate in hard-core sexcapades.

...Another one of the complexities in working for Danni Ashe is that she doesn't consider what she does for a living as pornography. I found it strange, if not downright disingenuous to hear her say, "I just hate the word pornography." She would refer to her work as "erotica," ...but since she freely offers her subscribers XXX-rated and hard-core material as long as it doesn't display her company's name or logo, she can't honestly get away with it. What we were doing was erotica, but it was also most certainly pornographic. It seemed absurd that a multi-millionaire pornographer found the word "pornography" distasteful.

...Danni and I did not accomplish our goals by ourselves, however. There was no way either of us could have achieved our objectives without considerable technical expertise and artistic assistance.

### Tits, Ass, and Techies

...A woman whom I glommed onto shortly after I got Internet fever, long before I came to DHD, was the first member of the team. She was directly responsible for my being at DHD, since she arranged my initial interview with Danni Ashe. This young woman, whose Web alias is Emily, provided the technical support I needed for everything I was to do at DHD until the very end of my tenure. ...Emily is a 5'7" Web whiz, with long brown hair and a body that is lean, svelte, and strong, who was in her late twenties at the time we were at DHD together. She's an avid rock climber, extremely intelligent, a lover of fine food, great books and good times. ...As a devout techie, Emily is not exactly the most overt individual, actually being quite shy about her looks and figure. ...[S]he personally hated and refused to get involved with...photos of voluptuous to large-figured females. Even the humongous-breasted pictorials sent Emily away wincing. She couldn't understand a person's preoccupation with huge hooters.

...The Internet is a 24/7 reality, so to say that Emily didn't have much of a life while we were at DHD together is an understatement. Emily is one of the several individuals at DHD who insists on her anonymity. Her family has no idea that she works for an adult porn company, and she doesn't ever plan to tell them. She is not able to talk about her work in detail with her family, which bothers her immensely. Emily will eventually have to decide whether she wants to continue working on a porn site, reconciling her own conscience with her family's philosophies about pornography. This is bound to make her dig deep within herself, or maybe she'll get comfortable with compromise in light of the big bucks.

...Another member of my original team was an irreverent rebel named Bishop. He was our webmaster after Shannon quit. He's a tall, adorable, sensual young man, who is very bright and was just hitting his thirties when we worked together. He has tons of talent, but his love for the late night L.A. club scene and partying, along with his inability to conform to a defined workweek, made him the most contrary member of what would become our team. ...Danni and Emily had originally hired Bishop. He was invaluable to me because of his multiple skills and technical range[.] ...His family didn't know he worked for an adult soft-core porn company, and they would have been hurt had they found out. ...He's long-gone from the porn world at the moment, though he has been known to design and maintain small stripper sites for a select few girls. Bishop is now a dad and has committed to a full-time, stable job.

...The gentleman I hired to be the new designer after Shannon quit, named Vaneyck, came to me through Danni, because he has been doing her print artwork for several years, including designing the DHD trademark "nipple." ...The females on the team hated that damn nipple with a passion and we never let Vaneyck forget it, teasing him relentlessly. (It was finally replaced at the end of 1999) ...Vaneyck was in his middle thirties when we worked together. He is around 5'7" tall, with a rock hard jock bod and deep soulful eyes. ...Vaneyck is good looking, very loving, and a gifted artist, with strong masculine presence, as well as a tender and understanding side as well. Few women could pass up taking a look at this man as he passed by. Unfortunately for them, Vaneyck is married to a former Playboy Bunny, who is a stunner in her own rights. ...And let me tell you, there's nothing like watching Vaneyck walk down the hallway. What an ass.

Sexist comment, isn't it? Well, sexist comments flew around the DHD office. Every time I interviewed someone for a possible position at DHD, I had to draw a clear distinction for them on what constitutes sexual harassment in mainstream industry and sexual harassment in an adult entertainment corporation, because almost all of my interviewees had never worked for an adult entertainment company. ...I mean, we would swap dialogue around the office about tits and ass, penis and pussy, with a little technical jargon thrown in, like medical students might do in an anatomy class.

Anyone wanting to work for an adult entertainment company, let alone a porn site, has to be prepared for a little spice in the office repartee. ...[S]exual innuendo and dirty jokes reigned supreme amidst this totally adult environment. Everyone who worked at DHD had a very good understanding of this, regardless of gender or sexual persuasion. Sex was our business.

There were other times when the conversation revolved around the pictures we were scanning and uploading onto the site, which was actually one of the most important jobs on the team. The young woman who became the artistic image producer, scanning and making online beauty out of still photos for me, was named Shellyn. This young woman, just in her thirties at the time, had quit her stagnant, yet secure day job to come temp and answer phones for DHD in the hopes that she might learn some computer skills, too. ...Shellyn is over six feet tall, an Amazonian femme with alabaster skin and large breasts, who is literate, sensitive, a bit over emotional, but someone with great potential. She just hadn't found an outlet for her artistic abilities yet. ...Bishop...agreed to help teach Shellyn the beginning arts of scanning, willing to take her through the ropes of

Photo Shop and image retouching details. The photo enhancement that Shellyn was responsible for would take on many forms, including smoothing out stretch marks when photos came in of models that had bad boob jobs. There were a lot of those. Danni's Hard Drive dealt with a lot of big-bust models with silicone implants, and when I say big bust, I mean it. Would you believe 42FFF and beyond?

...Shellyn would perform miracles on other parts of the female body, as well. She'd remove corns on feet appearing in foot fetish photo sets, smooth out tummy wrinkles, as well as do amazing things with derrieres. For instance, one day she came in to tell me about a miraculous touch-up job that she'd just done. ...She then showed me what she'd done, which included before and after shots of her work, which practically sent us both to the floor in laughter. She'd just made a very nasty hemorrhoid disappear from a porn actress's derriere so that the woman's bend-me-over backdoor close-up would be presentable. Our laughter brought in Emily, who was constantly amazed at what Shellyn's job entailed. I just shook my head, grateful that the detailing required for such a job didn't repulse her. Shellyn finally declared that she didn't know if she should be proud of the work she'd done or disgusted. ...Emily and I would often remark that she was the most talented Internet photo retoucher we'd ever seen.

...The original team, Emily, Vaneyck, Bishop, Shellyn, and I had a lot of raucous fun. All four of these people worked in one room, while I had an office just across from them. There was something very special that went on with the five of us[.] ...We had a lot of successes[.] ...We survived the stress of it all, which was considerable, by keeping a sense of humor and by my insistence that we take moments out of our day to pause and unwind. We were also merciless teases[.]

...As DHD grew and expanded, so did the team. The next members were to take us into full bloom as a creative force, adding dimensions to what we could do that went way beyond what any of us could have originally anticipated. ...When we ran the blind ad in *Variety* and the *Hollywood Reporter* for the new position of talent coordinator, I quite literally got ten pounds worth of resumes. I even got resumes from individuals who had worked with Johnny Carson, as well as the Disney Corporation. Of course, they had no idea they were applying to work on a soft-core porn site, which was something you just didn't advertise.

One resume in particular caught my eye out of them all. The first line on his resume stated that he'd managed the talent for Barnum and Bailey Circus. That was all I needed to know. Anyone who could manage circus talent definitely had the qualifications to coordinate the crew I needed managed, the strippers, models, and XXX-rated porn actresses of the adult entertainment industry. After spending ten minutes with Johnathan, I decided to hire him on the spot. ...Johnathan is an incredibly talented, professional and driven gentleman whom all the girls love. What is it they say about gay men? They're always the best looking and the first one you want to take home. Well, this gorgeous hunk of Texas has had more than one porn star propose marriage and fatherhood. Luckily he's smart enough to stay loyal to the (somewhat) saner sex.

...There were several latecomers to the team. One was Rick, who had never been involved in porn before, and who is married to a very educated gal. Rick came in as a designer, only to find his job description changed three times, twice in the same day. ...Rick, a seasoned professional, understandably found his constantly changing corporate role, as well as navigating Danni's changing marketing strategies, a little too unstable for his tastes. He left DHD after only four months, increasing his salary by almost 50 percent in the process.

...At the same time I hired Rick, I also hired a new webmaster to replace Bishop, a gal from the Midwest who had come to California to entirely change her personal and professional life. Sandi is a short, thirty-something female who had taught computer classes, but had never been part of a company like DHD. ...Sandi had certainly never been directly involved in pornography before.

...The last person I hired at DHD was for a new position being created as design assistant to Vaneyck. ...Ken had the job the moment I met him. ...Ken not only had the talent, but he also offered maturity and depth the team needed. ...Ken was in his forties when we worked together, closer to my age, which could account for some of the bonding that immediately happened, and was the most astute Internet Web designer I'd ever met. He and his lady partner had recently moved to Los Angeles. He also had never worked in porn before. ...Ken is an experienced designer and webmaster. He's capable of creating images that are visually striking, knows how to design so that his Web pages are easily navigated, sticks with Web-safe colors, and has a vast knowledge of browsers so he knows what a site will look like on different applications.

...The team had no direct responsibility for the adult content Danni was buying and providing. ...Danni was the bottom line on all content decisions.

...I didn't start out in my life to write about sex and relationships, let alone pornography. It all started quite differently. Of course, being editor to an adult smut site was quite a ride while it lasted and I don't regret a moment of it. It looks just great juxtaposed between Miss Missouri and being a phone sex operator! The phone sex operator came much later, when I began personally investigating the world of human sexuality, most specifically, anonymous connection. But even before I was a Miss America contestant I was interested in smut, from a purely investigative and voyeuristic point of view, which evolved as I matured and began writing down my adventures. I was Miss Missouri on the outside and Mae West on the inside, aspiring to someday integrate both characters into one woman that I could really live with and love.

...I've used a lot of different pen names, including "Anonymous," which I still sometimes use. ...Many women also chose masculine names, (like Taylor), to pen their stories under in order to hide their identity, enabling them to secretly procure funds with which to help them live unique, authentic, even incendiary lives, while still maintaining their proper façade. Image and reality have always been conflicting struggles for women, and that was never truer than with me.

As a phone sex operator I used several aliases, including Lisa and Taylor. When I was in Amsterdam interviewing prostitutes through different contacts I'd made in local pubs, I also used the name Taylor. Taylor was my secret, but today she is who I am. She is an extension of the girl from Missouri who had to create another life for herself in order to discover who she was. Seldom are things the way they seem on the surface and that was certainly true of me and the life I was experiencing. My given name, Michelle Marshall, is one that only my family and closest friends use. The people who have come to know me as Taylor Marsh, going back over fifteen years, can't see me as "a Michelle."

### Blast Off!

...From the very first day I walked into DHD, it was like being shot out of a cannon, and it would remain an unpredictable adventure until I dashed out the door a little over one year later.

I guess first off I must say that who I am contributed to the combustible nature of my relationship with Danni Ashe, as well as the inevitable outcome. Beyond that, let me also state that I have a deep-seated distaste for authority. ...[B]ut at Danni's Hard Drive I definitely knew who was in charge and did my damnedest to implement Danni Ashe's desires at all times, even when I disagreed strongly.

...The week I began at DHD the tension was palpable, due to an upcoming charity event that DHD was sponsoring. This charity event was just one instance of the high profile nature of DHD. Danni wanted the spotlight on herself and her company whenever possible. There was never a moment at this company when creating positive press wasn't part of her mission.

...My first challenge was to help organize the details of the upcoming event, Night Dance, which had been in the planning stages for over four months. The goal behind the event was to raise as much money as possible for Children of the Night, an organization that helps keep kids and teenagers off the street and away from drugs. My involvement included daily meetings regarding how to get more press for the event; lining up limousines for the strippers and porn Divas, preferably donated since this event was strictly for charity; as well as last minute details regarding the strip show spectacular, Night Dance.

...Danni Ashe was going through quite a lot to make certain that Children of the Night would benefit financially. She was intending to fly in the most popular strippers in the country, women she knew personally, to have a one-night-only strip tease extravaganza to benefit this organization. It was to be a strictly upscale affair, with tickets starting at $75, with other options available for giving larger amounts. You could get private dances with the strippers, buy items of clothing from them, including previously worn g-strings and bras, as well as take a private plane ride for a price that was auctioned off to the highest bidder. Also, dinner and limousine rides were available, which included a full night out with some of the guy's favorite strippers, including dancing, carousing, and lots of champagne. Men were coming from all over the world to attend this event. I was to help make it happen in whatever way that I could. My initiation was about to begin.

One night after a particularly tense day at work, Madison called me at home. The moment I heard her voice, I knew that something was up. She stated that she'd been cleaning out her office trying to get organized, and she'd noticed a package on the floor, which she'd forgotten all about. The star of the charity event, I'll call her "Star Stripper," had sent this package via overnight mail to the DHD offices. ...Madison then stated that when she had picked up the package something had moved inside of it, accompanied by a sort of sloshing noise like there was liquid inside of the package. Madison went on to say that she knew exactly what was in the package. It was an illegal, banned substance, a drug called GHB.

...I cannot say that I was surprised that one of the strippers was ingesting GHB, but I was horrified that she'd sent it via overnight mail to our corporate offices. ...This may seem like a small event, but to me it was not, especially considering that we're talking about the adult entertainment industry where drugs are rampant, and a charity event involving an organization whose primary goal is to get children off the street and off drugs.

...[Madison] next asked me what she should do. There was a long pause in our conversation. Was this a trick question? I'd been at DHD for three days, for God sake. It had already been made clear to me that Star Stripper was one of the most famous big-bust models in the world, worth a lot of money to DHD and the charity event. But what could I do? I told Madison to open the package and dump the substance down the kitchen drain immediately. In fact, I waited on the phone while she went to dump it. Madison came back relieved, but concerned how Danni would react. ...The next day, all hell broke loose.

...When Star Stripper called Danni to confirm her arrival time, ...she evidently threw a tantrum of seismic proportions[.] ...When Danni stated to me that she...thought Madison had done the wrong thing, I told her flat out that I'd given Madison just such orders and instructions. I then explained what I thought was obvious, that any corporation, but especially an adult porn company, cannot have any appearance of illegal activities, especially when it concerned banned substances that have been proven to induce comas and even death. I didn't bother to go into the other obvious elements. Like what the consequences would be if the star of a Children of the Night event, sponsored by a porn company, collapsed on stage because of a drug overdose.

...I then informed Star Stripper that she was fired form the charity event. ...So, Star Stripper was out and now Danni had to find a Diva of equal stature to replace her, which wasn't easy. Tawny Peaks, one of Danni's very best porn playmates, finally agreed to headline Night Dance.

Tawny Peaks is a legend and one of the most popular feature performers on the exotic dancer circuit. She is also a pivotal character in my story. Tawny is just five feet tall, and her measurements are 38DDD-26-36. Because Tawny is so short her breasts appear gigantic. In fact, her breasts got her into trouble in the summer of 1998. The story appeared in *USA Today* under the header, "He Should Have Known Better." The story was about a gentleman who had filed a law suit in Tampa, Florida, which stated that he'd been injured due to the size of an exotic dancer's breasts, when they were flung at him during her act. Tawny Peaks was the dancer named in the suit, whose performance, the guy claimed, had given him whiplash. Appropriately, the case ended up on television, with Tawny Peaks and the gentleman appearing on *People's Court*. Tawny won the case.

But even with Tawny Peaks hired to take over Star Stripper's role in Night Dance, we still had a lot more to accomplish before the night of the event, which at this point was less than one week away. The players involved at this point included one of The Palace's owners, which was where the event was to take place; the L.A.P.D., which meant Vice; the Alcohol and Beverage Control Board; and Madison and myself, representing Danni's Hard Drive.

The owners of The Palace had gotten very nervous over the appearance of impropriety that resulted from a clothed print ad of Danni Ashe, which had been brought to their attention by the L.A.P.D.'s Vice Squad. The ad was being used to publicize the upcoming charity event, appearing in several local papers, including the *LA Weekly* and *LA News Times*. Danni's sexy print ad brought out

The Palace owner's insecurities, as well as implied threats from the authorities that revolved around zoning laws and ABC club licensing requirements for clubs holding an event where location, alcohol, and stripping intersected.

The print ad in question showed Danni in a very short dress, her breasts bursting forth revealing ample cleavage, as she hiked her skirt up with one hand, seductively revealing a lot of exposed thigh and sexy lace panties. It was a provocative, suggestive, adult entertainment ad, but Danni was fully clothed. The authorities didn't like the ad, its inferences, and the fact that a strip tease event was taking place in a club serving alcohol. Zoning laws became their reason for interfering.

...After my very first meeting with the owner of The Palace, I saw we were in a real corporate-size dilemma. ...The Palace owner stated that what they really wanted to do was cancel the event immediately in order to head off any possibility of them losing their liquor license or the Vice Squad closing down the charity event, something they were convinced was a viable threat. ...After I informed Danni that I felt she was headed into big trouble, she became immediately fearful of what could happen if the L.A.P.D. Vice Squad or the ABC took a hard line on the night of the big party. That's when Danni shared a little inside information with me about what can happen when a bunch of strippers and adult actresses get together. She informed me that the women in this industry have a tendency, when they've been drinking and carousing together, to get a little loose and spontaneously drop their tops.

...At the very last minute, and after much hand wringing, Danni decided to cancel the charity event, and in its place threw a party to honor Children of the Night at a club up on Sunset Boulevard called Millennium. She offered everyone who had purchased tickets their money back since there would be no big show, but few asked for it, knowing that the proceeds were still going to go to a very good cause. The strippers came into Los Angeles on schedule looking forward to a short paid holiday and a little partying with girlfriends, if nothing else.

Minus the tickets already sold, the entire event came out of Danni's corporate pocket, which amounted to significantly more than she had originally anticipated, because Madison, who had been put in charge of pulling this monstrous thing off, had miscalculated on how many tickets had been sold. ...It's safe to say that Danni will think long and hard before she sponsors another corporate fundraiser. Soon after the charity event debacle, Madison was summarily fired.

...Although the time I spent at DHD was often chaotic, and even though our business relationship would never be stable, one of the things that kept me enthused about being managing editor for DHD, especially in the beginning, was my periodic creative meetings with Danni. They were actually brainstorming sessions about the company and where we were headed. For hours, we would hash out ideas and possibilities for new content, both of us excited about what was happening on the site. Each time one of these meetings would occur I'd get new energy for my job, plus renewed hope that I had a true business partnership with the president, my boss, something that had been strong at the start, when Danni needed my expertise the most. ...I was completely blindsided by the event that would scream, "Get out *now*!"

## I'm Outta Here

...[T]he content of Tawny Peaks's column for the September 1998 issue of Nippleodeon...would blindside me, and send me running for the exit. ...The column...was in such poor taste and so crossed the line of good judgment, I was dumbfounded there was even any question whatsoever as to what the proper decision was to make regarding publishing such content.

...."Tawny is posing nude where she went to elementary school, on her childhood playground." ...I looked at her in abject horror. "You're kidding. We can't use that," I stated bluntly. ...."It's a stripper exposing herself on an elementary schoolyard!" ...The written and audio portion of Tawny Peaks's September 1998 column, which went along with the pictures she had taken, revolved around a dare for her to pose nude romping around her childhood playground[.] ...Throughout her column, Tawny Peaks intimated feelings about taboo fantasies and longings that obviously referred to the voyeuristic pleasures of imagining an underage tryst and its pleasures. ...It was patently obvious that she knew exactly what she was doing and what her forbidden dare suggested. ...It seemed to me that it carelessly flirted with very sensitive issues.

...A school playground is intended to be a safe haven for children where nothing can threaten their educational growth, as well as their physical or emotional well-being. If cities and counties have zoning laws regulating strip clubs and adult bookstores, keeping such places a certain distance away from neighborhoods, churches, and schoolyards, I felt it was a safe leap for me to refuse to provide a forum where porn stars and strippers can expose themselves on an elementary school playground through pornographic photography, then expect viewers to pay money to see such exhibitionism, ultimately putting me in the position of seemingly advocating their behavior or worse, approving of such inappropriate conduct around children. ...There was no way in hell I could condone publishing Tawny Peaks's column. Would Danni agree with my decision? It was obvious to me I would no longer be able to ethically perform my job if Danni chose to veto my decision.

...Danni asked to read Tawny's column, after I stated firmly we could not publish it. [By the end of the] weekend, an email from Danni was waiting for me, stating there was no reason not to run Tawny Peaks's column. And that, as they say, was that. ...Then I resigned. Seemed like the only thing I could do. It certainly is Danni's prerogative to put whatever content she wants on her porn site, while walking the legal tight rope at all times, but I don't want to be associated with anything that includes the content subjects of elementary school playground, exhibitionism, and pornography.

...Perhaps my failures in this business relationship were due to who I am and what I intended to bring to the table as a writer and editor. Perhaps I served a purpose during a strategic time in DHD's history and it was time for me to leave. Or perhaps pornography has no place in it for a woman who is not a pornographer at heart.

...Many times when I would state to someone that I was a managing editor of a soft-core porn site, I would get disapproving looks and positively befuddled questions about why I was submitting myself to such work. My older brother even stated to me that when he told a close associate what I did for a living his response was, "Does she understand what she's doing?" The implication was that I was assisting in the moral decay of individuals on a large scale. ...On another occasion, one of my female friends asked, "Don't you feel that you're compromising yourself?" Once I was gone from DHD, this same girlfriend would ask, "In what ways do you feel that you compromised yourself by working for Danni, now that you're gone?" Invariably, I would state that I in no way compromised myself. ...[O]nce again, porn is a black-and-white issue. You either get what it's about or you don't.

...There is no mistake in my not being the managing editor of DHD anymore. But the real root of why I don't belong as editor to a site like DHD is because there is no philosophy, either erotic or political, that runs consistently through the site. There is nothing that even hints of the revolutionary sexual thinking that was pioneered by men like Alfred Kinsey, Hugh Hefner, and Larry Flynt, and that sent America into collective puberty in the late 1900s. ...I don't necessarily espouse any of these males' philosophies or completely agree with the means by which they promote individual rights, sexual emancipation, or social theory, but at least all of them were motivated by strong political and social motives, in addition to their capitalistic ambitions. It is the social theory behind revolutionary sexual thinking that gives erotica its core. ...The new smut peddlers multiplying daily online are bringing no hint of what resounded through the sexual insurrection of the past and through the 1960s onto their sites, opting instead for more, more, more, and offering nothing of substance at the core.

Some may argue proposing that porn needs political or philosophical meat at its base is preposterous, but I contend that the philosophical and political motives behind sexual repression inspires such lofty, intellectual, erotic posturing. Sexual freedom began through political and cultural revolution, whether written, spoken, or photographed.

...The views I hold about sex and pornography may differ from men like Kinsey, Hefner, and Flynt, but I share their political and philosophical drive to make erotica a genre of substance as well as flesh. The art of erotica and pornography is best exemplified when we are presented physically and emotionally naked and vulnerable to one another. The depiction of sexual intimacy between humans can include fantasy scenarios, power balancing acts, and graphic details of lovemaking from either gender's viewpoint, but there must never be disrespect or violence meant to physically harm either individual. The goal of erotica and pornography is to sexually empower, inspire, and fire the imagination through heightening the physical, emotional, and spiritual pleasure being experienced and sometimes shared by one or more human beings.

...I believe that healthy, sexually stimulating erotica and pornography serves a social purpose. The genre is especially important in America where Eros is not allowed out in the light of our daily lives, where violent and gun-ridden movies are accepted and rated less harshly than films with nudity and erotic love scenes. I've spoken with couples who have used smut to help them put the zing back into their marriage, as well as talked with women who have learned sexual techniques through watching porn. Erotic love scenes can liberate the most tight-assed individual, if she or he is a willing participant. ...But as far as peddling porn goes, I've had my fill for awhile. I've seen enough close-ups of human genitalia to last me a lifetime.

## ❖ Chapter Thirteen

# EroticaBiz: How Sex Shaped the Internet

## Lewis Perdue[*]

*As Lewis Perdue makes perfectly clear, "sex shaped the Internet as it exists today." This is not a surprise to most people, but the extent to which sex is woven into the entangled web of the Internet is rarely fully acknowledged, fully known, or, for that matter, fully knowable. Mainstream businesses would prefer to remain silent about their stake in the adult industry, and adult industry innovators seldom receive the credit they deserve for significant advancements in both technology and e-commerce. Yet, one thing is undoubtedly true: everyone who uses the Internet is in debt to the pornography industry—Lewis Perdue explains why.*

In 1998, I wrote two articles for a Silicon Valley magazine, *TechWeek,* dealing with the influence of sex on the Internet. The articles provoked an avalanche of reader mail split about one to four between those who wrote "How *dare* you cast the evils of sex and pornography in a favorable light!" and the vast majority who said, "You've just scratched the surface."

I responded to the first group that I had no intention of being porn's spin merchant or of trying to cast the sex industry in a good light. Neither had I set out to deliberately cast them in the worst possible light. But as a writer, business journalist, and technology entrepreneur, online porn seemed to be a substantial part of the content and profits on the Web, and for that reason it deserved to be looked at with a cold, hard eye that moved past the cleavage and sweaty bodies and to be given the same sort of analysis that was devoted to other sectors of the growing Internet economy.

After doing more research for several months, I decided that there was some substance here[.] ...Indeed, it seemed that perhaps the online sex industry's innovations may be influential far beyond its gross revenues (its critics say that *all* its revenues are gross). Indeed, porn has affected the lives of everyone who uses the Internet whether they've ever gazed at a salacious photo or not.

---

[*] Perdue, Lewis. 2002. *EroticaBiz: How Sex Shaped the Internet.* New York, NY: Writers Club Press. Pages ix, xiv–xv, 1, 3–6, 9–13, 26, 27–31, 33–42, 49–53, 57, 61–69, 72–76, 89–99, 101, 103–107, 109, 113, 123–124, 127–134, 137–139, 141–148, 151–156, 158–159, 164, 167–168.

...As you read farther, please keep the following in mind: whether you love or loathe the online porn industry, everything it has done in the past eight years, every success, each failure, and even the scams some have created have a very important lasting effect on your nonporn life. Web sex provided the only income stream to the nascent World Wide Web, revenues that developed the technology, and the market and funded innovation out of real profits. E-porn has also sustained many nonadult Internet companies during the Millennium Meltdown when so many DotComs went DotGone in 2000 and 2001.

Because of this, there are important lessons to be gleaned from the people in the online sex industry. We gain valuable context from their different ways of seeing the world. We learn valuable insights about e-business in general when we look at how they have approached the process of building Web businesses and developing technology that focus first on the user and usability. Valuable lessons of creativity and resourcefulness are even woven throughout the court records of those nailed for fraud.

### Introduction

...Sex shaped the Internet as it exists today. Whether you call it "adult content," "smut," "erotica," or "pornography;" whether you consider it disgusting or titillating, the facts are clear that without business and technical pioneers in the online sex business, the World Wide Web would never have grown so big so quickly.

Without consumer demand for big, bandwidth-hogging sex pictures and streaming video, Cisco would never have sold so many routers and Sun Microsystems so many servers. Without programming pioneers trying to perfect video streaming software that would deliver images of copulation and procreation to paying customers hooked up with a 28.8 kbps dial-up modem, it is unlikely that CNN would be effectively delivering news clips of global breaking news. Without sex-oriented chat and forums to sustain its early years, America Online might never have survived. The e-commerce payment systems that are so common today would be in a far more primitive stage of development, security, and usability. Indeed, without advertising from sex sites, Yahoo! Would be just another Web company with a bloody red bottom line.

At the foundation of any market niche is its customer base, one which is broad, deep, and global for online porn. Research firm Juniper Media Metrix says that of all the Internet users in the entire world in July 2001 (roughly half of whom are American), 21 million of them logged on to an Internet sex site. Those users averaged 85.5 minutes per month with the time split among five sessions.

This represents almost 35 percent of the world's Internet users, a number that has held fairly steady since 1998.

...Servicing all these millions of cybersex surfers, many of whom are seeking very specific niches and fetishes, requires a galaxy of sites. Research from Datamonitor and Forrester Research put the total number of Internet porn sites at 50,000 to 60,000, while Adult Check, an age verification service for sex sites, says it has more than 80,000 participating sites.

...All this indicates that—on the Web as with all the technologies before it—people have always been willing to pay for sex. Always. Companies that ignore this biological imperative do so at their own risk, something that electronics giant Sony knows all too well. At the 1998 Consumer Electronics Show in Las Vegas, Sony executives admitted that the key reason its technologically superior Betamax technology succumbed to VHS was the company's refusal to cooperate with the migration of porn flicks to home video. Having learned that lesson. Sony says they—and all their competitors, including arch-rival Pioneer—are cooperating to ensure the availability of adult content on DVD. Indeed, while DVD technology allows video producers to provide viewers with multiple camera angles, with very few exceptions, only adult video producers are actually delivering products that take advantage of this technical feature.

The compelling and demonstrable demand for online sex has provided profits for sex sites that have eluded all but a very small handful of other Internet businesses. ...Sex as been the only consistently profitable online sector because it started out with a product for which consumers are willing to pay. ...Adult site owners also figured out that the Internet could solve some compelling problems for consumers: access and anonymity. Further, sex and sexual desires represent a perfect subject for a medium where only a small market segment (let's say less than 1 percent who might want sexually oriented cartoons like XXX-rated Japanese anime') is actually a very large number of customers (when measured globally) who can be reached and served online.

Besides meeting a compelling need, a primary reason for the profitability of so many online sites is the lack of available outside investment capital. There are no venture capital firms with deep pockets behind adult sites. Most are bootstrapped by small entrepreneurs or built as an extension of an existing print or video porn business. As such, profitability, cost cutting, and serving the customer's desires have always come first for adult site webmasters. While many venture-funded companies operated in a fantasy land detached from the real needs of their customers, reality and necessity pushed adult sites into cost-effective innovations that cut a short path to a black bottom line.

This drove the development of easy-to-use payment systems, video streams that did not require a browser plug-in and worked on slower dial-up lines, real-time chat that actually worked, live Web cams, and business model innovations such as affiliate networks, performance-based advertising, traffic sharing, and even those pop-up console advertising windows that are annoying but highly effective.

The adult sites have also learned to use the minimum amount of technology to deliver their product. Many of the websites that tanked in 2000 truly deserved to tank. Take Boo.com: everything about the site was about using the latest, greatest, cutting edge technology. The result was a pathetic disregard for users, most of whose browsers did not support the site's engineering or the need for the sort of high-speed broadband connections found in less than 20 percent of American homes. Arrogant Web designers and engineers expected consumers to spend their valuable time downloading and installing additional plug-in software in order to have the privilege of slowly accessing their site.

In the wake of investor demands for well-run, reality-based Web operations in 2000, the profitability of adult websites started to produce respect and an un-accustomed degree of respectability for those in the digital sex trade.

### A Star Is Porn

...Understanding how adult content could shape a technological and cultural phenomenon as globally massive as the Internet requires an understanding of just how big the legal sex industry really is. But sorting that out in a cool, ra-tional, and realistic manner is a lot harder than it seems, thanks to the love-mostly-hate relationship Americans have with sex.

...The issue is far from a cool rational one. Political conservatives, most feminist organizations, and many religious groups have declared war on what they call obscenity and would like to see it aggressively prosecuted and banned as immoral, exploitive, and disgusting. To accomplish those goals, they need to marginalize the industry and cast both producers and consumers as a very small, despicable, and numerically negligible band of perverts in raincoats. For this group, smaller numbers make for an easier target and thus they argue for the smallest interpretation possible.

Liberals, Libertarians, and the porn industry itself may have just the oppo-site goal: to be seen as a large, crypto-mainstream industry with broad consumer (and voter) support that makes such a large financial impact that it can't be at-tacked without damaging the national economy and hurting a politician's reelection chances. What the adult industry wants most is respectability—precisely the one thing the other side wishes to deny them.

...So, how big is the American sex business? Big. Billions. But how many billions has become a vicious and continuing bone of contention between two New York journalism powerhouses. On May 18, 2001, the *New York Times* ran an article by senior writer Frank Rich that tagged the figure at $10 billion to $14 billion. A week later, *Forbes* magazine published a scathing deconstruction of the *New York Times*'s figure, ridiculing Rich's methodology and accusing him of sloppy reporting. The actual figure, *Forbes* countered, was more like $2.6 billion to $3.9 billion. The two publications dueled throughout the spring and summer, in print, on National Public Radio and online.

...In reality, both *Forbes* and the *New York Times* pieces...are...probably wrong. The problem with both estimates comes from the reality that neither of those publications takes the pornography industry seriously enough to assign a beat reporter to cover it. This despite the fact that even the lowball *Forbes* estimates acknowledge that porn is bigger than Major League Baseball ($2.8 billion in 1999, according to MLB Commissioner) and Broadway theater ($575 million in ticket sales in 1999, according to the League of American Theater and Producers Inc.).

Neither the *New York Times* nor *Forbes* knows with any degree of absolute certainty which of the numbers is closest to reality because the embarrassment and the "ick factor" have prevented all the usual news and research organizations from devoting enough time to researching the industry, getting to know its foibles, and developing source relationships that allow a reporter to accurately assess source credibility. Without someone assigned to thoroughly getting to know a beat, a publication can only engage in hit-and-run reporting. The adult industry, like many complex market niches, is absolutely immune to an outside reporter dashing in, talking to 13 people and then dashing off to write an accurate story. It took me two years of constant effort to reach enough of the right people to begin to understand the industry and help me sort the gems from the dregs.

...The lack of credible, independent data led me to develop my own independent analysis of sex-oriented traffic on the global Internet backbone...which was first published by the *Wall Street Journal Online* in March 2001 after two weeks of constant editorial scrutiny and relentless confirmation of sources. That methodology, which was reviewed before publication by top academic sources and corporate experts, indicates that the world of online porn is much, much larger than previously thought[.] [Based on my analysis, I estimate the Internet porn industry at] a total of $31.2 billion. [See Lewis Perdue's book for a complete and detailed discussion of his sophisticated methodology and a breakdown of the figures that comprise this phenomenal estimate.]

...As irrational as it may sound, most financial and technology industry analysts ignore the sex industry despite its financial clout because of an extreme embarrassment factor combined with stock-holder and upper-management pressures to ignore or minimize the industry. Whether you like the industry or loathe it, ignoring its financial realities is shortsighted and irrational because decisions based on incomplete or incorrect data are flawed decisions. ...But ignored or not, porn is here; it's big; it's here to say, and it will continue to shape the non-porn lives and technologies of the future.

### ePocrisy

...Sex has long given rise to widespread double standards and hypocrisy, but nowhere is that ambivalence more prominent than in the multi-billion-dollar symbiosis between nonadult technology and entertainment companies and the online sex industry. Indeed, the eagerness of very large publicly traded companies to get their hands on the profits from online sex coupled with their abject refusals to admit that they profit from lust and copulation constitutes nothing less than "ePocrisy."

...But with millions of stockholders, respectable board members in suits, and conservative institutional investors, it is not surprising that Cisco won't talk to anyone about the importance of sex to its sales. Neither will most of the biggest names in American business including Marriott, General Motors, Exodus, Concentric, Verio, AboveNet, UUNet (owned by MCI), Sun Microsystems, Yahoo!, AltaVista, Convad, Pacific Bell, Bell Atlantic, Real Networks, Microsoft, AOL, Earthlink, and many, many others that provide the software, infrastructure, and delivery systems for porn in all its many variations. ...Try as one might to explore the topic with industry or brokerage analysts, investment bankers, or venture capitalists, the ePocrisy gets deeper and ranker.

...The server hosting business is a substantial and growing one. Forrester Research puts 2000 revenues at $3.5 billion, 2001 at $6 billion and 2003 revenues at $14.7 billion. ...[T]hese awesome data centers are the core of the Internet. They are also the epicenter of the Web's sex industry. Indeed, data provided by PCData Online (www.pcdataonline.com) and derived from the Web-based services of NetCraft (www.netcraft.com) show that 14 of the top 20 adult websites are hosted by a handful of large, well-known public companies that never mention their adult clients: AboveNet, Digex (part of MCI), Exodus, Level3, UUNet (part of MCI), and Verio (owned by Japanese telecom giant NTT).

Exodux [sic], the undisputed leader in the market, has almost $900 million in revenues and a 15 percent share of the market. AboveNet, which is a subsidiary of publicly traded Metro Fiber Network, houses the number one adult site, Karaxxx.com (owned by RJB Telcom), which ranks as number 70 in the top 100 of all websites with 6.9 million unique users each month. For perspective, that's more visitors than WebMD.com (also hosted by AboveNet), PayPal, BarnesandNoble.Com, or AmericanExpress.com got in February 2001. The biggest player, at least among the top 20 adult sites, is MCI through its ownership of hosters Digex and UUNet. UUNet hosted adult giant Cybererotica, which logged 4.6 million visitors that month while one of Digex's units, Business Internet Inc., hosted the number two adult site, adultrevenuesservice.com, along with smutserver.com, sexspy.com, and amateurfreehost.com. Exodus (including the hosting business it bought from Global Crossing in 2000) provides a home for Top 20 sites sexshare.com and adultfriendfinder.com as well as Danni's Hard Drive (danni.com)[.]

...Because adult Web operations are more likely to be profitable, money-generating sites, it comes as little surprise that they frequently reside at the top of the list for trouble-free operation. At Verio, the longest running server in late February 2001 was adult site freegallery.com followed by valleyvehicles.com. The next three in order were free-xxx-pics-4u.com, fuck1.com, and topfucksites.com. A look farther down the list shows the irony of Web hosting. Number 18 on Verio's list of longest running servers is strongfaithbiblechurch.com and number 33 is the site for the Catholic Archdiocese of Atlanta, mostblessedsacrament.com. Not far aware are bestiality sites, horsesexpics.nu, beastfever.com, and sexanimals.nu.

With sex sites running the gamut from the mostly soft-core Danni's Hard Drive to those featuring bestiality, hosting companies have usually turned a blind eye to content and focused more on the steady payments from porn sites. "For most of us, our adult hosting division is something we try to leverage as much as possible, while drawing as little attention to it as possible," said Nash Hall, the e-mail pseudonym used by an executive with one of the country's major Web hosting firms. "In our case, a very small percentage of our customers are adult companies, but that small group results in a large portion of our revenues. To stay alive in our business [Web hosting] we have to do business in that industry." ...Not only are adult sites a reliable source of income for hosting companies, they are also the most profitable. "An average mainstream customer at our company spends $5,000 per month. This gets them a couple of NT servers, some storage and a Cisco switch," said Hall. "An average adult customer spends around $20,000 to $30,000 per month."

...Another reason for the superior hosting profitability of adult sites lies in the amount of bandwidth pornography requires. While there are trillions of HTML Web pages in the Web universe, most are text pages with small graphics and few of them exceed 15K to 30K in size. On the other hand, even relatively small porn images are rarely less than 100K and most are substantially larger than that. In addition, as of spring 2001, the Web's only tested and operational premium real-time streaming video operations are adult in nature.

"It's clear from log file traffic analysis that a very large number of our DSL customers have purchased the higher bandwidth services in order to view pornography," said a network supervisor at Pacific Bell, a division of SBC Corp. "It's never been a secret that our IP [Internet] backbone traffic is at least half porn if you measure it according to the file transfer amounts." ...Estimates of how much porn consumes of the Web's total bandwidth range as high as 80 percent but none put it lower than 40 percent—a staggering percentage for a market segment that most in the adult field would prefer to keep hidden in a closet just so long as it kept slipping large payments under the door every month.

...Telecom consulting firm RHK (www.rhk.com) estimates Internet bandwidth used for all purposes at 42 million Gigabytes per month. Andrew Odlyzko, head of the mathematics and cryptography research department at AT&T Labs, estimates that about 80 percent of the Internet bandwidth is used for the Web. Band X (www.band-x.com), a major bandwidth trading exchange, estimates that bandwidth sells wholesale for $4 per gigabyte and $20 retail. From this we can do some simple math: Total Internet traffic (42,000 Gigabytes) times the Web's portion of that (80 percent) equals 33,600 Gigabytes of Web traffic per month. If we use a lower-end estimate of the adult portion of this (50 percent), then the Internet carries 16,800 Gigabytes of porn every month. So, if adult traffic is 16.8 million Gigabytes per month, and we take a reasonably low estimate for bandwidth of $12 per Gigabyte (midway between wholesale and retail) and multiply that by the 16.8 million Gigabytes we get a very commanding number: $201.6 million a month, or $2.4 billion per year. If, on the other hand, 80 percent of Web traffic is adult (as many experts assert) then the annual revenues from sex-related bandwidth would be $4.8 billion!

**You've Got Male! (and Female, Shemale, Other...)**

..."AOL is the center of porn in America," said Gerard Vander Leun, head of Penthouse.com. "AOL is built on porn." Hard numbers and other evidence backs up Vander Leun's assertion that America Online is the largest online sex operation in the world. ...[T]he well-scrubbed, family-friendly portal was based in large part on its ability to satisfy urges and desires of a great many of its 30 million paying members.

...While AOL likes to promote its various news and other informational areas, real-time chat is the killer app that kept its lights on in the early days and remains one of the primary motivations for new members to sign up. ...AOL has acknowledged the role its wide-open, no-holds-barred chat rooms played in catapulting it beyond Compuserve and Prodigy, which closely monitored and heavily censored messages containing sexual content or vulgarity. But AOL chat went far beyond this level of sexual toleration in its official areas and allowed members to create their own chat rooms, one level of which is listed in their "People Connection" area and a third, very private area which is unseen by the general public and accessible by invitation only. And while AOL likes to promote the availability of accounts with up to seven screen names as a family-friendly feature, it allowed balding, overweight, over-the-hill, sex-starved members to choose the right screen name (stud69, babe4U) and suddenly become young, buff, and cyber-attractive in a nanosecond. ...In addition, AOL's private Instant Messaging, along with the unmonitored private chat rooms that AOL allows members to use, are vital enablers in the trading of addresses, selling or trading pornography (including child porn), and setting up offline sexual liaisons. ...Indeed, it is clear that the privacy to set up sexual liaisons, trade pornography of any sort, or simply carry on virtual copulation is built into the core of the AOL system—and not by accident.

...AOL users spend between 5 percent and 10 percent of all their online time in chat rooms depending upon which set of AOL's corporate pronouncements we use. ...But what part does sex play in all this chat? As we'll see below, it's a starring role. To determine the percentage of chat devoted to sex, I analyzed all of the public chat rooms, both official AOL room and member-created public ones, on five consecutive nights in September 2001 and found the following: On average, there were 1, 411 official AOL rooms and 2,832 member-created rooms. I dropped in on a minimum of 50 official chat rooms and found that the chat was predominantly sexual in about 30 percent of the rooms. Of the member-created rooms, all but 20 had sexually-related names and spot visits confirmed that these rooms lived up to their names and were hot with cybersex and swapping of pornographic images. ...Sex clearly dominates the chat rooms hosted by AOL's own members-only online service.

But translating how valuable that sex chat is to AOL's bottom line is somewhat less clear. While brokerage and industry analysts were reluctant to offend the AOL Time Warner behemoth and would speak to me only on a background or off-the-record basis, they all confirmed the importance of sex to AOL. They all agreed, to varying degrees, with the 1997 statement made by Alan Weiner, then an analyst for research firm Dataquest, who told the *Detroit News,* "If AOL eliminated chat, you'd see the subscriber base go from 8 million to 1 million faster than you could spit!"

"The situation is a bit different today," an analyst at a major New York brokerage house told me. "The AOL customer of 2001 is different from the AOL customer of 1997 and I think that while sex and chat are of fundamental importance to continued growth and long-term profitability, I think AOL would lose no more than 60 percent of its subscriber base today if it eliminated chat rather than the almost 90 percent Weiner estimated in 1997." Two other analysts with whom I spoke said that, based on their own research, they thought only about 20 percent of AOL's users would bolt if chat were eliminated.

...If we assume that 16 percent of this $6 billion in subscription, advertising, and e-commerce revenues are generated by people who would not be AOL subscribers without its sex chat rooms, that amounts to $960 million per year, almost half as large as the rest of the online sex universe combined. The numbers are smaller, but still substantial when measured against the 4 percent to 8 percent of all time devoted to sex chat. Those numbers yield annual sex-related revenues of $240 to $480 million per year, which at the high end make it the largest single online sex operation and at the low end puts it among the two or three largest online porn operations in the world.

Regardless of how small the number you choose to believe, it is clear that AOL used sex to survive in its early days and continues to operate and encourage company supported sex content as a vital part of its corporate profits. No matter how loudly the corporate *spinmeisters* scream "No sex please!" We're AOL!," adult material and pornography, some legal and some not, are just a mouse click away.

## Search Term: ePocrisy

...Ryan Jacob, portfolio manager of The Internet Fund in New York told CBS Market Watch that pornography accounts for 15 to 20 percent of revenues for portals and search engines like Yahoo!, AltaVista, and their competitors. Indeed, advertising revenues from adult sites are consistently among the top two or three largest categories for all advertising-supported search engines. This should not be surprising given that "sex" is the most frequently searched-for word on every Internet search engine. ...In fact, it's not a very well kept secret that as much as half of all search engine traffic is sex-related.

...Search engines ignore the income from adult sites at their own peril as Disney eventually found out. Disney's Go.com search engine (including Excite.com which Disney purchased), excluded all listings for adult-related sites from its directory and quickly went belly up in February 2001 for lack of adequate revenues.

...Yahoo! spotted sex as a path to profitability early on. From the earliest days, Yahoo!'s sex-related categories were extensive and varied. In 1997, the company even created adult-only chat rooms and aggressively marketed advertising space on them to adult sites. But as the number of sex-related sites proliferated, Yahoo! made it harder and harder for a site to get listed; even those that finally got in usually waited for months before their listing appeared. Yahoo! started charging a fee that speeded up the process but still did not guarantee inclusion. Faced with increasingly stiff odds against getting listed, adult sites responded by an increasing reliance on other methods of generating traffic and on getting listed with search engines that rely more on automated indexing robots—known as spiders—instead of humans as Yahoo! does.

The revenue picture deteriorated further for Yahoo! in early 2001 when it tried to dip its toes into the adult pond by creating a section of its site devoted to the sale of adult videos. But a group of conservative religious groups led by the Tupelo, Mississippi-based American Family Association (www.afa.net) blasted Yahoo! and initiated a blitz of more than 100,000 e-mail complaints, which forced the search engine to discontinue its sex video sales plans. In addition, pressure from these groups pushed Yahoo! into forcing its sex-related listings underground. ...All indexed links to sex sites previously listed in various search categories are still alive on Yahoo's servers, but they have made them harder to find by inserting intermediate links that don't lead directly to porn sites.

...Failure to cultivate and accommodate adult advertisers clearly contributed to Yahoo!'s deteriorating financial position and huge stock price declines in the spring of 2001 which resulted in the loss of its CEO and other key executives. ...But Yahoo! and other search engines and portals have a bigger problem with adult advertising than conservative religious groups: effectiveness. By 1998, the larger adult sites that could afford to buy banner ads on Yahoo! and other major search engines like AltaVista and Lycos, quickly found that the number of surfers clicking on their banners did not justify the money paid for the ad.

...In reality, surfers who visit a search engine tend to be task-oriented, hunting for a specific bit of information among the search results, and thus unlikely to click on an advertising banner. Search engines have responded with a number of "context-sensitive" strategies that display advertising banners or paid links that are related to the search terms. The theory is that surfers are more likely to click on a banner closely related to their intended searches. This has resulted in a thriving black market where advertisers actually buy certain words and search terms with the agreement that their banners—and often their site listings—will be displayed along with the search results whenever a surfer types in those words. Top search terms, including the word "sex," can go for more than $25,000 per year and higher in addition to the actual cost of the banner ad itself.

...Whether in desperation or a belated epiphany that sex makes the World Wide Web go 'round, AltaVista signed a precedent-shattering, performance-based deal in August 2000 with global pornographer, Private Media Group. Instead of a straight advertising arrangement, the deal with Private gives AltaVista a share of the revenues from subscriptions that are referred to Private's adult sites. While such revenue-sharing partnerships are the norm among adult sites, it is the first time a nonadult search engine has linked up with an adult site in this manner. Private CEO Berth Milton said that half of all searches on AltaVista are sex related and as a result, he expects the arrangement to give Private exposure on 25 million of AltaVista's 50 million daily search inquiries[.]

### Sex: The Key to Profitable Content

...Except for sex, content has been mostly a money-losing proposition on the World Wide Web. This seems to be especially true for big-time Web content ventures backed by big-time money and really big names like the *New York Times,* News Corp., NBC, and others. After a public relations orgy in 1998 and 1999, filled with self-congratulations and predictions of astronomical accomplishments, a lot of the big names began to sort of cyber-Dunkirk in 2001, pulling back or pulling out of the online content business after collectively losing hundreds of millions of dollars. Most of the big media names retreated to their legacy businesses to lick their wounds, a little wiser but, judging from their public statements, pretty clueless about what it would take to make an actual profit from the Web. Only the *Wall Street Journal*'s online effort seemed capable of actually getting people to pony up money for subscriptions[.]

...How is it, then, that the brightest minds in the world's biggest media companies working with huge investment budgets can't eke out a dime's worth of black ink while some bootstrapped 22-year-old with a ton of dirty pictures can make thousands in profits working part-time from his bedroom and bigger pornographers can easily clear $10 million or more every month? ...The biggest mistake nonadult Web content companies made was failing to understand that advertising in the legacy media world does not translate onto the Web any better than content.

The most familiar attempt at generating revenue and driving traffic on the Web is all those banner advertisements that plaster Web pages like bumper stickers and graffiti. The banner is the first and most enduring form of Web advertising, but it is also the most abused, especially by nonadult sites. The biggest problem for nonadult sites is their vision of a Web banner as something analogous to a television spot or a magazine advertisement. As a result, they sell their banner advertising on the same basis as these legacy media: the more eyeballs, the more money. By this logic, a banner advertisement on a page that is viewed by 400,000 people should command the same price as an advertisement in a magazine with a circulation of 400,000 people.

...In the early days of the Web, back in 1994–95, the model seemed to work fairly well[.] This legacy model held up for a while because there were so few websites in those days and banners were such a novelty that the click-through rates (the number of surfers who actually click on a banner advertisement divided by the total number of surfers who view the page on which the ad resides) averaged 2.5 percent and could reach into the low double-digits with a creatively tweaked banner.

...While the big players in the adult market—magazine publishers, video producers, and toy makers—watched from the sidelines, the Web quickly blossomed with sex, mostly from small mom and pop operations that included strippers and porn stars looking to take control of their own images, or strip and sex clubs looking for ways to attract more customers to their establishments. ...But while most of these pioneering pornpreneurs were initially as clueless as the nonadult world, they were more extremely pressed by the immediate need to make a profit. They began selling their traffic based on "hits" from their server log files or from visitor counters ("You are the 3,346,789th person to visit this page!") placed on their home pages.

Adult webmasters were the first to realize that raw server logs were misleading. What a server log records is every request from a user's browser to get something from a server. Let's suppose we have a home page with five graphic images on it. If a surfer clicks onto that page, the server log will record six hits: one for the basic HTML page, and five more for the graphics that go on it. It became quickly apparent that a "hit" was meaningless...this led to the development of server log analysis software, a long, involved, complicated and expensive partial solution to the problem.

Server log files are filled with line after line of what appears to be gibberish to the average person but actually carry a great deal of detail about visitors and what they came to see. These files can tell the website operator which website a surfer is coming from, which browser (and version) is being used, the Internet address of the surfer's computer, which pages are visited, and how long is spent at each page. Log-file analysis software processes this information to produce a more understandable picture for the website owner and potential advertisers.

...Fraud is also easy to perpetrate with log-file analysis software: simple scripts can be written to fatten up log files with bogus visits before the files are fed through the analysis software. The ultimate insult is that different log-file analysis software packages will produce significantly different numbers for the same log file. Because big money was at stake, the adult Industry developed a solution that was both simple for the webmasters and reliable for advertisers: the third-party counter.

...As with many other innovations, Cybererotica provided the first third-party counter—XXX Counter—that adult webmasters could put on their sites to measure traffic and signups. XXX Counter, now owned by counter firm Sex-Tracker, was launched in early 1996[.] ...The adult counter concept was the first implementation of what became known in the nonadult world as the "ASP" (Applications Service Provider) concept.

...[T]he development of good counters helped advertisers realize just how much cheating was going on in advertising traffic numbers. As a result, Cybererotica abandoned the practice of buying banner advertisements on a straight cost-per-thousand basis in August 1996. [Founder of Cybererotica,] Fantasyman[,] says Cybererotica's FastCash program was the first pay-per-clickthrough program on the Web. In a pay-per-clickthrough system, a site pays the referring affiliate site a small amount, typically $0.05 to $0.10, for every visitor who clicks through, regardless of whether that visitor actually buys anything at the destination site.

...While this technique is just now catching on with some nonadult websites (known as "performance-based advertising"), adult webmasters are already moving away from it because pay-per-clickthrough is so easily abused. Indeed, not long after the first pay-per-click system went into operation "clickbots" arrived: simple programs designed to automate the task of clicking on a banner ad with the intent of inflating the click-throughs and maximizing checks. Clickbots were also used to inflate the "hit counts" of nonadult websites trying to boast of record numbers of visitors back in the surreal heyday of the Web investment when the number of eyeballs a site could claim mattered more than profits. ...Cybererotica...caught on first and in late 1996 began paying only for click-throughs that came from unique IP (Internet Protocol) addresses. ...This arms race between the sites and scammers went on until pay-per-click, while still widely used in the nonadult world, was eclipsed by conversion-based performance systems: payments are made only for click-throughs that result in a purchase.

...The larger partnership programs also offer financial incentives for webmasters who refer other webmasters and for valid e-mail addresses that can be used for opt-in spam. Spam is a continuing source of frustration for all Web surfers, but it's an especially hot source of friction between the adult and the nonadult worlds. It's not uncommon for average people, including children, who have never visited an adult site to find their e-mail inboxes filled with salacious and unwanted e-mail. ...Webmaster revenue programs pay participating sites as much as $1 for every e-mail sign-up they send to the program.

Much of the traffic that is sold through these performance-based promotion systems is generated by exit consoles. When a surfer leaves an adult site, usually one or more "exit consoles"—new windows—launch on the screen. While annoying and seemingly random and endless, the adult industry invented and has refined exit consoles as a method of filtering surfer desires and profiting from the results.

"The industry uses consoles because they work," said Vander Leun [responsible for *Penthouse* online]. "You don't want bikinis? Okay, a new console pops and here's anal and Asians and African Americans. Don't like them? How about mature, plump, or amateurs? Not your dish? Okay, another console for gays, transvestites, midgets, legs, stockings, lingerie, and so on. The more consoles that pop, the greater chance there is that the surfer will find *something* they'll pay for."

...[N]onadult sites like Yahoo! and the *New York Times* online tried to emulate porn sites, but did it so badly it was obvious they did not understand the filtering principles. the *New York Times*, for example, doesn't wait for a surfer to exit before popping consoles; it pops consoles on nearly every page visited. Adult webmasters were unanimous that launching consoles at the beginning or during a surfing session was guaranteed to shorten the session at the site and reduce the number of pages viewed. Not only does the *New York Times* pop consoles throughout the surfer's session, but it pops the *same* console time after time. Thus, even after surfers indicate that they are not interested in the console's subject, the site fails to dish up something else that might have more interest. This process, then, fails to help filter surfer interests and fails to direct them to things that might be relevant. Finally, the *New York Times,* after irritating its visitors, commits the ultimate mistake and fails to pop an exit console that might sell the exit traffic to another content site or advertiser.

It's worth mentioning that adult webmasters can turn even the most mundane Web problems into revenue. There are several companies such as

Found404.Com which will pay for traffic sent from broken links, moved pages or typos. Most surfers have experienced a server error when accessing a Web page, the most common being a plain and usually cryptic plain white page that says something like "404 Error—Page Not Found." Surfers who don't type in a password correctly will get a "401—Access Denied" error as well. It is very easy to customize these pages, either to be more helpful or to offer a revenue opportunity. Apache, the server software used by most adult sites, lets webmasters easily configure their sites so that server errors display any page they desire. Instead of wasting a page view, savvy adult webmasters construct a page displaying their sponsor's banner ads and/or directing surfers back to the site's home page. They can also make $5 per thousand visits by directing that traffic to a site such as Found404.Com.

...While the percentages, bounties, and per-click payments vary from site to site, the principles of performance-based Web promotion are the same and its message for nonadult sites seeking profits shines brightly but still, for the most part, unheeded.

### Spam, Scams, and Flim-Flams

The world's most widely quoted bank robber, Willie Sutton, was consistently clear when asked why he robbed banks: "Because that's where the money is." The same irrefutable logic has attracted cybergrifters, con-men, crooks, scammers, and borderline business sharpies pushing the legal envelope to the Web as a whole. But despite lurid headlines and high-profile prosecutions of a handful of porn crooks, the adult side of the Internet seems to have produced an average level of complaints despite the fact that on the Web right now, sex is where most of the money is.

A close look through the Federal Trade Commission's actions and warnings on cybercrime (www.ftc.gov) and the statistics compiled by the National Consumers League's Internet Fraud Watch (www.fraud.org) shows that most Internet crime is pretty mundane and not related to adult sites. In fact, most cybercrime comes from the migration of garden-variety scams onto the Web: pyramid and Ponzi schemes, bogus offers to get rich stuffing envelopes at home, stock promotions, bait-and-switch merchandise sales, bogus vacation packages, crooked "charities" and get-rich-fast schemes.

...Just as the adult industry has been on the cutting edge of inventing and perfecting technology and business models that have broadened and enhanced the nonadult surfer's experience and offered nonadult businesses new paths to profitability, some online porn scammers have also paved a new, innovative, and decidedly crooked path to Internet fraud and consumer deception.

Porn fraud has, in its own way, also enhanced the nonporn surfer's experience by compelling law enforcement to develop new investigative techniques and devote more time to cyber-crime. It has also made the Web a little more secure for both surfers and merchants because a number of security holes, especially those related to credit card fraud, have been closed. For those reasons, it is instructional to look closely at the top scams, how they were perpetrated, and the ways they were shut down.

### What Part of "FREE!" Don't You Understand?

...Back in 1997 and 1998, Xpics founders Mario Carmona and Brian Shuster were on top of the world, raking in close to $10 million per *month* from the network of adult websites—xpics.com, sexmuseum.com, asswards.com, sexroulette.com, livesexstream.com, xxxsexphotos.com—that they had founded in 1996 with less than $1,000 of Carmona's money. For almost two years, Xpics remained one of the most frequently visited adult sites in the world as measured by Media Metrix. In fact, by May 1998, it was the 19th most frequently visited site on the Internet with more traffic—almost 5 million visitors—than Amazon.com. Two years later, it was dead.

What happened? Carmona and Shuster put it down to mistakes in judgment and a conspiracy among banks, credit card companies, and the federal government. The Federal Trade Commission says it was because "Free" didn't mean "Free."

...[I]n mid 1996...the two men followed a fairly typical routine for entrants into the adult Internet at that time: They started with a soft-core links site and then progressed to a hard-core links site that sent traffic to adult verification services. By late summer, they had started their own hard-core pay sites and within weeks, found themselves with 50 to 60 new memberships per day at $9.95 a pop. This is a significant return on a very small initial investment: at $500 per day, their site was producing $15,000 per month. $180,000 per year. All bootstrapped by two guys on less money than most people in Los Angeles pay per month for a one-bedroom apartment.

For the next year, they persevered in an increasingly crowded market. Then Shuster got the idea that got them into trouble: Free trials with an automatic conversion to a paid monthly recurring membership after the free trial expired. This was not terribly original: magazines had been offering "free trial issues" for years. ...But the concept has not been tried on the adult Web before and Shuster decided it was Xpics' path to riches.

Like most great ideas, success lies more in the execution rather than the inspiration. *Readers Digest* and the other thousands of magazines that offer free trial issues with follow-on subscription billing manage to avoid trouble because they offer a quick and easy way to avoid payment: A customer can simply write "cancel" on the invoice and send it back, keeping their free issue and whatever *tchotcke* incentive (calculator, miniature boom box, etc.) they received. According to the FTC's complaints, however, Schuster and Carmona turned their free trial offer into an e-roach motel where subscribers checked in and could not manage to find the exit.

The Xpics sites promoted themselves variously as "FREE, FREE, FREE! 100 percent Free," but to get the free trial, the site told customers that they had to provide a credit or debit card number and expiration date to verify they were of legal age. The site didn't disclose that the consumers would be paying a monthly fee unless they actively canceled the monthly billing. ...Then, according to the FTC, once Xpics had a consumer's credit card information they not only began charging $9.95 every month, but also "used a variety of tactics to make it impossible for consumers to cancel their registration," including overriding the controls on the consumer's browser to prevent them from reaching the cancellation page or by redirecting consumers to irrelevant pages. In other instances, the FTC said that consumers trying to cancel subscriptions got "error" or "access denied" pages and were unable to find the Xpics toll-free number. Even when consumers located the toll-free number, the FTC said that consumers were unable to leave a message because the voice-mail box was full or because Xpics did not respond to messages. What's more, the FTC said that Xpics had buried in its Terms and Conditions the provision that consumers who canceled their subscription would, instead, be automatically upgraded to a more expensive form of membership.

...Because getting in touch with the company was such an ordeal and getting a refund nearly impossible, consumers turned to their credit card companies to dispute the charges. ...Chargebacks are very expensive to merchants who must refund the consumers money, pay a penalty and risk losing their ability to accept credit cards at all. ...Xpics was paying $15 for every chargeback on top of the refund. In April 1998, chargebacks grew so numerous that Charter Pacific Bank revoked Xpics' merchant credit card account. Other banks followed suit and effectively put Xpics out of business. ...Webmasters who participated in Xpics' "Xcash" click-through revenue program were owed, and subsequently lost an estimated $10 million in revenues.

The FTC joined by the New York attorney general, brought an almost identical lawsuit against Crescent Publishing Group on Aug. 25, 2000, illustrating just how tempting "FREE!" can be to consumers and how easy it can be to make $100+ million per year on the adult Web. ...According to the FTC lawsuit, Crescent's "free" Web tours generated more than $188 million from 1997 through October 1999, with $141 million of that generated in the first ten months of 1999 alone. The FTC complaint alleges that Crescent promoted free tours of their websites and assured prospective customers that credit card numbers were being requested solely to verify that the surfers were of minimum age. However, the FTC complaint goes on to charge Crescent with billing those cards for monthly membership fees ranging from $20 to $90 per month.

...As with Xpics, the FTC said that Crescent's chargeback rates grew high enough for them to have their merchant accounts revoked. But instead of going out of business, the FTC said that Crescent used one corporate name after another to obtain new merchant processing accounts and when this was finally detected, moved their merchant credit card account to a bank in Guatemala. The FTC said that Crescent's chargeback rate was approximately 35 percent. The Crescent case was currently unresolved as this...was being written.

**Pagejacking: A Uniquely Adult Scam**

Back in mid 1999, parents who were surfing the Web with their kids looking for books about medieval history were shocked when search engine results links took them to hard-core sites instead. What's more, once they had landed on those sites, they were unable to leave without shutting down their browsers and, often, rebooting their computers. They had been pagejacked.

...By the time the Federal Trade Commission got wind of the scam in the summer of 1999, its staffers estimated that more than 25 million Web pages had been pagejacked. Following the process of exactly *how* the scammers perpetrated the crime offers a valuable insight into the clever, if illegal, minds of the people behind it.

...In the case of *FTC v. Pereira,* the U.S. District Court for the Eastern District of Virginia found, in September 1999, that Carlos Pereira, a resident of Odivelas, Portugal, did the actual pagejacking and sent the resulting traffic to a group of Australian adult websites run by Guiseppe Nirta. ...For his part, Nirta was a director of a company in Giralang called W.T.F.R.C. which, according to people who worked there, stood for: "Who The Fuck Really Cares?" For its part, W.T.F.R.C did business under a variety of names including Kewl Photographies and Kool Images and operated numerous websites including: taboosisters.com, taboohardcore.com, tabooanimals.com, shemen.com, and extrme-boys.com. Pereira's pagejacked visitors were sent to W.T.F.R.C's websites.

Pereira's role in the scheme was actually the most fiendishly clever part. He started the pagejacking process by copying the source code from existing pages and inserting a Javascript routine that instantly redirected surfers to one of Nirta's pages. The source code of a Web page is very easy to view and copy. Both Internet Explorer and Netscape provide "View Source" and "Save Web Page" which allow anyone to view the underlying HTML source code for the page and to save it to a file.

The pagejacking of Gloriana's Bookstore offers a great example of how the scam actually operated. Gloriana's Bookstore is part of Gloriana's Court (www.gloriana.nu), a site dedicated to medieval culture and spirituality run by Elizabeth G. Melillo, a British webmistress, scholar, and Internet consultant and designer. Unbeknownst to Ms. Melillo, Pereira hijacked one of her pages, www.gloriana.nu/kids2.html, saved it to his computer, and added the Javascript redirect code. Once that was done, Pereira uploaded it to his own server with the same page filename, so it appeared as www.atariz.com/kids2.html. Finally, he submitted the page to all the major Internet search engines for indexing and inclusion. ...So, when many users typed in a request for "children's medieval history" they ended up clicking on one of Pereira's purloined pages that directed them to one of Nirta's down-under, down-and-dirty sex sites instead of to Ms. Melillo's site.

But the diversion of visitors from Kind Arthur and the Knights of the Round Table to something less noble was not an isolated incident. Pereira, you see, automated the process with a script, a custom program, so that by the time the FTC shut down the scam in September 1999, the evil Portugese genius had page-jacked an estimated 25 million Web pages out of the approximately 1 billion in existence at the time.

Why? For the traffic, of course. And for this reason, pagejacking is a crime unique to the adult industry because it is, so far, the only industry where Web traffic is actually profitable. And where there is money there is temptation. ...While it is doubtful that any permanent damage was inflicted on the accidental visitors...the pagejacked sites were the real victims, having lost traffic, sales and readership that was siphoned off by the cyberpirates.

### Consumer Fraud: By Consumers

...While the Federal Trade Commission has halted some choice adult site scams which ripped consumers off for about $200 million over the last few years, the biggest *victims* of cyberscams are actually e-commerce websites, both adult and nonadult. Those websites are brutally squeezed between fraudsters and cyber-shoplifters on one side and an antiquated, uncaring, financially punitive, and often outright hostile credit card system on the other. These sites—predominantly *non*adult enterprises—are ripped off by consumers to the tune of $2 *billion* every year. This is an enormous burden on a struggling new industry that is trying—and often failing—to stay alive.

Porn sites, on the other hand, are disproportionately targeted by hackers (mostly underage, hormone-driven teenage boys) and dishonest adults so embarrassed when their smut purchases are discovered by a spouse or partner that they will lie about spending the money and having their credit card company reverse the charges (a chargeback). These factors, combined with a double standard by credit card companies that requires adult sites to have a smaller percentage of chargebacks than nonadult sites have forced online porn companies to develop significantly better fraud detection systems that could hold a big part of the chargeback solution for nonadult e-commerce. ...Central to the issue is a system that, in the United States, holds online merchants 100 percent liable for all Internet fraud and chargebacks while failing miserably to provide adequate methods to verify the validity of a transaction. Adding insult to injury, merchants face dismal apathy in trying to find justice even when fraud is clear and provable.

Typical of the vast majority of fraudulent chargebacks is the case of Le Anne Crounse of Gig Harbor, Washington, whose nonadult e-tailing site, Best NFL Store (nflstore.com) sells officially licensed NFL products such as caps, T-shirts, and jerseys. Crounse, who started her online business in 1999, sent a Jacksonville Jaguars kids jacket to a fan in Sacramento, Calif., in November 2001. ..."The lady then claimed that her boyfriend used her credit card and that she hadn't ordered the merchandise. And even though it was delivered to her apartment, she claimed they cohabitated, and that she was not responsible for the charge. We were charged back. Mastercard didn't make her press charges against the boyfriend or return the merchandise." Crounse said she had to eat the $52.95 for the merchandise and express shipping as well as a $15 chargeback penalty and another two or three hours of fruitless effort trying to fight the chargeback.

...With e-commerce revenues estimated at $38 billion in 2000, 2.64 percent of that equals a whopping $1 billion loss to credit card thieves and cybershop-lifters. ...Hard numbers on the total amount of chargeback fees paid by e-tailers is difficult to come by, but could be in excess of $500 million per year, according to an analyst at CyberCash, a major Internet payments gateway now owned by Verisign.

...E-tailers, industry consultants, and analysts confirm that credit card fraud and cybershoplifting flourish because neither the issuing banks nor the credit card companies have any financial incentive to stop it. ...A former Visa executive who is now an online payments system consultant told me in an interview that it costs the bank less than $6 to handle a chargeback, making their $25 to $35 fees very profitable. "The banks that issue merchant credit card processing accounts clearly have a lucrative financial incentive *not* to clean up their acts," said a transaction consultant with one of the largest accounting firms in the world who talked to me only on the condition that I keep him and his firm anonymous. "If you were raking in hundreds of millions in profits from chargeback fees, why in hell would you want to make security better? It would hurt you two ways: first you'd have to spend money to create a more secure system that the fraudsters couldn't game. And after you did that—if you were successful—you'd see a very profitable gravy train disappear.["]

...The adult industry's solutions may be just what the nonporn world needs because the problem is far more severe for adult sites and other Web merchants who sell "digital goods"—downloads of music, software, games, images, or video streams—because it's hard to prove that the person whose card was charged actually received the goods. ...One way that adult sites handle the situation is to turn the process over to specialized transaction companies with more experience than any one site can possibly develop on their own. Most adult sites don't even have their own merchant credit card accounts but instead use third-party processing companies such as iBill and CCBill (the two largest) which have a special merchant account that allows them legally to process transactions for others.

...The process of trying to detect fraudulent transactions before they are processed is known as "fraud scrubbing." It is a growth industry in both the adult and nonadult worlds, but clearly the struggle is even more intense when a legion of testosterone-intoxicated teen-age boys with technical savvy but without credit cards follow their biological imperatives into cyberspace oblivious to the laws they have to break to do it. ...[C]ompanies that handle credit card billing for adult sites have more experience dealing with fraud than nonadult billing companies. Fraud control technicians at three of the largest third-party adult billing processors told me that on average, 40 percent of all *attempted* transactions are fraudulent. Because of this, the processors and sites must develop technology to eliminate at least 97.5 percent of those fraudulent transaction attempts. To do otherwise would allow chargebacks to rise over 1 percent which, if allowed to continue for more than a month or two, could result in the cancellation of the merchant account. While this is serious for any individual site, it is truly disastrous for third-party billers that use their own merchant accounts to process transactions for hundreds, and sometimes thousands, of others. So, it's no surprise that adult billing processors have, by necessity, the best fraud scrubbing systems in the world.

## Piracy, Hijacking, Burglary, & Spam

### Piracy

...As of spring 2001, music remained the one notable exception to the negligible financial value of most nonadult content. The Napster controversy which began in 2000 highlighted better than any other situation the ease with which copyrighted materials can be pirated: copied and instantly made available to anyone in the world in clear violation of laws. In the real world, we call this theft. Napster tried to call it a business model.

The American legal system finally caught up to this charade in March 2001 when Napster was hit with an injunction that required it to filter out all copyrighted materials or be shut down. ...Napster wailed and tried every slick legal maneuver it could fabricate until the court essentially shut it down. Ironically, Napster could have complied instantly with the court's filtering order if CEO Hank Barry had returned Mark Ishikawa's phone calls. Ishikawa, you see, is the CEO of BayTSP which provides services that can track any sort of digital file, including music files, based on the file's "electronic DNA."

...Not surprisingly, BayTSP has its roots in the adult industry. Until the advent of Napster, porno was the only content on the Web that generated enough profits to make it worthwhile for the content creator to protect it. Using a highly protected system and computer algorithms, BayTSP processes the file—whether it's a photo, text, or music—and creates a mathematical profile unique to that file, the "electronic DNA." The company then stores that digital profile in its database along with licensing and copyright information, content management details, and a list of sites that are authorized to use the file.

BayTSP then uses a "spider" to search the Web for pirates. Spiders (also known as robots or 'bots) are actually server-based software programs that automatically visit websites, much like a human surfer with a browser, only thousands of times faster. Search engines make heavy use of spiders, sending them off to "look" at a website, following a site's links and indexing its pages according to the content and other unseen information embedded in the page's HTML code. But BayTSP's spider sees what others cannot: the digital profiles of images and other files. If the spider finds a violation, the BayTSP server then takes a "snapshot" of the site that contains the offending file and stores the information. BayTSP notifies the offending site and generates a legally binding copyright notice to both the site owner and the ISP informing them of the infringement. ...Every step of the way, the BayTSP system keeps time-and date-stamped records of the violations and amasses the evidence for court action if necessary. The BayTSP system can also automatically register works with the Copyright Office. ...BayTSP launched its service in June 2000 and by March 2001 had detected and sent warnings for more than 93,000 copyright violations.

Prior to BayTSP, the only protection for images was "watermarking," subtly altering an image to embed unseen copyright information. But since watermarking must be inserted into each individual file, the process is time consuming and cannot protect images that have already been placed on the Web. In addition, many watermarks are destroyed when an image is resized or digitally altered.

### Hijacking

...Back in the heady DotCom days before the train careened off the tracks into the financial abyss, foggy-headed venture capitalists financed companies that paid millions of dollars for a single domain name. eCompanies whizzed away $7.5 million for the domain business.com while pioneer Virtual Vineyards squandered $2.9 million on the name wine.com. By the end of 2000, most companies that did such foolish things had balance sheets worth less than the silly price paid for its domain names.

The money to be made in the adult sector produced one of the most bizarre and expensive cases of domain name hijacking: the saga of sex.com. ...The saga of sex.com started in 1994, when online pioneer Gary Kremen registered the domain name without really knowing what he would use it for. In retrospect, this might seem to have been an obvious thing to do, but remember that in 1994, a very large number of people thought the Web was just a fad along the lines of CB radio and pet rocks. At that time, it took some vision to think that a domain name might eventually be worth anything at all.

At the time Kremen registered sex.com, he was involved with building one of the first online dating services, match.com, which he eventually sold for $7 million to Cendant Corp. Unbeknownst to Kremen, his future nemesis, convicted felon Stephen Michael Cohen, was chilling in federal prison, serving three and a half years for bankruptcy fraud.

Court records indicate that Cohen got out of prison in February 1995. Nine months later, domain registrar Network Solutions received a letter transferring the sex.com domain name to Cohen. Network Solutions has repeatedly been accused of carelessness, arrogance, and incompetence so many times that their monopoly was shattered in 1998 when other companies were allowed to register domains.

But Network Solutions was at its sloppiest when it turned sex.com over to Cohen, who then proceeded to build a multi-million-dollar porn site. No one knows how many millions sex.com made from its beginning until November 2000 when the U.S. District Court in San Jose ruled that the letter transferring the sex.com name was forged and that the domain rightfully belonged to Kremen. Sex.com probably had gross revenues of somewhere between only $100 million and $200 million if the site was mismanaged, and upwards of half a billion dollars, according to Kremen and his legal staff.

In November 2000, the U.S. District Court judge also ordered Cohen to place $25 million in a court-controlled escrow account to ensure payment of a possible judgment that was to be determined at a court hearing on March 8, 2000. But Cohen never transferred the money to the court. Instead, he disappeared along with his money. On March 5, 2000, he was cited for contempt of court, and a warrant issued for his arrest. As I write this, he remains a fugitive from justice and was last sighted in Mexico.

## Burglary

Burglarizing someone's house with stolen keys is marginally better than breaking a window and leaving a mess behind as an insult on top of the injury. But theft is still theft whether the stolen key is a brass one for your Schlage or a digital one to illegally gain entry to a password protected pay site. ...Again, this is almost exclusively an adult site problem because of price and demand. There are no password sites specializing in stolen access data to the *Wall Street Journal* online or Playhouse Disney.

...The operators of password sites often try to paint themselves with the same Robin Hood paintbrush as Napster, just a bunch of good fellas trying to bring affordable porn to the masses who can't afford it. Others disingenuously claim they are a public service to pay sites, posting the stolen account information so the site operators will know their passwords have been compromised.

Password sites can be expensive in two ways: First and most obviously, they cost the pay site operator a paying membership. Second, the illegal free surfers use up bandwidth, something that ranges from an annoyance to a problem so serious it could put a small site out of business.

Cybererotica's owner estimates that more than 20 percent of all pay site traffic comes from unauthorized, nonpaying surfers using stolen passwords. But it's worse for a small pay site that has a cap on the amount of bandwidth it can use. An attack of free-password surfers could easily use an entire month's worth of bandwidth in a day, with the site operator paying hundreds or even thousands of dollars worth of additional bandwidth fees, all for traffic that returns no money at all.

Some thieves even use stolen passwords to enter a site and then run easily available "Burglar Bots" that quickly follow every link and harvest every image on the pay site, downloading them to the thief's own computer where they can either be posted for free on a news group or reused on the thief's own porn site.

Software is available to curtail access from stolen passwords. The software keeps watch over incoming IP addresses and if it notices multiple IP addresses using the same username and password, it can automatically disable that account's access.

Some adult webmasters fight back by scamming the scammers. Since they know that people are attracted to the free access provided by password sites, some post usernames and passwords to sites they have constructed specifically to handle password site traffic. After entering the password and user names, eager thieves using those deliberately posted "stolen" accounts frequently do not find a content-rich pay site, but instead are confronted by a page containing revenue program banners. Surprisingly, many users click on the banners, generating revenues for the site owners. Again, creative adult webmasters recognized that where there is traffic there is money and turned a bad situation into cash.

## Spam

For most people, a mailbox filled with spam is a mild annoyance and a good excuse for exercising the "delete" key. But a study by the European Commission found that spam costs European users 10 billion Euros (about $10 billion) per year in wasted time, bandwidth, and server operation.

Globally, one of the most annoying forms of spam is sex-related material that shows up unsolicited, often in the mailboxes of children. On the other hand, adult webmasters have found e-mail to be a lucrative source of new business, traffic, and memberships. To reconcile the two compelling interests, Cybererotica created the "double opt-in" system. To sign up, the user registers an e-mail address with the site and minutes later receives a confirmation e-mail to the address registered. The user must reply in order to be placed on the list. ...Spam complaints to ISPs and especially to AOL can get a site's IP address banned, blocked from servers entirely. Fantasyman said that his system, which has been widely adopted in the industry is the surest defense against a site being blocked.

## Dreamin' of Streamin'

...Hollywood studio Miramax thought it was a big deal when it announced on January 18, 2001, that it would make a forgettable 1999 film, *Guinevere,* available for download on the Web. Interested surfers with $3.49 and a high-speed connection could take half and hour to download the 500-megabyte file, then look at it as many times as they wished for the next 24 hours. Miramax won't talk about how many people actually bought into the process, but the absence of the usual self-congratulatory press releases and promotions may be an indication of the effort's lack of success.

Video rental Goliath Blockbuster thought it had just the same sort of movie mega-deal when it announced that it would use custom television setup boxes, DSL connections from Verizon and Pacific Bell, and computer services from Enron to connect consumers to a database of about 400 movies that they could select and play on demand. ...Nine months later, Enron whined that Blockbuster couldn't find enough decent movies for a lunch worthy of their technology and thus the two companies got a divorce.

And in mid August 2001, five Hollywood heavyweights—MGM, Paramount, Sony, Warner Brothers, and Universal—announced their own video on demand (VoD) partnership, which was soundly panned by all reviewers because the system worked just like the Miramax system.

*Business Week*'s Los Angeles bureau chief Ron Grover sums up the problems: "For starters, it takes more than 30 minutes to download a film over even the fastest Internet connection. Never mind that it will be four or five more years before even half the country has access to super-fast broadband. Even then, how much of a market will there be for watching movies on a PC screen while sitting ramrod-straight in a hard-back office chair? Oh, yes, and the picture on the screen is a four-inch square."

To be fair, Miramax, Blockbuster, and the Hollywood Five are just some of the many large companies that have disregarded the needs and desires of consumers and tried to impose their own unwieldy technology on the market.

These companies have a lot to learn, and they might turn their attention to the adult video industry for a solid lesson in how to deliver profitably a product that people are willing to pay for. Long before Blockbuster, Miramax, and others made their announcements, the adult Internet industry had been delivering *paid* video on demand, both live and recorded, over the Web for more than six years. Indeed, by 1994, the first real-time, live entertainment video feeds were coming from the sex shows at Amsterdam's Casa Rosso courtesy of David Vander

Poel's site Red Light District. Not only that but the Red Light District's feeds could be viewed (albeit jerkily) at the very slow 28.8 speeds of the day.

...[T]he Red Light District developed a system that required no extra browser plug-ins for the consumer to fiddle and hassle with. Vander Poel said the no-plug-in method was a first for the Web and was developed in less than a day when he bet his programmer a chocolate bar that it could not be done. It illustrates the ease with which consumers can be accommodated if companies are only willing to consider them. Vander Poel told me that the paying user base grew so fast that the Dutch government-owned phone company had to install dedicated ultra-high-bandwidth optical cables to their servers in order to handle the traffic.

...Today, Gamelink (www.gamelink.com) uses Media Player to encode the approximately 1,000 videos currently available to consumers. "We have another 3,000 licensed and in the process of being encoded," [founder Ilan Bunim] told me, "and we anticipate having 10,000 to 15,000 for sale in the next year or so." Each video costs, on average $7.99. Gamelink sold the Web's first full-length streaming, on-demand video—*Sin City: The Movie*—to Web surfers in 1997. The video, according to its producer Marc Goldman of Sin City Films, originally made in 1993, is one of about 450 of his company's films available at their VoD site (www.sincityvod.com) which is run by Gamelink. Unlike the Blockbuster and Miramax systems, which give purchasers a fixed time period in which to view the film, usually 24 to 48 hours, Gamelink's payment system allows a fixed number of minutes, generally 120, that can be spent by the purchaser in multiple sessions spread over as many days or weeks desired.

...Vivid uses the standard adult pricing model for its VoD, making them available only to members who pay $39.99 per month for access to its premium Web operation. AEBN [Adult Entertainment Broadband Network, www.aebn.com], on the other hand, offers access to all of its videos to users who pay for a given number of minutes, which can be used on any video on the system. The typical user buys 60 minutes of access time for $8.95 and can spend a minute on one video, five or ten on the next, skipping around and sampling as they like. This profit model is the precise counterpart of the old brick-and-mortar peep shows where users would plug quarters into a slot and get a few minutes of viewing time in a booth for each payment.

...By contrast, as of fall 2001, there is no record of any nonadult streaming video operation that operated at a profit. Even the over hyped and glitch-plagued Web broadcasts from Victoria's Secret (February 1999) and Madonna (November 2000) were publicity-seeking, money losing stunts that had no connection to profits. In addition, these streaming stunts were one-shot events that required months of preparation and millions of dollars to set up. IBM and its server facilities handled the Victoria's Secret broadcast while Microsoft built the system to handle the Material Girl. Despite paying $45 million for the rights, promotions, and computer and network facilities to handle a six-song, 29-minute performance by Madonna, the Microsoft broadcast performed like a virgin in a porn flick with slow, jerky, fuzzy images and frequent disconnects.

...However, there are signs that the studios are beginning to wake up to the success right under their nose. ...Akamai is one big-name Internet company that has openly turned to the adult Web in pursuit of profits. Akamai is a massive global caching company with more than 8,000 physical servers stationed at some 1,200 Internet Service Providers, connected to 700 different networks in 55 countries worldwide. What they offer is the ability to move content off of a centralized server on to many different ones located closer to the ultimate consumer of the content. This speeds up content delivery and decreases network congestion. ...Paying customers can then get a faster, higher-quality stream and all those big, high-bandwidth streams files don't have to hog bandwidth on Internet chokepoints such as the undersea fiber-optic backbone cables carrying Internet traffic from the United States to Europe or from the U.S. West Coast to the Pacific.

In March 2001, Akamai cofounder and chief technology officer Danny Lewin (who died in the September 11, 2001 terrorism) met with the technology gurus from 15 adult companies including Playboy, Vivid, iGallery, Babenet, and others and told them, "The adult industry is a significant market segment we can't afford to ignore."

Akamai does, however, put a firewall between sex and its nonadult customers like CNN, Nasdaq, Apple, Microsoft, Yahoo, CBS, and MSNBC by offering its services through a partnership with Directrix, a technology company spun off when Playboy bought the Spice cable sex network in 1999.

...While video on demand operations involve finished theatrical works, a similar phenomenon, the live Web cam, actually began long before streaming was possible and started not with movies or live sex shows from Amsterdam but with a coffee pot in the Trojan Room of the computer sciences lab at Cambridge University. The seven-story building had but one coffee pot, which meant that programmers frequently trekked to the room only to find the pot empty. In 1991, the creative, caffeine-deprived computer scientists then trained a digital camera on the offending coffee pot and wired it into the building's network. With their custom Xcoffee software, the pot level could be checked from any desktop. This system was the very first frame grabber software that looked at the video coming from the camera, selected a particular frame at the preset time interval and moved it along the network. The program required users to install special software on their workstations in order to view the liquid level. It was clearly the forerunner to David Vander Poel's Casa Rosso system although the sex show video went it one better by not requiring client software on the viewer's end.

The Trojan coffee pot went live on the Web in 1993, becoming the world's first Web cam. With the advent of a new computer sciences building, the coffee pot was retired in 2001. Not long after the Trojan Coffee pot and Casa Rosso went live on the Web, exhibitionists started rigging up camcorders with inexpensive frame-capture devices that uploaded the images to a Web server one frame at a time.

...In the mid 1990s, Logitech, which was best known for mice and trackballs at the time, came out with the first models of its QuickCam, a $100 video camera that looked like a very large eyeball, and software that made Web video child's play. The QuickCam also came along just in time to satisfy the growing "I'll show you mine if you'll show me yours" crowd of Web-savvy exhibitionists. To the eternal embarrassment of my alma mater, Cornell University, which invented the first consumer-ready Webcam software, CUSeeMe, the first uses were not business video conferences or family-oriented long distance chat, but sex chat complete with excruciatingly close-up images of various body parts.

QuickCam was somewhat more sanguine about the use of its products for sexual purposes. A company spokesman quoted by the *Wall Street Journal* in 1998 said, "We don't advertise the product that way, of course. But people are going to do what people are going to do." ...QuickCam and others in the field acknowledge that people using Web cams for sexual purposes helped drive the continued development and improvement of consumer Web cam hardware and software, which has increased quality and driven down prices and made them more widely available for nonadult uses.

But while the nonadult uses of Web cams tend to be small, home-oriented operations on personal Web pages, sex continues of dominate any sort of organized Web operation or videoconferencing portal. There is no better illustration for the frustrations this can cause than Microsoft's NetMeeting service. In 1996, Microsoft included NetMeeting videoconferencing software with Internet Explorer. That was coupled with an online directory where users could add their names to find other users. While Microsoft envisioned this as a portal for business users to videoconference, the service was almost immediately swamped with X-rated listings. When the word got around, the traffic brought the Microsoft servers to its knees. Microsoft eventually bailed from the space. Identical problems have beset similar enterprises like ICUii, CUSeeMe Networks (not affiliated with Cornell), and iVisit.

But again, where the nonadult players saw frustration and annoyance, pornepreneurs see profits and opportunity. One of the pioneers in sex-related websites, WebPower—which made an early mark with the amateurs.com mega-porn site—operates iFriends (www.ifriends.com), the largest Web cam site where people can set up their cams and be connected with interested viewers. ...And while iFriends offers hundreds of nonadult categories from home improvement to quilting, sex dominates. iFriends acknowledges that the vast majority of its traffic is adult-related. A typical day for iFriends shows 557 live video conferences of which 534 were sex-related.

The iFriends site, which has more than 2.6 million registered users, acts almost like a Napster peer-to-peer system where hosts fill out a profile of themselves and their specialty. When a visitor elects to enter a video chat with a host, the iFriends server hands off the connection so that the user and host computers are communicating directly with each other and not through iFriends. Because the connections are direct and are not handled by the host's computer, the video quality depends upon the host's connection to the Internet. ...iFriends does, however, handle billing for the hosts, which charge from $1.99 to $3.50 per minute for the connection with a two-minute minimum. iFriends keeps 50 percent of the revenues.

In addition to iFriends, there are thousands of Web cams operated by lone exhibitionist entrepreneurs, not all of which offer porn content. Jennifer Ringley, a young woman in Washington D.C., is now famous for her Jennicam which she started in 1996 while still in college and which continues as a subscription site costing $15 for a three-month membership.

Nowhere is the value of sex in driving profits more apparent than the demise of Cammunity.com, a portal for well-scrubbed, nonadult, family Web cams. The venture-funded portal had a network of 10,000 smut-free sites in its camera community in 2000. But at its height, it never drew more and 200,000 unique visitors per month and quietly shut its doors in 2001 leaving nothing but a home page and no forwarding address.

At the other end of the spectrum from the amateur or semipro Web cam operator are the slick, studio-quality operations from VoyeurDorm and Dancer-Dorm. Launched in 1998 by Tampa residents Bruce Hammil and David Marshlack, VoyeurDorm follows the lives of a group of 13 college-aged women living in a house in Tampa, Florida. In exchange for tolerating 55 cameras, which provide no privacy for even the most personal activities, the women, aged 19 to 23 years, receive stipends along with college tuition.

Some 800,000 Cyber Peeping Toms pay $34.95 per month to watch the women and to chat with them online. In addition, almost 40 percent of the subscribers pay an additional $16 per month for chat sessions with the women. That all adds up to almost $40 million per year. ...And, if the VoyeurDorm concept seems a bit familiar, you may be one of the 27 television viewers who actually watched CBS's reality TV show "Big Brother" which debuted in 2000. Hammil and Marshlack felt it was a bit *too* familiar for comfort and filed suit against CBS in May 2000, charging the network with ripping off their idea.

## How the Internet Is Shaping Sex

...Just as sex has shaped the Internet, the Internet also influences sex and our society in ways that could have very substantial cultural implications, including changes in the community standards definition of obscenity, empowering women working in the sex field, and moving adult material from its traditional male orientation to one that caters to women's desires as well.

The Internet has changed obscenity in the United States by untethering the definition of community from the purely physical to one which is bounded by bits and bandwidth. ...Global media, including the Internet, cable, and satellite television have effectively destroyed the ability of courts to define a community using geographic boundaries. [Lawrence G. Walters, a Florida-based partner of Weston, Garrou & DeWitt, a national law firm headquartered in Los Angeles that specializes in First Amendment cases] said that when porn was available only in print or on film or video cassette, "a small community could physically keep the material out through zoning or obscenity prosecution." But the advent of technology, he said, "means that anyone, in any community can have their porn available in the privacy of their own home—something the Supreme Court says is legally protected. Technology allows you to do this without imposing it on others. In America, we like our porn available but not in our faces," Walters continued. "We want access, but we don't want to have to see it in stores or on the street."

...Walters agreed with other legal experts that the acquittal of a Provo, Utah, video rental store owner on obscenity charges is one [of] the most telling cases of how technology has changed local community standards. ...The case started in 1996 when police raided Larry W. Peterman's two small independent Movie-Buffs video stores in American Fork and Lehi, Utah. The action was taken after more than 4,000 people in Utah County—which likes to call itself the most conservative county in the United States—signed a petition calling for Peterman's prosecution. Peterman's store was not an adult-oriented book and paraphernalia store, but like thousands of independent video stores across the United States, offered the complete gamut of videos that people wanted to rent. His store had everything from Disney's Dalmatians and Bruce Willis splattering blood and guts across the screen to an adult section in the back with Debbie Doing Everybody. Peterman testified that 11 percent of all rentals were adult in nature, somewhat below the national average of 16 percent. But that number, the courts would learn, is deceptively low.

Rather than simply not visit the adult section of the store, the 4,000 pious petitioners pressed for a pornography prosecution to prevent other Provonians from perusing Peterman's pornography.

Prospects didn't look terribly bright for Peterman until one day his attorney, Randy Spencer, was gazing out the courtroom window at the penultimate symbol of Mormon's mammon: Marriott. While Mormons try to keep their flock on the shortest of leashes, they'll never turn away from making a buck off selling forbidden fruit and drink to those who are already headed for Hell: alcohol, coffee, and tea as well as video sex are available for paying adults who stay at a Marriott.

Spencer's investigator, defense witness Richard Gale, testified he checked into the Provo Marriott, set up a tripod and a video camera, and recorded 11 adult movies that were offered over the in-room On Command service. Among the videos he testified recording were "Pamela Anderson and Tommy Lee: The Infamous Home Video," "Doing the Boss," and "Award Winning Triple X." After documenting the cornucopia of sex films available right in the middle of the nation's most conservative county, he then subpoenaed the Marriott's pay-per-view purchase records. John Garfield, who managed the downtown Provo Hotel, was called as a prosecution witness and pleaded his Fifth Amendment rights against self-incrimination.

Even though most Marriott guests who tuned into the in-room porn were presumably from beyond the borders of Provo, this is legally irrelevant, according to Walters and other legal experts. What's necessary in defining community standards, they say, is whether the material is available in the community.

But Peterman's defense attorney didn't stop with the video proclivities of Provo's visitors. He then went after local cable and satellite television providers' records on subscriptions and rentals of sex flicks by Provo residents. What he found was a nearly fathomless pit of hypocrisy: the citizens of Utah County rented far more porn flicks per capita than did people in the rest of the United States. Indeed, Spencer pointed out that satellite channels had sold more than 20,000 adult sex videos during the time period in which Peterman was charged with violating obscenity laws. Not only that, but the 20,000 was roughly twice the per capita number of sales as the rest of the United States. ...Provonians were privately purchasing porn from purveyors who were not visible to the community, thus allowing them pious deniability and the capacity of having their porn and prosecute it too. The jury acquitted Peterman after just two and a half hours of deliberation.

...In addition to changing how we define community standards, the Internet has confused local governments about whether they even have jurisdiction. The city of Tampa, Florida, tried to shut down VoyeurDorm, arguing that the home occupied by 13 scantily clad women and 55 continually webcasting cameras was an adult business improperly located in a residential neighborhood. However, in late September 2001, the 11th U.S. Circuit Court of Appeals sided with VoyeurDorm, saying that the actual "business" was conducted in cyberspace and not at the house. The court said, "The public does not, indeed cannot physically attend" activities at the house and thus, it "does not fall within the purview of Tampa's Zoning Ordinance."

Perhaps of even more cultural importance are the changes that the Internet is brining to the uneasy relationship between women and the public conception of how they should relate to sex. ...Before the advent of the Internet, most of the pornography business was controlled by men; there were very, very few women entrepreneurs. ...[T]he fact that there is a legion of female entrepreneurs working in this field—where there had previously been none—is due to an environment fostered by the Internet. These women are not simply content to go with the online flow, but are determined to use the technology to shape the face of sex and to create a new category of erotica that appeals to women. ...All the women I interviewed said that they hoped to redefine, or at least expand, the range of erotica offered on the Web by creating a different class of material that appeals more to women and couples. ...This is not to say that the old sex industry has disappeared. ...But the Internet and the availability of cheap accessible technology has offered women an opportunity they never had before.

...The market saturation of the online sex world brought new attention in 2001 to content that appeals to women and couples. Increased competition made adult webmasters look at some pretty stark numbers: while women are roughly 50 percent of U.S. Web surfers, they make up only about 3 percent of those accessing the adult Net. The reason, as pointed out by the women webmistresses [I interviewed], could be that the adult industry has not tried very hard to produce content that appeals to women.

The sex toy business shows that it doesn't have to be that way. A survey I conducted of the top five online sex toy sites (which, combined have more than a 50 percent share) indicates that women make up at least half of their customers because the sites have something to offer them. Women are also half of the customers at Hustler's upscale Hollywood sex toy boutique. The challenge for content producers is to match those kinds of numbers for their content.

# Chapter Fourteen

# Technology, Obscenity, and the Law: A History of Recent Efforts to Regulate Pornography on the Internet

## Stephen C. Roberds

*In the short span of one decade the Internet had already proven a trigger for significant social change in a wide array of social institutions. Perhaps nowhere is that provocative effect more evident than legal structures. As Stephen Roberds rightly suggests, technology, pornography, and legal definitions of obscenity are bound in a loosely stitched common history—understanding how and why the contemporary Internet pornography industry poses such a significant challenge to prevailing legal definitions of obscenity requires an understanding of this history—particularly print, television, and radio. Roberds neatly frames this history with special attention to significant rulings of U.S. federal courts that are especially relevant.*

For over five decades courts have been inundated with cases involving governmental attempts to ban or regulate obscenity, indecency, and sexually offensive materials. Early cases dealt with books, magazines, and film. Advances in technology and widespread growth in the dissemination of sexually explicit materials led courts to examine telephone, television, cable, and Internet mediums for the distribution of questionable materials. As technology has expanded the production, distribution, and access to sexually explicit materials, courts have been asked to address problems of definition and regulation. Far from trivial, these challenges have been an important part of the evolution of obscenity laws that have broad implications illustrating, among other things, how sex and technology exert a broad social and cultural influence. In this chapter, that influence is examined from the perspective of the law. While state courts are battlegrounds for much of the legal wrangling, this review will focus on federal courts in general and the US Supreme Court in particular.

Advances in technology always pose challenges to existing bodies of law. The Internet has brought about philosophical and legal issues concerning copyright, libel, and intellectual property law. Cases have come to the courts involving privacy, commercial and political speech, and creative property law. Advances in technology have posed problems for courts in dealing with non-First Amendment issues as well. However, there is nothing necessarily surprising or new about these kinds of contemporary issues pertaining to technology and the law. The ability to wiretap telephones has led to Fourth Amendment cases; drug-testing capabilities have posed questions involving personal privacy and search and seizure law; advances in prenatal testing led to maternal-fetal legal conflicts. Beyond criminal law and procedure cases, new technologies in firearms pose Second Amendment issues, and recording devices used in the White House led to a constitutional crisis and resignation of a president. In short, law often races to catch up with technological advances, in a contest that has no foreseeable end. As technologies change, so do public opinion, culture, and the composition of the judiciary. Attempts to summarize law and precedent in any issue area are doomed by the relativities of the date of publication. With this in mind, I turn first to an examination of obscenity law and technology in the United States.

In order to understand how courts deal with questions of Internet obscenity one must place the topic in the larger context of Supreme Court doctrine. The legal implications of new and developing technologies cannot be evaluated in a vacuum. Just as new technologies posed clouded issues regarding search and seizure law, Internet pornography posed serious issues in obscenity law. But courts do not start anew when new technologies arise. Courts have had to place police procedures using new technologies against existing precedent and attempt to determine, for example, if the use of listening devices constitutes a "search." Likewise, the courts have to make judgments as to whether the Internet is more like radio, television, the print media, cable, and so on. Courts also have to address definitional problems with pornography, and determine if pornography resides within First Amendment protections, as pure speech does, or outside, such as obscenity. Thus, the foundation for examining the development of Internet regulations must begin with early efforts to regulate non-Internet pornography.

### Early Development of Obscenity Law

Contrary to popular belief, suppression of sexually explicit materials was not historically rampant in England or the English colonies. In 1748, John Cleland's *Memoirs of a Woman of Pleasure (Fanny Hill)* was published without much fanfare, although *Fanny Hill* would undoubtedly achieve "best-seller" status by any measure. The Attorney General's Commission on Pornography *Final Report* noted that as the world entered the nineteenth century, "it remained the case that in most of the world there was greater tolerance for sexually explicit writing, printing, and drawing than there would be fifty years later..."[1] More often than not, law was used to prosecute sexually explicit works if those works were interpreted to be religious blasphemy or a challenge to political power—especially in Europe. Religious *and* political dissidence—not sexual deviance—were the typical grounds for banning or regulating works of expression. Likewise, by 1792 all of the new American states legislated against blasphemy and/or profanity. However, law and enforcement are not one in the same; prosecution of producers, distributors, and consumers of pornographic materials remained relatively rare.

Advances in technology in the 1800s made sexually explicit materials more readily available to the general population. The development of photography and improvements in printing technology made possible the dissemination of progressively more graphic materials. At the same time, societal norms and attitudes toward sexual morality were becoming increasingly conservative. In England, suppression of what was called "obscene libel" increased throughout the 1800s. Private groups such as The Society for the Suppression of Vice lobbied for prosecution of obscenity. Similar groups in the United States like The Watch and Ward Society of Boston, and New York Society for the Suppression of Vice, were prominent in leading the moral crusade. In the United States, a New York grocer, Anthony Comstock, played a central role in the passage of what became known as the Comstock Act of 1873. The Comstock Act was the first federal attempt to suppress the trade in and circulation of "obscene literature and articles of immoral use."[2]

Anthony Comstock fought against obscenity with the passion of a religious zealot. The Comstock Act was a strict federal postal law making the mailing of obscene material a federal offense. Shortly after the law's enactment, Comstock was appointed special agent in the Post Office Department and led efforts to vigorously enforce the act. At the time of his death Comstock was thought to have been responsible for the conviction of 3,000 individuals on obscenity charges and the destruction of 160 tons of obscene materials. Comstock was involved in intense struggle with Margaret Sanger and others revolving around issues of reproduction and birth control—circumstances that ultimately led to the undoing of this kind of increasingly unpopular "Comstockery."

Until 1957 the US Supreme Court had generally deferred to state courts in determining the constitutionality of obscenity laws. The Court had never rejected what was known as the *Hicklin* test. This standard for judging obscenity came from the 1868 English case *Regina v. Hicklin*. In *Hicklin*, Lord Cockburn stated that the test of unprotected obscenity was:

Whether the tendency of the matter charged as obscenity is to deprave and corrupt those whose minds are open to such immoral influences and into whose hands a publication of this sort might fall.[3]

The *Hicklin* test set a very low standard for judging materials obscene. The major prongs of the *Hicklin* test were:

1) Regardless of the intent of the writer/publisher, if the material had a tendency to corrupt the most vulnerable members of society (children)
2) based not on the entirety of the work but any of its parts
3) regardless of any social value of the work
4) and the material could possibly fall into the hands of the most vulnerable in society
5) the work is to be considered obscene and would be punishable

The Supreme Court upheld the Comstock Act in *Ex parte Jackson* (1878) and even extended its coverage to include materials discussing human reproduction. However, in 1957 a more liberal Warren Court struck down a state law that essentially used the *Hicklin* standard in *Butler v. Michigan* (1957). The Court ruled that basing obscenity on the standard of what might be harmful to children "is to reduce the adult population of the country to reading only what is fit for children."[4] The Court struck down the *Hicklin* test in *Butler*, but did not substitute an alternative standard until later in that term in *Roth v. U.S.* (1957).

In *Roth*, the Court held that obscenity was not constitutionally protected press or speech. The six-member majority noted that Congress had passed twenty obscenity laws from 1842 to 1956 and, as early as 1712, Massachusetts made it criminal to publish any filthy, obscene, or profane song, pamphlet, libel, or mock sermon imitating or mimicking religious services. In addition to holding that obscenity was not protected speech, the Court radically altered the standard for judging what is obscene. As opposed to the *Hicklin* test, the Roth majority ruled that the test would be "whether to the average person, applying contemporary community standards, the dominant theme of the material taken as a whole appeals to the prurient interests."

The *Roth* ruling brought about four major changes to the previous "test" of obscenity. First, *Roth* substituted the child test of *Hicklin* with the "average person test." Second, the work had to be evaluated in its entirety rather than judged by a single part. Third, the work had to be deemed as an appeal to prurient interests, rather than judged in terms of normal, healthy, lustful thoughts. Prurient interests require an appeal to the lascivious, shameful, and morbid interest in sex. Finally, contemporary community standards implied an appeal to evolving societal sexual morality rather than a static Victorian standard. Predictably, *Roth* raised as many questions as it answered. The Court was vague on what it meant by "community standards." Is community defined as the nation, a state, a county, or a town? What was meant by "dominant theme"? How much of the work could be obscene in order for authorities to judge the entire work as obscene? These questions plagued the Court for decades to come.

In *Jacobellis v Ohio* (1964) the Court defined the community standard as that of the entire nation. Local communities would have to abide by a national standard of obscenity rather than their own standards—be they more liberal or conservative. The Court also stated that to be judged as obscene a work had to lack any redeeming social value. In *Memoirs v. Massachusetts* (1966) the Court addressed the dominant theme ambiguity with reference to the necessity that a work has a "modicum of social value." In *Manual Enterprises, Inc. v Day* (1962) the Court ruled that obscene materials must appeal to prurient interests in a "patently offensive way." Taken together, the *Roth-Jacobellis-Memoirs-Manual* standard became "whether to the average person applying standards of the society at large, the material is utterly without redeeming social importance, possessing not a modicum of social value."[4]

The *Roth* test proved ironic: *Roth* imposed extremely high standards, yet little fails to pass the test of *some* redeeming value. To be sure, the Warren Court did uphold some attempts to regulate sexual material. In *Ginzburg v. U.S.* (1966) the Court upheld laws banning "pandering." In *New York v. Ferber (1982)* the Court sustained a law banning child pornography. But, in *Stanley v. Georgia* (1969) the Court struck down a state law making the mere possession of obscene materials illegal. Soon, public opinion became more conservative; Richard Nixon was elected president, and four Republican appointees joined the Court. Between 1969 and 1972 Warren Burger, Harry Blackmun, Lewis Powell, and William Rehnquist replaced Abe Fortas, Hugo Black, Earl Warren, and John Harlan II. These personnel changes dramatically altered the ideological composition of the Court. It was this much more conservative Supreme Court that ruled in the case *Miller v. California* (1973) and substantially refined the *Roth* test.

### *Miller* and Its Aftermath

Marvin Miller was convicted of mailing unsolicited materials advertising adult books, magazines, and film through the mail. The brochures included graphic pictures of men and women involved in sex acts and displaying of human genitals. Miller was arrested when one unsuspecting recipient of the material complained to police. The more conservative Burger Court used the *Miller* case as the occasion to revisit *Roth* and *Memoirs* and altered the obscenity test dramatically. The same day the Court handed down the Miller ruling they also ruled in

*Paris Adult Theatre I v. Slaton* (1973). This case involved an adult theatre in Atlanta, Georgia, that had shown films depicting fellatio, cunnilingus, and group sexual intercourse. Even though the theatre admitted only consenting adults age twenty-one and over, the Court refused to apply *Stanley* and upheld the conviction of the theatre manager.

At first glance the new standard set in *Miller* appears to be consistent with *Roth*. Under the *Miller* test material may be deemed to be obscene and outside the protection of the First Amendment if:

    (a)  whether "The average person, applying contemporary community standards" would find that the work, taken as a whole, appeals to the prurient interest;

    (b)  whether the work depicts or describes, in a patently offensive way, sexual conduct specifically defined by the applicable state law;

    (c)  whether the work, taken as a whole, lacks serious literary, artistic, political, or scientific value.[5]

The Court retained three important elements of the *Roth-Memoirs* standard. First, *Miller* retained the "average person" adult-standard rather than retreat to a child-standard of the previous *Hicklin* test. Second, *Miller* likewise stipulated that the material in question had to be viewed as a whole, in its entirety, rather than isolated passages or clips. Third, obscenity had to involve sexually oriented material that is patently offensive. Chief Justice Rehnquist, the author of *Miller*, even gave some guidance as to examples of what could be considered patently offensive. These included depictions of ultimate sexual acts, normal or perverted and patently offensive representations or descriptions of masturbation, excretory functions, or lewd exhibition of the genitals.

Despite retaining certain elements of the *Roth-Memoirs* test, however, the five-member majority in *Miller* made two important changes. First, the Court ruled that local standards, not a national standard, should be applied. Rehnquist noted that people in Maine and Mississippi might have quite different values and notions of what is acceptable than people in Las Vegas or New York City. The federal system permits people in various states to differ in tastes and attitudes, the chief justice argued. Thus, contemporary community standards would be local, rather than the national standard of *Jacobellis*.

The second major change in *Miller* was adoption of the SLAPS test in place of the "utterly without redeeming social value" test: the Court ruled that material that had serious literary, artistic, political, or scientific value must be protected regardless of public disapproval. While this appears to protect much that would be considered art, literature, and so on, it also lowered the bar dramatically. Material must have "serious" value, rather than, in the words of *Miller-Memoirs*, "any value." This "serious" standard along with "local" standards substantially altered the *Roth-Memoirs* standard, and both prongs of this test made it easier for local communities to prosecute and convict under obscenity laws.

The *Miller* decision and a more conservative Supreme Court gave wide latitude and extensive powers to local authorities. Between 1957 and 1969 the Court supported First Amendment claims in 88% of its obscenity decisions. Between 1973 and 1998 this percentage dropped to 32%. Clearly, the Court was much more deferential to local community standards and supportive of local ordinances and convictions.

In two subsequent obscenity rulings, the Court upheld a New York state law prohibiting obscene or nonobscene material that involved children under the age of sixteen (*New York v. Ferber* [1982]) and an Ohio law banning the possession and viewing of child pornography. However, in *Pope v. Illinois* (1987) the Court substituted the words "reasonable person" for "average person," a change that was welcomed by those who feared local tyrannical majorities and the imposition of intolerant attitudes. In the 1974 case *Jenkins v. Georgia* the Court stated that nudity alone was not sufficient to make material legally obscene. In ruling that the film *Carnal Knowledge* was not obscene, the Court warned local authorities that, "it would be a serious misreading of *Miller* to conclude that juries have unbridled discretion in determining what is patently offensive."[6] Thus, the Court sent signals that *Miller* still protected speech and that the justices were not about to leave total discretion to local communities.

Much of the application of Miller has dealt with bookstores, adult establishments featuring live entertainment, and zoning ordinances. The Court has upheld state laws prohibiting nude dancing in bars on the basis of a state authority to regulate liquor under their interpretation of the Twenty-first Amendment.[7] In *Arcara v. Cloud Books, Inc.* (1986) the Court upheld an ordinance that called for the closing of adult bookstores where the premises are used for solicitation of prostitution. In *Young v. American Mini Theatres* (1976) and *City of Renton v. Playtime Theatres, Inc.* (1986) the Court upheld local zoning ordinances barring adult establishments from operation, within certain distances of schools, churches, and residential areas. These rulings interpreted the ordinances as mere "time, place, and manner" regulations and upheld local authorities' concerns with attempting to control "secondary effects"—not expression or speech—of such establishments. In the 1991 case *Barnes v. Glen Theatre, Inc.* the Court upheld an Indiana public indecency statute that banned nude dancing and any public nudity. The Court ruled in *Barnes* that it was not an obscenity case but rather the right of a city to prohibit nudity. Whatever expressive speech there was in nude dancing, it was deemed to reside at the outer limits of First Amendment protection and did not trump the legitimate state interest in regulating nudity. Two final ways that governments have tried to address issues surrounding obscenity involve the applications of racketeering statutes (RICO statutes) and the withholding of government funds.

In *Fort Wayne Books v. Indiana* (1989) the Court upheld Indiana's application of RICO laws to businesses profiting from criminal acts. In *National Endowment for the Arts v. Finley* (1998) the Court upheld the authority of Congress to revise NEA funding policy to empower the agency to consider general standards of decency in the awarding of grants.

Whether through funding, zoning, considering secondary effects, redefining "community" standards to mean local community, applying the SLAPS test, or using the Twenty-first Amendment, the Court has found creative ways to regulate objectionable material. In these ways, the Court has followed a long line of governmental regulations regarding new issues and technologies. Before turning to the Internet, it is instructive to examine how past emerging technologies posed problems for those concerned with sexual, pornographic, or otherwise "indecent" material.

### Film, Telephone, and Cable Regulations

While the focus of this volume is Internet pornography, it is important to note that new technologies have always caused concern for those fearful of the dissemination of obscene or indecent materials or messages. Radio, telephone, television, and cable TV have all made the spread of objectionable material more possible. In this sense, the Internet is just one more new technology that gets caught up in a much broader political, ethical, and economic controversy. It is instructive, therefore, to understand how courts have tried to address previous issues with these technologies, and sheds some light on why courts deal with indecency on the Internet in the ways they do.

One of the earliest technologies to pose concerns for society and courts was the emergence of motion pictures. As early as 1915, the Supreme Court upheld an Ohio law that required film licensing. In *Mutual Film Corporation v. Industrial Commission* (1915), the Court ruled that films were not entitled to First Amendment protection and were purely commercial in nature. Because "commercial speech" is subject to governmental regulation, Ohio could censor films that might corrupt the morals of its population. It is important to note that at the time of *Mutual Film*, the First Amendment had not been incorporated and did not apply to the states. Not until 1925 in *Gitlow v. New York* was the First Amendment made applicable against state governments. Still, it was not until

1952 that the Court struck down a state law permitting licensing of films. In *Burstyn v. Wilson* the Court set aside a state law banning "sacrilegious" films on the grounds that it gave the government far too much power to suppress expression. The Court in *Burstyn* ruled that films were entitled to a degree of First Amendment protection.

Many cities and states developed regulations requiring that movie distributors submit films to local authorities for clearance prior to public showing. Prior viewing by authorities would ensure that the films were not obscene. While this would appear to violate the standard against prior restraint first developed in *Near v. Minnesota* (1931), the Court had left room in *Near* for prior review of possibly obscene material. In *Times Film Corp. v. Chicago* (1961) and *Freedman v. Maryland* (1965) the Court issued rulings that upheld requirements that films be submitted for review, but placed serious limitations on governments. The Court ruled that only a court had the authority to declare a film obscene, any restraint on showing the film had to be temporary, and there must be prompt resolution to the inquiry. Thus, boards and other agencies could not make judgments but only courts could declare films obscene, and the film in question could not be tied up in administrative limbo for an extended period of time.

Films have also been regulated, even when not obscene, through zoning ordinances. In *Young v. American Mini Theatres, Inc.* (1976) and *City of Renton v. Playtime Theatres, Inc.* (1986) the Court upheld zoning ordinances limiting both the number of adult theatres legally permitted within so many feet of one another and the location of adult theatres within so many feet of churches, schools, parks, or residential neighborhoods. In *Renton* the Court relied on the "secondary effects" justification for such zoning laws. This time, place, and manner limitation was imposed on adult theatres not because of the content of the films but rather because of the increased likelihood of secondary effects associated with adult theatres such as increased crime, drunkenness, and the like.

These limitations on film perpetuated a legal tradition that not only obscenity but also "indecency" could be regulated. The Radio Act of 1927 and Communications Act of 1934 make it a crime to broadcast obscene, indecent, or profane language. The Federal Communications Commission (FCC) is empowered to enforce federal standards of decency over the airwaves. While indecency is a vague term, the FCC shed some light on what was not permitted by stating that indecent material "describes or depicts, in terms patently offensive as measured by contemporary community standards for the broadcast medium, sexual or excretory activities or organs, at times of day when there is a reasonable risk that children may be in the audience."[8] The constitutionality of this FCC policy was challenged in 1978 in *FCC v. Pacifica Foundation*. At issue was a twelve-

minute George Carlin monologue played over a New York public FM radio station at two o'clock on a weekday afternoon. In the monologue, Carlin satirized
the words prohibited over the radio by saying repeatedly, in numerous contexts,
the words shit, piss, fuck, cunt, cocksucker, motherfucker, and tits. In a five-to-
four decision, the Supreme Court upheld the FCC ruling on two grounds. First,
because it was played in the afternoon, the monologue could have been heard by
minors, and parents would have no way of guarding their children from hearing
the "seven dirty words." Because of the nature of radio, one could tune in precisely at the moment the words were being aired and the damage could be done
before switching stations or turning off the radio could take place. Second, the
Court ruled that radio had a pervasive presence in citizens' lives and penetrated
the sanctity of the home, causing a conflict between the First Amendment and
privacy rights. The Court ruled that the FCC could constitutionally limit the
times at which such indecent programs could be aired.

In subsequent years, Congress and the FCC applied indecency standards to
television as well as radio and attempted to apply the indecency standard to a
twenty-four hour time period. In 1991, the D.C. Circuit Court of Appeals struck
down the twenty-four hour rule in *Action for Children's Television v. FCC*
(1988) on the grounds of overbreadth and ruled that there had to be some "safe
harbor" period when broadcasters could legally air adult programs. As of 2003,
the safe harbor time period remains ten P.M. to six A.M. However, whether the
news media were to be covered by the indecency standards remained an issue
until 1989. In that year, National Public Radio aired a news program which included part of an interview with an alleged mobster in which the words fuck and
fucking were used ten times. After a listener complaint the FCC ruled that the
broadcast was not legally indecent and merited constitutional protection based
on legitimate news content.[9] Finally, in 1991, the FCC clarified its standards by
stating that indecent material is that which describes sexual or excretory activities in a patently offensive way based on a national standard of the average listener or viewer. The FCC also considers the full context of the program and the
frequency and context of the language. Thus, the FCC uses a balancing test that
considers a wide array of contextual factors.

One of the justifications for regulations of the broadcast media was the limited number of frequencies available to be granted to broadcasters. The introduction of cable television posed new problems for regulators. So far, courts have
been unwilling to apply *Pacifica* to cable television. Generally, the courts have
granted cable operators similar rights as those in the print media. In *Wilkinson v.
Jones* (1987) the Court upheld a federal district court's ruling, striking down a
Utah law barring indecency on cable.[10] Similarly, in *Cruz v. Ferre* (1985) the

Court of Appeals for the Eleventh Circuit struck down a Miami ordinance prohibiting indecency on cable TV.[11] In these cases, the courts ruled that cable does not "intrude" into the home, but the subscriber must take affirmative steps to elect to have cable come into the home. Also, the subscriber must take additional steps to purchase extra programming, including movies. In addition, there is a wide array of channels unlike commercial broadcasting. Finally, parents have options to protect children including programming guides warning of vulgarity and nudity, and lockboxes that enable parents to prevent children from gaining access to certain channels.

Most recently, the Supreme Court ruled that section 505 of the Telecommunications Act of 1966 was unconstitutional. This section of the Act required that cable operators who provide premium channels primarily dedicated to sexually-oriented programming fully scramble or block those channels or limit transmission to the hours of ten P.M. to six A.M. This Act was designed to protect basic subscribers who did not desire the adult channels. However, scrambling is not precise and some video or audio might be received. Therefore, most operators opted for the safe harbor time period, substantially cutting into the number of hours the programming would be available to those desiring adult content. In *U.S. v. Playboy Entertainment Group* (2000) the Court struck down section 505 because it was content-based and could not survive "strict scrutiny." Under the strict-scrutiny standard, speech is awarded a high level of protection unless the government can show a compelling governmental interest and that the limitation imposed is the least restrictive means to achieve its goal. The majority asserted that the blanket restriction was too severe, not narrowly tailored, and the least restrictive means would be to block the channels on a customer-by-customer basis.[12]

Telephones have also been used as a means to communicate obscene or indecent speech and the courts have had to address regulations limiting that medium. In 1988, Congress amended the Communications Act of 1934 to make illegal commercial phone sex businesses and other sexually explicit messages over the telephone. In *Sable Communications of California, Inc. v. FCC*, the Court upheld part of the act that banned obscene messages, but unanimously struck down another portion banning indecent speech. While agreeing that indecency could be regulated, the Court pointed out that it could not be totally banned. Justice White said that the outright ban of indecent messages in order to protect children was just "another case of burning the house to roast the pig."[13] The Court said that placing a telephone call is not the same as turning on a radio broadcast. The caller must take affirmative steps to receive the message. Service providers could also use methods such as access codes to limit the availability to children. Since *Sable*, Congress has passed a statute banning dial-a-porn services to anyone under the age of eighteen. Courts have upheld requirements that dial-a-porn be restricted to those paying in advance by credit card unless the provider requires an access code available only to adults.[14]

It is against this backdrop of legal precedent that courts have had to address issues concerning the newest technology posing a threat to those opposed to sexually explicit images and words—the Internet. In the next section we review recent case law and Supreme Court decisions regarding Internet pornography. As with other media, the courts have had to deal with issues of whether this medium is more like publishing or broadcasting, whether users are captive or take affirmative steps to receive the information, and whether the regulations are narrowly tailored or overbroad.

### Indecency, Internet Regulations, and the Courts

From the beginning the Internet was an obvious vehicle for transmission of adult materials. In recent years the Internet has become a substantial medium for the dissemination of sexually explicit images, downloadable videos, interactive adult visual and audio transmission, message boards, chat rooms, and commercial sex businesses including dial-a-porn, prostitution, and video sales. Given the growth in home computer sales and the ease with which users can browse the Internet, it was inevitable that both children and easily offended adults would come face-to-face with sexually graphic websites. Governments, interest groups, schools, parents and others have shown considerable creativity in fashioning policies designed to regulate or ban such sexually explicit materials. This section will review the major court cases that deal with Internet regulation of obscene and indecent messages and graphics.

The first major congressional attempt to regulate obscenity and indecent material on the Internet came with passage of the Communications Decency Act of 1996. Two sections of the act were challenged by the American Civil Liberties Union and other interest groups. Section 223(a) criminalized the "knowing" transmission of "obscene or indecent" messages to any recipient under the age of eighteen. Section 223(d) prohibited the "knowing" transmission or display, to a person under the age of eighteen, of any message, "that, in context, depicts or describes, in terms patently offensive as measured by contemporary community standards, sexual or excretory activities or organs."

There were numerous issues in the CDA case. Opponents argued that while there were exceptions to the *Miller* obscenity definition for serious scientific, literary, artistic, and political materials, the CDA contained no exceptions to its "indecency" prohibition. Would the CDA ban medical and educational graphics and depictions on the Internet? Would crime scene photographs be considered indecent? Another question concerned which "community" standards should prevail. The standards of the entire nation? The standards of the local community in which a particular user might reside? A third issue revolved around defining the Internet medium. Is the Internet invasive like radio, or do users have to take sufficient affirmative steps to bring up sites, like cable television? These issues were addressed in the Supreme Court case *Reno v. ACLU* (1997).[15]

The Supreme Court ruled on an appeal from a three-judge federal district court. In a unanimous decision the federal district court had struck down as unconstitutional those sections of the CDA that addressed indecency. Because the CDA was a governmental restriction on speech, and was content-based, the level of review necessary was that of "strict scrutiny." In other words, the government would have to show a compelling governmental interest and that the regulations imposed were narrowly tailored and the least restrictive means to achieve its goals. The district court found that the CDA was not narrowly tailored, had a "chilling effect" on legal speech, and posed restrictions on adults who do have a right to view sexually explicit materials. Further, in the CDA Congress had not defined what was meant by "indecent" or "patently offensive." Thus the act was deemed vague, overbroad, and "profoundly repugnant" to the principles and values embodied in the First Amendment.[16]

In June 1997, the Court issued a seven to two opinion upholding the lower court's decision. Justice Stevens, writing for the majority, said that language in the CDA was imprecise, and that this imprecision made the CDA overly broad and would have a chilling effect on speech:

> We are persuaded that the CDA lacks the precision that the First Amendment requires when a statute regulates the content of speech. In order to deny minors access to potentially harmful speech, the CDA effectively suppresses a large amount of speech that adults have a constitutional right to receive and to address to one another.[17]

In addressing the government's argument that the CDA could be justified on grounds of zoning, such as in *Renton*, the majority pointed out that *Young* and *Renton* upheld zoning but not a complete ban. The Court also ruled that there were less restrictive means to achieve the government's purpose. Justice Stevens noted that parental controls, including blocking software, were available. The CDA's overbreadth would also make the act of a parent showing Internet sites to their children criminal if those sites might be deemed "indecent" by local authorities. The law as written made no exceptions for parents, or teachers, or clinicians, or others who might have the legitimate occasion to view or exhibit such websites. The Court also noted that the Internet could not be likened to radio where the scarcity of broadcast frequencies justified governmental regulations. Finally, citing *Pacifica*, the Court pointed out that indecency was not altogether banned in radio broadcasting, but simply limited to hours when minors were less likely to be listening. The CDA was a total ban and, therefore, failed the test of constitutionality.

Congress was determined to fashion an Internet porn act that would pass constitutional scrutiny and attached the Child Online Protection Act to a 1998 budget bill. COPA was directed at commercial pornographers. Rather than impose restrictions on the Internet itself, COPA targeted the producers of obscene and indecent content. The act provided:

> Whoever knowingly and with knowledge of the character of the material, in interstate or foreign commerce by means of the World Wide Web, makes any communication for commercial purposes that is available to any minor and that includes any material that is harmful to minors shall be fined not more than $50,000, imprisoned not more than 6 months, or both.[18]

The words "indecency" and "patently offensive"—both of which caused problems for the Court in *Reno v. ACLU*—were omitted from COPA. Instead, Congress defined harmful material as:

> Any communication, picture, image, graphic image file, article, recording, writing, or other matter of any kind that is obscene or that–
> (A)  the average person, applying contemporary community standards, would find, taking the material as a whole and with respect to minors, is designed to appeal to, or is designed to pander to, prurient interest;
> (B)  depicts, describes, or represents, in a manner patently offensive with respect to minors, an actual or simulated sexual act or sexual contact, an actual or simulated normal or perverted sexual act, or a lewd exhibition of the genitals or post-pubescent female breast; and
> (C)  taken as a whole, lacks serious literary, artistic, political, or scientific value for minors.[19]

Clearly the language of COPA was strikingly similar to the standard for obscenity set in *Miller v. California*. To protect adults and provide an affirmative defense for commercial sites trying to comply, COPA included a provision requiring use of credit cards, debit accounts, adult access codes, or other means that would verify age. Despite congressional efforts to satisfy the Court's objections to the CDA, the new act was immediately in the courts. Originally known as *ACLU v. Reno*, a federal district court issued a preliminary injunction stopping enforcement, and an appellate court agreed. In 2002, the U.S. Supreme

Court decided the case, by then retitled *Ashcroft v. ACLU*, by issuing a partial ruling and remanding the case back to the district court. The decision was anticlimactic and left most issues unresolved.[20]

The lower courts had ruled that COPA was overly broad, would have a chilling effect on protected speech, and that the community standards provision would essentially give a veto to the most puritanical community in the nation. The Supreme Court was badly divided and in *Ashcroft v. ACLU* five separate opinions were written. A majority agreed that the community standards provision did not automatically render COPA unconstitutional, and remanded the case back to the Third Circuit Court of Appeals with instructions to reevaluate (1) whether COPA was overbroad, and (2) whether it was vague or otherwise unconstitutional under the strict scrutiny test. In a concurring opinion, Justice O'Connor questioned whether a national standard might not be preferable to a local community standard. Justice Stevens wrote a dissent essentially agreeing with the appellate court's analysis. Justices Breyer, Kennedy, Souter, and Ginsburg believed that prior to any ruling the appellate court should closely examine what is meant by "commercial communication," and the very nature of the World Wide Web as a medium for communication.

On remand the Third Circuit Court of Appeals again found COPA to be unconstitutional due to overbreadth, lack of a narrowly tailored policy, and the availability of less restrictive means. The appeals court further noted that the reference "harmful to minors" did not distinguish among infants, those in their early teens, and those just shy of the age of eighteen. It is anticipated that the Supreme Court will revisit COPA in its 2003–2004 term.

In 1998, 1999, and 2003, federal courts were asked to review restrictions placed on public library access to pornographic Internet sites and a state law restricting state employees from accessing sexually explicit material on state-owned or -leased computers. In three decisions, federal courts sent mixed signals as to what is and is not constitutionally sound limitation on computer access to certain websites. First, in *Urofsky v. Gilmore* (1999), a Virginia law prohibited any state employee from accessing such sites without prior approval from supervisors.[21] Six public college and university professors had challenged the state law on grounds of First Amendment rights of academic freedom. The plaintiffs argued that accessing such sites was work-related and denial of access would substantially interfere with their ability to perform their jobs. In January of 2001, the Supreme Court denied certiorari to those wishing to appeal the appellate court's ruling. Thus, the ruling has legal applicability only to the Fourth Circuit, but the Court's denial of cert certainly leaves open the question of whether other states might follow Virginia's lead. Such restrictions would clearly affect the ability of sociologists, psychologists, legal analysts, and other academics to conduct legitimate scholarly research on campuses using state computers—including the works of nearly all the scholars who have contributed to this book.

The first of two major library Internet cases originated in Virginia. The Library Board of Loudoun County voted to adopt a policy entitled "Policy on Internet Sexual Harassment." The policy required that site-blocking software be installed on all library computers so as to block child pornography, obscenity, and other materials deemed harmful to children. Adults who wished to view blocked sites could submit a written request that included their name, telephone number, and detailed explanation of why they desired access to the blocked site. Library staff had unlimited discretion as to whether or not to unblock the sites. A number of residents sued and the case was decided by a federal court in the eastern district of Virginia.[22]

In *Loudon v. Loudoun County Library* (1998), a district judge upheld the portion of the policy blocking child pornography and obscenity, but struck down the provision blocking material deemed harmful to minors. The judge stated that the library was not obligated to provide Internet access, but once access is provided the library could not engage in censorship based on content. Further, the policy was overly broad, was not narrowly tailored, and was not the least restrictive means available to achieve its goals. The policy was over inclusive in that it limited access to adults and children alike, effectively limiting adult users to material suitable for a child. While the government does have a compelling interest in promoting a nonsexually hostile environment in libraries, the policy in question was not the least restrictive means available. The court pointed out that other remedies were possible, including privacy screens around terminals, filters that could be turned off when adults were using a computer, creation of separate rooms for adults-only and children-only computers, and creation of an acceptable use policy. In short, once again authorities had violated First Amendment rights by prohibiting adults from accessing legal nonobscene materials. But, in 2000, the Congress attempted to address public libraries and Internet usage by passing the Children's Internet Protection Act (CIPA).

To help public libraries provide Internet access, Congress offers two forms of federal assistance grants. These grants are extremely helpful to local public libraries that have limited budgets. Congress became concerned that adults and minors were using public library Internet service to access pornographic sites and passed the CIPA in 2000. The CIPA withholds federal grants from any public library that does not use filtering devices to protect minors from visual depictions deemed harmful to children. Thus, the act did not require libraries to use the software but any library that wanted to be eligible for federal grants would have to install such software on all of its computers. The American Library Association (ALA) and other groups filed suit and argued that Congress had exceeded its authority under the Spending Clause, that the CIPA was a content-based restriction on access to a public forum, that the act was over inclusive and not narrowly tailored, and that the act was not the least restrictive means to achieve the government's goals. A federal district court in Pennsylvania struck down the law as a violation of the First Amendment.[23] The Supreme court issued a decision on June 23, 2003 in *U.S. v. American Library Association*.[24]

The Supreme Court reversed the lower court and held CIPA to be constitutional. Six justices voted to uphold the law, but there was no majority opinion. Chief Justice Rehnquist wrote the Court's plurality opinion, which was signed by Justices O'Connor, Scalia, and Thomas. Justices Kennedy and Breyer wrote concurring opinions and Justices Stevens, Souter, and Ginsburg dissented. The Court's plurality argued that libraries were not obligated to offer Internet access, nor were libraries obligated to offer access to all Internet sites, just as they could limit which books are purchased or establish limits to their interlibrary loan services. Further, Congress could place limitations on grants and other funding based on the decisions in *Rust v. Sullivan*[25] and *National Endowment for the Arts*. In those cases, Congress withheld federal funds from any hospital that performed abortions and allowed federal agencies to consider content in funding decisions to artists. Justices Kennedy and Breyer wrote that as long as adults could request, and librarians agree, to remove the blocking software, the policy appeared to be constitutional at face value. However, if libraries did not or could not efficiently remove the software blocking so that adults, upon request, could access legal sites, then a future case would have to examine the application of the policy.

The dissenters disagreed and found the CIPA to violate the First Amendment. While agreeing that libraries out of necessity must make decisions on what books to purchase for the library, content discrimination was not permissible. Space and budget considerations are appropriate, but not content, and the Internet posed neither space nor budgetary issues. The minority also cited the ALA's mission of allowing adults access to all books in a library rather than limit their access in accordance with what is appropriate for minors. The dissenters also argued that there were less restrictive means available to the library board. But these arguments were to no avail; *U.S. v. American Library Association* marked a precedent that gave a victory to those wishing to limit adult access to legal websites in a public facility. This case, along with *Urofsky,* gives hope to those dissatisfied with the CDA and COPA rulings.

The most recent Court decision dealing with Internet pornography is *Ashcroft v. Free Speech Coalition* (2002).[26] What makes this case not only important, but in many ways unique, is that it addressed "virtual child porn," or computer-generated images even when actual minors are not involved in the material or images. In 1996, Congress passed the Child Pornography Protection Act (CPPA). Congress was concerned with three specific problems and attempted to address the issues with the CPPA. First, Congress was concerned with sophisticated technological advances that make possible the depiction of children through computer generated images and morphing. Second, these advances make prosecution of some actual child pornography difficult due to the difficulty of proving that a particular picture was produced using an actual child. Third, pedophiles could use these images to induce children to participate in sexual activities or to whet their own sexual appetites. While *Ferber* outlawed child porn that involved the actual use of children, CPPA would extend protections to the depictions of children through computer generated or other means.

The CPPA had two sections that were particularly problematic to civil libertarians. Section 2256 (8) (B) prohibited "any depiction, including any photograph, film, video, picture, or computer or computer-generated image or picture that is, or appears to be, of a minor engaging in sexually explicit conduct."[27] Section (D) prohibited any sexual image that is "advertised, promoted, presented, described, or distributed in such a manner that conveys the impression that it depicts a minor engaging in sexually explicit conduct."[28] A federal district trial court upheld the act but the Ninth Circuit Court of Appeals struck down the CPPA as overbroad and the case went to the Supreme Court. In April of 2002 the Court handed down its decision in *Ashcroft v. Free Speech Coalition.*[29]

In a five to four ruling the Court upheld the appellate court's decision striking down the CPPA. Justice Kennedy wrote the majority opinion, which was signed by justices Breyer, Ginsburg, Souter, and Stevens. Justices O'Conner and Thomas concurred in part and dissented in part. Justices Rehnquist and Scalia dissented in full. The majority ruled that the CPPA was inconsistent with *Miller*. The Court reasoned that the CPPA prohibited material that was nonobscene, did not require that the material appeal to the prurient interest, and did not require that the material be patently offensive. Further, the CPPA did not permit exceptions for material having serious literary, artistic, political, or scientific value, nor did it require that the work be taken as a whole. One scene or photograph, taken out of context, could make the entire work illegal. The majority noted that many classics, plays, films, literatures, and other creative expression would fall outside of the protection of the law because of adult actors playing the parts of minors and cited Shakespeare's *Romeo and Juliet,* the 2001 Academy Award-nominee *Traffic,* and the Academy Award Best Picture winner *American Beauty.*

Justice Kennedy also disagreed with the government's argument that *Ferber* justified the CPPA. The *Ferber* decision was based on "how" films were made—using actual minors who became victims—rather than the message being communicated. *Ferber* also relied on the distinction between actual and virtual child pornography. The CPPA could not, therefore, be saved by reliance on *Ferber.* As to the argument that the CPPA would effectively protect minors by eliminating virtual porn that could be used by pedophiles to whet the appetites of children, or that the virtual porn would arouse the appetites of pedophiles, the majority reasoned that legal speech cannot be banned because it may have a "tendency" to incite others. As to the argument that virtual child porn makes conviction of actual child porn difficult due to the difficulty of distinguishing the two, Justice Kennedy wrote:

> Finally, the First Amendment is turned upside down by the argument that, because it is difficult to distinguish between images made using real children and those produced by computer imaging, both kinds of images must be prohibited. The overbreadth doctrine prohibits the Government from banning unprotected speech if a substantial amount of protected speech is prohibited or chilled in the process.[30]

Justices O'Connor and Thomas wrote separate concurring opinions. While concurring in the judgment of the Court, Justice Thomas noted that the government's strongest argument was that actual child pornographers might escape conviction by claiming that the images used were computer generated. However, he noted that at this time the government was only asserting that the defendant might raise such defenses and not that any have actually done so successfully. Justice O'Connor disagreed with the majority as to the overbreadth of virtual porn, but agreed that the ban on nonvirtual porn where adults "appear as" minors was unconstitutional. Justices Scalia and Rehnquist dissented in full and would uphold the CPPA in its entirety.

*Ashcroft v. Free Speech Coalition* is the latest in a long line of Internet porn cases reaching the Court. Civil libertarians can find comfort in *Ashcroft* as well as Court rulings on the CDA and COPA. However, the current Court is badly fractured along ideological lines that affect decisions in not only Internet porn cases but also defendants' rights, religion, and privacy cases. Personnel changes on the Court could tilt the balance. It must also be noted that *Ashcroft* lacked any presentation of data or other evidence supporting the government's claim concerning potential difficulty in obtaining convictions of child porn. Should a similar case come before the Court where the government offers clear evidence, the outcome could be in question.

## Conclusion

In the four decades since *Roth* the Supreme Court has had to address numerous issues involving obscenity, indecency, technology, and adult entertainment. With the exceptions of actual child porn (*Ferber*), public nudity (*Barnes*), and library funding (*ALA*), the Court has generally supported First Amendment protections. The CDA, COPA, and CPPA all posed serious threats to legal nonobscene materials and in each case the Court upheld First Amendment rights. However, changes in Court personnel and public opinion could affect future decisions. Most risks would appear to come from regulations of virtual child porn and computer user policies in public institutions. The district court ruling in *Urofsky* should cause concern for those favoring broad protections for Internet use in libraries and on university campuses.

Attempts to limit and regulate Internet porn are hardly unique to the United States. Germany, Indonesia, Thailand, Japan, and Canada are all currently creating governmental policies that substantially limit the availability of nonobscene materials. However, given the international nature of the Internet, enforcement is problematic. With over 600 million users in over 140 countries, the Internet poses serious problems for any single government attempting regulations. As a result, many parents, interest groups, and state and local authorities are turning to blocking software and computer-user policies. Courts will continue to be inundated with cases involving these attempts to protect children and adults who object to sexually oriented materials.

The body of law is in the process of creation. Unlike most other bodies of law, Internet and obscenity law is relatively new. Just as the history of nonobscene seditious speech grew in stops and starts, beginning with *Gitlow* in 1925, so too is the historical evolution of law in these newer mediums of communication and expression. The major test for courts revolves around attempting to find where the Internet fits in terms of communicative speech. Restrictions will be judged at least partially on analogies between the Internet and cable, radio, television, and so on. Regulations are more likely to be upheld than complete bans. There will also be jockeying by those groups interested in Internet policies. Legislatures will learn from court rulings how to better write laws and policies so as to not run afoul of constitutional constraints. At the same time, distributors will find ways around laws to maintain sites, and civil libertarians will muster forces to creatively attack regulations. Staffing of the courts will thus be a hotly contested political issue. There is every reason to suspect that Internet pornography will continue to occupy a significant place on court dockets for years to come.

## Notes

1.  Attorney General's Commission Pornography, *Final Report* (Washington, D.C.: U.S. Department of Justice, 233).
2.  17 stat. § 598 (1873).
3.  Epstein, Lee, and Thomas G. Walker, *Constitutional Law for a Challenging America.* Vol. 2. Washington, D.C. *Congressional Quarterly Press.* 2004. p. 350.
4.  Epstein and Walker 355.
5.  *Miller v. California* 413 U.S. 15 (1973) 24.
6.  *Jenkins v. Georgia* 418 U.S. 153 (1974) 160.
7.  *New York State Liquor Authority v. Bellanca* 452 U.S. 714 (1981).
8.  Zelezny, John D. *Communications Law.* 4th ed. Belmont, CA: Wadsworth. 2004. p. 451.
9.  Ibid. 455.
10. 800 F. 2d 989, 13 Media L. Rep. 1913 (10th Cir. 1986) affd. Without opinion, 480 U.S. 926 (1987).
11. *Cruz v. Ferre*, 755 F. 2d 1415, 1420 (11th Cir. 1985).
12. *U.S. v. Playboy Entertainment Group, Inc.*, 529 U.S. 803 (2000).
13. *Sable Communications of California, Inc. v. FCC*, 492 U.S. 115 (1989).
14. *Information Providers' Coalition for Defense of the First Amendment v. FCC*, 928 F.2d 866, 872 (9th Cir. 1999).
15. *Reno v. ACLU* 521 U.S. 844 (1997).
16. *ACLU v. Reno*, 929 F. Supp. 824 (1996) (ED PA).
17. Ibid.
18. Child Online Protection Act, 47 U.S.C. §231.
19. Ibid.
20. *Ashcroft v. ACLU*, 535 U.S. 234 (2002).
21. *Urofsky v. Gilmore*, 995 F. Supp. 634 (E.D. Va. 1998).
22. *Mainstream Loudoun, et al,, v. Board of Trustees of the Loudoun County Library*, F. Supp. 2d 552 (1998)(Ed. Va.).
23. *American Library Association v. U.S.*, 201 f. Supp. 2d 401 (ED. Pa, 2002).
24. *U.S. v. American Library Association*, 123 S.Ct. 2297 (2003).
25. *Rust v. Sullivan*, 500 U.S. 173 (1991).
26. *Ashcroft v. Free Speech Coalition*, 535 U.S. 234 (2002).
27. 18 U.S.C. § 2256 (8) (B).
28. U.S.C. 18 § 2256 (8)(D).
29. Ashcroft v. Free Speech Coalition, 535 U.S. 234 (2002).
30. Ashcroft v. Free Speech Coalition, 535 U.S. 234 (2002).

# Part Six

# The Future of Internet Sex

Future is always fiction, at least from one point of view; time exists only in a perpetual present and everything else is an abstraction. Yet, as one moment becomes the next, most often we know the present will forever be made into the past as we move incrementally into a future with some measure of confidence about where we have been and where we are going. While we know that life is, in part, a lottery, most of us bank on this assurance. In this way, the past and the future are necessarily connected by the eternal present: the seeds of the future are sown in the past and cultivated in the present. In other words, clues to the future can usually be seen before our eyes, if we only have the right lens of vision.

Of course, anytime we discuss the future, having the right lens of vision is *the* problem; infinite combinations of endless variables from the past and present make for a boggling array of possible future configurations. Consequently, it often sometimes seems fortune cookies know better than human beings. Even so, contemplations of the future are well worth considering. It is often in discussions of the future that we see with greatest clarity our collective hopes and dreams, as well as our fears and nightmares. It is also in discussions of the future that we see clear statements about the things in the present that command attention. The readings in this Part Six are no exception.

Of all that Howard Rheingold has written, his musings on "teledildonics" are the most well known. As Rheingold (1991:345) describes in his best selling book *Virtual Reality*, his contemplations on the future of virtual reality and telecommunications struck a global nerve. Yet much of what Rheingold wrote is not particularly shocking, and he is probably correct that the "first fully functional teledildonics system will be a communication device, not a sex machine." After all, this is what we have already witnessed with Internet sex, and it is fair to assume that in the future people will continue to use computer-networking technologies to have sex with other *people*, not machines per se. And, as Rheingold also correctly points out, the future of Internet sex will be one that mines and navigates a contentious ethical terrain.

Although some may read Trudy Barber's account of the "sex tourist" of the future as a way-out (and sometimes cynical) fantasy, a little contemplation reveals that Barber has merely extended upon trends in society and culture that are already present. We are *already* technological sex tourists: out of amusement, curiosity, or genuine libidinal interest, an enormous plethora of sexual expressions are available for anyone willing to purchase the images, videos, phone-sex operator's time, Internet connection, or any number of other commercial products. The continued merging of media and the potential of virtual reality would only seem to extend upon the kind of sex tourism that millions of people already consume.

From the beginning, this book has explored the many and varied ways that technology, sex, and pornography have posed a unique and significant context for reflection on society, culture, and the people who may (or may not) be grounded in this extraordinary matrix of computer-mediated words and images. We have also explored the significant influence of Internet sex on a wide array of personal, interpersonal, and institutional phenomena. While no one can know precisely what the future holds, one thing is certain: the history of Internet sex promises some assurances on its future, a future of curious and sometimes disturbing novelties that will continue to compel the dynamics, issues, and reflections that have sparked the imaginations of millions of Internet users, the innovation of scores of entrepreneurs, and the curious inquiries of the social sciences.

## References

Rheingold, H. 1991. *Virtual reality.* New York, NY: Touchstone.

## ❖ Chapter Fifteen

# Teledildonics: Reach Out and Touch Someone

## Howard Rheingold[*]

*Based on this earlier essay, Howard Rheingold's best selling book* Virtual Reality *contains an entire chapter on "teledildonics"—the use of sophisticated computer and communication technologies for sexual pleasure. Rheingold's discussion of teledildonics" may be among his best-known works. Indeed, people everywhere are fascinated by the prospects. Rheingold explains where these technologies may be going and what the future of Internet sex might look like. Yet, as Rheingold also explains, it may be necessary to curb our enthusiasm; the future of Internet sex contains uneasy moral and ethical questions that cannot be overlooked. In this respect, Rheingold (1991) gives us all some good advice: "it is good to beware of looking at the future through the moral lens of the present."*

> There was a young man named Kleene,
> who invented a fucking machine.
> Concave or convex, it fit either sex,
> and was exceedingly easy to clean.

The first fully functional teledildonics system will probably *not* be a fucking machine. You will not use erotic telepresence technology in order to have sex with machines. Twenty years from now, when portable telediddlers are ubiquitous, people will use them to have sexual experiences with *other people*, at a distance, in combinations and configurations undreamt of by precybernetic voluptuaries. Through the synthesis of virtual reality technology and telecommunication networks, you will be able to reach out and touch someone—or an entire population—in ways humans have never before experienced.

Dildonics—it had to happen. It is the unnatural fruit of the marriage of lust and craft. The word "dildonics" was coined by visionary computer pontiff Ted Nelson in 1974. Ted is best known as the inventor of hypertext and designer of the world's oldest unfinished software project, appropriately named "Xanadu." As originally conceived, it described a machine invented by San Francisco hardware hacker How Wachspress: a device capable of converting sound into

---

[*] Rheingold, Howard. 1990. *Mondo 2000*. Issue 2/Summer:52–54.

tactile sensations. (Patent #3,875,932). The erogenic effect depends upon where you, the consumer, decide to interface your anatomy with the tactile simulator. Picture yourself a couple decades hence, getting dressed for a hot night in the virtual village. Before you climb into a suitably padded chamber and put on your head-mounted display, you slip into a lightweight—eventually, one would hope diaphanous—bodysuit. It would be something like a body stocking, but with all the intimate snugness of a condom. Embedded in the inner surface of the suit, using a technology that does not yet exist, is an array of intelligent effectors. These effectors are ultra-tiny vibrators of varying degrees of hardness, hundreds of them per square inch, that can receive and transmit a realistic sense of tactile presence in the same way the visual and audio displays transmit a realistic sense of visual and auditory presence. You can reach out your virtual hand, pick up a virtual block, and by running your fingers over the object, feel the surfaces and edges, by means of the effectors that exert counterforces against your skin. The counterforces correspond to the kinds of forces you would encounter when handling a non-virtual object of the specified shape, weight, and texture. You can run your cheek over (virtual) satin and feel the difference when you encounter (virtual) human flesh. Or you can gently squeeze something soft and pliable and feel it stiffen and rigidify under your touch.

Now, imagine plugging your whole sound-sight-touch telepresence system into the telephone network. You see a lifelike but totally artificial visual representation of your own body, and of your partner's. Depending where you go and where you are allowed and what you are willing to pay (or trade or do) you can find one partner, a dozen, a thousand, in various cyberspaces that are no further than a telephone number. Your partner(s) can move independently in the cyberspace, and your representations (aka "puppets") are able to touch each other, even though your physical bodies might be continents apart.

Every nook and protuberance, every plane and valley and knob of your body's surface, will require its own processor. Technically this is the limiting factor in the evolution of teledildonics: the development of extremely powerful computers to perform the enormous number of calculations required to monitor and control hundreds of thousands of sensors and effectors. Fiber optic networks can already handle the very high bandwidth that telepresence requires. But it may take decades to develop the mesh of tiny, high-speed, safe but powerful tactile effectors. Today's vibrators are in the ENIAC era. [ENIAC was the first electronic digital computer].

The tool I am suggesting is much more than a fancy vibrator, but I suggest we keep that archiaic name; a more sober formal description of the technology would be "tactile telepresence," and it is much more than a gleam in the eye of a horny hardware hacker. Part of the infrastructure for a dildonic system exists already in the form of computerized clothing and head-mounted displays that permit people to enter the fully three-dimensional illusion of an artificial reality.

Teledildonics is inevitable given the rate of progress in the enabling technologies of shape-memory alloys, fiber-optics, and supercomputing. Enormous market-driven forces will be unleashed when sex at a distance becomes possible. Questions of morality, privacy, personal identity, and even the very definition of Eros will be up for grabs.

If everybody can look as beautiful, sound as sexy and feel as nubile and virile as everyone else, what then will have erotic meaning?

If you can experience sexual frissons or deep physical communion with another person with no possibility of pregnancy or VD, what then of conventional morality?

If you can map your hands to your puppet's legs, and let your fingers do the walking through cyberspace, there is no reason to believe you won't be able to map your genital effectors to your manual sensors and have direct genital contact by shaking hands. What will happen to social touching when nobody knows where anybody else's erogenous zones are located?

Clearly we are on the verge of a whole new semiotics of mating. Privacy and identity and intimacy will become tightly coupled into something we don't have a name for yet. In Unix systems, files and programs and groups of users can be grouped into nested hierarchies by a system of "permissions."

The protocols of passions are something we can only guess at now. In cyberspace, your most public persona—the way you want the world to see you—will be "universally readable," in Unix terms. If you decide to join a group at a collegial or peer level, or decide to become informationally intimate with an individual or group, you will share the public keys to your identity permission access codes. The physical commingling of genital sensations might come to be regarded, in time, as a less intimate act than the sharing of your innermost self-representations.

Finally, with all those layers of restricted access to self-representations that may differ radically from layer to layer, what happens to the self? Where does identity lie? And with our information machines so deeply intermingled with our bodily sensations, as Ted Nelson might say, will our communication devices be regarded as "its"…or will they be part of "us"?

# Chapter Sixteen

# A Pleasure Prophecy: Predictions for the Sex Tourist of the Future

## Trudy Barber

*In many respects we have already witnessed an institutionalization of sex tourism, and nowhere is this more evident than on the Internet. Anyone with an Internet connection can tour a stunning array of sexualities and temporarily sample or otherwise vacation in erotic wonderlands of one's choosing. In addition, like tourism in real life, sex tourism on the Internet favors privilege: those who can pay get to play. Trudy Barber suggests that both aspects of sex tourism will shape the future of Internet sex and posits a provocative series of possible future scenarios.*

The counter-narrative to such way-out visions of future sex features a big dose of technofear and associated misgivings voiced by theorists and artists ranging from Marshal McLuhan to David Cronenberg concerning excess, the decline of real flesh experiences and a dread of what happens when men and machines fall in love.

—Laurence O'Toole, *Pornocopia*.

The fear of the decline of "real flesh" experiences, as expressed in the above quote by O'Toole, is visually paralleled by the now ironically aging Arnold Schwarzenegger, who represents the forever-young synthetic flesh of the "terminator" in his popular series of cyborg movies. In *Terminator 3*, the cyborg manifests itself simultaneously as young, naked flesh, but also as a declining and aging self-depreciating actor, being chased by the next-level upgrade of cyborg, which happens to be a young, blonde, female killing machine. Her ability to totally reconfigure her body, at a moment's notice, embues her with an unusual allure. By the same token, considering the female "Borg" character "Seven of Nine" from the *Star Trek: Voyager* series, "falling in love" with the machine appears to be inevitable (for fans and crew alike); her pert attributes are continuously subjected to nano-probes and aesthetically placed biotechnical devices.

Of course, these fictional characters are visually constructed in the offline world of everyday reality, where the actors are flesh and blood and undergo extensive reconstruction by talented makeup and special-effects artists. However, with the upgrade in animation technology through computers, the "virtual actor" as "avatar" becomes increasingly apparent in the twenty-first century. The avatar displaces and sometimes compliments the "need" for flesh actors. Examples of this are films like *Final Fantasy: The Spirits Within* (2001), and *The Matrix Reloaded* (2003). The "synthespian" takes over from the real flesh, created from a social and cultural construct of aesthetics and beauty by designers and computer artists that specialize in the hyperrealism of the moving image. The hyperreal implications, in this case, are not only those used by postmodernist thinkers such as Umberto Eco (1986) and Jean Baudrillard (1983), whose discourses included notions of "fake" and "simulacra," but also that of computer animators whose dominant aesthetic can "conflate the 'remediation' of live action film within animation (and photo-realism in CGI) [computer-generated imagery] with a rather indistinct notion of contemporary culture as increasingly virtual" (Lister et al. 2003:143).

More than just another technique of film magic, the virtual avatar can also be seen as a beginning of the movement toward a different kind of sexual future; a future where one will be able to not only fall in love with a "machine," but also fall in love with the product of the digital. This is the arena of the post-cyborg where, like the cinema that imitates a life that proceeds it, technology and fantasy come together to create a hybrid of sophisticated sexual phantasms and scenarios with high-tech autoerotic experiences. Combine this prospect with the already continuous upgrading of computer communication technologies merging with most forms of media and subsequent "scientific breakthroughs," and you have the ingredients for yet another upgraded technological "new frontier" to the consuming end user—not unlike the advent of the commercialized World Wide Web in the early 1990s. What will be the form and substance of this "new frontier" and how will it be marketed and used sexually? I suggest that the end user, whilst navigating this new sexual frontier, will be the "sex tourist" of the future. But what exactly is a sex tourist?

Sex tourism is a phenomenon that already exists, and perhaps always has. For example, many ordinary tourists today visit the Dutch city of Amsterdam in order to gain access to sexual experiences. The Far East is renowned for its bars, clubs, and underage sex workers. Sex tourists visit places like these for the sole purpose of having sexual titillation. Even London has an interesting reputation:

> Britain's capital, today, is in the culinary super-league and restaurant goers can sample the delights of kitchens from Amsterdam to Vietnam. For the sexual gourmand London is also a world café that offers delicacies and indelicacies that appeal to every palate and which serve an international market. London is a sexy and licentious city. There are bars full of strippers; clubs where girls will dance on your lap or perform with a pole; there are

peep shows, sex shows and bed shows; and an exhaustible number of bars and clubs that provide for every sexual perversity (Archer 2003:19).

Similarly, current users of sex, pornography, and erotica on the Internet can already be considered tangential to these real-life (offline) sex tourists. Offline sex tourism can involve notions of anonymity and financial restrictions, thus visits to easily accessible countries that offer cheap sexual services for specific predilections with a "no questions asked" attitude have proven very popular. However, consumer choice for the online sexual tourist brings global sexual service consumption directly from cyberspace into the user's own living room. Equally similar to offline sex tourism, anonymity and financial restrictions limit the type of sex service available. Introducing sexual services into the user's home through online sex tourism also introduces new issues concerning domestic consumption and production, as some online users will advertise their own sexual services for free, working with an online media link on their own PC from home. For some, the act of paying money for sex is itself a form of sexual arousal, so the superabundance of consumer choices for online sexual services creates an environment for arousal and excitement.

At this point let us project some ideas into the future, where computer fetishism has become a tool for creating new software and hardware, and communication technologies enable the "sex tourists" that we *already* are to make consumer choices that we never before thought possible. What follows are brief but sexually themed future extrapolations and conjectures of technology currently already available. Just what will be available for the sex tourist in this upgraded future frontier of cyberspace? This essay is a possible future of techno-sex: a series of pleasure prophesies. So, where would be the first stop for our future sex tourist?

## First Stop: The "Reproduction Restaurant"

The Reproduction Restaurant symbolises choice, not physical location. It refers to the tremendous and exciting reproductive options that will be available to future generations. But as many of those options will be available on the Internet, as many already are in the United States, doubtless some of the modern-day Internet Cafes will upgrade themselves literally into reproduction restaurants.

—Robin Baker, *Sex in the Future.*

In his book on the reproductive revolution, Robin Baker (2000) combines computer-mediated communications with reproductive choice. His idea of a "Reproduction Restaurant" is a place of online menus for invitro fertilization treatments and other reproduction solutions. Taking cue from Baker, for some sex tourists of the future, the first stop might be to deposit physical cells from their real-life flesh and blood body at a genetic cell storage company that is accessible online. The physical cells will be stored so that they can be used and/or sold online at a later date. The sex tourist would then have all their genes and physical features available online as part of a menu of choices for procreation. Software programs would be able to create visual images and avatars of prospective offspring by using the genetic information on the menu combined with information input by the prospective user, client, and parent to be. This is high-end, no mess, sterile and self-selective reproduction with multiple degrees of separation between the consumer and the end product—a child. The cell donors never meet each other in this process of selection, and surrogate wombs add another degree of separation—as they are also available online.

Users of the Reproduction Restaurant would be able to avoid all the physical stresses of the process of conception, pregnancy, and birth. The availability of the upgraded Internet café as the "Reproduction Restaurant" would also create mothers of virgins, and make fathers obsolete. However, one would need to be financially stable, as the creation of the baby as a commodity fetish will turn out to be a lucrative online business.

* * *

Thus, our sex tourist, having organized the prospect of having any future offspring, can now throw caution to the wind concerning sexual responsibility and narcissistically concentrate on his or her own pleasure. It is always global party time in cyberspace, so our intrepid tourist goes in search of a good time and hot "action."

### Second Stop: The "Play Palace" at the "Sin City" Resort

Through searching online, our sex tourist finds information about "sin cities," where all kinds of technosexual adventures are available. These adventures and services are set in "play palaces" to compliment online and offline preferences. Sex as interactive entertainment is big business, Las Vegas style. Our tourist instantly books an online sex package and decides to travel offline to the massive hotel complex. However, online teledildonic gratification is instantly available from the play palace web site, only as a "teaser" for what is available at the resort. Our tourist, seduced by the promises of the web site, wants to be at the play palace, in person, in order to get his or her money's worth of "action." Indeed, this prospect of recreational sex for the sex tourist of the future has already been considered by senior policy advisors to the World Health Organization (Mackay 2000:112):

> This is nothing new. History has shown repeated cycles of liberalism and conservatism towards sex. But, for the first time, new technology will introduce undreamt of possibilities in the sexual arena. World trade in recreational sex industries will increase exponentially as these new technological developments become available.

We can therefore expect that play palaces and "sin cities" will employ large numbers of people in these booming service industries. Not only will the pleasure industry need a variety of real-time offline sex workers for entertainment, but it will also need sex programmers and other technology experts to create and run the interactive and immersive entertainment software. Also, commercial sex in cyberspace means that more sex workers need to be computer literate. The sex worker will develop more advanced skills at "creating virtual realities, programming environments, plots, and sensations for the client" (Califia 1994:247). Hardware engineers will literally have to make sure that for some, their genital teledildonic attachments are working safely and to maximum effect, as the pleasure seeker who suffers from a "micro soft" (a simile that could be used for the inability of a male user to gain an erection) will probably hold the pleasure palace liable for not delivering advertised expectations. Sex work, pornography, and entertainment—in all its media forms—will converge, making fantasy and reality an immersive entertaining experience. The end user will be the consumer of a sex product that has been created by a vast number of sex technologists, sexologists, psychosexual analysts, sexual theaters, where the enactment of intimate sexual behavior takes place, and hardware and software designers.

* * *

On arriving at the pleasure palace, our sex tourist needs to decide on what type of experience to purchase, based on what is available and affordable. There is an urgent need to communicate bodily desires for fun, pleasure, and entertainment. But with whom will our brave tourist decide to spend some time?

### Third Stop: The Sensorama Celebrity!

> Basically, immortality is digitizing. The more of yourself you digitize, the more of yourself is going to be immortal. The more your actions and memories you get digitized, the more immortal you're going to be. I was one of the first people to discover this. My claim to fame today is that there is more of me in digital form than almost any other person in the 20th Century.
>
> —Timothy Leary, *Chaos and Cyber Culture.*

The popular cult of celebrity will involve the digital storing, recording, production, and construction of the "celebrity avatar" in cyberspace, through a process much like that expressed by Leary (1994) in the above quotation. The celebrity identity will become an all-encompassing commodity brand available for purchase, hire, and exploitation. A current example of this is the British soccer player, David Beckham, who has a cult brand status in Europe and whose image is used extensively in advertising. In the future, it seems likely such celebrities might earn a royalty, of sorts, from these kinds of hyperreal avatar uses of their images. They may even employ specific agents to manage their avatar commitments, opening up work for copyright, legal, and virtual employment issues. This is already beginning to happen in the sports and film-themed computer game market, where images and voices of real-life sports and movie stars are bought or sponsored and then developed as action avatars in the game. One very popular and obvious example of this is of course the Play Station® 2 console game, "The Lord of the Rings. The Two Towers" (2002).

So how will the concept of the avatar work? The term "avatar" is taken from Hindu religion and lore, meaning the descent to earth of a deity in human, animal, or superhuman form. In this sense the use of the godlike, untouchable celebrity might involve a similar kind of "descent" into the interactive avatar plaything for the average user. However, such avatars could be programmed with unimaginable and superhuman sexual capabilities. According to Davis (1998), the association of the term avatar with cyberspace is attributed to creative designer Chip Morningstar of Lucasfilm, and Neil Stephenson's cyberpunk novel *Snowcrash*. For Davis (1998:224), the avatar possesses a dual identity in that "on the one hand, they are separate from the godhead, receiving only a portion of its spirit," but also "indivisible from the godhead, because the gods remain in constant communication with everything they touch." For our tourist to be in constant communication with the celebrity avatar, the avatar will have to be constructed from a software package and move and react appropriately. Consequently, current software research into emotive movement and interaction has been ongoing, "which could lead to the development of a broader model that establishes a matching between a theory of emotions and the parameters that effect animation" (Vala, Paiva and Gomes 2002:223). The avatar permits the crossover between offline exclusion and online inclusion, and challenges the concept of separation, conceptions of the self, identity, and ontology (Barber forthcoming).

Consequently, our sex tourist will be able to buy or hire a celebrity-programmed avatar, and can exchange identities from one's own avatar in cyberspace by using immersive virtual reality and a teledildonic sex suit. This will mean that our sex tourists can also adapt themselves to appear polymorphous, androgenous, intersexual, ambisextrous, and probably several other forms of sexual expression that we have not yet considered. Indeed, a form of digital necrophilia with dead celebrities will be commonplace with recreated avatars of the famous deceased. One could go back in time for that special experience: sex nostalgia and nostalgia as sex!

\* \* \*

Having spent a wild couple of nights in immersive cyberspace with a favorite avatar, and experiencing some amazing sexual role-play with a number of long dead celebrities of the twentieth century, our exhausted sex tourist wants to keep a record of the trip—to reminisce, and to show their partner what a great time they had. Our tourist goes back online to order something special.

### Fourth Stop: Wet-Ware Online! Playback Your Pleasure for the Folks at Home!

Pleasure will be digitally recorded. Playback is through a subcutaneous chip connected to the pleasure centers of the brain. This may sound a little sinister for some; however, current experiments and debates are considering the intrusion of computing technologies into our own private "inner space" of the body. Indeed, it has long been a fantasy for many to be intelligently augmented by technology as expressed in the following:

> And who says we just have to upgrade our existing senses. Growing up I was disappointed when I realized that it appeared that I didn't have ESP, but I do know how to use a cell phone to talk around the world. How about adding radios to brains? (Gershenfeld 1999:244)

Kevin Warwick, Professor of Cybernetics at Reading University in the United Kingdom has been working on the symbiosis of flesh with the computer for some time. Part of Warwick's research involves the implantation of a computer microchip under his skin. The computer chip sends signals from his body to his working environment, enabling electronic devices to react to his movements. Warwick has also had a chip implanted in his wife, so that she can sense when he is stimulated and vice versa. Some may find this unethical and sensational. Fear and social exclusion debates surrounding computer-mediated communication technologies can be perceived as superstitious in argument, projecting Orwellian ideas of technology as "evil science" involving surveillance, control, and personal information. The embedded chip, if developed and used en masse, also has the potential to transform government of others by emotive control into the bipolarities of dominance and submission. By submitting himself to this form of experimentation, Warwick forces us to confront notions of emotional authenticity and freedom. The embedded chip is a tool for social control, compliance, and dissent. Consequently, Warwick has unintentionally created what could be called a "hegemony chip" (Barber forthcoming).

It would appear that research such as that of Warwick's not only introduces notions of the potential true synthesis of the techno-human, but also questions society's connections to, and power relationship with, technology. This begs the question as to whether one could trust any use of this form of technology. It would be the ultimate in surveillance techniques, a nightmare for civil libertarians. One could simply log on to the network and see life through someone else's eyes. Gershenfeld (1999:243) once more considers such practicalities:

> For the foreseeable future we've got a lot of work to do to create around people inanimate technologies that they can trust. Beyond that, it's impossible not to speculate about implanting them in people. Your body is already the ultimate wearable computer, why not move the heads-up display to your retina? Striking work is being done in augmenting people's sensory and motor disabilities in this manner, but I don't trust anyone yet to do these things on a purely discretionary basis.

All the experiences in the play palace are digitally recorded; however, for a little extra cash, you can have a pleasure chip inserted into your body that will relay your sensations to a mainframe system. You will then be able to purchase your physical and emotional responses that have been recorded onto a mini disc to replay and relive at a later date.

* * *

After spending so much money on the recording for use back home, our tourist decides to take in some of the sites around Sin City. Standing next to the dirty artificial fountain, underneath the painted skyline, our tourist sees something of culture at the far end of the sex mall.

### Fifth Stop: The Genital Museum: Sex as Art and Cultural Display

Physical sex will be viewed as part of sociocultural history. Sex for procreation will be displayed as a historical and nostalgic novelty. The open display of flesh on flesh contact will both disgust and titillate. The flesh becomes fetishised. However, the fetishizing of the flesh has already happened in the form of "fat admiration" by men and women (the feeders) who feed their lovers (the feedee's) until they reach the required weight for the feeders sexual arousal.

Feeders often use computer image enhancement in order to get a computer-generated preview of how their lovers will look when they have put on weight. (Gates 2000)

Sex technologists will be an essential part of cultural information gathering, contributing a great deal to the structure of education. Certainly, the Internet has had an empowering effect on female sexuality—not only for consumers, but also for female e-pornographers. One researcher into a social history of sex technology is Rachel Maines, who studied the vibrator. Maines (1999:122) suggests technology may reveal an extensive history and understanding of female sexuality.

> The vibrator and its predecessors, like all technologies, tell us much about the societies that produced and used them. The device remains with us, praised by some, and reviled by others, neither good, bad, nor neutral, a controversial focus of debate about female sexuality.

How sex and technology are combined also tells us much about the desires and wants of a society and culture. The idea of two separate sex organs and gender assignation will be seen as reflecting the sociocultural difficulties of past conflicts, such as the development of social control through gender product targeting by large global corporations for financial exploitation. It will reveal inequalities and oppression, but also raise new questions about sex, technology, and emancipation.

* * *

After this brief sojourn around various old computers, models of breast implants, and insertable vibrating and flashing devices, it is time for our tourist to be daring and reconsider a new "style" to surprise everybody back home. You can't leave Sin City and return home the same person when you left.

### Sixth Stop: The E-Skin and Body Augmentation Shop

Genetics and reconstructive growth surgeries will create new body parts for personal statement and simply for fun (much like body piercing and tattoos are often used today). This will be seen as an upgrading of the body, and will involve the creation of new and novel pleasure organs and personal displays that are made an intimate part of the body. New technologies such as animated tattoos and "electronic-skin" (e-skin) rental means that the body itself can be connected online permanently with selected body parts relaying commercials or whatever images are required. This will be seen as the extended upgrading of the current popular "craze" of exchanging ring tones, text, and images from mobile phones. However, instead of using an external mobile communications technology, the body will be the technology itself. This will be a large part of new consumer and youth cultures, as is already happening with the contemporary youth subculture of the "cybergoth."

"Cybergoth" is a youth subculture that is already influenced by the impact of computer-mediated communications and virtual reality. Cybergoths are unlike previous representations of youth subculture, in that they are not interpretations of class "favoured by and transmitted through the authorised channels of mass communication" (Hebdige. 1979:86). Cybergoths want to *be* the channels of mass communication. Cybergoths do not wish to be like Hebdige's punks, representing media rhetoric and crisis. Cybergoths, much like cyberpunks, *are* their own created media. Cybergoths deviate to innovate (Barber forthcoming). "Goth" and its subcultures "extol the esoteric and unusual. Its playfulness, theatricality and love of the arcane represent a direct affront to a dull consumerist culture and rigid work ethic" (Baddeley 2002:284).

Apart from the cybergoth, performance artist Stelarc has already considered and displayed computer technology as body modification by using cyberspace as a vehicle for his work. Stelarc (1998:116, emphasis in original) suggests:

> The obsession with the self, sexual difference, and the symbolic begins to subside in cyber-systems that *monitor, map* and *modify* the body. Increasing augmentation of the body and automation by transferring its functions to machines undermines notions of free agency and demystifies the mind. CYBER-SYSTEMS SPAWN ALTERNATE, HYBRID AND SURROGATE BODIES.

So, our sex tourist now has a hybrid body with brand new set of dual-sexed genitals, and a rented space by computer giant "Macro-Hard" proudly displayed on the forearm. The body e-skin rental surprisingly helped pay for the majority of the trip.

* * *

But, it's nearly time to go back home, to reality, and our brave sex tourist wants to do one more thing before returning to the mundane. Our daring, and shall we say even romantic, sex tourist has decided to get married.

### Seventh Stop: The Church of the Virtual Realist

As an upgrade to the present-day online chat room romance, the future could see a marriage and/or commitment to a virtual avatar that could be considered legally binding. In the Church of the Virtual Realist, cyberspace is sacred space. It is also a place where commitment is shared and declared between the user and the digital. Falling in love with the product of the machine will be commonplace, as are long-distance weddings online between real-life people. One can marry any avatar that portrays a person or object of desire. Narcissists can be reconstructed as avatars in cyberspace and even marry themselves, if they so wish, and anthropomorphists will be able to marry an engineered avatar representation of their pet or favorite animal cartoon character. For fetishists and those with other unusual predilections, the possibilities could be endless.

This is a serious moment for our sex tourist. She has contacted her partner back at home, who has succumbed to the romance of the "digital proposal." In the immersive virtual chapel, the environment is tacky, brightly colored, and loud. The avatar priest looks a little transparent, and one of his feet appears to be missing due to play palace software company negligence. Our tourist's girlfriend appears online from home at long distance. She has purchased the avatar of a young Elvis, a popular singer and movie star from the twentieth century for this special occasion, and our tourist has chosen to take the form of another singer. She has chosen the avatar of Michael Jackson, the one from the 1980s as there were apparently several Michael Jacksons to choose from. The two offline women exchange their online vows.

Our tourist now considers it time to go home, to physically be and live with her partner. However, how on earth is she going to explain to her partner the extra genital augmentation and the e-skin? What next, a digital divorce?

## Consequences

It is all too easy to see devastating consequences from such fantastical use of technology. There is pedophilia, addiction, rape, pornography, obscenity, sex murder, sex terrorism, and any other permutation of social fear and moral panic that can be projected onto the use of technologies of cyberspace. However, all such fears are readily realized. It is only to be expected that such problems will continue to manifest in cyberspace. However, cyberspace can also make such problems more visible. The Internet has revealed to us the insidious nature of the pedophile, and indeed through delicate policing operations such as "Operation Ore" online, worldwide pedophilia rings have been rooted out and arrested by multinational police cooperation. This also raises questions of consent, trust, and "sexual grooming." For example, as in the Shivaun Pennington and Toby Studabaker case, where a twelve-year-old British girl went to Europe with a thirty-one-year-old American male. It also makes us consider and question our real-life relationship values in comparison to online flirtations. At what point is there infidelity and will it have legal consequences? However, on the other side of the coin, computer-mediated communications have brought people together in love during times of stress and desperation, and help to keep long distance love alive and create new successful relationships despite the sensationalism that depicts otherwise in the tabloid press.

However, while we use the technology and are sometimes seduced by the hype and the promises of computing, other considerations should be recognized. The role of genetic selection in procreation has taken on a new purpose. Computer technologies are using the genetic selection process of parenting as a model for the upgrading process. Computers are now designing themselves.

In a personal interview with Britain's top futurologist, Ian Pearson describes ideas and possible adaptations of biological sexual procreation to be used as a methodology to enhance technological development. Pearson examines concepts of polyamory and group sex in comparison with concepts of genetic engineering and sexual selection. He describes possible ideas concerning computer-to-computer communication using the metaphor of genetic and sexual selection, thus introducing the concept of computer genetics (Barber forthcoming). This can be described in Darwinian terms as *unnatural selection* or *electronic selection*. As Ian Pearson suggests:

> So over a period of a million generations, which you could run on a computer on a weekend, you could start off with a very simple program which does half of what you're looking for, and you end up with a program which does exactly what you want in no time flat, minimum cost, and, ...no bugs. Self-evolving software, that's one of the primary uses of sex in industry as it were. You know we looked at it, and thought well, the idea of biomimetics is not to copy nature exactly, but to steal the idea and get hold of it. (Barber forthcoming)

Computer sex, net sex, cybersex, techno-sex, or whatever you wish to label it, will be a tool for creating future generations of computing that will in turn have greater impact on our offline and online lives. It is a new narrative contributing to a form of contemporary technological determinism. Woolgar (1990), writing in a paper concerning machine as text, considered that machines, in the case of computer technology, could be ascribed "behavior." That is, in order to upgrade the use and the development of computer-mediated communications and workstations, hardware and software developers were looking at creating new patterns of human computer interaction. By a "distribution of attributes" (e.g., computers could be said to be temperamental), users are granting intentionality to an inanimate object. In using the distribution of attributes usually considered within a metaphorical context or even as a literary device, Woolgar (1990:61) argues "that by setting parameters for the users actions, the evolving machine effectively configures the user." Woolgar

(1990:63) also asserts "accounts of action and behaviour are constrained by assumptions about the acting entity." According to Lister et al (2003) there are many viewpoints concerning technological determinism founded on cultural approaches to technology extrapolated from theorists such as Williams (1974), McLuhan (1967) and Latour (1993). In the plethora of approaches to the historical narrative of technology such as agency, physicalism, linear and non-linear causalities, it is easy to neglect the possibility of the inclusion of the subject of sexuality and arousal within determinist narratives (Barber forthcoming).

Current "net sex" is a mirror of our needs and reflects what is going on in our global society. However, the future holds something new for the upgrading of technology and, in the process, sociocultural change. The birth of super-generated, "unnaturally selected" microscopic nano-computers influenced by our sexual behavior will become part of organizing our existence and will invade our very being. As fantastic as this claim is, the way in which sex has already been *the* driving force for the development of Internet technologies suggests that this is already happening. Technologies innovated by the Internet porn industry have already become a part of how we organize ourselves—at least for those people or institutions who use the Internet. Consequently, there should be no fear of the future that has been proposed by these fictional pleasure prophesies. Neither should we fear falling in love with "the digital" or "the machine," as suggested in the quotation at the beginning of this essay; because, similar to our brave and intrepid sex tourist of the future, we are in a committed relationship with it already.

## References

Archer, C. 2003. *Tart cards. London's illicit advertising art.* New York, NY: Mark Batty.

Baddeley, G. 2002. *Goth chic. A connoisseur's guide to dark culture.* London: Plexus Publishing.

Baker, R. 2000. *Sex in the future. The reproductive revolution and how it will change us.* New York, NY: Arcade Publishing.

Barber, T. (Forthcoming). *Fetishism@Cyberspace: Sexual innovation on the internet.* Oxford and New York: Berg.

Baudrillard, J. 1983. *Simulations.* Trans. Foss, Paul, Patton, Paul, and Beitchman. New York, NY: Semiotext(e).

Califia, P. 1994. *Public sex: The culture of radical sex.* San Francisco: Cleis Press.

Davis, E. 1998. *TechGnosis. Myth, magic, and mysticism in the age of information.* London: Serpents Tail.

Eco, U. 1986. *Travels in hyperreality.* Orlando, FL: Harcourt Brace Jovanovich.

Gates, K. 2000. *Deviant desires: Incredibly strange sex.* New York, NY: RE/Search Publications.

Gershenfeld, N. 1999. *When things start to think.* London: Coronet Books (Hodder and Stoughton).

Hebdige, D. 1979. *Subculture the meaning of style.* London: Routledge.

Latour, B. 1993. *We have never been modern.* Trans. Catherine Porter. Hemel Hempstead: Harvester-Wheatsheaf.

Leary, T. 1994. *Chaos and cyber culture.* Berkely, CA: Ronin Publishing Inc.

Lister M., J. Dovey, S. Giddings, G. Iain, and K. Kieran. 2003. *New media: A critical introduction.* London: Routledge.

Mackay, J. 2000. *The Penguin atlas of human sexual behaviour. Sexuality and sexual practices around the world.* London: Penguin Reference.

Maines, R. P. 1999. *The technology of orgasm: "Hysteria," the vibrator, and women's sexual satisfaction.* Baltimore, MD: Johns Hopkins University Press.

McLuhan, M. 1967. *Understanding media: The extensions of man.* London: Sphere.

O'Toole, L. 1999. *Pornocopia: Porn, sex, technology, and desire.* London: Serpents' Tail.

Stelarc. 1998. From psycho-body to cyber-systems: Images as post-human entities. In *Virtual futures. Cyberotics, technology, and post-human pragmatism,* ed. J. Broadhurst Dixon and E. J. Cassidy. London: Routledge.

Vala M., A. Paiva, and M. R. Gomes. 2002. From virtual bodies to believable characters. *The Interdisciplinary Journal of Artificial Intelligence and the Simulation of Behaviour* 1(2):219–224.

Williams, R. 1974. *Television, technology, and cultural form.* London: Fontana.

Woolgar S. 1990. Configuring the user: the case of usability trials. Paper for discussion at Discourse Analysis Workshop, University of Lancaster. In *A Sociology of monsters. Essays on power, technology, and domination,* ed. J. Law 1991. Sociological Review Monograph 38. London and New York: Routledge.

# ❖ Contributors

**Trudy Barber** is an artist who recently completed her Ph.D. in sociology/cultural studies at the University of Kent at Canterbury, UK. She is the author of the forthcoming book *Fetishism@Cyberspace: Sexual Innovation on the Internet*. She exhibited what is likely the first immersive Virtual Reality Sex environment as an art installation in the early 1990s while a student at Central Saint Martins College of Art in London. She is a specialist of cyberculture, cybersex, cybersociology, fetishism and deviation, new media, and the arts. She has lectured worldwide and has extensive broadcast experience. For further information see: http://www.trudy-barber.com

**Joel Powell Dahlquist** is the director of criminal justice at Minnesota State University Moorhead. He continues to pursue his interest in popular erotic arts and is also researching narratives of innocence and wrongful conviction.

**Mark Douglass** was an assistant professor of sociology at Ridgewater College and Saint Cloud Technical College until his unfortunate death in 2002. Between 1996 and 2002 Mark's scholarly contributions include research on Internet chat and cybersex. Mark is fondly remembered and sorely missed by all who knew him.

**Keith F. Durkin** is an associate professor of sociology and director of the Institute for Social Research at Ohio Northern University. He holds a Ph.D. in sociology from Virginia Tech. He has authored or coauthored articles that have appeared in *Deviant Behavior*, *Federal Probation*, the *Journal of Alcohol and Drug Education,* and the *College Student Journal*. He has served as a contributor to the *Encyclopedia of Criminology and Deviant Behavior* as well as the *Handbook of Death and Dying.*

**Charles Edgley** is a professor of sociology at Oklahoma State University. He has authored or coauthored numerous articles; his recent books include *A Nation of Meddlers* and *Life as Theater*. His primary scholarly interests include health and medicine, death and dying, and dramaturgical sociology.

**Donna M. Hughes** is a professor and endowed chair in the Women's Studies Program at the University of Rhode Island. Her research interests include sexual exploitation, trafficking, women's organized resistance to violence, religious fundamentalism and women's rights, and issues related to women, science, and technology. In addition to extensive scholarly publications, she has also written numerous articles for various journalistic publications including *The Washington Post, Wall Street Journal, The Prague Post, National Review Online, FrontPage Magazine,* and *The Weekly Standard.*

**Lauren Langman** is a professor of sociology at Loyola University. He is primarily a social theorist writing in the tradition of the Frankfurt School. His substantive interests and research concerns dialects of political economy, culture and identity (specifically concerning relations of consumerism), and identity and the reproduction of domination. His work has explored the grotesque, body modification, and goth/punk subcultures.

**John Leonard** and **Naomi McCormick** are clinical psychologists who specialize in sexuality and sex therapy.

**Taylor Marsh** is an author, columnist, and currently hosts a Las Vegas radio talk show. A former Miss Missouri, singer, dancer, and actress, Taylor was also a former managing editor for Danni's Hard Drive. She has been covered by *USA Today, L.A. Times, Reuters, Las Vegas Weekly, Las Vegas City Life, Newsbytes,* and *Playboy TV.*

**Erica Owens**, assistant professor of social and cultural sciences at Marquette University, specializes in identity, narrative, and family sociology. She has been an associate editor of the *Journal of Family Issues* since 2000. Most recently, her research has focused on how an individual's self is affected during marital separation. Her publications include works on love and alimony.

**Lewis Purdue** is a California technology executive and Internet pioneer. He is a former columnist for *TheStreet.com, Wall Street Journal Online, CBS Marketwatch,* and has written for *Forbes ASAP, Barron's, The Washington Post, Los Angeles Times, Boston Globe, Washington Monthly,* and various other publications.

**Howard Rheingold** is a well published futurist and veteran observer of technology. His numerous books include *Smart Mobs, The Virtual Community, Tools for Thought, Virtual Reality,* and *The Millennium Whole Earth Catalog.*

**Stephen C. Roberds** teaches political science at Southern Utah University. He earned his Ph.D. at the University of Missouri-St. Louis and specializes in constitutional law, voting behavior, and research methods. His scholarly interests include the effect of candidate scandals on congressional elections and how courts address emerging issues of Internet pornography.

**Claudia Springer** is a professor of English and film studies at Rhode Island College. Her research interests include film studies, cultural studies, postmodern theory, and literature.

**Jim Thomas**, professor of sociology and criminology at Northern Illinois University, specializes in research on prison culture. He was an observer and participant in computer underground culture from 1988–1992. He was editor of *Computer Underground Digest* from 1990–2000, an electronic newsletter that focused on cultural and legal issues related to cyberspace. He has published on research ethics in cyberspace and hacker culture. In addition to online teaching, he also serves as a Unix system administrator.

**Phillip Vannini** teaches media and popular culture in the Sociology Department at the University of Victoria. He has published works on Internet subcultures and Internet bulletin boards. Among his latest projects is an ethnographic non-participant observation of computer-mediated communication among "weather junkies."

**Lee Garth Vigilant** is assistant professor of sociology at Minnesota State University at Moorhead. He received his Ph.D. in sociology at Boston College in 2001. Dr. Vigilant has taught sociology at Boston College, Tufts University, and Framingham State College, and is the recipient of the Donald J. White Teaching Excellence Award for Sociology at Boston College in 2000 and the TCU Senate Professor of the Year Award at Tufts University in 2001. He publishes and teaches in the areas of health and illness, sociological theory, thanatology, and the sociology of the body. His most recent publications appear in the *Handbook of Death and Dying*.

**Dennis D. Waskul** is an assistant professor of sociology at Minnesota State University at Mankato. Dennis has published extensively in areas of computer-mediated communication, with special emphasis on online chat and cybersex. He is the author of *Self-Games and Body-Play: Personhood in Online Chat and Cy-*

*bersex* (Peter Lang, 2003). He has also published his research in *Symbolic Interaction*, *New Media & Society,* and *Sociological Spectrum.*

*General Editor: Steve Jones*

**Digital Formations** is an essential source for critical, high-quality books on digital technologies and modern life. Volumes in the series break new ground by emphasizing multiple methodological and theoretical approaches to deeply probe the formation and reformation of lived experience as it is refracted through digital interaction. **Digital Formations** pushes forward our understanding of the intersections—and corresponding implications—between the digital technologies and everyday life. The series emphasizes critical studies in the context of emergent and existing digital technologies.

Other recent titles include:

Leslie Shade
*Gender and Community in the Social Construction of the Internet*

John T. Waisanen
*Thinking Geometrically*

Mia Consalvo & Susanna Paasonen
*Women and Everyday Uses of the Internet*

Dennis Waskul
*Self-Games and Body-Play*

David Myers
*The Nature of Computer Games*

Robert Hassan
*The Chronoscopic Society*

M. Johns, S. Chen, & G. Hall
*Online Social Research*

C. Kaha Waite
*Mediation and the Communication Matrix*

Jenny Sunden
*Material Virtualities*

Helen Nissenbaum & Monroe Price
*Academy and the Internet*

To order other books in this series please contact our Customer Service Department:

(800) 770-LANG (within the US)

(212) 647-7706 (outside the US)

(212) 647-7707 FAX

To find out more about the series or browse a full list of titles, please visit our website:

WWW.PETERLANGUSA.COM